HE
8846
.I64
S62
1982

Sobel, Robert, 1931
Feb. 19-

I.T.T.

DATE DUE

I·T·T

I·T·T

The Management Of Opportunity

Robert Sobel

A TRUMAN TALLEY BOOK

for
Stewart Holbrook (1893–1964)
and Ralph Hidy (1902–1977)

Published by *Truman Talley Books* · *Times Books*, a division of
Quadrangle/The New York Times Book Co., Inc.
Three Park Avenue, New York, N.Y. 10016

Published simultaneously in Canada by
Fitzhenry & Whiteside, Ltd., Toronto

Library of Congress Cataloging in Publication Data

Sobel, Robert, 1931 Feb. 19–
  I.T.T.: the management of opportunity.

  Bibliography: p. 409
  Includes index.
  1. International Telephone and Telegraph Corporation—
History. I. Title. II. Title: ITT.
HE8846.I64S62 1982   384'.065   82–50039
ISBN 0–8129–1028–1

Manufactured in the United States of America
10 9 8 7 6 5 4 3 2 1

Contents

Contents

Preface

MY initial contact with ITT came in the spring of 1978, when Jean Keaveny, of the public relations department there, called to learn whether I would be interested in undertaking a history of the corporation. Our talk was cordial, the first of many we would have during my researches and interviews over the next four years. Mrs. Keaveny told me ITT's management was interested in sponsoring a full-scale work; offered some suggestions as to style, approach, and content; and wanted to know how much such a manuscript would cost.

I replied that subsidized histories were of limited and questionable worth, since the payment of funds establishes a dubious nexus between the writer and his subject. I was willing to write an unsubsidized book and offered to locate a publisher who would enter into a contract with me that wouldn't require or involve any direct or indirect ITT subsidy. ITT, for its part, would have to assure me I would have complete access to records, files, and individuals, except for matters in litigation. The corporation would have the right to see the finished manuscript and to comment on questions of style and content, but could not demand or require changes or alterations of any kind. All this was done.

Later on I learned that at a board meeting a few months afterward, Rand Araskog, ITT chairman, was asked, "How's our book coming along?" To which I am told he replied, "It's Professor Sobel's book, not ours."

Mr. George Delhomme, manager for editorial services, and Mrs. Keaveny opened all doors. Some of the interviewees clearly would rather not have spoken with me, but they did, after hearing what I soon learned were the magic words: "Rand would like you to see him."

Several decisions made early in the research dictated this book's direction, and two in particular should be mentioned here.

First, I decided to concentrate on the management of the corporation, which would become the organizing theme. For most of its history ITT had been led by two titans of American business, Sosthenes Behn and Harold Geneen. Each had a unique approach to management, and each developed strategies and tactics and created an organization to carry them forth. They entered into relationships with governments and financial institutions that called for examination, analysis, and explanation. This became the focus of the book.

The second decision also involved the matter of emphasis. As will be seen, ITT is a highly complex organism, with hundreds of units grouped within five general areas. To examine all of these, or even to explore in proper detail the five component parts, would occupy the lifetimes of scores of researchers and writers, the results of whose labors would fill a dozen or more volumes. For example, such large ITT companies as Sheraton, Rayonier, Grinnell, and Continental Baking could well have their own histories. There already is a study of the largest ITT unit: Hawthorne Daniel's *The Hartford of Hartford* (New York: Random House, 1960). A number of histories might be written about components of ITT's huge overseas telecommunications and electronics operation, International Standard Electric. In the United Kingdom, Peter Young has recently completed one on Standard Telephones and Cables, the second largest ISE unit, and others remain to be done.

For these reasons I decided to concentrate on the management of

Preface

ITT itself and have devoted less space than some might wish to other aspects of the corporation and its components. It is akin to undertaking a political history of the United States, one that doesn't stress military efforts or aspects of the individual states and other political units.

From time to time I would send drafts of chapters to ITT to be photocopied and distributed to interested parties. On a half dozen occasions I met with ITT readers to discuss matters of fact and interpretation. Never was there any suggestion I shade a judgment, alter a phrase, omit or tone down an embarrassing episode, or include anything that might place the corporation in a more favorable light. Almost all the comments involved questions of fact, chronology, and the like.

This, then, is a "warts and all" presentation, and ITT has more than its share of warts. That it has cooperated so fully and that its officers have been so candid amazed many of my colleagues in the press and in academia, some of whom entertain decidedly negative views of the corporation. They read selected chapters—especially those concerned with ITT's dealings in Washington and Chile— and though they occasionally disagreed with interpretations, they conceded that the facts upon which they were based were accurate, verifiable, and complete.

Interestingly, I had a similar reaction from several ITT'ers who read the same chapters, though their sentiments were understandably different from my colleagues'. They were pleased to learn that earlier accounts claiming ITT had actively cooperated with the Nazis were either incorrect or exaggerated and certainly hadn't drawn upon documents readily available at the National Archives and elsewhere. On the other hand, they were dismayed by certain newly-revealed aspects of ITT's behavior during the Nixon era, the full story of which I attempt to set down here for the first time.

One such ITT executive, who had been in the midst of things during several of the more embarrassing Nixon/Chile episodes, read the manuscript but made no comment on the damaging sections. Curious, I asked for his reaction. "There's nothing to say," he replied. "That's the way it was."

No historian could hope for a more satisfying comment.

ROBERT SOBEL

New College of Hofstra
July 1982

I·T·T

Introduction to ITT

CONJURE a combination of feudal Europe *circa* 1100 and the
United States of America under the Articles of Confederation.
Place it under a power structure redolent of both the Holy Roman
Empire and the League of the Iroquois. Provide the system with a
diplomatic corps to deal with other nations and business empires.
Add an infrastructure of more than three hundred lending institutions and an internal staff to deal with the flow of liquid assets into
and out of the various parts of the enterprise. Give it an organizing
unit whose major function is to harmonize efforts and allocate resources. Then throw in a nervous system composed of telecommunications plus an admixture of corporate jets and fleets of limou-
sines. Imagine all of this and you will have just begun to
comprehend the essential nature of ITT.

It does little good to attempt to analyze this organization by the
standards of other familiar giants, such as Exxon, General Motors,
IBM, Citicorp, or Metropolitan Life, for these have more of an

internal consistency and a central mission than does ITT. Some observers have compared it with the large Japanese trading companies, such as Mitsubishi and Mitsui, and South Africa's Anglo American Corporation. But this is misleading, for ITT is a particularly American creation with no real counterpart elsewhere in the world. Stated simply, it falls within no previously existing paradigm.

Outside world headquarters, at 320 Park Avenue in New York, ITT is more an organizing principle and a force than anything else. Venture from the building, to as nearby as 67 Broad Street (the old headquarters is still home for ITT World Communications, which among its other duties operates the Washington-to-Moscow "hot line"), and you will discover that most there have loyalties to and maintain identification with the subsidiary far more than with the parent. Even second-tier executives rarely have much to do with the home office.

Consider the following items, typical of ITT but rarely found to this degree at other firms, even some of the conglomerates:

· An old-timer at Grinnell (acquired in 1969) fairly high in the pecking order is surprised to learn, ten years after the fact, that ITT owns O. M. Scott (acquired in 1971).

· A Sheraton senior executive is asked whether people in the field ever think in terms of making a move to corporate headquarters. For a few minutes he is confused; to him the world revolves around Sheraton's Boston operations, not ITT's in New York. Upon understanding the question, he replies, somewhat incredulously, "Why would they want to go to New York?"

· At world headquarters a prominent ITT'er offers an important distinction: A check given the San Diego Convention and Visitors Bureau in the Nixon era came from Sheraton, not ITT. There is a difference.

· A middle manager at Bell & Gossett (acquired in 1963) is asked to name ten other ITT companies. After some prodding he offers seven, three of which aren't in the ITT family.

· An officer at Standard Elektrik Lorenz AG, ITT's most important overseas operating company (parts of which were acquired as long ago as 1929), is asked whether SEL shares information and knowledge with other ITT entities in Europe, such as Standard Eléctrica, S.A., of Spain, and the United Kingdom's Standard Telephones and Cables Public Limited Company, which came into the

Introduction to ITT

system in 1925. He smiles and answers, "Of course not." Similar responses to the same question are given at SESA and STC.

· Virtually every senior executive outside New York refers to his own company when using the pronoun "we" or when talking about "our future."

· These executives can recite with ease the facts and figures regarding their operations but often won't hazard a guess as to those at some of ITT's most important and well-known subsidiaries.

Much of this is changing, in large part because of the efforts of the corporation's current administration. But with the problems of size, complexity, competing loyalties, and simple inertia, even a partial harmonization of the various segments probably won't become apparent for many years, perhaps not in this century. Diversity without much in the way of actual cohesion, then, is one of the hallmarks of ITT today.

A corollary of this is a curious combination of high visibility and an absence of knowledge of just what it is the corporation does. ITT is one of the handful of American companies readily identifiable by its initials alone, along with IBM, RCA, and GE. But whereas most people know that International Business Machines is involved with computers, Radio Corporation of America with television, and General Electric with electrical products, they are confused about International Telephone and Telegraph. For one thing, it isn't a major operator of telephone companies; the sole link to this part of the past is a small company in the Virgin Islands accounting for a minor fraction of one percent of total revenues. Nor are telegraphs part of ITT's present or future plans. Unlike other familiar "initial companies," then, ITT's name offers no hint as to its current businesses.

Yet its products and services are ubiquitous; few Americans and Europeans can go through a day without coming into direct or indirect contact with several ITT operations, though few are labeled as such. The person who hasn't the foggiest notion about ITT's business may live in a home constructed of wood from one of Rayonier's forests, containing hardware turned out by Grinnell, and insured by a company in the Hartford group. Possibly, the lawn was fertilized with Scott Turfbuilder, its borders edged with flowers from seeds ordered from the Burpee catalogues, the garden maintained by other products from both ITT firms. In the larder could be Wonder bread, Hostess cakes, and Twinkies (of which more than a billion a year are sold), all from ITT's Continental Baking. The telephones in the house and the wires and cables carrying messages in and out of it could have been turned out by ITT companies, along with the poles on which the wires were strung. Books on the shelves might have been published by ITT companies, printed on Rayonier-derived paper, and used in technical and vocational schools owned by the corporation. Even the heating oil could have come out of a well owned and managed by Eason, yet another subsidiary, and the electricity generated from coal mined by Carbon Industries, one of the more recent ITT acquisitions. The family's automobile probably contains several components turned out by other ITT companies, and the Sheraton hotel or motel at which they stay might be owned, managed, or franchised by that part of the corporation. Yet the family could purchase and use all of these products and services without even a notion that they came from units that are part of ITT.

In all, ITT owns more than a hundred individual companies (not counting their subsidiaries), ranging in size from The Hartford, currently the seventh largest entity in insurance with revenues of $5.9 billion and assets of $16.6 billion, to small electronics and hardware firms in Europe, each with less than one hundred workers. Most carry the corporate logo, but many, including The Hartford and Sheraton, do not. A few use the ITT designation for some purposes but not for others. Today the subsidiaries have a large degree of freedom in this matter, but there was a time in the 1960s when management insisted all be identified as ITT holdings—when one of the reasons for buying Continental Baking was to have the ITT brand in many American kitchens.

This experiment at fashioning intercompany solidarity came to an end in the early 1970s, when in some quarters ITT was castigated as a renegade corporation, engaged in corrupting domestic politics and contributing importantly to the overthrow of a foreign government. Headquarters in New York and elsewhere were picketed and worse, as management came under attack and developed a siege mentality. Without fanfare many subsidiaries dropped the logo, especially where consumer goods and services were involved. Several foreign holdings sold portions of their equity to nationals, so as to place distance between themselves and the parent. Thus, the worker at the plant or office and the user of the product often didn't know of the ITT connection. But, by now, this period has ended.

Introduction to ITT

These factors contribute to the apparent random nature of ITT, and upon cursory glance at the components an outsider might reasonably conclude that the various companies were established or acquired in a serendipitous fashion: Such a grab bag of unrelated units couldn't have been thrown together with any plan in mind. Or so it might appear. Yet there was a plan; in fact, there were two of them, each an overarching vision of an extraordinary businessman, and there is a third in the making. The second was superimposed upon the first but didn't dissolve it, and the third is to build upon this base.

Col. Sosthenes Behn founded and developed the International Telephone and Telegraph Corporation after World War I. During the 1920s he acquired a group of operating telephone and telegraph companies, most of them in Europe and Latin America, tied them together with cable interconnects, and purchased a group of factories that turned out telephonic and telegraphic gear. Behn called this "The International System," and others believed he had set out to create an international version of American Telephone and Telegraph.

Along with many other such dreams, this one came to an end with the arrival of the Great Depression, during which Behn saved ITT from bankruptcy several times through last-minute maneuvers. The International System couldn't survive in a period of growing economic nationalism, and its demise was signaled by the start of preparations for World War II. Now Behn turned to the domestic scene, and for a while ITT prospered by manufacturing products for the armed services. The Colonel hoped to concentrate on the American market after the war, but had little success. Meanwhile, the European operations recovered, and by the mid-1950s they were again the engine that powered ITT. These operations remain the essential legacy of Behn's original vision.

Telecommunications and electronic products and services—most of which are turned out and marketed in Europe—account for approximately a third of ITT's revenues and profits. The two most important European operations, Standard Elektrik Lorenz (SEL) and Standard Telephones and Cables (STC), provide more than half the revenues, earnings, and dividends, and today ITT owns a majority, but not all, of the stock in both, having sold shares to nationals in recent years. Each company is a leader in its field and one of the top twenty industrial firms in its country.

I·T·T: The Management of Opportunity

The German facilities are centered in a huge complex on the outskirts of Stuttgart; STC headquarters can be found along London's prestigious Strand. These companies operate independently of each other, as do Bell Telephone Manufacturing (BTM), of Belgium; FACE Finanziaria, of Italy; Standard Telefon og Kabelfabrik A/S, of Norway; Standard Eléctrica (SESA), of Spain; and their counterparts in Austria, the Netherlands, Denmark, Portugal, Switzerland, Sweden, Finland, and Greece. This was a hallmark of Behn's International System, which attempted to harmonize national interests with overall direction from New York. Long before it became fashionable, the ITT companies overseas had nationals as chief executives and operating officers, and few Americans could be found on their boards of directors. But the holding company for these foreign firms, International Standard Electric (ISE), is headed by ITT's chairman, and its board is composed entirely of Americans from the home office. This, too, follows the Behn pattern.

Harold Geneen arrived at ITT from Raytheon in 1959, and after overseeing a period of consolidation and pruning, he set about creating his version of the corporation. Within a few years ITT had become a conglomerate, the exemplar of the breed and one of the fastest-growing large enterprises in America. By the late 1960s he was acquiring companies at the rate of more than one a week, and some of these were several times as large as ITT had been when he arrived.

Geneen later claimed to have taken the best of what was available, suggesting a businessman on a shopping tour in some gigantic mall, buying whatever attracted his eye. This simply isn't borne out by the facts; for, like Behn, Geneen, too, had a vision—in fact, two of them. One of these, the creation of a major telecommunications-electronics-entertainment corporation along the lines of RCA, was thwarted in 1967, at which time he turned with a passion to the second vision, the creation of the giant conglomerate so familiar a few years later. Had he succeeded in the former pursuit, the latter would have developed quite differently, if at all, and the Geneen legacy would have been altered considerably.

As a conglomerateur Geneen hoped to strike a balance in several areas: between domestic and foreign sales, capital-intensive and labor-intensive industries, consumer goods and capital equipment. Always there was this sense of balance, for Geneen expected his ITT to be self-sufficient, capable of weathering any political or economic blow. In addition, there was a strong element of *synergy* —a popular word during the conglomerate era. One holding would complement and augment the other. The nexus between such firms as Sheraton, Continental Baking, a group of parking lots, Avis, and Canteen Corp. was obvious. So were relationships between publishing companies and schools, Rayonier and Levitt, with Hartford and Grinnell providing financial services and fire-protection equipment for all. That Avis, Canteen, Levitt, and portions of Grinnell were divested in settlement of an antitrust action doesn't detract from this vision. Geneen ever was a man who saw connections, and for him ITT was a gigantic jigsaw puzzle, and his major task was to locate, and then whittle to size, pieces for the picture that would never be completed but would continue to grow. In fact, there was no greater advocate of growth than Harold Geneen, in an age when this quality was prized.

The heart of his ITT can be found along the lines of a roughly shaped parabola that runs through New York, Connecticut, Rhode Island, and Massachusetts. It begins at the Continental Baking headquarters in Rye, New York, just across from the Connecticut border, in a bucolic setting, not far from the amusement park for which the town is best known. The building is large but not particularly impressive, and might easily be mistaken for a regional junior college were it not for the small sign at the entrance. Continental operates fifty-five bakeries from this location and several other minor operations. Sales and revenues for 1981 were close to $2 billion. Were it a separate entity, Continental would be as large as such companies as Koppers, Olin, and National Distillers & Chemical.

A few miles across the Connecticut border, in Stamford, are the recently relocated headquarters of Rayonier, an important supplier of wood and paper products, with total sales approaching $1 billion. Travel along Route 95 into Rhode Island and you'll arrive at Providence, base for Grinnell, an old-line manufacturer of a wide variety of valves, castings, hangers, and other hardware used by the utility, construction, capital-goods, and related industries. In what most consider a mature industry, Grinnell has managed in five years to double sales, which, like Rayonier's, now stand close to $1 billion. Each of these companies, if independent, would be in the Fortune 500, around the 300 mark, slightly smaller than Louisiana Land and Exploration, G. D. Searle, and Libbey-Owens-Ford but larger than Becton Dickinson, Joy Manufacturing, and Kaiser Steel.

I·T·T: The Management of Opportunity

The Sheraton Corporation, housed in a modern Boston sky-scraper, oversees close to 500 hotels and inns worldwide with a total of more than 120,000 rooms. Although behind Holiday Inns in number of rooms, Sheraton is far ahead of its old rival, Hilton. More than $2 billion in sales went through the Sheraton system last year —approximately the revenues gathered in by Abbott Laboratories or Revlon.

Sweeping back into Connecticut, to Hartford, one can easily locate the insurance company of that city's name. Its central building is a huge Greek-revival edifice constructed in 1920. Behind it are newer buildings, including a modern skyscraper that houses most of the employees and an immense data-processing operation, one of the industry's largest, so powerful that the energy throw-off from it helps heat the buildings in winter and air-condition them in summer.

Taken together, these five companies—Continental, Rayonier, Grinnell, Sheraton, Hartford—contribute close to half of ITT's revenues. They represent Harold Geneen's corporation much in the way the International Standard Electric units represent Sosthenes Behn's work between the two world wars.

Other Geneen units are scattered across the nation, but not overseas. In his two decades at ITT, Geneen acquired only one sizable foreign concern, Teves, a manufacturer of auto parts (there are, however, a number of overseas plants). Domestic units range from the ultramodern Qume facility in San Jose to the more traditional Bell & Gossett plant near Chicago. At Qume a small force composed of skilled technicians is developing components for highly complex computer readouts, while half a continent away the rough young men at Bell & Gossett are engaged in fabricating a wide variety of pumps and heat-exchange units. Notices on the Qume bulletin boards offer "rewards" for those who can persuade a scientist to take a post there; the assembly-line workers at Bell & Gossett are gratified to have jobs during economic downturns.

Parts of Geneen's ITT are creating the technologies of the twenty-first century, whereas others are manufacturing products based on models almost two centuries old. Neither group is much aware of the other.

Geneen's corporation includes Carbon Industries and Pennsylvania Glass Sand, both headquartered in West Virginia, the former in Charleston, the latter in Berkeley Springs. Eason Oil is in

Introduction to ITT

Oklahoma City; Bobbs-Merrill, the publisher, is centered in Indianapolis, Indiana. One of Geneen's major accomplishments was the resurrection of Behn's domestic unit, Federal Electric, housed in a sprawling complex of offices, laboratories, and factories in New Jersey, across the Hudson from New York City. (In fact, there are ITT facilities in every state and close to a hundred foreign countries, all of which, in one way or another, bear the Geneen brand.)

That Geneen was an authentic genius, or at the least a brilliant manager, is conceded even by those who harshly criticize other aspects of the man's personality and many of his actions. He was an innovator of the first rank, perhaps a counterpart in the private sector to Robert Moses in the public. But his legacy was that feudal landscape described earlier, held together in large part by the force of his personality. At such major firms as Grinnell, Rayonier, Sheraton, and Continental are the earls of the empire, and at Hartford, the largest and most independent of the units, chairman and president DeRoy Thomas has ducal powers. The barons at Standard Elektrik Lorenz and Standard Telephones and Cables paid homage to headquarters, as did the knights at such units as Terryphone, Electro-Physics, and Bell & Gossett, and they still do, though Geneen has all but passed from the scene. The decision as to how much control should be centered in New York and how much retained at the units is one of the most crucial to the body and its parts.

Even with his enormous capacity for work, his clear and penetrating intelligence, Geneen couldn't possibly keep up with the minute details of the activities at so many companies. Much of his time was spent in providing overall direction, sketching long-term objectives, keeping tabs on managers in the field, and boosting spirits and offering critiques. In addition, he would decide on allocations of capital, defend ITT against outsiders, oversee the acquisitions program, and occasionally (and reluctantly) agree to divestitures.

Meanwhile, the operating companies were pretty much able to go their own way, with the clear understanding that management would be rewarded for outstanding performances and penalized for failures. Most of all, they had to contribute to the flow of information. There were seemingly endless reports, meetings, conferences, and consultations, all of which were designed to ensure smoothness of operations. Geneen often said, "I want no surprises." There were few within the corporation during his tenure in New York. As will be seen, the major surprises—and blunders—of that era came not from the divisional managers but from Geneen himself.

Geneen stepped down as chief executive officer in 1977 and two years later relinquished the chairmanship as well. He remained on the board, but for all intents and purposes his time had passed. The legacy remains visible, but even that is fading. In fact, a new ITT appears about to emerge, and in some respects it may resemble that of Sosthenes Behn more than it will the conglomerate created by Harold Geneen.

Rand Araskog has been ITT's leader since 1978 and is currently chairman, president, and chief operating officer as well as chief executive officer. His patrimony is enormous, complex, varied, and in some ways flawed. Araskog seems to understand this, and he has a program to alter the situation.

Just as Geneen had done before him, Araskog spent his first years in power sorting things out, preparing to institute his own policies. That he already has initiated a third phase of ITT's development is only now becoming evident. Part of the program depends on the sale of assets, mostly those gathered in by Geneen. The money will likely be used to cut back on long-term debt, clean the balance sheet, and be devoted to the core of the corporation, telecommunications.

During his tenure Geneen attempted to harmonize efforts at the ISE companies, in particular to bring together the French, Belgian, British, and German firms, which seldom communicated with one another. Each was most concerned with obtaining a share of the national market within which it operated, and each, more often than not, had closer relationships with other national telecommunications entities than with its own ISE partners. Thus, SEL, the largest member of the group, worked in tandem with Siemens, whereas STC wooed the British Post Office, which entered into telecommunications contracts with it and other domestic firms. Only Bell Telephone Manufacturing showed much interest in foreign markets, and this was due to the small size of its local telephone operation as much as anything else. Geneen wanted to unite the research capabilities of the Paris laboratories, the development expertise and marketing skills of BTM, and the manufacturing facilities in Germany and the United Kingdom, but his attempts failed, dashed on the rocks of nationalism, the peculiarities of the markets, and tradition.

Much of this is now changing, as several ISE companies are

Introduction to ITT

sharing information and responsibilities for System 12, ITT's most ambitious venture in telecommunications. The corporation's technological future may have been wagered on this new switching operation, and it has brought together SEL (Germany) and BTM (Belgium) as never before. But not STC, which has united with its British partners to perfect a rival technology, thus hewing to the old ways and hedging ITT's bets in that large market. Moreover, France has nationalized ITT's historic Compagnie Générale de Constructions Téléphoniques, CGCT; how the System 12 program will be affected remains to be seen.

In this, as in so much else, ITT remains a bewildering entity, even to insiders not directly involved with telecommunications. To give it manageable coherence—a much more rational shape than the corporation has had in the recent past—is perhaps Araskog's most important task. Like his two larger-than-life predecessors, he will have to respond to developing political and economic events while acting upon management, structure, and evolving opportunity.

1

The Brothers Behn:
The Early Years

LIKE many other major enterprises, International Telephone and Telegraph originated in a series of insights on the part of an exceptional individual who had the natural gifts and the experience to put them into practice. Sosthenes Behn was also fortunate to have arrived on the scene at a time when this was not only possible but almost mandated by expressed needs, technology, and organization.

Under the terms of its articles of incorporation ITT would be empowered to acquire controlling shares of two small Caribbean telephone companies, but the very name indicates that its founders must have had more than this in mind. From the first they intended —assuming all went well—to initiate, acquire, or manage communications companies throughout much of the world. They were to start in Cuba and Puerto Rico with the little they already had. Much more was to follow, however.

Because of the nature of the telephone industry during this period, most of the growth would have to be accomplished through acquisitions and cooperation with governments rather than by creating new entities in the private sector. The vast majority of telephone companies outside the United States were government owned and run, often as adjuncts of the postal services.[1]* From its inception, then, ITT was wedded to politics, and its operations and strategies had to be geared to this as well as to economic factors. ITT's leaders would have more dealings with rulers than with businessmen, at least in the beginning. This was a circumstance firmly established at its birth and not a post–World War II development, as is sometimes assumed.

Telecommunications was growing rapidly in the aftermath of the Great War, and starting such an enterprise not only appeared viable but in retrospect seemed an obvious step, one talked about for years by such men as Alexander Graham Bell, Thomas Edison, and Clarence Mackay, and even by J. P. Morgan and E. H. Harriman. Major corporations such as American Telephone and Telegraph and Western Union played with the notion. United Fruit had visions of a global telecommunications network being utilized by its ocean-going vessels. General Electric and Westinghouse thought of the profits to be realized by supplying an international version of AT&T with equipment. Before turning to other matters, the young Radio Corporation of America also considered such an enterprise.

The possibility was discussed in those hobby magazines catering to radio enthusiasts, and in some articles can be found predictions that in the near future it would be possible to place a telephone call to almost anyone in the world with as much ease as making a direct call within a neighborhood. The technology for such a system already existed, and in some parts of the world cooperation between companies was a reality.

Within the industry it was generally believed that a global network would consist of a federation or confederation of national firms, each distinct and independent, tied to the others by means of long-distance lines. That such a system might be owned and operated by a single giant corporation wasn't seriously considered. In the nature of things governments hardly would relinquish control over so important an enterprise as a telephone company.

Sosthenes and Hernand Behn had no such grandiose ambition in 1920, when they organized ITT. But they did intend to acquire as

*Superior figures refer to the Chapter Notes, which begin on page 393.

many companies as they could and perhaps, eventually, become dominant leaders in global telecommunications.

This was a vast undertaking, even for the largest of corporations, and certainly the ITT of that period wasn't at all in this category. Their Cuban Telephone Company serviced only 33,000 customers in 1920, and Porto Rico Telephone had less than a quarter of that number. (In contrast, AT&T had more than 10 million telephones in operation.) Given what they began with, the obstacles in their way, and the nature of the industry, the Behns did remarkably well for themselves.

This was the beginning of what would be an American decade; the country's economic might and international reputation never appeared brighter than in the aftermath of the Great War. This was duly acknowledged throughout the world, and if businessmen didn't consider the period to be the high noon of American industrial capitalism, it was because they expected better things to come.

In London the *Times* grumbled that the major reason Britain had fought in 1914–18 was to maintain its world position against an expanding German empire. That country had been defeated, but in the aftermath of victory the United States had seized Britain's position and was now replacing it as the leader in world commerce. Large American companies were aggressively setting up factories and offices in Europe, Asia, and Latin America. Wherever the British businessman looked, there were three or four Americans eager to displace him, offering superior goods and lower prices, and out-maneuvering him at every turn.

This appeared evident in telecommunications, where Sosthenes Behn would soon best his British counterparts at Marconi and Eastern Telegraph and earn a reputation as a master strategist and brilliant tactician. He also was somewhat of a mystery man, a well-known entrepreneur who never granted interviews, a dazzling original in a period when at many organizations corporate pyrotechnics were being subordinated to a penchant for teamwork and chief executive officers took pride in their abilities at arriving at consensus. Behn would have none of this. ITT was to become an extension of his personality and would receive his stamp in much the same way International Business Machines reflected Thomas Watson's creed and Ford Motors did that of its founder.

Behn seemed always on the go, wheeling and dealing, charming kings and politicians, spending months at a time overseas engaged

The Brothers Behn: The Early Years

in a wide variety of ventures that appeared romantic and even dangerous to a generation eager to believe the best of its business tycoons. Behn was in his element negotiating with counterparts at foreign companies or leading government figures at sumptuous banquets or private dinners aboard ocean liners to and from Europe. The traditional arena of operations for American businessmen was the boardroom, where deals were struck across long, dark, document-laden tables around which were arrayed batteries of lawyers and accountants, after days of negotiations. Europeans often conducted their most important discussions in a more casual way, over brandy and cigars after a gourmet meal, and the Latin Americans followed that tradition. It was in such a setting that Behn was a master, and those who witnessed him in action on his own ground were so impressed that they recall small details of such encounters more than four decades later.

Europeans and Latin Americans who dealt with Behn saw in him a familiar figure and at the same time tended to consider him a typical American, referring to his drive, dynamism, and swiftness in coming to conclusions. But in America he was looked upon as a European, and New Yorkers who met him for the first time were often surprised to learn he wasn't French or English. One told an ITT officer, "He does not dress like an American; he does not eat like an American; he carries his handkerchief in his sleeve, which no American does."[2]

For some writers of the period Behn became the prototype of the tycoon they expected would dominate the emerging world business community in the second quarter of the century: glamorous; involved in exciting new technologies; a polymath in close rapport with leading political, business, and scientific leaders on all continents; international in style and prepared to move swiftly from place to place. Hardly a probusiness publication, *The Nation* saw this in him. In the spring of 1928 it was said in its pages that "Sosthenes Behn may, a century hence, loom considerably larger than Calvin Coolidge."[3] It was, for the time, the supreme accolade.

And he was successful. The following year ITT would post revenues of more than $100 million and profits of $17.7 million. Under its corporate umbrella were nine telephone companies in Latin America and Spain with more than 580,000 stations; a major cable and telegraph operation; and factories in Belgium, France, Norway, Spain, Italy, the United Kingdom, Austria, Argentina, Japan,

China, and Australia. ITT's common stock had been one of the standouts during the great bull market of the decade, having risen from 64 to 281 in less than five years. The Behns' reputation remained bright even after the crash of '29. The following year, when other businessmen were in eclipse, *Fortune* published a major article on the brothers, noting they had "built one of the world's most spectacular enterprises."[4]

With all of this, little is known of the Behns' origins and early lives, which only enhanced the fascination they commanded. Sosthenes in particular was the kind of individual about whom elaborate, farfetched stories were told. Even those that were factual smacked of romance.

It is known, for example, that Louis Richard Sosthenes Behn was born on the island of St. Thomas, in what was then the Danish West Indies, on January 30, 1884. These are the name and the date that appear on his certificate of baptism. Yet even his closest friends weren't aware of his true given name. Years later, when Sosthenes first sought employment, he attempted to appear more mature by growing a beard and adding two years to his age. When in middle age, he would tell people he had been born on the same date as Franklin D. Roosevelt: January 30, 1882.

Hernand was almost two years his senior. There was another, older brother, August Wilhelm ("Willie"), who died of lockjaw after having stepped on a rusty fishhook while walking on the beach with his father, and a half-sister, Madeleine, later the wife of the Norwegian minister to Canada.

During the 1920s and 1930s some newspapers and magazines carried stories claiming the Behns were an old Danish family. In 1931 Sosthenes told a reporter that one of his ancestors was Aphra Behn, a female writer of some note at the court of England's Charles II. Her picture hung in the family home, and Sosthenes owned a yacht named *Aphra*. There is no other evidence of the relationship, however. During this time some business rivals whispered that the Behns were converts from Judaism—again, without evidence.

It is fairly certain the family had German roots, and that the Behns spread out all over Western Europe. The father, Ricardo Augusto Guillermo Behn, came from a branch of the family that had originated in Germany and later migrated to Venezuela. He was born in Venezuela in 1840 and sent to school in Hamburg, probably because he had relatives there. Guillermo, as he was later

The Brothers Behn: The Early Years

known, settled in St. Thomas in 1868, after having been in business for a while elsewhere in the Caribbean. According to most accounts, he became a ships' chandler, selling supplies to captains who used the island as a stopping place. Guillermo owned the only ice house on St. Thomas and also dabbled in other ventures, such as land, the sugar and tobacco businesses, and shipping. In 1872 he married Louise Mendes Monsanto, the daughter of a well-to-do St. Thomas merchant. Her family was French, and at least one of the brothers' close associates believed it to have been distantly related to the Eiffels of Paris.[5]

The Danish West Indies was in economic decline at the time of Sosthenes' birth. The islands' fortunes rested upon sugar and tobacco grown on St. Croix and to a lesser extent on St. Thomas, and the planters there hadn't been able to compete successfully with their more efficient counterparts in Cuba and Puerto Rico. At one time the St. Thomas harbor of Charlotte Amalie had been one of the busiest in the Caribbean, but now it was in danger of becoming a backwater port. The commercial spirit remained strong, but there was little promise for bright, ambitious young people, and many members of the upper and middle classes wanted to leave.

Havana was the economic and cultural magnet for the region, and there was a direct telegraphic link between that metropolis and Charlotte Amalie, so that news from the outside world tended to have a Cuban flavor. Few West Indians felt the urge to migrate to Havana, however. Despite centuries of Danish rule and proximity to Spanish-speaking lands, English was the native language for islanders of all social classes, and it was used in government as well.

The educated aristocrats hoped to go to Europe for cultural experiences, but the American influence in St. Thomas was stronger, with even month-old U.S. newspapers in great demand. A colonial council member of the period, Charles Taylor, spoke for many when he expressed his admiration for the Americans: "It has been a pretty general opinion that if the island were to change owners, and some such prosperous nation as the United States of America were its possessor, its condition would improve and its prospects would be better."[6]

It isn't difficult to imagine Hernand and Sosthenes as small boys in this kind of environment, swimming at the beaches, taking small boats for trips to the other side of the island, fishing off the docks in Charlotte Amalie and watching the ships arrive and depart, and playing outside their father's chandlery. Perhaps they realized, in a faint way, that business was declining, for they could have seen this in the traffic at the Behn establishment and learned of problems by listening to casual conversations along the docks. But the land and climate were beautiful, with perpetual summer and few challenges or threats, and the business slump was gentle and so might easily be ignored. Charles Taylor thought that all the merchants in St. Thomas knew the situation was worsening but that they lacked the energy, power, and imagination to do anything about it. He could have counted Guillermo Behn among this number: "But did they seek to adapt themselves to the altered condition? Did they lower their prices? Did they seek to attract buyers or to establish some new industry to prop up their fortunes? Not at all."[7]

Guillermo Behn might have noted all of this, but he also would have observed that these conditions hadn't altered the way he and his family lived. The Behns were middle class to the core, with friends and relatives in local government and on other islands in the region. In addition there was money in Louise's family, and this source might have been tapped in case of an emergency. Had things continued along these lines, Hernand and Sosthenes might have entered their father's business and, with their intelligence and abilities, gone on to become important merchants in the Caribbean trade or in the sugar business. Whether they would have broken out of this mold cannot be known, but it is highly improbable. That part of the Caribbean was hardly an incubator for prominent world figures.*

Little more is known of Guillermo Behn, who died in 1889, at the age of forty-nine, and was buried alongside Willie in St. Thomas. Sosthenes used to tell associates and his sons that Louise blamed Guillermo for their oldest son's death. Had they not been walking on that beach, Willie wouldn't have stepped on the fishhook, and would have lived. She had been devoted to him and after the funeral spent all of her afternoons in the family mausoleum, never again to speak to Guillermo. Sosthenes implied that this might have contributed to his father's death.

A year later Louise married Sosthenes Luchetti, the French con-

---

*Alexander Hamilton, who was born in the British colony of Nevis and educated on St. Croix, was one of the small handful of islanders who left the area to go on to great fame. He arrived in New York more than a century before the Behns were born.

The Brothers Behn: The Early Years

sul in Charlotte Amalie, a neighbor and an old family friend. Luchetti had been Sosthenes' godfather, and the boy had been given his name (it is Greek and means "life strength").

Sosthenes Luchetti was the last of nine children. Many of his five brothers were businessmen with interests in the Caribbean—Cuba, in particular—and this might have explained why he sought and obtained the diplomatic post at St. Thomas. A more worldly and sophisticated person than Guillermo Behn, Luchetti had relatives and business connections in Italy, France, and the United States as well as in the nearby islands of the Caribbean; he wasn't the kind of person likely to plant roots in an out-of-the-way post such as the Danish West Indies. Those who knew Madame Luchetti, as she came to be known, remarked on her forceful personality and the close relationship she had with her sons. Apparently Luchetti had a similar temperament, and he got along well with both boys, especially so with Sosthenes. He was determined that they should have a Continental education and then a good start in whatever business or profession they selected.

When Hernand and Sosthenes were old enough, they were sent to a private school in Ajaccio, the capital of and one of the larger towns in Corsica, where Luchetti had relatives who could look after them. Afterward they attended the Collège Ste. Barbée, a secondary school run by a religious order. It was on the outskirts of Paris, an especially exciting city for young people, and it must have suited Sosthenes' personality and interests and contributed much to his Continental mien.

Hernand graduated in 1896 and returned to St. Thomas, where he served as his stepfather's assistant, leaving Sosthenes on his own at Ste. Barbée. Early in 1898 Luchetti left the diplomatic service and moved the family to New York, where in midyear they were joined by Sosthenes. Their familial ties were strong, and the young men were practicing Catholics—Hernand more than Sosthenes—but in many other ways they, too, had become somewhat rootless. In time the more sedate Hernand would prefer to stay in one place, but Sosthenes became restless when long in one city. Only sixteen years old, he had become addicted to travel and the company of worldly, sophisticated figures, and would remain so for the rest of his life. He also was quite urbane, fluent in English, French, and Spanish, and confident—almost cocky—regarding his abilities and prospects. All that remained of his years in the West Indies were stories he would tell friends of how he and Hernand had played as boys and a strong preference for daiquiris.

Apparently one of the reasons Luchetti had moved to New York was that that city was a major entrepôt and listening post for the Cuban-American trade. In the mid-1890s he had become involved with several properties in Cuba, a railroad being the most important, and in addition he saw troubles brewing between the United States and Spain regarding the future of the island. Luchetti was part of a circle of individuals with similar interests, among whom were George Hopkins, William Burt, and Walter Ogilvie, fairly well known in Manhattan and Cuba as investors and managers for properties owned by others. Valuable at the time, they would become even more so should the guerrilla fighting then erupting on the island be contained, and especially if Cuba were to come under American protection.

The United States declared war on Spain in April, and two months later the first marines landed in Guantánamo Bay. By early July there were more than 25,000 American troops in Cuba, with more on the way. And in New York, Luchetti and the others wondered about the condition of their properties and looked for ways both to take care of them and to obtain contracts relating to the war effort.

In late July the Cuban & Pan American Express Company was formed in New York, with Hopkins, Burt, and Ogilvie its president, vice-president, and treasurer–general manager respectively. Into it were placed some of the holdings these men controlled—most involved with commerce and a delivery service that crisscrossed the island and could serve as an information network. Hopkins was able to win an Army contract to ship military and other supplies to Cuba, and in addition his company was given primary responsibility for the military payroll. This meant its agents had to keep in close contact with all units, which presumably would put them in a good position to make certain the partners' properties were protected.

Cuban & Pan American was a privately owned entity, and there is no way of knowing whether or not Luchetti had an interest in it. But he may have asked Ogilvie, as a favor, to find employment for Sosthenes. (Hernand was already working for the French Telegraph & Cable Co. in New York.) At the time a junior messenger in lower Manhattan, Sosthenes was eager for a challenge and leaped

The Brothers Behn: The Early Years

at the chance to become a clerk at the company's office in the financial district.

Business was booming. Not only were the Cuban properties secured, but the holding company itself was a huge success. Seizing the opportunity, Hopkins set up a subsidiary, International Express, which performed the same services for American forces in the Philippines. Cuban & Pan American continued on after the war, when it seemed the partners had in mind a global delivery operation, one that engaged in a variety of somewhat bizarre tasks, such as shipping Chinese corpses home for burial.

Sosthenes was to leave Cuban & Pan American shortly after the war ended. For him this company wasn't much more than a school, a place where he discovered an interest in international dealings and developed a desire to continue in this kind of business. In little more than a year, according to Walter Ogilvie, he had become involved in all aspects of the operation, though he never rose much higher than clerk-messenger. Later Ogilvie worked under Behn, and on occasion he remarked that Behn had been one of the most industrious people he had ever known at Cuban & Pan American; still, Ogilvie must have exaggerated when he claimed that prior to his departure the young man had advanced to the stage where he might have managed the business himself.[8]

At the time, Behn must have felt that he could do better, learn more, and advance rapidly at some other job, and Ogilvie apparently agreed. He encouraged Behn to seek another position and recommended him for one at the Morton Trust Company, a medium-size Wall Street house with a good reputation in the financial community. Although primarily concerned with underwriting domestic railroads and industrial companies, Morton did have a small foreign desk, and it was there Sosthenes sought employment. Initially rejected as too young, he applied again a few months later. He had grown a beard and "officially" added two years to his age, and this time he was hired. As a clerk in the foreign-exchange office he demonstrated the same drive and abilities he had at Cuban & Pan American. Soon he was named assistant to the head clerk, and in 1903, at the age of twenty-one, he became head clerk himself.

Sosthenes was restless in this post. Although the financial education he was receiving at the Morton Trust was priceless, and the business contacts he had made would serve him well in the future, he yearned to travel and, most important, to run his own operation.

I·T·T: The Management of Opportunity

An assignment from a group of Wall Street bankers took Sosthenes to Mexico in late 1903, and from there he went to Puerto Rico to see Hernand and to gauge for himself the island's potential.

Puerto Rico had become an American possession as a result of the Spanish-American War, and business had developed rapidly with the inevitable infusion of new capital. Luchetti controlled a small railroad there as well as sugar plantations and a large tract of land on the outskirts of San Juan. While Sosthenes had been learning high finance in lower Manhattan, Hernand was involved in managing these properties and exploring new opportunities for the Luchetti interests. Delighted to be together with his brother again, Sosthenes considered his own future on the island. Puerto Rico easily might become a major source for sugar, especially since as an American territory its products could enter the mainland duty-free. Along with the expansion of the plantations would come the growth of the railroad, and the port of San Juan would prosper, making land there quite valuable. In addition, a rapidly developing Puerto Rico would be a natural customer for a wide variety of American goods, from clothing to coal. All of these activities would require banking and brokerage services, as well as expertness in dealing with American businesses, something Sosthenes felt he had acquired in New York.

Sosthenes decided to remain in Puerto Rico, where he worked with Hernand and several of Luchetti's relatives in managing properties and in making certain the railroad ran in good order. But soon he became bored with this kind of work, finding himself with a good deal of spare time. Sosthenes spoke with one of his uncles about the demand for farming equipment on the island. He proposed to import such merchandise, and demonstrating a fine skill at negotiation, he managed to borrow $1,000 for the venture, which turned out well. Sosthenes then reinvested his profits in additional stock and repeated the operation on an enlarged scale; additional profits were realized. Within less than a year he repaid the loan and had $40,000 in capital.

Sosthenes had utilized the training he received at Cuban & Pan American and the Morton Trust, and at the age of twenty-two he was about ready to strike out on his own—but not quite. From his earliest childhood he had dreamed of working with Hernand. Not only were they bound together by genuine affection, but their personalities complemented each other. Sosthenes was becoming a

The Brothers Behn: The Early Years

daredevil promoter, whereas Hernand, always more conservative, had demonstrated talents for management. Each provided characteristics deficient or lacking in the other, and this became immediately evident to those who came into contact with them. "Hernand is the more deliberative and philosophical; Sosthenes is the quicker, has more nervous energy," thought a reporter after an interview with them years later. And he added, "There seems to be a peculiarly close bond between them." It was, then, a natural match, one of the most fortuitous and harmonious in American business history.

In 1904 Hernand and Sosthenes pooled their savings, inheritances, and a bequest from their mother, and used the funds to organize their own firm, Behn Brothers. This partnership engaged in a wide variety of activities, almost all of which involved sugar, brokerage, banking, commerce, and warehousing. In time it owned docks in San Juan and storage facilities in many parts of the island. Puerto Rico's once diversified economy was being transformed into one based on sugar. Old plantations were expanded and new ones organized, and all but the largest required assistance in marketing and financing crops and receivables. Behn Brothers would advance funds, taking as security crops yet to be harvested and sold. In addition, the firm arranged credits for those planters in need of them and offered investment assistance for the more prosperous ones. It was a risky, highly competitive business, demanding a keen knowledge of crops, markets, credit terms, and people, but the brothers did well at it. Hernand's earlier good relations with the planters contributed to the success; more might have been due to Sosthenes' ability to master the intricacies of the sugar and factoring business and to utilize his New York contacts. The Behns were on their way to amassing a fortune, though just how much they made and the extent of their holdings is unknown, since the firm's papers have been lost or destroyed long ago. By 1913, Sosthenes was president of the San Juan Stock and Produce Exchange as well as founder and president of that city's chamber of commerce. It wasn't a particularly large pond—San Juan's population was around 70,000 —but Sosthenes Behn had become one of its biggest and most prominent fish.

By then Behn Brothers had become one of the largest agents for American companies on the island. Sosthenes traveled back and forth to the mainland to service accounts and to maintain banking and other contacts, and there were jaunts throughout the Caribbean as well. Hernand generally remained in the office, taking care of management while Sosthenes worked on new deals. Sosthenes was president of the partnership and chief operating officer. It was a pattern both men had created, with each doing what he enjoyed and was best at.

In June of 1914 the Behns appeared as directors and officers of the newly created Porto Rico Telephone Company. This much is certain; there are records of them as members of the board and officers. But the details of the transaction, and of how they came to the company, are more in the province of myth than of fact. This isn't because the brothers had anything to hide but rather because of the lack of documents, faded memories of events that took place so long ago, and Sosthenes' tendency to embroider the tale when recounting it to friends, associates, and journalists. He had a flare for the dramatic, and it must have pleased him to tell of how a $100-million corporation began as the settlement of a debt.

According to their story, the Behns accepted the company in lieu of money owed them by a client. It appears that this person, a cane grower, had himself obtained the telephone company in lieu of a debt payment, and now he proposed to unload it in the same way. The Behns thought this better than nothing. Hernand had learned about the business at French Telegraph & Cable. Perhaps he could do something with the property.

They really didn't know what was involved. Shortly thereafter the Behns went to the central station to assess the situation. There they found little more than a shed, from which originated 250 telephones. This was the entire system. Dismayed, Sosthenes turned to his brother and remarked, "You were in the telegraph business for a while, Hernand. Now let's see what you know."[9] And that, said Sosthenes, was how International Telephone and Telegraph was born.

But the actual events were more complex than those related in this tale, and far more revealing of the ways the Behns did business.

Contrary to Sosthenes' account, the brothers hadn't acquired Porto Rico Telephone—which didn't even exist at the time—but rather South Porto Rico Telephone, a minor operation that serviced the towns, villages, and plantations in that part of the island. This company wasn't in as bad shape as Sosthenes later claimed, but it certainly fit the general description he gave reporters. The actual date of the acquisition cannot be determined, but apparently it was in 1905 or 1906. Nor is there any way of discovering how the brothers managed to run the operation and its finances, how many telephones were installed, what rates were charged. More is known of the island's other telephone company, Porto Rico General, which operated in San Juan and other parts of the island where the large majority of the wealthy people lived.

Under ordinary circumstances South Porto Rico might have gone under, perhaps to be taken over by its larger and more successful neighbor. This didn't occur. Instead the Behns managed to turn it into a profitable property. When merger talks were initiated, they entered from a position of some strength. Porto Rico General remained several times larger than South Porto Rico, but the Behns clearly had demonstrated skills that impressed the former company's board. Thus, though originally minority stockholders, they assumed leadership of the newly created Porto Rico Telephone.

Given the time and place, Porto Rico Telephone was a sizable operation. The enterprise had assets in excess of a million dollars and net earnings of close to $50,000, out of which was paid a dividend, in 1914, of $36,000, or $6 a share.[10] The Behns had parlayed what must have been a small investment in a minor entity into control of a much more significant one. This was quite fitting. Perhaps the most merger-minded corporation in American history, ITT originated in an acquisition engineered by a businessman who would emerge during the next decade as one of the era's shrewdest bargainers and negotiators, one whose purchases and sales of utility companies overshadowed the kind of management he provided those under his umbrella. Yet none of this would have been possible had it not been for the nursing to health of a firm that prior to the Behns' arrival had been a rundown, almost valueless property.

Sosthenes started by raising additional capital through a Wall Street bond offering, and Hernand used the funds to improve and expand services and to integrate South Porto Rico into the new entity. By 1917 gross revenues had risen by almost 50 percent, to more than $300,000 from $228,000 in 1915; the dividend had been boosted to $8 a share; and the company reported that it had a retained-earnings account of more than $25,000.[11] Clearly the Behns had shown themselves to be as adept at running a utility as they had been in factoring, finance, and trade.

They had also shown that the talents, strategies, and tactics suited to commerce might be adapted to the management of a telephone company. Their two businesses were quite different, after all, and on the surface they would appear to have demanded strikingly different approaches.

Behn Brothers might expand wherever opportunities existed and resources allowed, just as it could stagnate if new opportunities were not sought out. It might have taken on new products, performing a wide variety of services for clients and worrying little about government interference or, in that period, regulations. This kind of operation was well suited to Sosthenes' talents, to his outgoing, freewheeling approach.

In contrast, most utilities function under fairly rigid sets of rules established by political entities, and they are answerable to them in such matters as financing, operations, and rates. For example, Porto Rico Telephone had been granted a franchise that would run out in fifty years and was limited by it to the creation, maintenance, and operation of the telephone system; nothing else would be permitted. Furthermore, the government had the right to purchase the company in 1934, or at ten-year intervals thereafter, at a price to be fixed by an independent board. Later the Behns would have to obtain government approval for bond offerings and to petition for rate increases.

At Behn Brothers, Sosthenes had dealt with businessmen, in competition with other bankers and factors. As leader of Porto Rico Telephone he had a monopoly, and his most important transactions would be on the governmental level. He would negotiate with political agencies in the knowledge that victory in any head-on confrontation was unlikely. Behn Brothers might withdraw from an area or business, taking its holdings with it. Under terms of the franchise, Porto Rico Telephone had to live up to a certain level of performance and wasn't free to deploy assets elsewhere.

As constricting as this must have been for Sosthenes in a business sense, it was even more disturbing personally. With his proclivities he couldn't have relished the idea of devoting himself to a business that would limit his geographic horizon. He yearned to expand, but Porto Rico Telephone was island-bound; it couldn't set up operations elsewhere in the Caribbean. Future development would of necessity be internal—within Puerto Rico itself.

But the Behns might acquire other telephone companies, in areas outside of their home base. Each would have to be kept distinct,

The Brothers Behn: The Early Years

separate from the others, for governments would hardly accept intrusions such as this into what they now considered sovereign territories. From this might develop a family of companies but not a giant, monolithic corporation. Even American Telephone and Telegraph, which under the leadership of Theodore Vail had started or acquired dozens of local companies throughout the United States and tied them together with long-distance lines, was having difficulties on this point, with litigation a chronic problem and squabbles with state and local authorities a generally accepted part of the business. If it was so difficult to have a unitary system in a federated republic, it would have been close to impossible to have one that operated in several countries.

The Behns mulled over this idea and considered their own possibilities, and that of the region. The United States exercised hegemony in the Caribbean, but as yet owned only Puerto Rico. There was no direct telephonic connection between the island and the mainland; certainly Washington would look favorably upon such a link. The line might originate in San Juan and run underwater to Santo Domingo, where it would connect to a land-based system in Haiti. There could be a second submarine cable to Cuba's eastern shore, and then overland to Havana. A third cable would connect that city to Key West, Florida.

Such a project would require the direct assistance of the Woodrow Wilson Administration and intervention in three Caribbean countries. It would appear rather farfetched for Washington to use its muscle for so small an entity as Porto Rico Telephone. For the time being, at least, the idea was shelved.

Porto Rico Telephone was doing well, however. In less than a year their work had attracted the attention of other regional utility executives. The Behns were turning around the Puerto Rico operation; perhaps they could do the same with others.

The Cuban Telephone Company was in need of assistance at this time. It had been organized in 1908 as a consolidation of several smaller units, but the merger hadn't jelled, either technologically or in terms of management. The booming Cuban economy required additional lines and units, and these were slow in coming. Revenues were rising steadily, but they were eaten up by interest charges resulting from unfavorable bond placements. Management insisted upon a generous common-stock-dividend payout, which emptied the treasury and made necessary further debt issues.

On top of all this the service was poor. Havana's businessmen and the island's sugar and tobacco planters complained that their operations were being harmed by the lack of reliable communications facilities. The company's 1915 revenues were a record $1.2 million, and by manipulating the figures it showed a profit.[12] In reality, Cuban Telephone was close to insolvency. Both the common and preferred dividends were passed that year, and their prices on the Havana and London stock exchanges collapsed. Management found it impossible to raise additional capital, either locally or overseas. Outside help was needed.

The managers couldn't approach American Telephone and Telegraph. Under the terms of a commitment worked out by that company and the U.S. Department of Justice, AT&T was restricted from acquiring new units. In any case, AT&T wasn't interested in this kind of expansion; nor were any of the independent American telephone companies. Since the United States maintained what amounted to a protectorate over Cuba, and frowned upon entry by other countries, the Behns seemed a logical choice. By then the brothers had become American citizens as well as prominent figures in the American Caribbean outpost. Moreover, they were experienced telephone executives with a record of success. Finally, the Behns had a good reputation on Wall Street, without which nothing else might have mattered. Cuban Telephone's banker was National City, and that institution urged its directors to seek help from the brothers. This was done, and negotiations began in late 1915.

Any records that might have been kept of negotiations and arrangements have been either lost or destroyed, but the following year the brothers took command at Cuban Telephone. Applying lessons learned in Puerto Rico, they restructured the debt, upgraded operations, and within two years created a healthy system. Revenues for 1917 came to $1.7 million, arrearages on the preferred stock were cleared, and the common dividend was three times what it had been in 1913. With all of this, Cuban Telephone had for the first time an adequate depreciation account as well as a comfortable cash reserve.

American influence was growing in the Caribbean, and so was its presence. Soon Wilson would purchase the Behns' birthplace from Denmark and rename it the Virgin Islands. Yet Cuba was the centerpiece, not only the largest island in the region but also the wealthiest. In addition, it had the closest economic ties to the United States. Prospects for growth were excellent, in spite of political instability. Bumper sugar and tobacco crops brought high prices on the world markets. The Cuban-American commercial and investment communities in New York were busily seeking new ventures on the island. An American military intervention there was interpreted by Havana businessmen as a sign from Washington that stability would be maintained, while United States Army expenditures contributed to the island's prosperity. This situation not only benefited Cuban Telephone but encouraged the brothers to consider expansion, especially a cable link to the mainland.

Such a connection would be of limited value, and perhaps even impossible, without the full cooperation and support of American Telephone and Telegraph. The cable would have to link with that company's lines, after which there could be a direct Havana connection from almost anywhere in the United States. In addition, the Behns lacked the financial resources to undertake the project on their own, and AT&T would be a logical partner. Finally, they were interested in arriving at some kind of relationship with that company, one that would benefit their expanding Caribbean enterprises.

Through mutual associates at the Morgan Bank the Behns contacted Theodore Vail and in turn were referred to Nathaniel Kingsbury, AT&T's first vice-president and lead negotiator. The talks went smoothly, with Kingsbury immediately recognizing the benefits to be derived from such a project. Shortly thereafter the two companies became equal partners in a new entity, the Cuban-American Telephone and Telegraph Company, which was to construct a cable between Havana and Key West. This not only provided the brothers with access to a major market but gave them a common interest with the world's largest telephone company, which meant added recognition and prestige.

Planning was to have begun in 1917, with the actual construction to take place the following year. This schedule was interrupted by the American entry into World War I. Sosthenes enlisted in the Army shortly after President Wilson declared war, in April 1917. A year later Hernand joined the Naval Reserve, but he spent the period at the telephone companies.

In recognition of his experiences Sosthenes was assigned to the Signal Corps, where he served in various executive capacities. He arrived in France in time to participate in the final offensive of the war and achieved the rank of lieutenant colonel; at the time of the armistice Behn was assistant chief signal officer for the First Army.

Never in any real danger, he did see limited action in several key battles, for which he was awarded the Distinguished Service Medal and membership in the French Legion of Honor. By early 1919, however, Sosthenes was back at his desk in San Juan, once again working in tandem with Hernand in the telephone and banking businesses.

But this military experience left a permanent mark on the man. It altered his self-image, the kind of associates he sought, and even the structure of the business he hoped to shape. Now he would be Colonel Behn, or, to his close friends and business allies, simply "the Colonel." He gloried in the title, all of the military trappings, and even the supposed glamour of combat. This could be seen later on when he surrounded himself with former military and naval officers, many of whom he had met during the war. At headquarters in New York one often heard references to generals and admirals as well as to the Colonel. Most were engineers or professional managers; others were retired soldiers or sailors to whom Behn had taken a liking.[13]

Finally, the respite from business had provided Behn with time to consider his own future and that of his enterprises, to obtain a measure of perspective not possible in the Caribbean, and to witness, learn about, and make innovations in the most advanced techniques in telecommunications.

He was also to consider a move to a wider stage. In 1917 it appeared that Behn's old dream of an inter-island network was possible. Haiti by then was a virtual American protectorate, and Santo Domingo was occupied by an American military detachment. Behn-dominated telecommunications companies in those countries as well as in Cuba and Puerto Rico seemed capable of being organized. By 1919, however, he had scrapped the concept in favor of a much more ambitious one, which had incubated in France and developed in conversations with engineers and technicians who worked in the field for the armies.

Probably Sosthenes would have ventured elsewhere in any event; the wartime experiences helped jell elements already present in his personality and intellect. The Behns soon set about creating the vehicle that would take them out of the region of their birth and apprenticeship and in the process transform Sosthenes into a world-famous entrepreneur.

2

The Colonel:
The Early Acquisitions

ALWAYS vital in armed conflicts, communications played a decisive role in World War I. For the first time, naval combat patrols
utilized ship-to-ship and ship-to-shore wireless in engagements, and
by the time of the armistice, contacts were possible between surface
vessels and submarines. Airborne radiotelephony was perfected in
1918, so that observer craft might report findings to artillery installations and direct their barrages. Trench warfare in the West brought
about the rapid development of field-telephone units.

Long-line cables between the fronts and headquarters had been
laid by engineers of the Allied and Central powers in 1915 and 1916,
and the Americans would do the same once they entered the conflict. Wartime demands for telecommunications were increasing
exponentially. Shops and factories in Britain and France that in 1914
produced small amounts of switches and "radio telephones" now
became major installations utilizing mass-production techniques.
Europe's manufacturing facilities were strained, and soon those in

the United States would feel the impact of requisitions. Yet suppliers scrambled to obtain contracts, which not only were lucrative in themselves but would provide them with decided advantages in the postwar competition that was sure to develop.

Technological advances and plant expansion during the conflict would set the stage for rapid growth afterward. Europe's governments might control their telephone systems, but most of the equipment they used came from private suppliers. Such industry leaders as L. M. Ericsson and Siemens and Halske understood this, as did their counterparts at International Western Electric, a subsidiary of AT&T's Western Electric, which had facilities in many countries at that time.

Such opportunities were also perceived by Sosthenes Behn, whose work in the Signal Corps had brought him into close contact with representatives of these and other equipment manufacturers. While in France he became conversant in the latest technologies and heard of ongoing researches, in addition to meeting the men involved in both.

Behn knew about the rapid spread of telephony in the United States, and his Caribbean experiences had shown him how underdeveloped the systems were in that region. Now he learned of the enormous potential of the European telephone market. Compared with that of the United States, it was an almost virgin field, with the industry barely established at this time. According to one census, the United States had almost 64 telephones per 1,000 inhabitants in 1920; that year there were fewer than 9 per 1,000 in Germany, and fewer than 5 and 3 per thousand in Great Britain and France respectively. This was a part of the world he intended to enter, though at the time the means of doing so weren't at all clear.

Toward the end of the war representatives of Europe's telephone operations met with American bankers to discuss reconstruction and development problems. President Wilson sent observers; he had become interested in telecommunications, and in particular he wanted to make certain no foreign company or country controlled any significant portion of the American market. Assistant Secretary of the Navy Franklin D. Roosevelt was in Europe at the time, and he may have attended the discussions. Outspoken in his belief that foreign ownership of any part of American telecommunications would prove dangerous in any future war, he would later formulate a plan whereby the British Marconi interests in the United States would be taken over by a new entity, Radio Corporation of America. Admiral William Bullard, who was present at the conferences, learned there of projects for setting down a transatlantic telephone cable and came away determined "that if possible this new form of international communication should remain in the hands of the Americans."[1]

Whether or not Behn attended is not certain. The meetings weren't secret, and with his rank and position, he easily might have arranged an invitation. Furthermore, he already knew the representatives in attendance from the Morgan interests and National City. He wrote to Hernand about plans for entry into the European market, probably knowing that Washington was prepared to support if not sponsor American telecommunications companies involved in such projects.

This surely was more important and exciting than anything occurring in the Caribbean. Cuban Telephone and Porto Rico Telephone wouldn't be ignored, however, and the first order of business would be to construct the cable to Key West. But while awaiting the ship that was to return him to Havana from France, Sosthenes' thoughts were likely more with Europe than with the islands.

Both of the Behn telephone properties had prospered during the war, a period when commercial activities were high and demand for communications expanded rapidly. Under Hernand's management Cuban Telephone had gathered a sizable reserve, and Porto Rico Telephone's finances had never been in better shape. The Colonel had no difficulty in picking up where he had left off. Now that the fighting had ended, work on the cable could begin. Demand for such a link had increased during the past few years, however, and together with AT&T executives the brothers decided to construct two additional lines. Hernand supervised the work, which was completed on April 11, 1921.

In the meantime the Colonel had been in New York, attempting to organize and finance a new company, whose object would be to assume control or management of other existing telephone and telegraph companies, presumably through exchanges of stock. This was in early 1919, and during the immediate aftermath of the war, prospects appeared bright and money for new projects still wasn't difficult to come by. But Behn had little more than an idea and his own record to offer—no assets, organization, or carefully worked out strategy. He was turned down by several banks, among them his old associates at Morgan and National City who had helped finance the Cuban and Puerto Rican operations and to create Cuban-American. Undaunted, he came forth with another proposal. The new corporation would be composed of all three of these companies—or at least those shares of the Cuban and Puerto Rico companies controlled by the Behns as well as the indirect 50 percent equity in Cuban-American. This would be a holding company in that its only assets would be stock in the operating units plus some furniture and a lease on an office. Once this was organized, Behn hoped to raise money by selling new shares as well as floating a bond issue. The money thus obtained would be used to purchase control of additional companies.

This plan would be easier to implement than the original one. The offering would be conventional enough, to the casual observer little more than a shuffling of paper, certainly not the creation of a major new corporation. Individual investors purchasing shares would in effect be getting partial ownership of the Caribbean telephone companies. But the objective remained a far larger entity, one that would break out of the area and operate on a vaster scale.

Hence the name. There is an old ITT story to the effect that the Colonel selected it in the hope that investors and others would confuse his new company with American Telephone and Telegraph, and perhaps this was a consideration. More likely the "International" reflected his clearly stated ambitions and objectives. But in the original July 19, 1920, prospectus there is to be found a more modest goal. ITT intended to exchange its shares for those of the Cuban and Puerto Rican companies, to manage these firms "and any other desirable telephone and telegraph companies in Latin-American countries."[2]

Enough owners of shares in the operating companies accepted the offer so as to make ITT a viable entity; within a year and a half it held 90 percent of Porto Rico Telephone and almost as much of Cuban Telephone. But it was a small firm, having started out with cash items of $10,954 and a basket of securities the brothers valued at more than $12 million, though actually worth perhaps a quarter of that amount.

ITT might acquire additional firms through exchanges of stock or through outright cash purchases, and in 1920 neither method appeared promising. As yet there was no public market for the stock, and in order to create one the Behns would have to locate an

The Colonel: The Early Acquisitions

underwriter interested in selling a new issue to investors and speculators. The country was in the midst of an economic decline that year, one that continued on into 1921, and the securities markets plunged; no Wall Street house was willing to take on an ITT stock issue. Nor was it possible, in this kind of an environment, for a new firm to float bonds so as to raise funds in this way. The Colonel was able to place a $4.3 million Cuban Telephone bond issue with National City Bank, but only after agreeing to pay what for then was the almost usurious rate of 7½ percent. This money was used to help finance cables to Key West and a thorough revamping of the Havana lines, which had fallen into disrepair during the war. But the parent company languished, unable to do much more than manage existing properties until the Behns obtained sufficient capital.

In May 1921, the Colonel married Margaret Dunlap, of Philadelphia, who was related to the Berwind family, one of Behn Brothers' first and most important clients. After a short honeymoon he entered into negotiations regarding the possible purchase of the entire Chilean telephone system, and later Behn came close to taking over the telephone operations in Montevideo, Uruguay.[3] Both deals were aborted when ITT was unable to raise the necessary funds. The Colonel persisted; much of his time was spent among the New York bankers, attempting to develop new methods of raising capital.

ITT was placed on a 6 percent dividend basis in October, this in spite of a poor balance sheet. The Colonel was mistaken if he thought this would impress the Wall Street bankers. He was able to raise some additional cash the following year, however, by means of a program whereby new shares would be offered directly to Cuban Telephone's workers. At year's end, close to 1,300 individuals —most of them officers and employees—owned slightly more than 150,000 shares. By then the balance sheet had improved somewhat, and bankers were starting to take notice of the company's growth.

Despite a continuing dismal scene on Wall Street, Behn was able to interest several underwriters in his shares. In April 1923, E. B. Smith and Dominick & Dominick underwrote a 50,000-share offering of common stock at $68.50 a share, and the issue sold out in less than a week, giving ITT more than $3 million in new capital. Immediately Behn filed for listing on the New York Stock Exchange, and after approval was granted, trading began on April 25. ITT not only had achieved its initial breakthrough in the capital market, but its shares were now traded on the nation's premier exchange. These were necessary prerequisites for expansion, and the Colonel was in a stronger position when bargaining for acquisitions. Shortly thereafter he organized the International Telephone Securities Corporation, wholly owned by ITT, as a vehicle to assist in his work, and then embarked on what amounted to a shopping tour of Latin America and Europe.

Hernand remained in Havana, overseeing ITT's operating properties. Under a mutual arrangement he was president of Cuban Telephone and executive vice-president of the parent company. Sosthenes was on the boards of both Cuban and Porto Rico Telephone and was nominally president of the latter company for a few years. He was president of ITT itself, an entity that at the time consisted of a suite of offices on Broad Street and a small staff.

The Colonel demonstrated little interest in the actual day-to-day management of properties; this was Hernand's responsibility. Monies earned at the two operating companies would be used to service the debt and pay for expenses. What remained was remitted to ITT in the form of dividends. In 1922 these came to half a million dollars and the following year to more than $800,000. To this would be added the funds Sosthenes raised through securities offerings. The money piled up. By the end of 1924 he had the means to initiate a whirlwind program of takeovers.

In May, Behn announced that he expected shortly to report "the acquisition of substantial interests in the telephone systems of one European country and one Latin-American country."[4]

It was an open secret on Wall Street that Spain was the European country involved. At the time, the national treasury was almost bare, and Spain was on the brink of chaos. In September, King Alfonso XIII gave his approval to a military coup led by Gen. Miguel Primo de Rivera, in the aftermath of which there was a measure of stability. Now Spain's bankers moved in to attempt a restructuring of its debt and to keep the country afloat financially. National City was a leader of the consortium, not unusual in a period when the major New York banks were expanding throughout the world, elbowing aside their European counterparts.

International Telephone and Telegraph was among National City's newer and more rapidly growing clients. On Wall Street the company was viewed as part of the bank's "constellation" and a vehicle whereby additional business in Europe and Latin America might be obtained. Just as National City was engaged in competition with the European banks, so ITT was about to enter into contests with Europe's leading producers of telephone equipment. The two American companies were natural allies.

Spain's nationally owned telephone system had always been one of Europe's worst, famous for undercapitalization and mismanagement. Now it was almost completely closed down, with more than half of its 90,000 stations inoperable and the rest in service sporadically. The Madrid government lacked the resources to bring it back to life, and so Primo de Rivera looked abroad for help.

Several major European equipment manufacturers, among them Ericsson, Philips, and Siemens, were interested in taking over the telephone operations. None of these firms had significant experience in operating a major utility, but on their staffs were individuals who might have handled such tasks. They appreciated that much of the system would have to be reconstructed from the ground up and that this would involve major contracts for equipment. A firm like Siemens might have been willing to take losses on operations, knowing that these would be recoverable through the sale of a wide variety of hardware. In the beginning a clear favorite, Ericsson understood this and was prepared to accede to almost any conditions laid down by the government.

ITT was in a completely different position. By 1924, Cuban Telephone had only 50,000 stations and the Puerto Rico company a fifth that number, but Hernand and some members of his staff had been at their jobs for many years. Although it was true that no one there had been involved in so large an enterprise, ITT still had an edge in this regard over its Swedish and German counterparts. On the other hand, ITT lacked manufacturing facilities, and should the company obtain the Spanish concession, it would have to purchase equipment from other firms, at least initially.

Given the nature of the competition, International Western Electric Corporation (IWEC), AT&T's European subsidiary, might appear to have been the obvious candidate for this role. Clark Minor, an IWEC vice-president, had acquired an intimate knowledge of the Spanish situation and was eager to work with Behn on the project.

IWEC was solidly entrenched in several European countries. It could be traced to the International Bell Telephone Company, which had been founded by several of Alexander Graham Bell's associates in 1879 to introduce the telephone into Europe. Mainly an importer of American equipment at first, it was located in Antwerp,

Belgium. Soon thereafter the American Bell interests purchased Western Electric, which promptly took responsibility for IWEC. Now IWEC became a manufacturing company, largely by acquiring the Bell Telephone Manufacturing Company of Antwerp. By 1924 it was one of the most important telecommunications suppliers in Europe, and a willing partner for ITT.

As has been seen in his development of Cuban-American, Behn wasn't averse to joint ventures when they suited his purposes. Whether he had this in mind in the Spanish case cannot be known. Nor are there any records of conversations between him and representatives of Ericsson, Siemens, IWEC, or any other firm. But ITT did notify the Madrid government late in 1923 that it was interested in obtaining the concession, and early the following year Behn arrived to take charge of negotiations. Once there he would be in close contact with the National City Bank contingent, as well as with Clark Minor. The U.S. Commerce Department had an office in the capital, and the Colonel came to know and work with its assistant trade commissioner, James Burke, who was willing to help ITT in its efforts. At a crucial point in the discussions he enlisted the help of American ambassador Alexander Moore as well.

With the support of National City the Colonel purchased control of three small but important Spanish telephone companies: La Madrileña, which had the concession for Madrid; La Telefonía General, with lines in other major cities; and La Peninsular, a long-lines company. Out of these he organized the Compañía Telefónica Nacional de España (CTNE), whose board was headed by the influential Duke of Alba and contained several government officials. With this kind of support and these allies, it is little wonder Behn felt confident of success.

This was his initial foray into the major league of international business, and the Colonel performed superbly. His fluent Spanish and courtly manner impressed King Alfonso, Primo de Rivera, and others with whom he came into contact. Capable of entertaining lavishly and then working through the night after his guests had left, the Colonel soon outdistanced his European rivals. National City Bank applied pressures when they were needed, and additional Spanish politicians and noblemen were added to the CTNE board when help was required from that quarter. Ambassador Moore went out of his way to assure the government that "the American telephone system was not equalled anywhere," and Burke killed stories inimical to ITT's interests.

The Colonel: The Early Acquisitions

King Alfonso approved of the concession on August 25, and four days later Primo de Rivera made it official. CTNE promised to create a national telephone system within five years and to employ as many Spanish technicians as possible. The government pledged not to attempt a takeover of the company for twenty years, and ITT agreed to accept a profit margin of 8 percent. CTNE was capitalized at more than $45 million. ITT retained a controlling interest in the company, while a large number of preferred shares were owned by Spaniards, especially those close to or in the government. On December 5 ITT organized the International Telephone and Telegraph Corporation (España), which was to provide technical and financial assistance for CTNE. A few months later a jubilant Colonel Behn told stockholders that by 1935 Spain would have approximately 400,000 stations and its system would be one of the most efficient in the world.[5]

So ambitious a project would require large amounts of capital investment and equipment. The money wasn't too much of a problem. The great bull market was going full blast on Wall Street, and ITT's stock was considered one of the leading glamour issues. Shares that sold for 64 in 1923 went over 100 in early 1925, when the Behns raised almost $9 million through a rights offering. At the same time, National City made it clear there would be no difficulty placing a large new bond issue.

More troublesome was the way some of this money had to be spent. Not only did Ericsson and Siemens demand high prices for their equipment, but the Colonel thought much of it inferior to American counterparts. He knew, however, that importation of telephonic materials from the United States would pose problems. For one thing, under the terms of the concession, contracts had to be given to Spanish factories whenever possible; for another, the logistics of the work necessitated having suppliers on the Continent. Everything pointed in the direction of further acquisitions, this time of equipment manufacturers, whose major installations were in Europe.

The Colonel decided on a bold move. He would attempt to purchase all of International Western Electric from American Telephone and Telegraph. Although only a minor segment of the giant Western Electric—which in 1924 posted sales of close to $300 million —IWEC was a major operation in its own right, with sales and earnings that year of $44 million and $1.5 million respectively. Like its parent, IWEC was a holding company, with equity in operating firms in Great Britain, France, Belgium, the Netherlands, Norway, Switzerland, Austria, Hungary, Estonia, Egypt, South Africa, Canada, Brazil, Argentina—and Spain. Not only was IWEC more an international company than ITT, it had revenues in excess of seven times those of Behn's properties.

IWEC was engaged in manufacturing telephone equipment, mostly by using Western Electric's patents; it had no research arm, and a tenth of its sales were of equipment imported from the parent company's factories. It wasn't as profitable as Western Electric, and in some years actually posted losses. Part of this was the result of the mismanagement and undercapitalization of some subsidiaries; Western Electric tended to look upon IWEC as a form of corporate orphan. More important, Europe's telephone companies usually favored suppliers wholly controlled by nationals; often the same individuals appeared on both boards. IWEC would be turned down for contracts later awarded to national firms producing the same items under Western Electric's patents.

IWEC's indifferent earnings record and the need to invest additional funds in subsidiaries meant that remittances were required from AT&T itself. Indirectly, then, American telephone customers had to subsidize the growth of the foreign installations, and there was no way of knowing when dividends would be paid. The American government frowned on such a practice and pressured AT&T to divest itself of the overseas operations, preferably by selling them to another American company. Behn must have known of this; National City was a banker for both AT&T and ITT.

After concluding his business in Spain, the Colonel returned to New York for a meeting with Charles DuBois, president of Western Electric, to discuss a possible purchase. Recently turned down for the AT&T presidency in favor of Walter Gifford, DuBois wasn't of a mind to see his position diminished, and he rejected the advances.

Blocked at Western Electric, Behn next explored the situation at International Automatic Telephone, a Chicago-based firm with important overseas interests that was controlled by the Strowger Corporation. International Automatic was one of Cuban Telephone's major suppliers; Behn knew the management and suspected it would be willing to sell some of its European properties. But Strowger had assigned manufacturing rights to much of its equipment to Western Electric, and the connections between those two firms were so intimate that a sellout was impossible.

The Colonel: The Early Acquisitions

No other American manufacturer had the capabilities and patents required to restructure the Spanish telephone system. For a while it seemed Behn would be obliged to deal with the Europeans on their terms and in the process lose any chance for significant profits from CTNE. He did have one last opportunity, what amounted to an end run around International Automatic. Margaret Behn was related to a partner in the French banking house of Morgan Harjes, and through him the Colonel learned that the Compagnie Française pour l'Exploitations des Procédées Thomson-Houston might be willing to spin off its telephone-equipment-manufacturing arm, which consisted of two plants, two thousand workers, and also a large number of manufacturing rights obtained from both General Electric and International Automatic. Behn rushed to Paris to negotiate a deal, out of which came the Compagnie des Téléphones Thomson-Houston, at first a wholly owned subsidiary of the Compagnie Française but one in which ITT quickly obtained a substantial interest. In time it might become an important element in a manufacturing complex, but by itself this segment of Thomson-Houston couldn't handle CTNE's immediate requirements.

Still, it was an interesting situation. Provided with sufficient capital, Thomson-Houston might become the nucleus for a major new equipment company. Behn had learned the Paris city government was considering granting a management contract to some outside concern, and this too might be won if he had a French base of operations. In other words, Thomson-Houston could prove a perfect vehicle for entry into the lucrative French market. All of this would take time, however, and Behn was anxious for quick results.

While the Colonel was in Paris, the American government's pressures on AT&T to divest itself of IWEC were intensified. Eager to put fears of Justice Department prosecution behind him and at the same time to throw off a low-profit operation controlled by his former rival, Gifford agreed to sell if the proper purchaser could be located. National City Bank and J. P. Morgan & Co. brought Gifford and Behn together, Behn making one of his by then customary transatlantic dashes for the meeting.

The two men were introduced at the Morgan Bank, with DuBois fuming in the background. They agreed in principle to the sale, and that summer negotiating teams from both sides met regularly to work out details. Meanwhile, ITT's representatives visited the

European factories so as better to understand their capabilities and to assure executives there that programs in progress would continue and that new contracts were on the way.

The final problems were worked out by mid-September. IWEC would retain its Western Electric patents for several years—an important matter, for without them the Behns would be unable to use its equipment for CTNE. In return for this, Gifford received concessions on the purchase price and terms of payment. All that remained were minor housekeeping details.

The agreement was announced in September 30. AT&T would hand over ownership of IWEC for $30 million, a low price considering the assets involved and the potential of several of the units, in particular Standard Telephones and Cables, Ltd., the British subsidiary, and Le Matériel Téléphonique, which would fit in well with Thomson-Houston. Only $5 million of this amount would be in cash, with the remainder in the form of thirty-year convertible 5½ percent bonds. The convertibility was such that by making the exchange, AT&T might have a powerful, even controlling interest in ITT were it so inclined. This wasn't considered a serious problem, for such a move surely would invite prompt Justice Department action. Moreover, the two companies were on excellent terms, having, in a sense, divided the world between themselves. AT&T agreed not to compete overseas, and on his part the Colonel wouldn't erect telephonic-equipment plants in the United States.

ITT announced that there would be a name change, from International Western Electric to International Standard Electric (ISE), but that there would be no immediate significant alteration in operations. Shortly thereafter Behn established research facilities in Paris and London and prepared to consolidate its many independent units.

The acquisition of CTNE and International Standard Electric transformed ITT from a smallish regional utility into a medium-size, fully integrated operating and manufacturing complex. Behn not only could supply the Spanish telephone network with whatever equipment it required but in time might challenge Ericsson and Siemens elsewhere. He believed other countries in Europe and Latin America would soon appreciate the financial and operating benefits of private ownership of their lines. ITT's subsidiaries would provide him with entry into the bidding should this develop. Furthermore, he could become more aggressive in seeking acquisitions now that he could claim the capability of meeting all demands.[6]

ITT's next move was into Mexico, a country with a revolutionary tradition that included expropriation, poor relations with the United States, and a chaotic array of telephone companies. Several cities had systems of their own, few of which were connected to the others by means of long-distance wires. Franchises would be awarded only to be revoked once a new government came to power. Identical rights would be granted to two companies, so that in some parts of the country there were competing lines while in others, where services were needed, there were none at all. Moreover, each company used different equipment, so that interconnections weren't possible even if they were sought.

For example, the Mexican Telephone and Telegraph Company, organized by Boston financiers associated with the Bell system, had obtained a concession in 1903 to operate in the federal district that included Mexico City and from there to construct lines to other parts of the country. Five years later the government granted a similar concession to Empresa de Teléfonos Ericsson S.A., which soon had lines in the federal district and fought it out with Mexican Telephone in terms of service, price, and bribes to officials. Empresa de Teléfonos used Ericsson equipment, while Mexican Telephone's was supplied by Western Electric and IWEC.

Under the terms of Mexico's federal constitution each state had the right to establish its own system, and the privilege was extended to several districts as well. The state of Vera Cruz entered into a contract with the British-controlled Vera Cruz Telephone Construction Syndicate to establish a company in that city and to send long-distance lines into Mexico City. Soon there were three connections between Vera Cruz and the capital—one each from Mexican Telephone, Empresa de Teléfonos, and Vera Cruz Telephone—and none was working. Meanwhile, there was no service between Monterrey and Mexico City.

In 1915, a year when American troops invaded the northern part of Mexico, the Mexican government seized the assets of Mexican Telephone and operated the company as a national entity for the next five years. In this period there were few improvements, and even simple maintenance was ignored for months at a time. Meanwhile, Empresa de Teléfonos expanded rapidly, so that by 1925 it was the largest and most efficient system in the nation.

Behn had explored the possibility of acquiring the Mexican Telephone operation as early as 1923, and discussions toward that end were resumed two years later, shortly before the old concession was due to expire and at a time when the government hoped to improve its relations with the United States. The firm then had slightly more than 17,500 stations, most of which offered infrequent and unreliable service. Mexican Telephone's plant was said to be worth more than $5 million, but this clearly was overstated. Cash items were less than $50,000, and revenues came to less than $500,000. The company hadn't paid a dividend on its preferred stock for eleven years and had never made a distribution to its common shareholders. It was close to defaulting on its bonded obligations.

The picture was bleak, which perhaps was one reason why Behn had so little trouble in obtaining the concession. He talked glowingly of establishing an ISE plant in Mexico City to produce equipment, and promised cash advances to cover expenses until Mexican Telephone could be put back on its feet. Under the terms of the revised concession the company would be permitted to expand throughout Mexico, and within months ITT managers and engineers were planning for automatic exchanges in Mexico City and Tampico and for long-distance lines to most other cities. There was to be a direct connection with AT&T lines in Texas and, in the future, linkages with Cuba as well.[7]

Everything was falling into place, and ITT's prospects were excellent. Work on the revamping of Mexican Telephone began in early 1926. By then the CTNE had a new president, the Marqués de Urquíjo, who was close to King Alfonso and key members of the government and the army. ITT had organized Standard Electric S.A. around its ISE holdings in Madrid, and this company was charged with producing much of the equipment for the modernization and expansion effort, the initial step for which would be the creation of an automatic exchange system for the capital. In Paris, ITT representatives were negotiating for the remainder of the Thomson-Houston shares, and that firm had just received a new contract from the city's telephone company. Additional stations were being added in Cuba and Puerto Rico, and Hernand already was planning for a fourth submarine telephone cable from Havana to Key West.

In a period of slightly more than five years ITT had grown from a corporation with gross revenues of less than $3 million and assets of below $14 million on two Caribbean islands into one with revenues of more than $17 million and assets of slightly less than $100 million, with systems on two continents and manufacturing plants and offices throughout the world. The Colonel had triumphed in competition with major, well-entrenched European corporations. Siemens and Ericsson soon noted a new vigor at the major ISE installations. In Paris, London, and Berlin, ITT was viewed as one of the more important spearheads for a vigorous, powerful, and expanding American international capitalism. Other communications companies were monitoring the situation in Spain and Mexico, considering whether they would benefit from becoming part of an expanding ITT constellation.

While in France toward the end of the war, Behn had started to devise a strategy the implementation of which would bring under his control a major worldwide telecommunications corporation. His ambition hadn't been realized by early 1926, but the groundwork had been laid. He now had the structure that would bring him to that goal.

3

The International System

IN discussions with bankers and politicians, in speeches, interviews, and reports to stockholders, Colonel Behn often referred to "the International System." This wasn't a mere slogan but rather a rational, well-thought-out and tested idea that developed out of experiences during the 1920s and that toward the end of the decade was inculcated in every new executive and manager. This International System was a reflection of its founder and so provides a window through which to understand Behn's ambitions and methods of operation.

As he saw it, ITT would develop in a specific fashion, with no diversions or forays into unrelated fields. Additional national telephone companies would be acquired, and whenever and wherever possible they would be joined with other ITT-owned or -controlled means of communication. In those countries where the need existed, one or more ISE manufacturing facilities would be established, whereas in others, equipment would be imported from factories within the ISE constellation. It was all of a piece, and so described by the Colonel in an annual report of that period: "There appeared to be a fruitful field of service to be rendered in bringing together under one general organization electrical communications systems, and the extension by the parent company to the associated companies of the technical and financial facilities and direction that might be needed for their intensive and efficient development."

The Colonel made a careful distinction between the parent company, which of course was ITT, and the associated ones, of which Compañía Telefónica Nacional de España was the largest and prime example. Run by American officers and staff, ITT was to be centered in New York (and wherever Behn happened to be at a particular time) and would coordinate efforts, oversee the system, set strategic goals, run the interconnecting operations, and in general harmonize the businesses. The actual day-to-day problems of directing the telephone companies would be left to their individual officers, who were given a great deal of leeway in most matters. Already in control at Cuban and Porto Rico, Hernand would play a similar role at Mexican Telephone. But CTNE and other national systems acquired in the 1920s would always be led by prominent citizens of the countries in which they operated.

This wasn't unusual; in fact, it was the kind of approach utilized by American Telephone and Telegraph, itself a holding company that treated its operating units in pretty much the same way. But there were two obvious and important differences. AT&T didn't have to be concerned about national sensitivities, and although it functioned in many jurisdictions, above them was the nation-state, stable and deeply involved in the establishment of overall policies. In other words, Walter Gifford didn't have to worry about expropriations and was fairly isolated from corrupt politicians and completely so from revolutionary ones.

Sosthenes Behn was troubled by such matters. There could be revolutions and seizures of properties about which he could do little. A significant outburst of anti-Americanism could result in the liquidation of his holdings, and with the isolationist mood of the period, little help might be expected from Washington. The Colonel was acutely aware of the need to have excellent relations with host countries. This theme runs through all of the annual reports to stockholders during the 1920s. In early 1926, for example, when ITT was about to acquire additional telephone companies in Latin America, Behn declared, "It is the purpose of the International Corporation to develop really national systems operated by the nationals of each country in which the International Corporation is or may be interested." The following year Behn spoke of his "declared policy of developing the most efficient service so as to afford general satisfaction to the governments and people served." In presenting the 1927 annual report, he said, "In the development of the International System, there has been and will continue to be the ever-inspiring motive of rendering a high order of service in the different countries to which our activities are extended. Moreover, the best American practices have been suggested, but never imposed. On the contrary, the management has always been ready and quick to adjust American practices to local conditions and to adopt such local practices as were conducive to the successful development of the various entities." These exact words were used again the following year, and so may be considered the clearest and most definitive statement of the Behn point of view on the relationship that should exist between ITT and its national telephone subsidiaries.

The same approach was applied at the various ISE subsidiaries, but there Behn merely continued practices initiated by Western Electric. For a while he experimented with American managers at some of the companies, most notably at Standard Telephones and Cables, which had an American chief executive, Henry Pease, in the late 1920s. This was unusual, however; for the most part Behn preferred to hire and retain nationals as the heads of his manufacturing facilities. But there was an important difference between his practices and those of Western Electric's leaders. All of the latter, Charles DuBois in particular, tried mightily to keep the foreign companies on short leashes, an old AT&T tradition. This approach usually failed and might have been a reason for IWEC's generally poor overall performance.

The situation changed when IWEC became ISE. As much for reasons of temperament as anything else, the Colonel gave plant managers considerably more leeway in setting and implementing plans. He usually knew what was happening at their operations but rarely interfered if all was going well. An ISE chief executive officer or manager knew he would be free to operate as he saw fit so long as generous dividends were remitted regularly to the parent company, and he put on a good show whenever the Colonel came to inspect.

The International System

The managers and workers at the ISE facilities thought in individualistic and national terms. In some ways this was salutary, for it encouraged a spirit of entrepreneurship that otherwise might have been lacking. But it also implied that there really wasn't a true International System. For all of his talk about harmonization of interests, cooperation between ISE facilities in different countries, and the elimination of duplications of effort, the Colonel wasn't able to achieve any significant successes in integrating national manufacturing entities into anything resembling a coherent whole. In this period, the infancy of the modern transnational corporation, one hardly could expect Englishmen or Austrians to be wholly loyal to what in fact was a foreign holding company. Furthermore, in this particular industry, dominated as it was by national telephone companies, it would have been most unusual for a Belgian operation to purchase much equipment from a factory located in the Netherlands when it might be obtained locally. On several occasions during the next decade and a half, Behn managed to crack barriers to such sales, but when he did the story appeared in newspapers and magazines, so unusual was the development. Thus the ISE affiliates, like the national telephone companies, would remain more independent than might have been expected had the International System been truly effective.

Behn did better in attempts to have scientists share knowledge, but this was traditional among such individuals and not the result of the International System's approach. Technicians at the Laboratoire International in Paris cooperated with their counterparts at the ITT Laboratories in Hendon, England, but there was far less of this, in the beginning at least, between Le Matériel Téléphonique and Standard Telephones and Cables.[1]

This, then, was the situation in the mid-1920s. While talking of the International System, Behn was constructing what really was a confederation of telephone and manufacturing companies, bound together by financial controls and his own charismatic personality, to which soon would be added a third element—the interconnections between the systems.

In late 1926 the Colonel entered into negotiations with several major stockholders of All America Cables with an eye toward purchasing that company. This was an old, somewhat stodgy entity, which owned and operated telegraphic cables that ran between the United States and a good deal of Latin America and which would fit in perfectly with expansionist plans in that part of the world. All America would mesh with the ITT properties in Cuba, Puerto Rico, and Mexico. Furthermore, it would provide Behn with entry into Brazil, Argentina, and other countries whose telephone companies might be acquired.

At All America was a cadre of executives familiar with the situations in most Latin American countries and on good terms with their leaders, and they would prove useful additions to Behn's somewhat thin staff. For example, John Merrill, the company's president, had been at All America since 1884 and was well known in Mexico City, Buenos Aires, Rio de Janeiro, Lima, and Montevideo. Members of some of the nation's most prominent business families were on the board, which included William Emlen Roosevelt, Cornelius Vanderbilt, Percy Pyne, John Auchincloss, Russell Leffingwell, and Francis Higginson. Association with such individuals would provide the young ITT with a cachet that could prove invaluable later on, in addition to opening doors on Wall Street and in Washington.

Still, All America was a small company, with revenues of only $8.7 million in 1926. As befitted its conservative reputation, All America was in a highly liquid situation financially, with more than $13 million in cash and marketable securities and no debt. Since the Colonel was proposing to exchange ITT shares for those of All America, he would really be getting that company's operations for some of his own paper and in addition obtaining control of funds that later might be remitted to the parent in the form of dividends.

In late February, William Roosevelt, who was All America's chairman as well as its leading stockholder, met with Behn at the offices of Morgan & Co. Soon after, the two men told the press that Roosevelt and others on the All America board would accept four shares of ITT for every three of All America they owned. Virtually all the shares were tendered during the next month, so that on April 1 the company became an ITT subsidiary.

Roosevelt now stepped down as chairman and was succeeded by R. Fulton Cutting, a distinguished aristocrat who was seventy-four years old at the time and more interested in helping run the Metropolitan Opera than in directing the corporation. The Colonel became chairman of the executive committee, with his brother as vice-chairman. Given Sosthenes' many travels, this meant that Hernand became, in effect, All America's chief executive officer. Merrill remained as president and chief operating officer, and several ITT

men came over to help in the operations. This wasn't onerous, since
All America's headquarters were on Broad Street, just a few steps
from ITT's. Moreover, the cable business was quite stable and all
but ran itself.

The acquisition of All America completed the basic structure,
really a triad around which ITT would be developed during this
stage of its history. All America itself would become the foundation
for a major worldwide telecommunications empire, which at one
point appeared capable of dominating the field. Substantial additions would be made in the telephone-operating sector. As for the
ISE companies and Thomson-Houston, these would be expanded
and augmented, as would the laboratories. From this point on, the
pace of acquisitions would be hastened as the Colonel raced from
one negotiation to another on three continents.

The raw statistics provide a simple and an impressive demonstration of this accomplishment, and clues as to how it was achieved.
In 1926 ITT reported consolidated revenues of $22.7 million; these
would rise to over $100 million by 1929, and in the period net earn-
ings went from $7.1 million to $17.7 million and assets from $131
million to $535 million. Some of this growth came from internal
expansion, but most derived from takeovers made possible by the
issuance of new stock and debt, at a time when both were easy to
sell. The funded debt rose from under $9 million to close to $64
million, and the number of common shares went from 512,000 to
1,952,000. ITT's various subsidiaries raised additional funds through
the issuance of preferred stock, in much the same way as had been
done at CTNE. Some $8 million in face value of preferred was
outstanding in 1926; by 1929 the amount had grown to close to $40
million.

The Colonel's initial objective was to take over as many telephone
companies as possible in Latin America, wresting them from their
former concessionaires. The acquisition of All America was a prelude to the move southward; even while negotiating for that company, Behn had other deals in the making. All America would be
his beachhead, as it were, a means of introducing him and ITT to
the rulers of the area. As before, Behn would be assisted by officers
of J. P. Morgan and National City, and as had been the case in Spain,
his opponents would be Europeans, who increasingly found themselves being displaced by American businessmen in the aftermath
of the Great War.

Prior to 1914 Britain had been the leading trading partner and source of investment for many Latin American countries, and in fact it was Germany's attempts to invade what the British considered their special sphere of influence that helped set off the rivalries between these two European nations. British businessmen controlled railroads in Argentina, copper and nitrate mines in Chile, coffee plantations in Brazil, tin smelters in Bolivia, and telecommunications operations in these and other countries. Behind them were the leading London banks, which also floated government loans and provided a variety of services for the region's rulers. Assisting and protecting them all was the Royal Navy. A battleship was sent as a warning to the Guatemalan government when it failed to service loans floated by several London banks. After receiving an ultimatum from Whitehall, Haiti's leaders agreed to compensate a British citizen for losses suffered during a revolution. In 1914 a projected loan to Brazil was held up until outstanding claims were settled.

There was no doubt the British business community considered Latin America a prime area for investment. At the time direct holdings there came to around $3.5 billion, or as much as was placed in the United States, and the figure was growing rapidly.[2]

The war altered all this. Some British investments were liquidated, the power of the London banks was enlisted in the conflict, and merchants and manufacturers weren't able to service their clients. Now their American counterparts entered the breach. For many years active and even dominant in the Caribbean, they mounted an economic assault on much of Latin America. The banks led the way, with the mining and manufacturing companies not far behind. Morgan and National City were among the leaders and were well entrenched by mid-decade, having displaced British banks in several key refinancings. South American government and corporate bonds were the darlings on Wall Street in 1927, when Colonel Behn dramatically expanded out of his All America beachhead.

Within a period of two years ITT acquired a half-dozen of the continent's telephone companies, in each case displacing either a British concessionaire or a dominant investment group managed from London. This was accomplished with the help of the two American banks and their correspondents, which would arrange financings and later float bonds of the subsidiaries on Wall Street.

Behn started in Uruguay, which at the time had two competing companies, the Sociedad Cooperativa Telefónica Nacional, with 4,000 stations in the capital, and the Montevideo Telephone Company, Ltd., South America's fourth largest with more than 14,000 stations. Paradoxically, Nacional was a local operation and Montevideo functioned throughout the country. The Colonel soon united the two and joined them with the All America offices in Montevideo. As was becoming his custom on such occasions, the Colonel alluded to a large-scale construction program soon to be initiated, the establishment of manufacturing facilities, and linkages with other ITT systems. Then he hurried off to his next acquisition, leaving direction of the new operation to local businessmen drawn from the staffs of the predecessor companies.

Chile had been one of the more striking examples of how in the postwar period South America started moving out of the British financial orbit and into the one centered on Wall Street. By 1924 the country's bonds were being floated in New York by a consortium headed by National City, and the following year its central bank was reorganized along the lines of the Federal Reserve System. Gen. Carlos Ibáñez led a coup against the Emiliano Figueroa government in 1927. Both men were considered pro-American, but Ibáñez was more aggressive economically. Hoping to industrialize his country through an expansion of revenues from copper and nitrates, he wooed the American bankers assiduously, and one of his tokens of good faith was the award of the Chili Telephone Co. Ltd. concession to ITT. At the time South America's third-largest such operation with 27,000 stations, Chili Telephone was also one of the continent's more modern lines, and in addition a most promising situation. Chile clearly had a bright economic future, and expansion of its communications network was one of Ibáñez' more important interests.

The Colonel now attempted to move into Brazil. He only nibbled at the national operation centered in Rio de Janeiro, knowing that its Canadian concessionaires were too solidly entrenched with the regime of Washington Luiz Pereira de Souza to be displaced. This was the largest South American telephone system, one that Behn would pursue unsuccessfully for the rest of the decade. But he didn't leave Brazil empty-handed. Like Mexico, this was a federated republic, each of whose constituent states had the right to establish its own telephone facilities. Brazil had several other operating companies. One of these, Companhia Telefônica Rio Grandense, ran slightly more than 8,000 stations in Rio Grande do Sul, a state under the control of Getulio Vargas, one of Pereira de Souza's rivals. Behn was able to win this small concession, and with it in hand he attempted to move in on the Canadians, with little initial success.

The next step was Argentina, the wealthiest and most powerful nation on the continent and the one in which the British were most involved. While losing influence and prestige elsewhere, Britain not only retained its hold on leading segments of the Argentine economy but actually expanded upon it during the immediate postwar period. In 1928 Great Britain accounted for more than half of the total direct foreign investment in the Argentine of $2.1 billion. Yet here too the situation was changing.

For more than half a century Argentine politicians had dreamed of a time when their country might challenge the United States for hemispheric leadership, and they weren't likely to welcome American businessmen or bankers to their land. Both Hipólito Irigoyen and Marcelo Alvear, who alternated in the presidency for most of the 1920s, were decidedly pro-British. By mid-decade, however, President Alvear came to realize that Wall Street had a decided edge over London in the matter of government financing. Britain continued to dominate the private sector, but New York bankers were solidifying their influence with government officials.

ITT was no stranger in Buenos Aires. Its All America Cables building was a landmark in the capital, and it had a small ISE plant on the outskirts of the city. Chili Telephone's lines joined with those of Compañía Telefónica Argentina, a long-lines operation controlled, as were most of the utilities, by British banks.

Behn's ultimate objective was the United River Plate Telephone Company, which was centered in Buenos Aires but had lines in all parts of the country. With more than 200,000 stations, River Plate was not only the second-largest South American system but bigger by far than ITT's premier company, CTNE. At one time well managed and maintained, River Plate had declined significantly during the war owing to lack of repairs, and the British group that controlled and managed it during the early 1920s hadn't done much to alter this condition.

Although there is no way of knowing precisely how Behn proceeded, given his methods of operation and the situation at hand, he would have had to approach both the British owners and officials in the Alvear government. Utilizing the facilities of Morgan and National City as well as his managers at All America, he would have discovered what the price would be for River Plate, and whether Alvear would accept a change in the concession. An agreement wasn't possible in late 1927, however, and so Behn tried another approach. In March 1928 ITT purchased a controlling interest in Compañía Telefónica, whose 4,000 stations in Buenos Aires were dwarfed by those of River Plate but which did provide him with entry into the capital.

Irigoyen was returned to office by election a few months later, and negotiations were reopened. This time the government went along with the concession sale, and the British investors accepted Behn's offer of £12 a share or a smaller amount of cash plus ITT stock for their holdings, which came to approximately $60 million. In order to finance the purchase, ITT issued a $57.3 million convertible bond offering paying 4½ percent interest, a low rate at the time, indicating the company had an excellent credit rating and market acceptance. As before, the issue was floated by Morgan with National City a member of the syndicate.

By then stories about the Colonel appeared regularly in newspapers and magazines. *The New York Times* called him a "wizard at negotiations," and *The Washington Post* thought some of his deals "astonishing" and his vision "deep." *Time* said he was a man of exceptional abilities, observing that within weeks of completing the River Plate takeover, ITT engineers had started work on long-lines connections between Buenos Aires, Valparaíso, and Montevideo.

> Col. Behn's great design thus became obvious to the most casual observer. I.T.&T. cables stretch to the west coast of South America. Here they connect with the domestic telephone systems of Chile, Uruguay, and now Argentina. Thus a fast message may be relayed from New York to a house in the suburbs of Montevideo without once leaving I.T.&T. wires.[3]

Even while augmenting his Latin American telephonic network, Behn expanded upon the second leg of his triad, the manufacturing companies. Thomson-Houston, Standard Telephones and Cables, and Le Matériel Téléphonique were enlarged. Standard Eléctrica S.A., which provided equipment for CTNE, had plants in Madrid, Barcelona, and Santander, and from practically nothing had become the fourth-largest ISE subsidiary by 1930. ITT obtained interests in manufacturing facilities in Austria, Hungary, and Yugoslavia. In the spring of 1928 Behn completed negotiations for a controlling interest in Creed & Co., Ltd., an important British manufacturer of teleprinter apparatus. Early the following year ITT took a similar position in Ferdinand Schuchardt Berliner Fernsprech und Telegraphenwerke, A.G., a small manufacturer of telephonic gear and supplies with an office and factory in Berlin. This was to be his initial foray into Siemens' territory, a direct challenge to the Continent's leading electronic-equipment manufacturer that soon would be followed by additional moves into the German market.

What at the time appeared the most important acquisition took place in the United States and involved a dramatic restructuring of the telegraph and cable businesses. In early 1928 Behn entered into serious negotiations with Clarence Mackay, who controlled a holding company that bore his name, which in turn operated telegraph, cable, radio, and equipment-manufacturing concerns, the largest and best known of which were Postal Telegraph and Commercial Cable. The latter company owned and managed seven submarine cables that ran between the United States and Europe and one transpacific line that connected San Francisco to Hawaii, Midway Island, Guam, and the Philippines and then went on to interconnect with Japan and the Asian mainland. Postal Telegraph was Western Union's only significant American competitor, while some of Mackay's plants turned out a variety of radio hardware.

The corporation was in bad shape. In 1928 Mackay had assets of over $91 million, on which it reported consolidated revenues of slightly more than $39 million and net earnings of only $470,000. Mackay was generally considered a weak enterprise, capable of being revived but badly in need of fresh management and capital infusions, both of which the Colonel was prepared to provide.

Mackay himself was one of the legendary figures in American telecommunications. The son of a miner who had struck it rich during the California gold rush, he was celebrated in his lifetime as a reputable businessman much beloved by associates, but today he is probably best known as the reluctant father-in-law of songwriter Irving Berlin. Mackay had established Postal Telegraph early in the century as a vehicle first to challenge and then to absorb Western Union. Always audacious, he also attempted to seize control of American Telephone and Telegraph.

These bold plans came to nothing, and Postal Telegraph was

unable to develop into anything more than a marginal operation in the industry, and Commercial Cable performed only slightly better in its field. By 1927 Postal Telegraph had approximately 17 percent of the business; Western Union claimed the rest.

Much of Postal Telegraph's revenues derived from Commercial Cable. A businessman in London wishing to transmit information to someone in Cleveland, Ohio, might utilize Commercial Cable's wires. The message would be transmitted to the company's Broad Street station in New York, and from there sent on via Postal Telegraph to Cleveland, where it would be delivered by the familiar messenger boy. Western Union's domination of the domestic market scarcely could be challenged, but the Mackay operations in international communications did offer some advantages. Provided with proper leadership and new financing, and united with other systems, they could be turned into valuable properties.

Mackay was considering retirement in 1928, and several businessmen tried to buy him out, with little success or encouragement. Behn was different, and so was ITT. The Colonel wooed his man assiduously, in boardrooms and at his sumptuous dinners. Mackay was impressed, not only by the man and the way he had constructed ITT but also with his vision; in some respects Behn resembled the Clarence Mackay of a quarter of a century earlier. In addition, Mackay knew and respected John Merrill and appreciated how Commercial Cable would complement the All America operation. As for the Colonel, acquisition of Mackay Companies would not only greatly augment his cable business—in effect complete the All America network—but would also provide him with his initial entry into the United States. Under the terms of his agreement with AT&T, he still couldn't manufacture telephone equipment domestically, but there was no reason he couldn't engage in other, related activities.

Negotiations proceeded smoothly and were successfully concluded in a short time, considering the stakes involved. Under the terms of a fairly complicated plan, ITT organized the Postal Telegraph & Cable Corporation on May 18, 1928, a shell that was to take control of the Mackay Companies. With the help of Morgan and National City, Postal Telegraph issued $52.3 million in bonds, which were exchanged for the Mackay Companies' preferred stock. Every four shares of Mackay common were to be turned in for three shares of a new 7 percent preferred stock and one of ITT common. Thus,

ITT owned Postal Telegraph & Cable, which in turn owned the old Mackay Companies. Mackay and others of his team joined the ITT board, and he became chairman at Postal Telegraph, with Sosthenes as chairman of the executive committee and Hernand its vice-chairman. Some of All America's officers went on the Postal Telegraph board, and Mackay took a place on All America's.

The new ITT that emerged from the Mackay Companies merger and other acquisitions in 1928 had assets of more than $389 million, and consolidated earnings that year would come to $21.2 million. In fact as well as name, this was a global operation, and each of its three major components was larger than the entire company had been four years earlier.

ITT's role as one of the vanguard of the American business invasion of world markets was coming to be appreciated and its growing power recognized and respected. First with curiosity and then with concern, the London financial community watched as the Colonel bested his British counterparts in Latin America. His acquisition of All America was interpreted as a threat to the cable empires headquartered in that city and took on far greater substance when news arrived of his discussions with Clarence Mackay.

At the time, the major British radio, telephone, and cable companies were united in a loose alliance known as the Electra House Group. Disturbed by what they correctly interpreted as a challenge to their positions, several came together to form a new community of interests, the initial step in the erection of a giant telecommunications trust, which would be known as Cable & Wireless. Two months prior to the Mackay acquisition Sir William Plender of Eastern and Associated Cable Company and Sir Gilbert Gernsey of Marconi Wireless announced their intention to assume leadership in the movement. A new corporation would be erected on the old foundation; while each component would retain its identity for the time being, they would work "in the common interest." There was no mistaking what this meant: When and if ITT and Mackay came together, they would face stiff British opposition in cables, and other American communications firms intending to make forays overseas would meet the same response. Thus, Britain counterattacked.[4]

This new entity would have posed no challenge to AT&T, which by then had left the international arena. But it might adversely affect Radio Corporation of America, at the time competing with

The International System

Marconi for shares of the European radio-equipment market. The American firm also had a long-term contract with Marconi under the terms of which it handled all radio traffic between the United Kingdom and the United States, and indications were that the new British telecommunications corporation might seek to abrogate the arrangement, diverting business to its cables. Western Union was also in the cable business and had contracts with several British firms to carry messages from overseas to the United States; these, too, could be canceled, as could agreements entered into by Commercial Cable. The Americans would be dwarfed by this new alliance. Eastern and Associated was already the world's largest cable corporation, and with the others in the group it would own and operate some 141,000 miles of cables, far more than half the world total of 260,000 miles. In contrast, ITT, after the Mackay acquisition, would have slightly less than 63,000 miles, and although it was strong in the Pacific, it was in danger of being completely outclassed in the Atlantic. Moreover, a concerted British effort in Latin America might be part of a counterattack against American business on that continent, and might strike directly at All America.

The Wall Street investment community was prepared to meet this challenge. In 1928, when the business outlook appeared unclouded and the Great Engineer, Herbert Hoover, was running for the presidency, nothing seemed beyond its grasp. Confidence in American strength and in the country's ability to meet challenges was at its highest level in history, and the experiences of the past decade had confirmed Wall Street's belief in its power. In telecommunications, this meant that if Britain could put together a giant in the field to carry the national banner, so might the American bankers.

Ever since its founding in 1919, there had been rumors to the effect that RCA was intended to be the nucleus of a major international communications empire, and that it would begin by taking over Western Union's overseas operations. RCA had made gestures in this direction on several occasions in the 1920s. What would have been involved was an exchange of RCA stock for the relevant portions of Western Union, which would have left that latter company with its domestic operations plus a stake in RCA and the right to name new directors to its board. Nothing came of this, however, and the matter was dropped.

RCA's leaders were keenly aware in 1929 of the implications posed by a major British consolidation. The company's honorary chairman and one of its founders, Owen D. Young, was familiar with the companies involved and with individuals who would be in charge. A renowned international lawyer and sometime diplomat, he had played an instrumental role in obliging the British owners of American Marconi to sell their interests to what eventually became RCA. Young appreciated the magnitude of the British challenge and was prepared to assume leadership of the American business community when it came to organizing a response.

Gen. James Harbord, who was RCA's president, agreed with Young. By then, however, it had become evident that RCA's greatest growth would lie in domestic radio. The corporation's rising star, executive vice-president David Sarnoff, urged Young and Harbord to deploy assets into receiver manufacturing and broadcasting, and so they did, albeit reluctantly. By 1927 transoceanic communications and marine radio services accounted for only $4.8 million of RCA's gross income of $65 million, and international sales and services had a small part in the corporation's strategic thinking.

A similar situation existed at Western Union, a pioneer in the transatlantic-cable business that also competed with Commercial Cable in Latin America. In the early 1920s the company had announced plans for new and improved systems and for a while flirted with the idea of entering radio telecommunications in competition with RCA and Marconi. By 1928 Western Union was in trouble, and its president, Newcomb Carlton, had abandoned such expansionist plans for a defensive strategy. Four years earlier it had completed work on a new cable between the United States and Britain, which through interconnects went to the Continent as well. This expensive system had drained Western Union's treasury, and now, just when it was earning a good profit, came the challenge of the British consortium. Carlton had no ironclad guarantee that the British and other users would continue to utilize Western Union's facilities once the new company was in place.

Western Union was still large, and in some ways even powerful, but it was being challenged by Postal Telegraph and Commercial Cable on one flank and by AT&T on the other, and now this adversary loomed ahead. In a period of major growth in telecommunications, the company performed sluggishly. Revenues and profits edged forward slowly from 1922 to 1924, and even afterward, when business picked up somewhat, it lagged badly behind ITT and

RCA. Carlton realized he hadn't the resources to compete in the international field, even had he the desire and ambition to do so. Like David Sarnoff, he would just as soon concentrate on the domestic market, but for different reasons.

In February, Harbord dispatched Sarnoff to London, where he was to scout the situation at Electra House, discuss matters of common interest with Marconi's officers, and then report back with his findings. Carlton set off on the same ship, and with similar objectives. Referring to agreements with British firms then coming up for renewal, he told reporters, "How far these contracts are to be affected is a matter of great interest." More important, however, were Carlton's discussions with Sarnoff, for apparently, while on board, the two men reopened the matter of merger. After returning to America, Carlton admitted that he and Sarnoff indeed had talked of "finding some means of increasing our respective facilities," but dismissed rumors of takeovers. "So far as I know, Radio and Western Union are as far apart as the earth and the moon."[5] Yet within weeks Western Union's banker—Kuhn, Loeb—approached RCA, which referred the matter to its banker, Morgan & Co.

Thomas Lamont of Morgan urged RCA to reject the offer and suggested instead that Young and Harbord seek some kind of accommodation with another client, ITT, which had just taken over at Mackay. Knowing that these two had reluctantly concluded that RCA wouldn't become a major factor in the field of international telecommunications, Lamont asked them to help create a new American entry in that field, to be erected around ITT. According to Lamont, after negotiations were concluded, Morgan would float a new ITT bond issue, which then could be given to RCA in return for its overseas businesses, the proceeds to be used to expand domestic radio networks. This done, Morgan could approach Western Union with an offer for its international facilities and repeat the operation.

With Sarnoff's support, Lamont was successful. In early June, 1928, the New York and national business presses reported that negotiations toward this end had been opened between ITT and RCA. There followed a brief flurry of interest and activity, during which the stocks of both companies soared to record highs. Little more was heard of the matter for the next half year, though the talks continued and progress was being made. RCA in particular was positioning itself for some kind of deal while at the same time concentrating its attention on domestic business. On January 3, 1929, the company organized RCA Communications, Inc., as a wholly owned subsidiary, into which was placed the entire international operations of the firm. The following day RCA made a tender offer to the Victor Talking Machine Company, seeking to acquire that firm's phonograph and record businesses. Shortly thereafter discussions were entered into with General Electric and Westinghouse Electric & Manufacturing whereby the three companies would unify their research and manufacturing facilities for the production of radio receivers. Evidently the stage was being set for the sale of RCA Communications, the money for which would be used in the Victor takeover and for the development of new receivers.

On March 29 *The New York Times* carried a front-page story headed "International T.&T. Acquired R.C.A. Communications, Inc., To Add to Great World Chain." The price would be $100 million in ITT stock, to be transferred to RCA, which would make that company its largest shareholder. With this move ITT would become the "greatest organization in the telegraph business under a single ownership in any land." But not for long. The Electra House leaders were still working on their merger, and the *Times* thought it could be completed within a few months. Then the two giants would enter the contest for domination of world telecommunications.

The day after the *Times* story, Behn and Harbord issued a joint announcement that they were "in accord as to the desirability of a consolidation of their communications interests," and that a tentative plan toward that end had been drawn up. Nothing concrete had been decided on, but negotiations had got to the point where representatives of both companies had gone to Washington to discover whether the administration would consider such a merger in violation of the antitrust acts. Then, once again, the matter disappeared from newspapers and magazines.

October rolled around. The stock market collapsed, the British company still hadn't emerged, discussions between ITT and RCA continued, and in the Senate the matter of antitrust in telecommunications was being considered. The Committee on Interstate Commerce heard witnesses on both sides, the most forceful of whom was Owen Young. Not only should the government support such a merger, he said, it might actually consider direct participation. The time had come, thought Young, to set aside certain antitrust strictures and accept the need for government-business part-nerships, especially in the international sphere. "If you have any hesitation about unifying our external communications in the hands of a private company," he added, "then I beg of you, in the national interest, to unify them under government ownership in order that America may not be left, in the external communications field, subject to the dictation and control of foreign companies or governments." Young thought this as much a matter of national interest and pride as anything else. Simply stated, "In international communications the United States ought to be supreme."[6]

Through all of this, Colonel Behn was positioning himself for the grand move; he was eager to play such a role, having prepared for it for more than a decade. News of the British consolidation had only whetted his appetite, and the Mackay takeover was concluded with this in mind. Even the River Plate acquisition, completed in 1929, paled when set beside the vision of a united trust in telecom-munications headed by ITT. That company was the natural and even acknowledged leader, the rallying point, for such an entity, one that truly would become a world version of AT&T. Moreover, if Young had his way, it would be created with the support of government and the cooperation of former rivals.

Less than four years earlier Behn had taken over International Western Electric through government intervention and with a will-ingness on AT&T's part to leave the foreign field in order to con-centrate on domestic interests. Now it seemed to be happening again. Despite delays, hints of nationalized operations, and myriad frustrations, Behn was close to acquiring the foreign affiliates and subsidiaries of RCA, after which those of Western Union might fall into his lap. The following year Sarnoff would assume the RCA presidency; he was willing to cooperate. So was Harbord, who moved into the chairmanship. Owen Young was being considered for cabinet posts and ambassadorial assignments, and he used his influence on their behalf. Continued talk of a British consolidation prodded Congress into action, convincing members of the need for an American entry. When that appeared, the International System would be realized.

All that was needed was time.

4

Fighting for Time:
The Great Depression

ON March 6, 1931, the boards of directors of ITT and RCA issued the following joint press release:

> The accord made public by the two companies on March 30, 1929, for the consolidation of their respective communication interests when the law permitted, has been dissolved. This decision was necessitated by the fact that despite the increasing influence of communication mergers in foreign countries and the obvious advantage to American communications interests from consolidation of their services, no legislative action has been taken to eliminate these handicaps or facilitate the consolidation. The managements of the two companies have, however, in no way altered their sincere conviction, announced in their public statements of March 20, 1929, that the unification of American record communication services would be to the interest of our country and people.

There was more to it than an unwillingness on the part of some congressional leaders to go along with the merger. Although it was

Fighting for Time: The Great Depression

true that owing to the federal nature of the RCA charter, such permission would have had to be granted prior to the sale of overseas assets, other factors were of greater importance. For one thing, even though Cable & Wireless was eventually put together, the new entity proved incapable of expanding significantly upon the base created by its component companies. ITT was able to keep pace with it despite a rate war in 1930, and after a while Cable & Wireless simply abandoned most competitive tactics for a tacit agreement regarding market share. The general peace in transoceanic telecommunications and the lack of a serious British attempt to alter the status quo took pressures off Congress to come up with an American response.

Then there was the matter of terms for the takeover and the effects of delays on the participants. Although there was some talk of the issuance of 1.2 million shares of ITT common in exchange for RCA Communications, nothing definite had been decided, and as each side shifted ground the other grew increasingly disillusioned with the entire package. On his part, Colonel Behn became involved in other European discussions, some of which appeared more promising than the acquisition of RCA Communications or of segments of Western Union. Never a particularly patient negotiator when new prospects beckoned, the Colonel may have mentally written off the deal several months prior to the announcement to the press.

More important than either of these factors, however, was the advent of the Great Depression and all that it entailed for world business and finance. Although scholars today disagree as to when the economic decline actually began, clearly most American big businessmen of late 1929 expected it to be short-lived and not particularly disruptive. General Motors chairman Alfred Sloan said, "Business is sound," and Henry Ford reduced the prices of his cars in a gesture of confidence. Frederick Ecker of Metropolitan Life denied there was "any important change in fundamental conditions." "All the evidence," said President Hoover on March 7, 1930, "indicates that the worst effects of the crash upon unemployment will have passed during the next sixty days." To which John Edgerton, president of the National Association of Manufacturers, added, "I can observe little on the horizon today to give us undue or great concern."

In a report to stockholders in late May, 1930, the Colonel appeared quite optimistic and made no mention of the decline. He celebrated the River Plate acquisition; the purchase of controlling interest in the Compañía Peruana de Teléfonos, which was the leader in Peru's telephone system; and a foray into Turkey through ownership of the Constantinople Telephone Company. Behn was proud of the opening of new offices in ITT's own building on lower Broad Street, "one of the most modern edifices located in the downtown section of the City of New York," with a breathtaking view of the harbor. He observed that the corporation had obtained a major beachhead in the German market, that modernization of CTNE facilities was proceeding at a rapid clip, and that various ISE subsidiaries had turned in excellent performances. The Colonel appeared confident there would be further increases in revenues, earnings, and backlogs. Additional acquisitions were in the works. The present appeared pleasing, the future bright.

Behn issued the 1930 annual report in May of 1931, at a time when the business community had come to realize its perilous position. His summary of corporate developments was subdued, if not somber. Behn described 1930 as "a period of financial and economic crisis which, originating before the beginning of the year and extending after its close, spread throughout the world." He said that management had adjusted to these new circumstances, and there was more talk of "conserving existing plant and maintaining positions already taken" than of major new programs and plans. This is not to suggest that additional takeovers weren't in the works. In February 1930 Morgan was able to float a $50-million 5 percent bond for ITT, this money earmarked for Latin American and German acquisitions and for expansion of CTNE. ITT clearly wasn't hunkering down for a prolonged siege, but the Colonel expected further poor economic and financial news.[1]

Acquisitions and mergers aren't fostered by this kind of business climate. Under the terms discussed during preliminary negotiations with RCA, that corporation was to receive approximately $100 million in cash, bonds, or stock—or a combination of all three—in return for its communications operations. By mid-1930 money had become difficult to raise, and the situation worsened the following year, a period of financial stringency on Wall Street. But even had this not been the case, ITT couldn't have returned to the money markets so soon. The corporation's long-term debt had by then reached $188 million, and ITT had guaranteed an additional $27 million in notes issued by subsidiaries; in contrast, the debt had been under $34 million at the end of 1926. Interest charges alone came to more than $9.4 million annually, which was more than half the company's 1928 profits.

Behn had acquired this debt in the belief that the good times wouldn't come to an end and that the expansion of the 1920s would reach into the following decade and beyond. In the process he had erected a major international corporation, but one with decidedly weak financial underpinnings. He had gambled heavily, and in 1930 appeared to have lost. In other words, ITT was badly positioned to meet a major depression. Not only couldn't Behn afford to borrow funds so as to acquire RCA Communications; he could face insolvency unless the economy picked up soon.

Nor could the Colonel offer ITT paper in return for the RCA subsidiary. Despite a brave but reckless effort at maintaining the $2.00 dividend, the stock's price collapsed; in fact, ITT's shareholders were among the hardest hit of the bear market, and the corporation lost its credibility on Wall Street. The common stock peaked at a fraction below 150 just prior to the 1929 crash. Within a year the price had plummeted to 17½. In late 1930 the dividend was cut in half, soon to be eliminated entirely. By then ITT's 5 percent gold bonds had fallen from 100 to 33, a striking indication that investors were betting the company wouldn't be able to meet its obligations. This was hardly the kind of paper Behn could use for acquisitions. Moreover, he probably wouldn't have issued additional stock for RCA Communications even had that company been willing to accept it. There were rumors that Sarnoff intended the sale as a preliminary move to taking over ITT. Perhaps these weren't true, but Behn wouldn't offer shares to a person perceived as a rival in his field.

Thus, the Colonel's dream of creating a dominant world-telecommunications corporation was deferred, if not actually dead. After 1931 ITT sold off or shut down operations; no longer was there a frantic search for new properties to augment the International System. In the late 1920s Behn had taken weak companies under his wing, promising to resurrect and expand them, and his record in this regard had been excellent; during the Great Depression he sought allies who were or appeared to be stronger than himself, in the hope of utilizing their assets to salvage what had become a battered and crumbling empire.

As has been indicated, there would be one final expansionist gasp prior to the decline, which appeared logical and sensible at the time but would prove embarrassing later on. The 1929 purchase of Ferdinand Schuchardt, that minor factor in the German telephonic-equipment industry, was followed by further investigations of that country's markets.

In order to appreciate fully the implications of these developments, one must first know something of the situation in Germany at the time, especially the relationships that had developed between the German and American governments on the one hand and between businessmen in both countries on the other. Important as these were in their own right, they take on added significance in the light of the roles played by American corporations in Germany after Hitler came to power in 1933.[2]

In early 1929 Germany appeared a bastion of economic strength and political democracy in Central Europe. In February the coalition government of Social Democrat Hermann Müller accepted the Kellogg-Briand Pact outlawing war. That summer the French army of occupation evacuated the Rhineland, a move important in its own right but also symbolic of a new spirit of harmony between the two nations.

Foreign capital continued to pour into Germany, which had experienced strong economic growth after the immediate postwar period. As was the case in so many other parts of the world, Wall Street bankers led the way, followed by their American clients. They couldn't function there as they had in Latin America, for even in defeat it was clear that Germany wasn't destined to become an economic colony such as Argentina or Uruguay. The German government would seek loans, for which it would pay preferential interest rates, and German businesses would go to Wall Street for meetings with investment bankers who floated their bond issues. Several German companies and portions of companies were sold to foreign interests, but these operated strictly within local laws and regulations, almost always with nationals in command.

That the Germans were attracted to Wall Street because of America's clear financial domination of the postwar world is obvious, but there was more to it than that. France was an ancient political and even a cultural enemy, and prior to the war Germany and Britain had clashed repeatedly for markets. Both France and Britain were too close and antagonisms were too fresh for either to play much of an economic role in Germany, even had they the power. Moreover, French, British, and other European businessmen had little experience in investments there and less desire to acquire it after the war.

Fighting for Time: The Great Depression

The Americans were different. They had been popular in Germany prior to 1914, and even though the United States had joined the Allies in 1917, there was a surprising lack of antagonism between the two countries after the armistice. Like many of their German counterparts, American businessmen operating internationally had attempted to displace the British after the turn of the century; perhaps this common experience united some of them. German businessmen seemed to admire the American verve and imagination, and the Americans praised German dependability, efficiency, and respect for structure. Whatever the reasons—cultural affinity, economic opportunism, political necessity—there was a strong American presence in Germany during the 1920s and afterward, while on their part some German businessmen started to invest seriously in the United States.

In the ten years prior to 1931 German businesses floated more than $826 million worth of bonds in the American capital markets, and of this amount, National City, a lead ITT bank, took $186.5 million. Many American firms purchased all or parts of German companies, entered into partnerships or working arrangements with them, or established subsidiaries in that country. Among these were Dow Chemical, International Business Machines, Aluminum Company of America, and the Texas Company. Ford and General Motors aggressively expanded into automobiles. E. I. Du Pont, which prior to the war had close relationships with several German companies, renewed and strengthened them in the 1920s. Standard Oil of New Jersey shared patents and research with major German enterprises in this period. General Electric purchased shares in Allgemeine Elektrizitäts Gesellschaft (AEG), Gesellschaft für Electrische Unternemungen, and other companies, with most of the business conducted through National City Bank, and at one point even attempted to buy into Siemens & Halske.

While this was happening, Owen Young, General Electric's chairman, was selected to head a commission to study various means of restructuring and limiting Germany's war debt. Out of this came the Young Plan, unpopular in France, where it was considered too lenient, while the British financial community bitterly denounced the plan as tying Germany even more closely to the United States. With reluctance both France and Britain gave their assent. The German people approved of the plan in a referendum held in December 1929, sending a signal to Wall Street that additional loans

71

and investments would be welcomed and dealing a defeat to Adolf Hitler's National Socialists, who had campaigned against it.

Under the circumstances, then, it was both natural and prudent for ITT to seek further inroads into the expanding German economy, and so it did. Given its past relationships with National City and the close ties that had developed between Behn and Owen Young—and through him, with General Electric—it also made sense to work with and through these entities.

In 1930 ITT purchased Mix und Genest Aktiengesellschaft, Süddeutsche Apparatefabrik Gesellschaft, and Telefonfabrik Berliner, all of which were engaged in the manufacture of telephonic, telegraphic, and electrical equipment. Then the Colonel joined with General Electric to organize Standard Elektrizitäts Gesellschaft (SEG) as a holding company, into which he put these three companies, their subsidiaries, and Ferdinand Schuchardt. This new, somewhat smallish enterprise thus would have a relationship with the giant AEG, and for a while it appeared that General Electric and ITT would unite in a drive to displace Siemens as Germany's premier electrical company, but nothing came of this. Instead General Electric sold its share of SEG to Behn, thus providing ITT with what could become a major base of operations in that country.

In a separate but related move the Colonel purchased from the Dutch firm of Philips all but a fractional share of C. Lorenz, AG. A medium-size radio-equipment manufacturer, Lorenz had become an important competitor of Siemens in several fields, even though operating in Germany under governmental constraints and being chronically short of capital. In 1930, when it appeared the American economic slump was ending, Behn thought Lorenz could be provided with ample funds and, through his relationship with Young, freed of at least some of the controls.

Behn seemed positioned to carve out a slice of the German telecommunications-equipment market. He and his associates understood there was no chance of obtaining a telephone concession in that country, but equipment manufactured by Lorenz and SEG had a share of the strictly controlled German telephone-equipment market. Moreover, like many other American businessmen, Behn was entranced by the technological proficiency of German scientists and engineers and eager to control laboratories and research centers in which they worked. Finally, Germany was the traditional supplier

Fighting for Time: The Great Depression

of telephonic equipment to much of Eastern Europe, and through SEG and Lorenz, ITT might gain entry to these markets.

All of this has to be kept in perspective. In 1934, a year when the German economy was recovering rapidly, under 4 percent of ITT's assets were invested in that country—less than in Great Britain, Mexico, or Chile, a quarter of the investment in Spain, and only slightly more than had been committed to Cuba. Over a quarter of ITT's investments were in Argentina, and that country's affairs involved a proportionate amount of Behn's attention.

Viewed from the Continent, ITT's machinations in Germany appeared only a small part of a gigantic American program directed from Wall Street to take over the European electrical-equipment market, a movement opened up by Morgan and National City and led by General Electric, with ITT a minor ally, there to cover one of its flanks. Just as apprehensions regarding a triumphal American communications empire had prodded the British to organize Cable & Wireless, so there was talk of a unified operation in the electrical-equipment industry to meet the General Electric challenge. Siemens and Ericsson, rivals competing for the German electrical and telephonic businesses, now joined in an informal alliance, which some observers thought might be a prelude to the creation of a binational giant along the lines of Royal Dutch Shell, the British-Dutch petroleum combine that vied worldwide with Standard Oil of New Jersey for crude sources and markets.

At the time, Ericsson was controlled by Ivar Kreuger, a Swedish businessman who was one of the most spectacular and audacious international financiers and manipulators of modern times. From his base in Kreuger & Toll he had put together a combination of companies in construction, mining, ball bearings, wood pulp, and newspapers, but he was best known as the "match king," as he controlled some 250 factories throughout the world that turned out 30 billion boxes of matches a year—three quarters of the market. In Europe, Latin America, and the Orient, Kreuger tried to obtain concessions under which he would have a monopoly of the market in exchange for legal and illegal payments to governments and their officials. Much of this was financed by the sale of securities, and in the middle and late 1920s his main arena was Wall Street. From 1923 to 1929 Kreuger sold some $148 million of International Match stock and bonds through the New York bankers, and there were other placements for several of his properties, Kreuger & Toll included.

Almost all of this was transferred to Kreuger, to be used to make other acquisitions.

Kreuger had taken a small position in Ericsson in 1927, and he expanded upon it two years later to the point where he had control of that company. Although battered by the Depression, it was still a major factor in world telecommunications. Ericsson had the telephone concessions in Poland, southern Italy, Sicily, and parts of Argentina and Mexico, so it competed with ITT in the last two countries. There were manufacturing complexes in England, France, Hungary, and Poland as well as in Sweden. It could prove an excellent springboard for Kreuger, who apparently hoped to function in the communications industry in much the same way that he had in matches—initially as a competitor, then as the dominant force. "The telephone, as far as I am concerned, has the same qualities as matches," he wrote to a friend. "With the arrangement and management of telephone organizations, I can get State concessions and monopolies just as I can with my little wooden soldiers."[3]

Kreuger appeared secure, confident, and solvent in early 1931, a time when Wall Street buzzed with rumors of his "coup" in Italian government bonds, and he met with and offered advice to President Herbert Hoover on how best to deal with the Depression. There were profiles of Kreuger in leading magazines, including the most popular one of the day, *The Saturday Evening Post*, in which he was called an "authentic genius." And all the while talk of the Ericsson-Siemens combination continued in Europe and on Wall Street. J. P. Morgan & Co. was ready for it. Thomas Lamont, who had never trusted or liked Kreuger, consulted with Behn to plan a common approach, and in those days prior to the banking collapse Morgan was prepared to throw its resources behind ITT in what appeared to be a developing struggle for control of the German telecommunications market.

That May, in what was a sudden and unexpected reversal of form, Kreuger approached the Colonel with a proposal either to sell his Ericsson holdings or to exchange them for ITT paper. Surprised but certainly interested, Behn relayed the information to Lamont. ITT was in a poor condition to make a cash tender, and under the circumstances its stock couldn't be too attractive. But then Kreuger came up with a preliminary offer that could be met. As an initial step he would transfer 600,000 Ericsson shares—a majority—to ITT in return for 400,000 shares of that company's common stock in addition to $11 million in cash. This seemed a low price for so attractive a property. Ericsson had lost ground during the Depression, but there was no reason to believe it couldn't recover once the world economy turned around. The vision was appealing. If all went well, ITT could come out of the discussions the world's leading manufacturer of telecommunications equipment.

In all of this were echoes of the situation that had existed three years earlier, when the Colonel was prepared to acquire RCA Communications and take a central position in transatlantic radio and cable. Once again, this time in the midst of a deepening depression, he had an opportunity to expand greatly through a major takeover. In his view the fact that Kreuger would become a prominent stockholder in ITT and take a seat on its board was the price one had to pay for so large a prize. What was going on in Behn's mind cannot be known, but given Kreuger's reputation and presumed wealth, he couldn't have thought the Match King needed the money badly.

Yet such was the case. Kreuger required that $11 million, and much more, to put his affairs in order. Throughout the 1920s he had shifted funds from one operation to another, put off auditors, dissembled and falsified, so as to keep what truly was a paper empire intact. The financial stringencies following the 1929 crash were almost too much for Kreuger & Toll to bear. Now he was attempting to shore it up with cash transfers, of which the $11 million from Behn would be only one of several.

After a series of meetings with Lamont, during which the banker warned Behn of Kreuger's devious methods of operation, the deal was arranged. Morgan would assist in raising the funds through the issuance of short-term notes, even though it would mean straining ITT's already weak credit. "We were anxious to make the deal," recalled ITT controller Edwin Chinlund years later, "even though some felt we shouldn't push it through in bad times with short-term borrowed money." Chinlund along with the others thought "it seemed a good idea" to pool the resources of the two companies. Kreuger placed his 600,000 shares of Ericsson in escrow, along with the 400,000 of ITT, and was given the $11-million check. The next step, prior to the final sale of Ericsson, would be to have that company's books inspected by the accounting firm of Price Waterhouse.

During the next half year Kreuger rushed back and forth across the Atlantic attempting to juggle books and raise funds while not arousing suspicions as to his precarious financial position. In a reckless move necessitated by increasing pressures, he removed $7 million in cash from the Ericsson treasury, replacing it with depreciated bonds. Then Kreuger tried to keep the Price Waterhouse accountants at bay until he could return the money, presumably by raising it from another of his companies in a similar fashion. Meanwhile he was struck down by the banking collapse in Central Europe, which spread westward and then hit the United States. Kreuger clearly couldn't raise additional funds, and he was no longer able to put off the accountants, since both Price Waterhouse and Behn were growing suspicious of his actions. The books were turned over, the switch discovered, and Behn apprised of the situation.

This was a difficult period for the Colonel. ITT's earnings were melting, and its balance sheet was in a parlous state. Like Kreuger, he was fighting for time. The Ericsson acquisition easily might turn out to be the most important of his career, but unless it was completed quickly, everything might fall apart. Already there was talk that ITT was approaching insolvency, in part owing to the need to repay the $11 million in short-term notes. Behn needed that $7 million he assumed was in the Ericsson treasury. News of the replacement must have come as a shock.

In early February, 1932, the Colonel called upon Kreuger for an explanation. Each man was in a precarious position, but Kreuger's hadn't been uncovered, and so Kreuger might have thought himself the stronger of the two. In the past, with other businessmen and bankers, he had relied upon his reputation and glibness to cover often-shady operations, and once again he tried to brazen it out. But Behn was insistent; he had to be, under the circumstances. Unless the $7 million was returned, the deal would be canceled and Kreuger would have to give back the $11 million. Other meetings followed, with Kreuger maneuvering for time and position while the Colonel pressed for the money. It was evident that an impasse had been reached when they last met on February 19.

Shortly thereafter Kreuger returned to Europe, and on March 12 he committed suicide in Paris by shooting himself in the heart.

The sudden collapse of the Kreuger empire shocked the international banking community and sparked a sell-off on Wall Street. "Everybody's unloading but the cannibals in Africa," was the comment of *The New York Times* reporter who covered the story. A subsequent investigation showed that Kreuger's only clear assets were around $100,000 in personal property; the rest had vanished or never existed. There was no sign of ITT's $11 million. In light of this, it appeared that Colonel Behn might soon have to file for corporate bankruptcy.

CONSOLIDATED ACCOUNTS FOR ITT, 1930–1934

(millions of dollars)

Year	Gross Revenues	Net Income	Assets
1930	102.8	13.7	604.4
1931	87.8	7.7	615.5
1932	67.5	(3.9)	566.1
1933	74.0	.7	584.6
1934	79.3	2.1	581.0

Source: *Moody's Public Utility Manual, 1935*, pp. 2013–19.

Behn would have been in trouble even without the Kreuger fiasco. Those companies best positioned for survival during the Great Depression displayed several characteristics notably absent in ITT. They tended to have strong cash positions and not much in the way of debt, a low ratio of assets to sales, and they were in industries in which major infusions of capital either weren't required or might be deferred. By its very nature telecommunications demanded major investments simply to remain functioning, much less to expand. Additional financing would have been difficult to arrange even without the issuance of that $11 million in short-term notes and the linkage in the public mind of Ivar Kreuger and Sosthenes Behn. Now such financing was impossible.

Even this might have been borne if some of the ITT subsidiaries had been able to remit large sums in the form of dividends to the parent company, but such was not the case. The corporation's only important American company was Postal Telegraph, and rather than providing earnings, that firm reported losses every year after 1929.

For a while in 1932 this problem appeared capable of being resolved. In April, shortly after the Kreuger suicide, Behn met with Western Union's president, Newcomb Carlton, to revive discussions begun three years earlier regarding a merger. Both companies were in difficulty, and a combination made sense. Out of this came a plan whereby Western Union would acquire Postal Telegraph and in turn unite with ITT to create an entity with assets of more than a billion dollars. Elimination of duplicate facilities would create a profitable telegraphic system, one capable of paying substantial dividends to the parent firm in addition to providing better service. But the special legislation required before two communications companies could merge didn't gather sufficient congressional support, and the plan died.

Three years later Postal filed for bankruptcy, but even then its troubles weren't over. In 1937 the Justice Department launched an antitrust crusade, the most massive in American history, and one of the actions involved Western Union and Postal Telegraph. These two ailing firms were charged with conspiring to monopolize the telegraph industry. Nothing came of this, and in 1939 Postal was reorganized and recapitalized. Under the terms of a complex agreement with the bondholders and owners of preferred shares, there was created a new entity, American Cable & Radio, which acquired control of Postal Telegraph, All America, and the Sociedad Anónima Radio Argentina. ITT would have a two-thirds interest in the new company, and the rest would go to Postal's creditors and preferred stockholders. Behn hoped a revitalized operation might soon pay dividends, but this wasn't to be. The losses continued, and in 1944, with barely a ripple of protest from Washington, the remains of Postal Telegraph were sold to Western Union. In a period when ITT needed dollars, then, nothing could be expected from this source.

Most of the overseas businesses were profitable, and these declared dividends, always in local currency. But those that were tied to the pound sterling declined in relation to the American dollar in 1931 after Great Britain went off the gold standard. Furthermore, several of ITT's most solvent and important subsidiaries were in countries where controls had been placed on repatriation of earnings; these included Germany, Spain, and Rumania. In some cases host countries had regulations that obligated ITT to accept dividends in the form of commodities rather than cash, and these at prices fixed by local agencies.

Almost all of the parent corporation's revenues came in the form of dividends declared and submitted by subsidiaries, and under normal circumstances Broad Street could determine these insofar as size and timing were concerned. Conditions were hardly normal in this period. It was possible for a subsidiary to post excellent earnings but, owing to political factors over which it had no control, to be unable to declare a dividend, or to declare one only to have it blocked and placed in an escrow account. There were regulations that forbade the sale of foreign assets or repatriation of proceeds from sales to the United States.

The effects of all of this could be seen on the balance sheets. In early 1935 ITT had cash items of $33.3 million, but of this amount $23.8 million was in blocked accounts.

The situation was grim in the early 1930s. In 1932 ITT posted a loss of $3.9 million, and the company's assets had to be written down by $36 million so as to present a more realistic picture of its condition. Yet Behn had to meet obligations entered into with host countries under threats of forfeiture of concessions. Such was the situation in Argentina and Chile, where ITT had two of its most important holdings. In Spain there were powerful elements demanding the nationalization of CTNE, and this was one of the countries blocking repatriation of assets and earnings. In 1929 Behn had entered into an agreement with the Rumanian government to acquire its company, the Societatea Anonima Romana de Telefoane, and the concession was in danger of being taken away in 1932 because of ITT's inability to meet commitments.

Behn raised money by ordering larger-than-warranted dividends to be paid to ITT by ISE, All America, and Commercial Cable, placing those companies in tight financial positions. Some funds were even shifted out of Postal Telegraph, though that firm was hemorrhaging and appeared on the brink of bankruptcy. Funds for expansion in Latin America had to be raised locally under the most trying circumstances, and by 1933 even this practice had to be curtailed in several countries. With all of this, some of the subsidiaries had better credit ratings than the parent. ITT was able to raise badly needed short-term money in 1933 by having its notes cosigned by River Plate, and securities of that company were placed in the hands of lenders as collateral. But it had to be done. Even though revenues were down and losses posted, ITT was committed to the expansion of telephone operations under the terms of its concessions.

Expenses at headquarters and in the field were slashed to the bone, resulting in savings of $9.3 million in 1932. Virtually everyone accepted salary reductions that ranged from 10 to 25 percent, and on several occasions Behn went without pay simply because there was so little money on hand. There were times when employees were asked not to cash their checks for a day or so, since the money to cover them hadn't been deposited in the bank. The work week was cut from five and a half to four days, and salaries were adjusted accordingly. Some factories were shut down entirely, and operations at others were transferred elsewhere. Consolidation and economy were the order of the day. Chinlund remarked, "We had to work all day 365 days in the year just to get in enough cash to meet interest charges. The patient managed to keep alive, but not with much to spare."[4]

In fact, there wasn't a single bright spot in the ITT picture in 1932–1933, a time when insolvency was a chronic threat. There wouldn't be much in the way of improvement during the next few years, even though business picked up somewhat in 1934. Behn couldn't even console himself with the remains of the Ericsson affair. Clearly there was no way of regaining that $11 million, so, attempting to make the best of things, he offered to renounce the money in return for the 600,000 shares of Ericsson that Kreuger had placed in escrow. The Swedish courts agreed to the settlement but reduced the voting rights to one third, which meant that ITT became a minority stockholder in a company that itself was in poor shape and wasn't paying dividends.

On top of all this came a personal loss the Colonel found almost impossible to bear. In early 1932, as the negotiations with Kreuger were coming to a head and ITT's finances were in shambles, Hernand fell ill, and on several occasions he had to be hospitalized with stomach disorders. By September he could no longer continue on in New York, and together with his wife and children he went to Paris to consult with doctors. Afterward Hernand traveled to the family vacation home at St.-Jean-de-Luz, in France, where he was under almost constant medical care. By late summer of 1933 it became evident that he wouldn't recover, and the Colonel rushed to St.-Jean. He was at the bedside when Hernand died, on October 7, at the age of fifty-one.

This was a shattering blow for Sosthenes. The brothers always had been close. There was only one picture on the Colonel's desk in New York—one of Hernand—and it remained there for the rest of his life. He wore a black armband for more than a year. Sosthenes ordered calling cards and notepaper edged in black, and he used them for years. Of course, he had a wide circle of close friends, and he never suffered from loneliness. His verve, his zest for business and good living, remained. But those who knew him best said the Colonel never fully recovered from the loss of Hernand.

5

A Matter of Survival:
Spain and Germany

THE AMERICAN ECONOMY appeared well on the way to full recovery in 1936. The gross national product that year came to $82.5 billion, the fourth successive annual increase. Although the unemployment rate of 17 percent appears horrendous today, it should be considered that this was the first time since 1931 that it had fallen below the 20 percent level. Prices were inching up as well, and this was viewed as a sign of economic vitality in Depression America, an indication that demands for goods and services were increasing.

There was a great deal of jockeying for position in Western Europe, as the British, French, and Italians pondered Hitler's renunciation of the Locarno pacts and the reoccupation of the Rhineland. Yet there was a general belief that war could be avoided, not only because the memory of the 1914–18 conflict was so fresh but also because of the economic revival of the mid-decade period. At a time when unemployment was shrinking and factories were reopening, Europe's leaders thought that Hitler could be pacified and that the

A Matter of Survival: Spain and Germany

German people themselves would reject a conflict that could bring an end to their new prosperity.

There was one major trouble spot on the Continent, however. Spain was in turmoil. The cabinet headed by moderate Alejandro Lerroux fell in late 1935, the Cortes (parliament) was dissolved, and as a result of an election held the following January, a coalition of left-wing parties, the Communists included, came to power, this amid rumors of coups and countercoups.

In New York, Colonel Behn celebrated the revival of his company's fortunes. Despite the bankruptcy of Postal Telegraph, frustrating currency and investment controls, the residue of uncertainty left over from the Kreuger affair, and his own mourning for Hernand, he was optimistic that May as he presented stockholders with the 1935 annual report and offered thoughts regarding the future. ITT's consolidated gross revenues had risen to $58.9 million from $53.6 million the previous year, and net income had gone from $3.5 million to $5.8 million. The company's backlog for manufactured items at the end of 1935 came to $31.9 million; a year earlier it had been $24 million. In addition, ITT's short-term debt had been reduced from $41 million in 1931 to $27.2 million at the end of 1935, and the Colonel was able to borrow at regular rather than distress rates. There was no talk of acquisitions in the works, but neither was there serious consideration of a possible corporate collapse, which was a pleasant change from the situation two years earlier.

The price of ITT's bonds had moved up; the bellwether 4½s maturing in 1939 went from 20 to 88 in less than three years. The common shares had performed even better, and their price was approaching the 20 level as the Colonel addressed the meeting. There was no thought of resuming the dividend, but at least one financial writer believed there might be a token payout in 1937, assuming the recovery continued.

None of this would be possible—the company's financial viability, its increasing liquidity, the dividend—without success in Spain. CTNE operated more than a third of ITT's telephones and accounted for better than a quarter of its revenues and earnings. In 1935 it remitted $1.6 million to its parent; without this amount Behn would have been unable to clean up his short-term indebtedness. Little wonder, then, that he monitored the situation in that country and kept in touch with his two closest associates there, Lewis Proctor, CTNE's vice-president, and Capt. Logan Rock, the company's managing director, considered by many to be the most knowledgeable American in Madrid and a fine diplomat fluent in Spanish.

During the previous five years Rock had managed to steer a middle course in relation to Spanish governments, friendly with all but supportive of none, foiling those that wanted to nationalize CTNE while remaining on speaking terms with leaders of all factions. If not actually liked by the reformers and radicals, Rock was at least trusted and respected. Thus, he was well placed and informed, capable of dealing with whoever came to power.

On February 18, 1936, Manuel Azaña, a Catalan nationalist and socialist, became prime minister at the head of a Popular Front government that proclaimed a far-reaching program of social reform. While in office in 1931 Azaña had attempted without success to renegotiate the CTNE concession, and now he appeared ready to try again, in a period when Spanish politics were in disarray, with leftists gaining power almost daily.

On April 10 the Cortes voted to remove from office President Alcalá Zamora, generally considered a moderate monarchist. A month later Azaña was elevated to the presidency, with the support of a coalition further to the left than the one that made him prime minister. Azaña helped organize a new government under Santiago Quiroga, whose Ministry of Communications asked for a revision of the CTNE concession. After having obtained the support of American Ambassador Claude Bowers, ITT protested strongly. The Spaniards apologized for the "misunderstanding," and for the moment at least CTNE seemed secure.[1]

Logan Rock was under tremendous pressures during this period, keeping in almost constant contact with Spanish officials and the American embassy and at night conferring by long-distance telephone with Colonel Behn and others on Broad Street. The strain exacted a price. After a brief illness, he died, on June 20.

Rock's assistant, Fred Caldwell, assumed the late director's duties. An able man who understood the situation, Caldwell nonetheless lacked Rock's experience and contacts, and didn't have the confidence of many Spanish leaders. ITT vice-president Frank Page also was in Madrid, and he assumed some of the work, but it soon became evident that Rock truly was irreplaceable. Bowers called his death "a serious loss," and President Azaña, who often had clashed with Rock, thought it would be difficult to find a person with his "tact and conciliation."

A Matter of Survival: Spain and Germany

The Colonel had rushed to Madrid on learning of Rock's illness and, typically, decided to remain there and take personal command of CTNE in this crisis period. The government continued to move to the left politically, and there were unmistakable signs of opposition on the part of military commanders. The great powers—Britain, France, Germany, Italy, and the Soviet Union—were jockeying for position. Rebellion was in the air during the summer of 1936. Madrid was a dangerous but exciting place to be. Doubtless the Colonel wanted to be there to protect CTNE, without which ITT might be seriously, even fatally, wounded. But in addition he must have enjoyed the challenge. He probably wouldn't have gone to Spain were it not for Rock's ill health, but under the circumstances he might not have been able to resist the lure, especially after mid-July, when the Spanish Civil War erupted with a rebellion in Morocco that soon spread to Cádiz, Seville, and other garrison cities.

The Colonel didn't keep a journal, and any letters he might have written from Spain have long since been discarded or destroyed. But he clearly favored the generals at the beginning of the Civil War. At the time, it was known they had important support from Germany and Italy, while the government would soon be backed by the Soviet Union. A devout Catholic and staunch anticommunist, Behn was emotionally bound to the insurgents. As a businessman he had been faced with threats of cancellations of concessions for several years, and he must have thought he could do better under their government. Accustomed to being in command, the Colonel often could be blunt and direct. Thus, he abandoned Rock's policy of evenhanded neutrality for one of partisanship.

Had he lived and remained in charge of affairs in Madrid, Rock might have done the same, but certainly in a less forceful, obvious, and daring fashion. His temperament was quite different from Behn's, and although the results might have been the same, the execution would have been more subtle. As it was, Behn all but offered his services and those of the CTNE to insurgent generals Francisco Franco and Emilio Mola. The most knowledgeable students of the period believed Behn helped the rebels maintain contact with each other, which accounted for the smooth coordination of efforts in different parts of the country and which helps explain early Franco successes.[2] Publicly neutral at first, Behn nonetheless did what he could to assist those forces that he had reason to believe would reward CTNE if they gained power.

It was a touchy situation. Madrid remained in Loyalist hands, and Behn directed his operations from the company's headquarters there. Loyalist bands that knew what was going on seized several CTNE installations, and with the support of Ambassador Bowers the Colonel demanded protection from the very forces he indirectly was helping to overthrow.

The U.S. embassy in Madrid closed down in November as the insurgents pushed on in central Spain. Rather than remain there without Bowers' protection, Behn ordered Page and Caldwell to the new Republican capital at Valencia, and then he left the country to oversee operations from his summer home at St.-Jean-de-Luz, not all that far from the border.

Apparently convinced the war would soon end with a Franco victory, Behn openly voiced proinsurgent sentiments. After a meeting with him in mid-December, Bowers wrote, "Both Mr. Caldwell and Colonel Behn have been warm partisans of Franco from the beginning." He noted that Behn planned to return to Madrid once Franco captured that city. "He proposed that the Telephone Company shall recognize the Franco Government without waiting on the American Government." Bowers believed CTNE would be nationalized in the event of a Loyalist victory, primarily because of Behn's statements and actions. "If the Constitutional Government wins nothing can prevent the cancellation of the Company's contract." Several weeks later the Ambassador had a conversation with Caldwell and came away convinced the ITT official was "rabidly pro-Fascist."[3]

By then, however, Behn had become involved in playing a double game. Through his contacts with Franco he had come to realize the General couldn't be trusted to protect ITT's Spanish interests. Behind Franco were the Germans, and they clearly would expect rewards should the insurgents win. Chief among these might be the telephone concession—seized from ITT and bestowed upon a German firm, which would obtain its equipment from Siemens and not from ISE. Thus, while remaining on good terms with Franco, Behn did all he could to placate the Loyalists, to indicate to them by deed if not by word that his sympathies weren't wholly with the insurgents. For example, the telephone system continued to operate in those parts of the country held by government forces, not so much to collect revenues (which in any case couldn't be repatriated) but to be as well positioned as possible in case of a Loyalist victory.

A Matter of Survival: Spain and Germany

The Colonel tried to make the best of an impossible situation, to salvage as much of CTNE as he could. Some of Franco's associates saw through his actions and criticized him roundly, whereas the Loyalists refused to grant Behn a visa to reenter the country, backing down only after pressures were exerted by Claude Bowers. This continued for several years. By early 1939, when it seemed the Loyalist cause was doomed, Behn tried to move into a closer alliance with Franco. But even then it appeared such an approach would do him little good. Caldwell, whom Bowers once considered "pro-fascist," now said that CTNE might anticipate "less trouble with the Government than with the rebels."[4]

Such indeed proved to be the case. In victory Franco moved to reward his German allies, and for a while it appeared this included a transfer of the telephone concession. Once again the U.S. State Department came to Behn's rescue, and after vigorous protests and threats of rejection of Spanish applications for funds from the Export-Import Bank, Franco backed down. But CTNE's earnings and assets were frozen, and the company reorganized so as to include several important Franco associates on its board. Behn was permitted to return to Madrid, where he oversaw the restructuring. Those Americans who remained knew they were mistrusted by the government, under surveillance, and in constant danger of having their visas lifted.

ITT learned many lessons from the Spanish experience, and these would affect the corporation's activities throughout Europe and Latin America. One of the most important of these was a recognition of Germany's powers and Hitler's thrust. Clearly Germany was the most vital nation on the Continent, and the chancellor was the key political figure. Both would be taken into account by ITT during the years that followed.

After World War II there would be open and veiled charges that Behn had been pro-German in this period and later on, that under his leadership ITT had gone out of its way to assist in the German war effort. Even then, so it was said, SEG and Lorenz were producing materials for that country's military machine. Sympathies cannot easily be proved or disproved, but the German companies indeed did turn out military equipment prior to the war, although by then Behn had almost no control of operations. It should also be recalled that this was a period during which the United States and Germany maintained normal diplomatic relations, when many prominent European leaders (among them Winston Churchill) not only lauded Hitler for having taken Germany out of its depression but also considered him a bulwark against the advance of world communism. Prominent American businessmen visited Germany and returned to praise the man. Hitler bestowed high honors on several of them, including Henry Ford and Thomas Watson. This was a time when General Motors' Opel plants were producing most of Germany's tanks and military vehicles; when General Electric, Du Pont, and Standard Oil of New Jersey were transferring technology and capital to Germany; and when a well-known motto in the West was "You *Can* Do Business with Hitler."

In other words, Behn was one of many who hoped to turn their German operations into profitable ventures. Moreover, for ITT's factories to have rejected government orders for military production not only would have invited retaliation from the host government but would have been opposed by ITT's German managers and their staffs. Finally, Behn could not repatriate earnings from his German subsidiaries in the form of marks to be exchanged for dollars, and after 1937, under German law, he couldn't sell them or make transfers without specific approval from high government authorities. Such approval was not forthcoming, though attempts were made in this direction.[5]

To suggest, as some writers have, that the Colonel gladly left his investments in Germany, and even added to them when he might have sold them to others, is to fly in the face of what was happening at ITT during most of this period. As has been indicated, the company often was on the edge of bankruptcy, with Behn devoting a good deal of his time to efforts at raising cash. On January 1, 1939, $37.7 million of ITT's long-term 4½ percent bonds would be redeemed. Under ordinary circumstances most of this money would have been raised through the remission of dividends from subsidiaries and the sale of new bonds on Wall Street. By 1937, however, ITT's situation had become strained. The Spanish dividend had been eliminated, Postal Telegraph remained in bankruptcy, the German assets were all but frozen, and the company's cash reserve had fallen to $5 million. In the face of all this the bankers understandably were unwilling to make new commitments. Behn would have sold almost anything under these circumstances, using the funds to preserve what remained.

A Matter of Survival: Spain and Germany

Behn learned of the bankers' attitude at one of his famous lunches that summer. Attending were Russell Leffingwell and Arthur Andersen of Morgan & Co. and Gordon Rentschler of National City Bank, all of whom were also ITT directors and as such conversant with the company's condition. Several ITT vice-presidents were at the luncheon, prepared to answer questions and discuss problems. Toward the end, over cigars and coffee, the Colonel outlined his program for the next few years, indicating his capital needs and the way he expected to refinance the bond maturities. The bankers were reluctant to go along with him, all but recommending that he look elsewhere for funds. This is not to say that Morgan and National City abandoned the company but rather that they weren't prepared to risk more capital in ITT in 1937.[6]

Obviously Behn couldn't have poured additional sums into overseas operations that year, or at any time for the remainder of the decade. Instead he worked feverishly to repatriate as much as he could from foreign holdings. He sold $30 million of River Plate bonds in Argentina, Sweden, and Switzerland and used the proceeds to pay off some of that utility's short-term debts, then brought the rest back to America. Behn then exchanged ITT paper for those of subsidiaries held by New York banks, and when the notes came due he deposited the funds in the parent corporation's account. He also repatriated funds by means of paper-shuffling that altered financial structure but not operations. For example, in 1938 he sold $18 million of ISE debentures in the Netherlands and Switzerland and then ordered the money used for the purchase of several small holdings from ITT itself. In effect, the properties were switched from one account to another, while ITT obtained the funds. The same year, ITT sold Thomson-Houston, Creed, and its Ericsson shares to ISE for $12.9 million, and of this amount some $9 million was brought back to New York.

Behn all but emptied his treasury of stocks, bonds, and notes issued by other corporations, taking for them whatever liquid capital he could get. When several of ITT's operating units remitted dividends in the form of commodities, he established a unit to trade in these markets, and the funds received were set aside to service the debt. Finally, in late 1938, when it appeared the Colonel still wouldn't have sufficient cash to meet ITT's obligations, he managed to sell $10 million of ten-year bonds to the Export-Import Bank. In this way he was able to squeeze out of the situation. The alternative, of course, was bankruptcy. This was why contraction, rather than expansion, was the rule in the late 1930s.[7]

Nowhere was this more evident than in Germany. Working through contacts there, Behn maneuvered to exchange his holdings in the Reich for the assets of General Aniline and Film, an American-based firm controlled by the giant I. G. Farbenindustrie Aktiengesellschaft. General Aniline produced a wide variety of chemicals and photographic equipment and supplies, so it had no obvious place in the kind of corporation ITT had become by that time. Perhaps the Colonel thought to diversify further, but more likely he would have sold off General Aniline for that much-needed cash.

Together with vice-president Frank Page, Behn shuttled between New York, Washington, and Berlin, hoping to close the deal before the outbreak of war, and there were additional meetings in Switzerland. According to one State Department memorandum, Page said, "The value of each of the two companies was approximately the same, and the exchange would be of advantage to the I.T.&T. in that they would have their money transferred into an American asset." But nothing came of these initial negotiations, and ITT still controlled SEG and Lorenz when war came in September 1939. But all evidence shows that this wasn't Behn's intention. The suggestion that ITT remained in Germany before the war through choice strains credulity and contradicts the evidence. Behn and Page continued to seek a swap of ITT's German holdings for General Aniline at least into the spring of 1941, doing so with White House approval and with awareness of the current status of SEG and Lorenz. On June 19 Herbert Feis, the State Department's adviser on International Economic Affairs, sent a memorandum regarding the proposal to James Dunn at the European desk. "In view of the fact that the German government already had completely effective control of the ITT properties inside of Germany, I do not see any ground for objecting to the consummation of this transaction." The transfer never took place, of course, and ITT continued to own if not control its German companies when that country declared war on the United States a half year later.[8]

Finally, when one reviews Behn's often-stormy relations with Franco and his contests with the Germans in Spain for the *Caudillo's* favor, it becomes clear that whatever else he might have been doing in Europe, the Colonel certainly wasn't receiving benefits from

A Matter of Survival: Spain and Germany

Hitler for services rendered. Nor was he on more than proper terms, under the circumstances, with others in the Reich's top echelon.

Baron Kurt von Schroeder and Dr. Gerhard Westrick were Behn's most important German representatives. Both men had impeccable Nazi credentials and were considered high up in both party and government hierarchies. A member of an ancient Hamburg family that controlled the influential Stein Bank of Cologne, Schroeder had been one of Hitler's earliest and most ardent supporters in the financial community and a person with contacts in most European countries as well as in the United States. One of the Schroeders had relocated to London prior to the turn of the century, and J. Henry Schroeder & Co. of that city, an important merchant bank, was an outgrowth of his activities, as was the J. Henry Schroeder Banking Corporation of New York. All three worked in unison, though ownership was separate, and the directors of the New York bank had dealings with Morgan & Co. There also were ties with National City through Henry Mann, one of America's most experienced international bankers, who also worked with Behn. Mann brought Schroeder and Behn together sometime in the mid-1930s and from then on acted as their go-between.

Schroeder's star began to ascend soon after Hitler took command in 1933, at which time Behn appointed him to the boards of several of ITT's German companies, where he was supposed to serve as what amounted to a "conservator" of interests. It was through his good offices that Behn was able to repatriate some of the earnings from Lorenz and SEG, and Schroeder was adept at preventing the seizure of ITT assets in 1939, a year when those of many other foreign-owned concerns were in peril.

Schroeder had been in the United States in 1914, a member of the so-called "von Papen group," which engaged in propaganda for the German Empire and, later on, in espionage as well. Westrick was one of his associates at the time, and another was Dr. Heinrich Albert, a bright young attorney who also served as a commercial attaché. After the war Albert and Westrick organized a law firm that specialized in funneling American government and private loans to Germany, often through Schroeder's Stein Bank and Morgan and National City. Like Schroeder, Westrick came to know and work with Henry Mann, that ubiquitous banker involved in German-American relations. During the 1930s Westrick represented many American corporations with interests in Germany, among them Texas Company and General Electric. Like Schroeder, he was drawn into ITT's affairs, and on the eve of World War II Westrick was a director of all of the corporation's German affiliates, in addition to serving as Behn's legal counsel there.

Schroeder, Westrick, and their circle—not the Colonel—managed the affairs of SEG and Lorenz after Hitler came to power, and certainly from 1937 to the end of the war. This is not to say that the German subsidiaries were completely autonomous, or that Behn had no clear idea of what was going on in the boardrooms and factories. He was in contact with his German directors and was able to provide them with guidance in a general fashion, but he also understood that they were loyal Germans and Nazis who would support their country when its interests clashed with those of ITT. By 1938 these national managers had more authority over the business than did the New York staff. Westrick and Schroeder were to operate them in what theoretically was the ITT interest, but they, and not Behn, were to be the ultimate judges of just what that was.

For a while, however, this didn't cause the Colonel any deep misgivings. In 1938 he still thought a general European war might be avoided, this despite warnings to the contrary from his most trusted and knowledgeable associates elsewhere in Europe.[9] He continued to believe that Hitler might be appeased even after Germany marched into Austria that spring. Behn dismissed all Jews from management positions in his German companies, even though some of the subsidiaries, especially those in Berlin, had been founded by them. In so doing he acted much as had other American businessmen with German affiliates, though it would appear ITT kept its Jewish executives longer than most.

Through the intervention of Henry Mann, Behn was able to visit Hitler in Berlin, and he remarked that the chancellor was "more of a gentleman" than he supposed he would be. Was he charmed into a sense of security? Perhaps. Behn's hopes for peace remained strong in early 1939, at which time he invited a group of his European managers to the United States, where they were to consult with one another and listen to his ideas regarding the future. This proved a fiasco, with the Germans keeping to themselves while the others refused to talk with them outside of the boardrooms.

A few months later Westrick informed Behn that "the Poles' permanent threat to Germany [could not] be ignored, as they might well be capable of suddenly switching to measures of attack." Now the Colonel finally realized war was imminent. He told his foreign managers that he appreciated the difficulties of their situation and expected each of them would act as nationalists in the coming struggle. For that matter—as will be seen—so did he.[10]

There is no detailed account of activities at SEG and Lorenz during the 1930s, but it would appear that these companies continued producing telephonic, telegraphic, and radio equipment and that they took an increasing amount of military orders. Lorenz contributed importantly to the technology of avionics. In 1936 the company developed a highly sophisticated system of instrument landing for both civil and military aviation, which quickly won acceptance at airports throughout Europe. By the end of the year thirty-five of the units had been installed and some two hundred aircraft had been equipped with the devices. There was some interchange of ideas between Lorenz, Le Matériel Téléphonique, and Standard Telephones and Cables in this period, though shortly thereafter all communications between the laboratories and researchers were halted on orders of ITT's German managers. But the work continued at Lorenz, resulting in important contracts and grants from the Luftwaffe. This could have been the reason Lorenz bought a quarter interest in Focke-Wulf Flugzeugbau, a leading manufacturer of passenger planes and a growing factor in military aviation. The cost wasn't made public. Schroeder later claimed it was the equivalent of $50 million in marks, but clearly this estimate is too high for such a property at that time. Whatever the amount, it was paid by Lorenz from blocked accounts in Germany, and on orders from the national managers.[11]

In addition, Lorenz purchased half the common stock of Huth, a German manufacturer of radio and electrical equipment, probably to gain facilities and expertise for its growing avionics business. One of the Lorenz systems was brought to America in 1937, tested by the Department of Commerce, and given a trial at the Indianapolis Municipal Airport. In its annual report for that year Behn spoke glowingly of the product, and in the financial statement there is mention of a $108,390 advance to Focke-Wulf, an indication that ITT had lent that firm the funds out of its German reserves to help finance expansion made necessary by the growth of both its civil and military businesses.[12] Later claims that ITT attempted to hide this information simply do not square with this evidence.

The facts on hand are reasonably clear, even though the picture remains incomplete. The Colonel cooperated with the Nazi government after it came to power and for the rest of the decade. There were party members on the boards of his German companies, and these men had greater authority there than did counterparts at most other subsidiaries. ITT made financial contributions to German organizations and officials, as well as to the government. Behn located Nazi officials with close contacts in the hierarchy and made use of their services. As much had been done elsewhere, in Argentina, Spain, Mexico, Rumania—virtually everywhere the corporation functioned. ITT's affiliates in ISE had nationals in charge, and there, too, prominent political figures appeared on the boards. Standard Telephones and Cables and Le Matériel Téléphonique weren't much different in this regard from Lorenz or Mix & Genest. These companies helped Britain and France prepare for war, just as Lorenz and SEG did for Hitler. But there was a difference, at least insofar as profits were concerned. In 1939, when factories throughout Europe were busily turning out materials that shortly would be used in war, ITT received a dividend of $3.6 million from ISE, with most of the money coming from the British and French operations. That year—as in previous years—nothing came in from Germany. If ITT profited from preparations for war, these profits came from the Allied side and not from the Germans.

This said, it must be noted that there exists no evidence that the Colonel attempted in any way to prevent his German companies from playing important roles in that country's prewar armament efforts. Might he have done so? Perhaps before 1937, but certainly not afterward, when Westrick and Schroeder had control of operations in Germany. Just prior to the fall of France, three years later, Westrick was given general power of attorney over all ITT properties that might come under Hitler's control during the war. In this way Behn safeguarded the corporation's holdings.

The experiences in Spain and Germany and the tenor of politics in Europe toward the end of the decade resulted in the collapse of Behn's International System. Such a concept might exist and be implemented in a world at peace, especially one in which the United States was a dominant power, but it couldn't survive during armed conflict, when each utility in a nation at war was in jeopardy. Now that Behn had come to believe a generalized war couldn't be avoided, he saw that it was only a matter of time before the United States would be drawn into the struggle. In such an eventuality

A Matter of Survival: Spain and Germany

ITT's telephone operations in enemy lands and even those in pro-Axis countries would be completely exposed, liable to be confiscated immediately or whenever it suited the host country. New factories might be erected in secure zones, research personnel could be relocated, but nothing could be done to protect extant telephone companies and existing installations from seizure.

In early 1940, prior to America's entry into the war, Behn drew up a plan for the corporation to follow once the fighting ended. Germany appeared strong at the time, and its influence in Latin America—especially in Argentina—was growing. In those months prior to France's downfall it seemed a negotiated peace was possible, one from which Hitler would emerge as the Continent's most powerful leader. When that happened, Franco doubtless would seize CTNE and give it to the Germans, and the Rumanians might do the same for the Societatea Anonima Romana de Telefoane. An Argentine government friendly to Hitler could abrogate the River Plate concession and the Germans might move in there as well. Thus would the Germans receive tribute at the expense of ITT.

Under such circumstances ITT would be doomed. Little wonder, then, that Behn proposed a major switch in the International System, one away from telephone companies overseas to manufacturing operations in the United States. In effect, this was to involve a major "deinternationalization" of the corporation. Geoff Ogilvie, one of his chief lieutenants who had a hand in drawing up the five-year plan, said as much to Clyde Dickey, an executive at CTNE. Dickey recalled the conversation more than a quarter of a century later. Ogilvie had drawn him aside and said, "Clyde, there's no provision in the five-year postwar program for operating telephone companies. The Colonel plans to go into more manufacturing; he's going to transfer his earning power to the United States because he got badly burnt during the Depression and later years, and the remission of funds, foreign exchange controls, and everything."[13]

Any lingering hopes Behn might have had of getting something out of Germany were dashed during his visit to that country in mid-1940. This was billed as an inspection tour, and, as on previous occasions, there would be high living and celebration, as the Colonel demanded. Such had been the case even during the Spanish Civil War, when Behn employed a French chef to prepare elaborate meals at his besieged Madrid headquarters. But not in Berlin in 1940. The Colonel was not only shunted aside in the matter of lodgings but also denied entry into what after all were still legally ITT properties. Appeals to Westrick and Schroeder failed. Given their position at the time, these men might have arranged something better. So there were no luncheons, no meetings with top Nazis, no cocktail parties. Instead Behn had to content himself with a driving tour around the Berlin plant observing what he could from the outside.[14]

From Berlin the Colonel traveled to Switzerland, and then to France, to help move scientists, technicians, and machines out of the country. Some went to Britain, others to the United States.

ITT remained a transnational corporation in late 1940, but for all intents and purposes the International System had been laid to rest, an early victim of World War II.

6

Repatriation and Rebirth

COLONEL BEHN'S talents at extricating ITT from what at times appeared disastrous situations evoked admiration (and some suspicion) in business and journalistic circles. Yet even those who questioned several of his maneuvers had to concede that the dramatic empire builder of the 1920s had demonstrated extraordinary ability at the art of survival during the following decade.

The corporation had overcome a series of major difficulties ever since the collapse of efforts at erecting an American-controlled entry in world telecommunications. Always there was that nagging need to raise additional funds without which expansion and modernization would be halted and concessions canceled, to convert overseas earnings into dollars, to protect exposed assets, and to carry through on pledges to foreign leaders who by the end of the decade might have expropriated ITT's holdings without much fear of retaliation.

The Colonel demonstrated a rare sangfroid through these difficult times. Those who worked with him during this period remarked that he was able to maintain his composure throughout the Kreuger episode, the interminable Spanish crises, and the moments when it appeared the corporation might go under for lack of funds. Some years later, in an article fittingly entitled "The Nine Lives of I.T.&T.," a *Fortune* writer observed, "The amazing thing is not that Colonel Behn sees so much as he surveys his domain, but that he sees anything at all."[1]

At no time was this ability more needed than in 1940. ITT's manufacturing operations in Belgium, Denmark, France, the Netherlands, Yugoslavia, and Norway were seized by the Germans, who of course controlled SEG and Lorenz as well. Exchange restrictions prevented the transfer of funds from these countries to ITT, and the same situation prevailed in regard to the repatriation of capital from Great Britain, Spain, Hungary, and Rumania. Commercial Cable was cut off from its connections on the continent, and revenues declined sharply. In 1939, when ITT had received a $3.6-million dividend from ISE, it had shown a net income of $1.6 million. The dividend the following year came to $600,000, and the parent corporation posted a loss of $1.8 million.

Behn was able to remain afloat through assistance from two sources, the first of which was quite ordinary and expected. ITT's ten-year notes, most of which were owned by the Export-Import Bank, were due to mature on the last day of 1940. Prior to that time he arranged to have the payments deferred until 1948, a common-enough practice during that period and under these conditions. In addition, the Bank granted ITT a $1.5-million line of credit, of which $500,000 was taken initially. This sufficed to keep the company intact through the first months of 1941, after which ITT would have been in tight circumstances were it not for the sale of a European asset.

Societatea Anonima Romana de Telefoane hadn't loomed importantly in ITT's affairs, but in terms of stations it was the third-largest telephone company in its constellation, with more than 100,000, twice the number when acquired in 1930. Almost all of Romana de Telefoane's financings had been arranged in that country. Its operations were quite profitable, and in early 1940, before exchange restrictions were clamped down, it had remitted a dividend of almost $150,000 to the parent company. So it was a desirable property, though clearly in danger of being seized, either by the

Rumanians themselves or by any armed force that might invade the country.

In order to understand and appreciate Behn's problems, one must first know something about the situation in Rumania at the time. The country had been in a state of near collapse for several years. Torn between the forces of a vacillating King Carol, the dwindling ranks of the Liberal and Peasant parties, and the growing coalition of the rabidly anti-Semitic Christian League, it was a land rent by uprisings, demonstrations, shutdowns, and political assassinations. The Iron Guard, a military organization that was trained by native fascists and that gained experience by fighting on the Franco side during the Spanish Civil War, was prepared to seize power on the slightest pretext, while Carol's advisers urged him either to come to terms with the fascists or to establish a royal dictatorship.

The anti-Semitic riots—worse than those in Germany itself—had brought business to a crawl. The left-wing parties hoped for assistance from the Soviet Union while the Iron Guard and the Christian League plotted for intervention by Germany. The king was thought to be on the fence, eager to preserve his throne, and in late 1938 he appeared to be swaying in the direction of some kind of alignment with Hitler.

By then Britain and France had determined to stop Germany's drive into Eastern Europe. In March they guaranteed Poland's territorial integrity, and the same was done for Rumania the following month. Carol and newly installed Premier Armand Călinescu accepted this arrangement but almost simultaneously concluded a new commercial agreement with Germany. Thus the government attempted to work with both sides, hoping for favors from whichever one came to dominate that part of the world. And in the background was the Soviet Union, its forces prepared to invade once war came.

The United States had virtually no influence in Rumania, and so could do little to protect its nationals or their property. Along with other foreign businessmen, Americans who had assets in that country did what they could to dispose of them. ITT shut down some facilities and sold off holdings of Rumanian government bonds. Behn remitted whatever earnings and assets he could from Bucharest, but of course he could do nothing to safeguard the main properties of Romana de Telefoane, which remained in operation through all of this.

The Iron Guard took power when war came, forcing King Carol to leave the country and to abdicate in favor of his son, Michael. Then a pro-Nazi dictatorship was installed, under the leadership of Marshal Ion Antonescu. Rumania clearly had taken sides in the war, a fact duly noted in Washington. Late in 1940 all of that country's dollar holdings in American banks were impounded. The Rumanians protested that this was an act of war, but Secretary of State Cordell Hull was adamant. The money couldn't be touched until peace was realized or some changes were made in Rumania—at least, that is, by the Antonescu government.

The Colonel must have known that this situation presented ITT with an opportunity to liquidate its precarious holding. Might the State Department approve of the sale of Romana de Telefoane for part of the impounded assets? Clearly he meant to get an answer to that question.

Any contact with Washington on this matter probably was oral, for there is nothing in the corporation's archives to indicate Behn worked in tandem with anyone at the State Department or at any other agency. Nor is there correspondence at ITT between officials there and the Rumanians. Given the close relations between the Antonescu regime and the Germans, nothing of consequence could have been done without Berlin's approval. That the Germans were involved in the negotiations from the start was taken for granted; it would appear that Westrick or Schroeder—or perhaps both of them, along with associates—assisted in the talks.

Representatives of the Antonescu government met with ITT officials in late 1940, probably in November, to settle on details. One of ITT's harshest critics later claimed that the Rumanians were eager to make the purchase, but under the circumstances they hardly could have wanted it more than Behn.[2] In any case the talks went smoothly and swiftly, probably with the assistance of State Department officials. Their conclusions were made known in late December and went into effect on January 1, 1941.

Under the terms of the agreement ITT sold Romana de Telefoane to the Antonescu government for $13.8 million, all of which would be paid from blocked accounts in American banks. The transfers were made soon thereafter, with the parties involved acting in unusual haste. The reason for this was evident. German forces had arrived in Rumania in early October, and for all intents and purposes the country had become a Nazi satellite. Within a few weeks of the signing Antonescu acceded formally to the takeover. Of all the American firms with interests in Rumania, only ITT had been able to repatriate assets.

The sale of Romana de Telefoane was hailed as a prime example of Behn's astuteness. Together with additional funds from the Export-Import Bank, the money was used to reduce ITT's long-term debt, cutting annual interest payments by more than $600,000. The corporation was in better financial shape in mid-1941 than it had been for half a decade, though there would be further refinancing problems ahead. All of this was to Behn's credit. But the episode also indicated that more than most American businessmen of the time, he had close relations with the Germans and had been able to use them to his company's benefit. Of course, the United States still was a neutral country in late 1940 and early 1941, and in no way had Behn violated any American law or regulation. In fact, the sale couldn't have been consummated without the cooperation and approval of the Roosevelt Administration. Still, it would provide ammunition for those who years later claimed the Colonel had significant contacts with the Nazi high command.

The sale of Romana de Telefoane was important not only in that it provided ITT with the funds needed to clean its balance sheet but also because it was the initial step in the restructuring of the corporation. Prior to 1941 Behn had sold several minor manufacturing facilities, shut down holding companies, and of course had participated in the legal machinations regarding Postal Telegraph's bankruptcy. In the past, however, he had clung tenaciously to the telephone operations, ITT's original business and long considered its central interest. Now all of this was changed. Romana de Telefoane had been the last important telephone company to come under the ITT umbrella, and it had been the first to go. Others would follow, whenever Behn had the opportunity to divest at the right price. Never again would he even try to enlarge his operating holdings overseas.

Shortly after completion of the Rumanian sale, Behn attempted to find a buyer for CTNE. The Spanish government wasn't involved this time, but Franco located a group of German businessmen interested in the acquisition. With Westrick acting as intermediary, the Germans indicated a willingness to pay approximately $63 million for the property, the funds to come from accounts in the United States. Frank Page was the ITT vice-president charged with government relations, and he contacted the U.S. State Department to learn of its attitude toward such a sale. "From every aspect the proposed transaction seems completely counter to the national interest of the United States" was the response. Under the circumstances, however, there was little the government could have done had ITT gone ahead with it. But Behn cut off negotiations. "That's all I wanted to know," wrote Page to the State Department. The sale, which would have been of enormous benefit to ITT at the time, didn't take place.[3]

Despite this, from 1940 on the Colonel concentrated on domestic manufacturing rather than foreign telecommunications. This was a radical switch for ITT, necessitated of course by the coming of war, and one Behn undertook with some reluctance. Yet it probably would have been done even had the war been avoided, though the process would have been slower, less painful, and accomplished in a less-dramatic fashion. Economic nationalism had grown steadily throughout the world during the 1930s. Few countries in a position to do anything about it were willing to tolerate control of their telecommunications networks by foreign interests. No matter how sincere and convincing the Colonel might have been when discussing the International System, pressures would have developed for divestiture, in spite of the fact that more than almost any other American firm ITT had placed national managers and technicians in prominent posts and paid them well, and notwithstanding its generally excellent record in developing, financing, and operating its subsidiaries.

The Colonel had come to appreciate this in 1939 and 1940, before the United States became involved in the war as a belligerent. As significant as the changes would be, however, there was one important aspect of the basic approach of the old ITT that would remain in the new: The corporation would have nothing to do with the open, competitive marketplace for consumer goods.

Throughout the 1920s and 1930s ITT had acquired and managed utilities and factories and laboratories geared to supplying them with equipment and technologies. Behn and his associates were accustomed to dealing with politicians; ITT's managers knew how to gain concessions and franchises and how to keep government officials either as allies or at bay, as circumstances required. No part of the parent corporation, or any of its subsidiaries, produced and marketed products for the individual consumer. This orientation

Repatriation and Rebirth

would continue under the new dispensation. After 1941 Behn would use revenues derived from his utilities along with additional borrowings to expand in the manufacturing area, to create military products for governments.

At first the Colonel had to improvise. His British and French laboratories cooperated fully with one another between the declaration of war in September 1939 and the German march on Paris a half year later. Behn dispatched several of his officers to France to assist in relocation operations should these prove necessary, and they went into action in the spring of 1940. Some of the scientists and technicians came out by way of Spain and Portugal, while others crossed the English Channel and proceeded to London. A number of them remained in Britain, to work at STC during the war, but a majority continued on to the United States, where the Colonel was busily engaged in establishing his first important domestic manufacturing facility.

ITT might have entered this area in several ways. It could have purchased an operating company, or started from scratch, or Behn might have expanded one of his domestic holdings. Given ITT's parlous financial condition, an outright purchase was out of the question, even had one been available. The Colonel had to make do with what he had on hand, and in 1940 his most important asset in this regard was a group of talented scientists and technicians, most of whom were French, headed by Maurice Deloraine and Henri Busignies.

ITT also controlled several small factories in the United States, units that had come along with the Mackay acquisition. None had been considered sufficiently promising to develop, even when ITT had the money to do so, and the factories had been left on their own during the Depression, when demands for their products were low and the parent corporation was badly in need of funds. In any case, as a result of the AT&T agreements, ITT had promised not to compete with Western Electric in the United States. But the arrangement didn't cover items for the military, and so Behn felt free to enter this market.

Federal Telegraph Company was one of these firms. A minor operation that manufactured radio-telegraph transmitting and receiving equipment at its small factory in Newark, New Jersey, Federal had received some military orders in late 1939, but its sales the following year would come to less than $2 million, and about 20 percent of these sales were to other Mackay subsidiaries. It was a profitable and well-managed company, however, with a good reputation in its industry, but one that was generally left on its own, ignored by the parent. Although the plant was only a short drive from his Broad Street offices, Behn apparently hadn't visited it during the 1920s and '30s, leaving its direction to the Mackay officers.

All of this changed in 1940. Colonel Behn arranged for the transfer of Federal from Mackay to ITT itself, and assumed personal direction of its revamping. He organized the Federal Telephone & Radio Laboratories and sought a proper location for its facilities, preferably not far from Federal's main plant. During the next year ITT bought a site in Great River, New York, on which was erected a laboratory. Additional land was obtained in New Jersey, and new plants were constructed. Behn rented other factories and offices in Newark and purchased two small firms, primarily to acquire facilities and work forces. All of this was done through a wholly owned subsidiary, International Telephone Development, whose name soon was changed to International Telephone & Radio Manufacturing. Behn had little difficulty obtaining orders, and that year Federal's sales came to $5.5 million. Shortly thereafter the Colonel consolidated most of his domestic operations into a single firm, which he named Federal Telephone & Radio and to which he devoted most of his attention.

During this period it was perhaps inevitable that ITT should turn so strongly to manufacturing. There was little that Behn could do to preserve his telephone concessions in Europe and Latin America other than attempting to remain on good terms with political leaders, most of whom were of dubious reliability, given the circumstances of war. The CTNE concession was due to expire in 1945, and although Franco clearly wouldn't expropriate the company before then, neither was he expected to renew the grant if the Allies were on the defensive at that time, and there was no way of knowing whether Spain would pay a fair price for assets. River Plate was more secure, but given the pro-German proclivities of the Argentine government, its future, too, was in doubt. A similar situation existed in Chile. Cuban Telephone was of marginal profitability. ITT's other Latin American holdings were of little consequence.

On the other hand, those International Standard Electric companies in unoccupied areas were expanding rapidly, turning out military supplies for the Allies. Most of the ISE units specialized in telephonic, telegraphic, and radio equipment, for which demand was intense, but several Standard Telephones and Cables plants turned out specialized electrical and electronic gear as well. By 1945 ISE subsidiaries were producing military and related supplies worth more than $117 million. In contrast, ISE's 1939 revenues had come to less than $60 million, and that year's figures included sales for all the occupied European facilities.

Federal's growth was even more impressive. Sales for 1944 came to $90.8 million, and earnings were $3.6 million. This company had grown during the war from practically nothing to achieve the status of a major operation, by far the largest and most profitable in the ITT constellation.

The transformation at ITT was striking. In 1939 Behn had still spoken publicly of an International System based on telephonic operations. By 1945 ITT's major business was industrial, with the utilities of decidedly secondary importance. Telephonic equipment remained its most significant product, but the Colonel was branching out into new fields as well. It was as though American Telephone and Telegraph (to which ITT continued to be compared) had been reduced to Western Electric, the Bell Laboratories, and utilities operations in a dozen or so states.

Federal produced a wide variety of products. Initially most of these were based on conventional technologies related to communications: automatic telephone-exchange systems, telephone receivers, and radio transmitters, for example—and the company became the leading producer of field telephones. It also manufactured a unique selenium rectifier perfected by ITT just prior to the outbreak of war. Soon after, however, Federal turned to military devices that had little to do with its earlier business.

More than ever before, Behn recognized the need for higher levels of research-and-development spending. During the late 1930s ITT had subsidized experiments at several American universities, hoping in this way to nurture inventions and to lure researchers to its staff. These expenditures were increased and bore fruit, as a steady though small stream of new ideas and technicians flowed from the schools to Federal. The company was insufficiently glamorous at the time to attract leading American scientists, however, and so its research arm was dominated by those Europeans from Continental ISE installations who trickled into New York in late December of 1940 and the following January. This was a period during which the company was still in the process of turning itself around, attempting to become a military supplier. Despite much confusion, several mishaps, and suspicion on the part of American military officers regarding their loyalties, the Europeans were put to work and were soon turning out important products for use in the war effort.[4]

Deloraine and Busignies were the key scientists at ITT. Both men and their staffs were installed at Manhattan hotels. Soon they were at work in makeshift laboratories created for them on several floors of the ITT Building at 67 Broad Street, where they would remain until the New Jersey facilities were ready. Most of their work involved perfection of instrument-landing systems and direction finders for aircraft. Busignies had been involved with these projects in Paris during the 1930s and had become one of the world's most prominent scientists in this field. Before the end of the war, Federal's systems were not only in use in American avionics but were accepted by the Allies as well.[5] Even more important was the application of the principle to oceangoing shipping, troubled by German submarines throughout the war. Busignies perfected a high-frequency direction finder, known as HF/DF, or "Huff-Duff," which was of incalculable value in locating submarines. Out of the Huff-Duff technology came several families of electronic devices and radio equipment, which provided Federal with a reputation as a leader in these fields. The company expanded rapidly, so that by the end of the war it operated some sixty installations in the Newark area alone.

In the early summer of 1941, as he prepared for a European tour, Behn realized the United States soon would become involved in the fighting. Now he established the means whereby he could obtain information regarding the status of seized ITT factories on the Continent. Behn visited Zurich in June, meeting with ISE's managing director for Switzerland, G. Edouard Hofer, who would be his most important European contact during the war.[6] Hofer was to receive information from Westrick and Schroeder, as well as other ITT personnel in Germany and occupied countries, and in turn to transmit messages to them from Broad Street.[7]

Several officials in the State Department knew of this arrangement. As was the case with all other Americans in his position, Behn must have been aware that his telephone calls and cables to and from Switzerland were being monitored; copies of and references to them can be found in the National Archives, and, as might have been expected under the circumstances, they are quite innocuous. Occasionally Behn would inform the State Department directly of developments at ITT's holdings in occupied Europe, as he did on August 15, 1942, when he transmitted a letter from ISE president Henry Pease referring to Westrick's intention to establish a new management structure for the German companies.[8] This, too, would have involved Hofer, and perhaps others at ITT's Swiss offices.

Although the State Department doubtless knew of transmissions between New York and Zurich, it would have had little information regarding those passing between Swiss cities and Berlin. In this period SEG, Lorenz, and the other German companies, as well as those in occupied Europe, turned out quantities of telephonic and telegraphic gear, in addition to radio sets, guidance systems, and related military supplies. Westrick and Schroeder continued to have primary responsibility for installations under the control of the Reich. Even so, there was a measure of coordination of efforts if not outright cooperation between Broad Street and Berlin. Moreover, this was known at the State Department, for Behn kept officials there apprised of the situation.

The State Department had a strong concern about keeping Spain neutral, and ITT hoped to retain its properties in that country. The two worked together, with Behn taking directions from Washington insofar as operations at CTNE were concerned, while the American embassy safeguarded ITT against seizure. "The story of the successful diplomatic negotiations to protect American property and interests in Spain is one which I wish I could send to our 66,000 stockholders scattered throughout every state in the Union, as well as to the stockholders of all other American companies which have interests or property in Spain," wrote Page to Secretary of State Cordell Hull on June 14, 1940, and Hull responded by thanking Page for his "cooperation" in transmitting information regarding developments in Spain to his offices. Notes, letters, and reports on Spanish conditions were sent to the State Department at regular intervals.

Two years later, when America was at war with Germany, Behn wrote to the secretary of state to ask permission for CTNE to buy equipment from Le Matériel Téléphonique and ITT's German affiliates. He observed that these supplies weren't available from the

United States, an allied country, or a neutral. He hoped that under these circumstances Hull would agree to the purchases, adding his fears that unless the special gear was obtained, telephone services might suffer, and Franco could use this as an excuse to cancel the concession.[9]

Behn was more concerned with preserving his Spanish properties than with getting orders from the French and German companies. In this period CTNE and the Spanish ISE installations were valued at well over $75 million, whereas the State Department estimated the value of the German holdings at $17 million. The fact that Behn asked for permission would appear to suggest that he was willing to accept Hull's decision in the matter. The letter also shows that Behn must have known that Westrick could supply the materials. Whether the information came to him via Spain or Switzerland cannot be learned, but it does indicate that the Colonel probably had contacts with his German managers by way of Madrid as well as Zurich.

Still, Hofer remained his prime agent, and it was through him that the German managers learned of how Behn wanted to deploy their profits. Alexander Sanders, who was comptroller for the German operations during the war, has said that Behn wanted all reserves to be used for the purchase of land—not for the expansion of facilities or anything else of this nature.[10] This doesn't necessarily mean the Colonel expected to hinder the German war effort, though it would have been the result. He probably expected Germany to be flattened by Allied forces. Land couldn't be destroyed. Historically, it had been a good storehouse of value.

Sanders was in a position to know of such matters, and he has said that Westrick carried out Behn's wishes. But the tactic backfired. As it turned out, most of the property obtained during the war was in the eastern part of Germany—and was to be seized by Soviet occupying troops. Later, however, ITT was awarded compensation by the Foreign Claims Settlement Commission for its losses.

ITT might have squeezed some money out of continental Europe by means of shipping goods from its factories there to purchasers in neutral countries—Sweden, Switzerland, and several nations in Latin America. Payment would have been in local currency and deposited to ITT accounts there. Later such funds might have been repatriated in the form of dollars. Did this actually occur? Hans Kehrl, one of the German officials responsible for controlling such firms as SEG and Lorenz during the war, concedes it was possible, and Sanders agrees. But neither man had any direct knowledge of ITT's engaging in the practice.

Anthony Sampson has charged that ITT's operating companies in Latin America were used by Axis agents to transmit information to Berlin. In a section of his book *The Sovereign State of ITT* entitled "Telephones and Treachery," he describes ITT's involvement with Nazis and their sympathizers, and even notes the number of calls made through River Plate's lines to Germany.[11]

This certainly was the case. German agents did send their findings to Berlin by means of telephone and cable facilities owned and operated by ITT subsidiaries. Moreover, there seems little doubt that some—perhaps many—of the companies' employees sympathized with the Axis cause. Sampson failed to take account of three important matters, however. In the first place, River Plate and the other Latin American telephone companies had government concessions, and failure to transmit calls would have led to prompt cancellations and confiscations, in which case they would have continued to handle such operations, probably with the same personnel. Then, too, much of Latin America favored the Axis in the war, and given ITT's policy of using nationals whenever and wherever possible, it is likely that its companies had a number of them on their payrolls, some in top management posts.

Behn understood this, as did Secretary Hull. Henri Busignies, one of the Colonel's closest associates in a position to know of these matters, has said that Behn contacted the State Department early in the war and offered to do what he could to halt or slow down such communications, but was told not to interfere. By then all the transmissions were being monitored, enabling Washington to discover just what it was the German agents were telling Berlin.[12] Behn also entered into an agreement with Secretary Hull whereby loyal ITT personnel would report on activities in their countries, similar to the one worked out with CTNE officials in Madrid. Not only did Behn know of the telephone calls from River Plate and other companies to Berlin, he helped tap them and reported to Washington in detail on operations. It is from this material that Sampson and others were able to learn precisely how many calls were made, and to whom.

The same was true for cable messages. Page started sending them to Laurence Duggan, chief of the State Department's Division of the American Republics, on June 18, 1940, and continued to do so throughout the war. In 1943 he reported directly to assistant secretary Breckinridge Long on radio-telephone calls from Buenos Aires to Berlin. By then he had established close contact with Joseph F. McGurk, head of the Office of American Republican Affairs, through whom ITT officials in Latin America would submit regular reports on conditions in those countries in which they functioned. ITT managers also reported on activities of employees suspected of working for the Germans. On a more mundane level, clerks at the Latin American operating companies clipped newspaper and magazine articles that their employers believed would be of interest to the State Department.[13]

Whether any of this had a discernible effect on the war cannot be known. But it does seem clear that State Department intelligence regarding activities in Latin America and Spain was more complete as a result of cooperation by ITT. Discussions of ITT activities in areas for which there are no records belong in the realm of fancy and imagination rather than history.

Shortly after the Normandy invasion of June 6, 1944, Behn tried to obtain permission to accompany the troops, particularly the advance elements headed in the direction of Paris. He probably had several reasons for making the request, which after a short delay was granted. For one thing, it was to be a romantic escapade. Behn was to travel in battle dress, mounted in the back of a jeep, but always safely behind the lines, never in great danger. He stopped at familiar inns and hotels along the way to sample the cuisine, something he had missed sorely during the war. According to associates, he managed to find what he wanted in this regard. In other ways, however, this "tour" resembled his foray into Spain during that country's civil war, which is to say he wouldn't have gone were it not for a desire to check on the status of his factories and laboratories and to direct their operations.[14]

Behn hoped to obtain contracts from the Allied military authorities to produce equipment for them in those facilities that were liberated. Later on other ITT officials went to Europe with this in mind. Mark Sunstrom and Kenneth Stockton were successful in getting such business, the result being that the transitions in operations at the French, Belgian, and Dutch factories went remarkably well. It would appear that at some installations goods were being produced for the German forces one week, and the next the same kinds of materials were being shipped to the Allied armies.

Repatriation and Rebirth

There was little manufacturing of any kind at the German facilities, which by then had been almost completely destroyed. Most of ITT's plants had been located in and around Berlin, which had been heavily bombed and among the last to be taken by the Allied armies. Lorenz had utilized more than 3 million square feet of factory and laboratory space; almost all of this was in rubble. The Mix & Genest plant was bombed out. What few pieces of machinery remained were taken by the Soviets and shipped east.

In the autumn of 1945 ITT workers in these areas were attempting to revive their plants. Under the circumstances they hardly could resume fabrication of old products, and so they turned to new ones. Mix & Genest turned out trowels and dust pans, and Lorenz began making frying pans, small stoves, bread knives, and stove lighters.

In this period stories started to appear on American radio and in newspapers regarding ITT's activities in rebuilding Germany's industrial might. Max Lerner and Drew Pearson charged that improper pressures had been applied to American military-government forces by ITT personnel and that the corporation protected Nazi officials. *Philadelphia Enquirer* reporter Pat Frank wrote that ITT was one of those American companies involved in resurrecting German industry, this at a time when most public-opinion polls indicated a fear that such a policy would result in a revival of Nazi sentiment and perhaps even lead to a third world war.

Rumors and allegations continued into the autumn. That October, Johannes Steel, a New York–based radio commentator, reviewed charges of improper behavior on the part of several large American corporations and the complicity of the military government. "It is high time that a senatorial committee investigated the matter and cleaned house," he concluded. "If the world really wants peace, then American economic policy, or rather German economic policy, cannot be determined by American officers who in private life are associates of General Motors, Alcoa, I.T.&T., Dillon, Read & Company, and other similar interests."

Sunstrom responded to these and related charges in a lengthy memorandum intended for ITT's executives. Noting some errors in fact, he also explained that supposedly secret and clandestine meetings with Westrick and others were held at the behest of the military authorities, and with Army officers present. Records of such conversations were on file, and some came out during the Nuremberg trials. Westrick had asked Behn to vouch for him. The Colonel refused to do so; he had had no contact with Westrick in the postwar period. Sunstrom said that talk of major production efforts at ITT plants in liberated areas was vastly exaggerated, and he produced statistics to support his position.

Rebuttals were simple affairs in some cases. A Los Angeles radio commentator, Arthur Gaeth, claimed that Sunstrom, Stockton, and one other ITT official were army generals in Europe. No ITT manager or board member on leave for military service achieved a rank higher than that of colonel. Other charges, such as one alleging that ITT protected Nazis, were difficult to answer, since they were vague and imprecise.

How was ITT to respond to this assault? Sunstrom thought actions might be filed for libel and slander, but he recommended against it. "I.T.T. has a real case, if it could prove damages, but if it sustained any damages as a result of libel, what is the measuring stick?" Both Stockton and he had suffered "a certain amount of humiliation and embarrassment as a result of the unjust charges, implications, innuendos, etc.," Sunstrom continued, "but we are still drawing our salaries and enjoying reasonably good health so I cannot see the basis for any supportable claims for damages."[15]

Behn must have agreed, or for some other reason he preferred to let the matter drop. There would be no official response to the various charges. This created new problems, however, for some commentators took the silence as a tacit admission of complicity, and further allegations resulted.

More serious charges were made regarding larger corporations such as Du Pont, the Texas Company, General Motors, General Electric, Ford Motor, and Standard Oil of New Jersey. It was demonstrated, for example, that the last two maintained relations with I. G. Farben during the early stages of the war, though the full extent of these relations remained unclear. Leaders at these and other firms so charged either ignored the charges or offered *pro forma* responses and then let the matter drop, expecting that in time they would be forgotten or simply ignored. ITT did much the same, but in its case the allegations surfaced again in the 1970s, and in such a way as to distress those in the board room and corporate suites deeply.

One might reasonably question the motivations of some of the journalists involved. Doubtless most of them were sincerely convinced there had been collusion between certain American corporations and the Nazis, whereas others simply were tracking down leads or reporting on rumors then current. Big business had been castigated by many of the same journalists for having exacerbated if not actually caused the Great Depression, and they may have been carrying on their antibusiness crusades on this new battlefield. And of course in this period there was a strong national determination that Germany never again be given the opportunity or power to start another war.

This wasn't a unique or an unusual reaction. After World War I there had been congressional investigations during which businessmen were charged with having pressured President Wilson into declaring war in order to increase profits. At the time, the executives were labeled "merchants of death." It wasn't quite the same in the late 1940s. Still, businessmen were said to have assisted the recent enemies and profited from investments in German industries.

Virginia Swartz, a writer for *Time*, may have been typical of such journalists. In July 1945 she was assigned by her editor to put together a story on the activities of ITT in occupied Germany. She obtained an interview with State Department official Robert Terrill in which she asked about the rumors and charges then being broadcast and written about. Terrill shot them down, one after another, noting that they simply had no basis in fact, were distorted, or resulted from incomplete and highly suspect intelligence. In his memo on the interview Terrill wrote:

> Miss Swartz intimated that I was attempting to "white wash" Mr. Sosthenes Behn and the IT&T and asked why I was so disposed. I replied that in view of what seemed to be certain inaccuracies in her present story and in view of the fact that IT&T was a private company whose affairs could not be disclosed by me, I thought she should seek to verify the details and in particular should consult the Company itself. She replied that they would simply "deny everything." I answered that they would then have to live with their own denials.
>
> I further stated to Miss Swartz that it seemed desirable to keep a proper prospective [*sic*] in matters of this sort and not to generalize from any one case; that many American concerns had acquired foreign subsidiaries in countries all over the world and that of course with the intervention of war they were necessarily placed in an embarrassing posture, often

through no fault of their own; that a "smear" campaign would not be a service to the reestablishment of the liberal and cosmopolitan world trading community which this country favored.[16]

Perhaps because of this interview, *Time* decided not to run the story, although there might have been other factors that were more important in the determination of publishing priorities. Some felt the charges should be aired, and so they were. None was proved, but suspicions lingered. Traces of them remain to this day.

7

A Matter of Succession: The Heir Apparent

BECAUSE of an upset world, our Corporation decided, just prior to the last War, to develop its research and manufacturing activities in the United States to a point where instead of more than two-thirds of our revenues being derived from foreign subsidiaries and services, at least two-thirds of our revenues would eventually originate in the United States.

This was Colonel Behn's message to the ITT stockholders in April 1947, his way of informing them of the progress in carrying out the postwar five-year plan previously discussed. Notification of this kind really wasn't necessary. In a series of rapid and dramatic moves reminiscent of those he had executed in the 1920s, Behn had positioned ITT so as to enter a new phase of its development. Out of the chrysalis of a company founded on the concepts inherent in the International System would emerge a high-technology electrical and electronics firm. The role played by CTNE and River Plate in the prewar ITT would be taken by Federal Electric and other domestic manufacturing companies. The initial moves in this direction had already been made, and the Colonel was reporting on them to the stockholders, with no small pride in his accomplishments thus far.

The first important step came in Spain in 1945. CTNE had grown substantially since the Civil War, and by 1944 it had more than 400,000 stations. That year it handled more domestic calls than all the other ITT telephone companies combined, and its facilities were in excellent condition.

In large part this was due to the fact that Franco had frozen the firm's assets and refused to allow Behn to repatriate earnings from any of his Spanish properties. Rather than leaving them in local banks, ITT used the money to improve and expand operations, perhaps in the hope that by so doing, it would win Franco's favor. This wasn't to be. Although Franco grew increasingly pro-American as Allied victory became evident, he had no intention of permitting ITT to retain control of CTNE once the concession expired.

In 1944 Madrid issued a series of decrees requiring CTNE to hire only Spanish personnel and paving the way for majority ownership of its common stock by nationals. Behn took this to be a prelude to cancellation of the concession, and after discussions with State Department officials he sent Fred Caldwell to Spain to negotiate the best settlement possible. This Caldwell did, with the help of the Madrid embassy.

Under the terms of the agreement, signed in May 1945, Spain was to pay ITT $33 million in cash and $50 million in 4 percent bonds. Whether this was a fair price cannot be determined, since statistics for CTNE had been unavailable since the late 1930s, but it was some $20 million more than Behn might have taken out of Spain before the war. In light of the valuation afforded similar assets in other countries, it would appear to have been in line with economic realities.

In addition, ITT was to receive a service and technical contract that provided it with what amounted to a monopoly insofar as CTNE equipment was concerned. ISE's Spanish subsidiary, Standard Eléctrica S.A., wasn't included in the sale, and its factories continued to produce equipment for CTNE and to export to other parts of Europe and Latin America. Moreover, ITT was given the right to repatriate profits, whenever appropriate, in the form of dividends.

A Matter of Succession: The Heir Apparent

Under the circumstances, ITT came out of its Spanish venture quite well. In 1939 Behn had indicated a desire to ease the corporation out of utilities ownership and management and to concentrate on manufacturing. Such was the case in Spain.

Behn now attempted to sell ITT's River Plate holdings in Argentina, a more delicate task given the situation in that country.

Even more than Spain, Argentina had been pro-German during the war and was considered the most important Axis listening post in the hemisphere. As has been indicated, information gathered there was transmitted to Berlin via ITT facilities in Buenos Aires.

ITT's manager in that city, Henry "Bill" Arnold, was one of the Colonel's personal favorites. He enjoyed the city and was devoted to River Plate and so rejected offers to return to New York for a high staff post that might have placed him in line for the succession. Arnold understood Argentina better than most Americans there and maintained close relations with important political leaders. He certainly was on good terms with President Edelmiro Farrell, an outspoken pro-Nazi, and his vice-president, Juan Perón, who had similar feelings. These relations continued after Perón was elected president, in February 1946.

Official American policy toward Argentina in this period was somewhat confused. Just prior to the cessation of hostilities that country had declared war on Germany, more in order to get into the new United Nations Organization than for any political reason or belief. The State Department had no desire to exacerbate relations with Argentina and hoped for an improvement under Perón. Ambassador Spruille Braden disagreed and openly opposed Perón both during and after the election. For his part, the new president was eager to appear anti-American. Complicating matters were the statements and actions of his wife, Eva, who made no attempt to disguise a strong dislike for Americans. Publicly, Argentine-American relations were at a low point but behind the scenes conditions were much better than they seemed.

Anthony Sampson has claimed that Behn and Arnold were strong supporters of Perón, implying that this was in line with their generally favorable attitude toward such people. Given their position, however, they weren't in any way able to influence official policy. Moreover, ever since the beginning of World War II Kenneth McKim, the assistant vice-president for ITT in Buenos Aires, had been sending reports on the political situation to Page, who forwarded them to the State Department. These were long, often complicated affairs, and in retrospect McKim's assessments of Perón appear remarkably accurate. In November 1945 he wrote that Perón was bound to win the forthcoming election, and recommended that the United States "step aside with a bow, instead of remaining in the ring in the ungracious capacity of referee." "The analysis is good," wrote a State Department official on the margin of the letter, "but the conclusions are bad."[1]

Argentina had prospered during the war, largely by selling grain and meat to the Allies. This provided Perón with more than sufficient funds to acquire River Plate—if he so desired. Much of this money was on deposit at the New York Federal Reserve Bank, and Ambassador Braden pleaded with Washington to freeze these assets. Perón had no clear idea of what might happen under these circumstances. He looked upon Arnold as a friend, and both he and Eva were disposed to use part of the funds to purchase River Plate before Braden and his allies might win support from the White House for their proposals. The situation, then, was somewhat similar to that which surrounded the sale of Romania de Telefoane in 1940.

Behn traveled to Buenos Aires at the head of a team of executives to negotiate the sale. This was one of the few times he went to South America, an indication of how important he considered the transaction. River Plate was ITT's major utility. The company was in excellent condition, with almost 520,000 stations in operation and applications on file for 125,000 more. Cia. Standard Electric Argentina, S.A., Industrial and Commercial, was ITT's largest and most important manufacturing complex south of the equator, providing River Plate with all of its equipment and selling substantial amounts to other ITT telephone companies in Latin America. As had been the case with CTNE, Behn wanted to make certain the relationship between the utility and his factories wouldn't be harmed.

The negotiations went well, and in early September, 1946, River Plate was sold for almost $94 million, to be paid out of Argentine deposits in New York—a figure about one fifth of that country's dollar assets.[2] ITT retained an interest in a small telephone operation outside Buenos Aires that connected the city to Santiago, Chile, but the government received everything else. Behn also concluded an arrangement under which ITT was to act as technical adviser to the new Argentine Telephone Administration for ten years, while

A Matter of Succession: The Heir Apparent

Standard Electric Argentina would continue to supply the company with all of its equipment.

The similarities between the River Plate contract and the one signed by the Spaniards is evident, but more striking was the parallel with the agreement entered into with the Rumanians. Within less than five years almost all of Argentina's dollar holdings had been exhausted, and by then anti-American sentiment in Buenos Aires had grown to the point where direct expropriation, not purchase, might have occurred.

The disposition of River Plate and CTNE removed from ITT its two major prewar holdings and revenue producers. In 1944 the corporation had 1.3 million toll stations in its various systems; two years later there were less than half that number in operation. Now its largest telephone company was Compañía de Teléfonos de Chile, barely a fifth of the size of River Plate and growing much more slowly. Behn hadn't taken ITT out of the telephone business, but under his direction major steps in that direction had been made.

In addition to filling ITT's treasury by these sales, Behn restructured the debt to take advantage of lower interest rates available owing to changing market conditions and the new financial strength of the company. The effects from all of this on the balance sheet were quite dramatic. In its consolidated statement for 1945, ITT reported cash items of $16 million; within a year the corporation had more than $96 million, all but $3 million of which was held by the parent operation in New York, with more to arrive before the year was over from the River Plate sale. Some of this was used to reduce the long-term debt, which went from $72 million in 1945 to slightly more than $20 million two years later. Most of the rest of the money was earmarked for investments in domestic manufacturing operations.

The way seemed clear for a smooth transition, the third major alteration in the corporation's history. Behn had navigated ITT through what at times appeared more difficult situations, and on the surface at least it seemed he would be able to do as much this time. The problems he had to face in 1947 were quite different from those he had dealt with earlier, however, and for that matter so was the man.

The Colonel had started out after World War I with an overarching concept, a plan to fashion an international version of American Telephone and Telegraph. The technology was available; the federal government was prepared to assist in such ventures, and so were the New York banks. Within less than a decade the young, vigorous entrepreneur had come close to realizing his ambitions. Then the nation and world were struck by the Great Depression, which forced Behn on the defensive. During the 1930s he focused most of his attention on keeping his creation intact, and he performed admirably. The coming of war obliged Behn to alter his strategy, to concentrate on domestic manufacturing rather than international and foreign utilities operations, and this, too, he had done. Allied requirements for telecommunications equipment and other products that came out of the ITT laboratories and plants enabled Federal and the ISE companies to prosper, and both expanded during the war. When peace arrived, Behn proceeded to sell off parts of his utilities operations, and this was accomplished skillfully. In a quarter of a century, then, the Colonel had first fashioned an industrial empire, then preserved it, and finally altered it substantially to the demands of a wartime emergency.

The challenges posed in the late 1940s were somewhat akin to those of the early 1920s, in that they called for a major effort of imagination and creation. Behn talked of ITT's becoming an industrial giant, quite a different kind of company from the one he had molded. The ISE companies might adjust without too much difficulty, since they could return to the prewar business of producing telephonic, telegraphic, and radio equipment to be sold to operating companies under government control. But what of Federal Electric, the key to the emerging domestic ITT, which itself was expected to become the heart of the entire corporation? The requirements for military equipment declined sharply in the immediate postwar period, and Federal was in trouble. This was hardly a unique situation, for many military suppliers experienced difficulty in converting their operations to meet the demands of a peacetime economy. In Federal's case, however, it was more a matter of entering additional lines of business than of recapturing former ones.

Federal had been a small company prior to the war, with almost all of its products sold to other firms within the ITT complex or to a group of old customers. Now it had to seek new markets. Given Federal's product lines and expertise, the obvious ones would be those telephone companies not controlled by AT&T. This meant competition with Western Electric and other suppliers. ITT had

A Matter of Succession: The Heir Apparent

had some experience with this in Europe, but none in America. Clearly a major switch in marketing would be required.

Then there were the opportunities in radio. Deloraine, Busignies, and other ITT scientists had developed and perfected advanced frequency-modulation equipment, opening the way to sales to radio stations. This would be a new area for Behn and his New York associates. There was also talk of entering the market for consumer radio equipment, and perhaps television as well. Busignies was certain many civilian uses could be found for a wide variety of electronic equipment produced during the war, but the old ITT leadership had no experience in these areas.[3]

Colonel Behn was a healthy man in 1947, but he was sixty-three years old, an age when many top corporate executives consider stepping down. In the past Behn had done little to prepare the way for an orderly succession in case of his death or incapacity. Several of his vice-presidents were ambitious for advancement—among them Fred Caldwell, Harold Buttner, and Frank Page—but the Colonel didn't encourage any of them. After the war, however, he assumed the title of chairman in addition to president. To some this seemed a mere formality, for Behn had been chief executive as well as chief operating officer ever since Hernand's death. But there was more to it than that.

One reason Behn might have made this move was to solidify his position in the event of a stockholder insurrection. ITT hadn't paid a dividend since 1932, and in light of its newly acquired wealth, it appeared reasonable to expect a payout of some kind. Behn adamantly opposed this, at least until the transition was completed. When one of his bankers suggested the time had come, the Colonel instantly shot back, "How? Do you want me to cut flesh from a growing body?"[4]

A more likely explanation for his assuming the title of chairman was Behn's need to gather as much prestige and authority as possible in dealings with other corporations, for by 1947 he was once again on the prowl for acquisitions. The situation was different from what it had been during the 1920s, and so was Behn's position. During the earlier period almost all of the Colonel's takeovers had been foreign operations, which already had or were given national officers who knew they were expected to remain where they were and would not be transferred to a staff post in New York. American

Cable & Radio and Mackay had aged leaders, and it was understood from the start that none of their officers would take an important position at the parent corporation. In 1947, however, Behn was seeking a domestic company, one that could complement or supplement Federal. Such a firm was bound to have a leader younger than Behn and eager to assume command at the merged entity. The Colonel would have none of this: another reason for the additional title. Perhaps he had in mind to take the chairmanship and the role of chief executive officer, leaving the presidency and the tasks of chief operating officer to the leader of the acquired company, who might become the heir apparent if all went well.

This would have made sense, for by then Behn had come to appreciate that Federal's troubles couldn't be handled by the existing management, and that more skilled hands were needed. The company experienced delays in construction in 1946, and its New Jersey installations were disorganized. Orders were flowing in from the independent telephone companies, but Federal was unable to fill them on time. The company was losing more than a million dollars a month. In 1944 Federal had been ITT's leading money earner; two years later it was hemorrhaging badly. In a desperation move Behn took personal command of the factories, going so far as to live in a house on the site. Soon it became evident that he lacked the temperament needed for such a task. Moreover, he was too old to change his ways. As much as anything else, this episode taught Behn that new leadership was needed.[5]

For a while it appeared the Colonel might dip into his treasury to purchase Sylvania Electric Products, a manufacturer of light bulbs and radio tubes as well as an emerging force in the promising television industry. Sylvania had come through its conversion experience in good shape, a tribute to management. Almost all of its business was domestic, and by acquiring the company, ITT would have achieved Behn's goal of drawing two-thirds of its sales and earnings from the United States. There was a nice mesh of Sylvania's products with those of Federal. Talks between the two companies began in 1946, but they were soon broken off, probably because of issues relating to the leadership of the merged corporation. Price also played a role: One of Behn's close advisers thought that at one point a difference of $2 million in cash separated the parties.[6]

The following year ITT entered into negotiations with Raytheon, which during the war had been a smallish manufacturer

A Matter of Succession: The Heir Apparent

of electrical and electronic gear and whose scientists had worked with Federal's on several projects. Raytheon was badly in need of money to complete its conversion efforts, and for that reason among others its leaders were willing to unite with ITT. There appeared to have been an agreement that ITT would be the dominant partner should the merger occur. Laurence Marshall, Raytheon's president, approved of the move. Years later he told an interviewer, "Together we could build microwave systems—broad bands that could pipe television and completely change the communications system in the nation."[7]

Behn got along well with Marshall, perhaps because the Raytheon chief indicated a desire to retire when and if a merger took place. Both men were entrepreneurial rather than managerial by temperament, and they shared many of the same ideas and dreams. Behn was also intrigued by Raytheon's technology. He knew, however, that the company had little else to offer, and that in many ways it suffered from the same problems that bedeviled Federal and at the same time lacked ITT's financial resources. What Behn wanted was a strong management team, and there was none at Raytheon. Marshall would resign in 1948, at a time when his company was still struggling to set itself aright. Discussions between the two corporations continued for several years, and although nothing of substance came of them, personal relations were forged between members of the boards that would have a profound effect upon ITT a decade later.

It was in this period that the anticipated stockholder uprising took place. Demands for a dividend were a cover-up for more important objectives. (Stockholders unhappy with management indicate their sentiments by selling out, not by entering into prolonged, expensive campaigns and litigation.) There was nothing spontaneous about this assault upon the Behn leadership, and it couldn't have taken place without careful, coordinated planning and execution by individuals intending to seize control of the corporation.

The attack might not have occurred at all without the appearance on the postwar scene of a remarkable group of businessmen-reformers, some of whom operated as an informal, loosely knit community of interests. Their supporters considered these individuals responsible organizers hoping to revitalize American capitalism, whereas critics considered them little more than corporate raiders.

Robert Young was the most prominent of their number. A former stockbroker who had become interested in railroading, Young hoped to create a truly transcontinental line and thus to help bring order out of the chaos in that industry. His vehicle in this was Alleghany Corporation, a holding company fallen on bad times, which Young had resurrected with the aid of his principal ally and financial backer, the Woolworth heir Allan Kirby. Young's cousin Robert McKinney, chairman of Davis Manufacturing and a member of the board of the Missouri Pacific Railroad, was another associate, and more of them could be found sprinkled through the business community. They had little in common except youth, ambition, wealth, and a zeal for reform.

Clendenin Ryan was one of the group. The grandson of financier Thomas Fortune Ryan, he was a rich man in his own right. Ryan was deeply concerned with New York politics. He had served as one of Mayor Fiorello La Guardia's lieutenants and later on as his commissioner of commerce. After distinguished service in the Navy during World War II, Ryan returned to New York, hoping to reenter politics. The time wasn't right for such a move, however, and Ryan looked about for other outlets for his energies.

How and why Ryan selected ITT as his target is unknown, but he did so with the help of Robert Young and Robert McKinney. One of Behn's executives later suggested that all three men were interested in transportation and that communications was a related field. This explanation is rather farfetched, but in any case Ryan initiated open-market purchases of ITT in 1946, and within less than a year he had accumulated more than 100,000 shares, representing a personal investment of approximately $2 million. Through his allies and Alleghany Corporation he controlled another 500,000, for a total of 600,000 out of ITT's capitalization of 6.4 million shares, or a little under 10 percent.

In the late summer and early autumn of 1947 Ryan first asked for and then demanded representation on the ITT board. He was brushed aside by Behn, who considered this an attack on his position. Thus rebuffed, Ryan organized a stockholders' committee, retained former Senator Burton K. Wheeler as its counsel, and laid siege to the corporation. His announced intention was to rally independent stockholders to his banner, expecting to succeed by promising them a dividend and cutting back on what he termed the Colonel's "exhorbitant" expenditures. In addition, Ryan was quoted in *The New York Times* as criticizing the corporation's lackluster per-

A Matter of Succession: The Heir Apparent

formance, saying, "In the last nine years Behn and his board of directors . . . have received more than $3,700,000 in salaries and fees while the . . . stockholders . . . have received nothing."

Comparing ITT's postwar record with that of other corporations, Ryan suggested that management had proved itself incompetent. Yet he denied having any ambitions of his own for leadership. Rather, Ryan initially said that he expected to place his nominees on the board, pay the dividend, and then monitor the corporation's future performance before deciding what next to do. After a series of cross-charges in mid-December, highlighted by the Colonel's first press conference in more than twenty years, Ryan changed his mind on this last point. At the May 1948 annual meeting he would vote his shares and those pledged to him to "pick a management that will operate in the interests of the stockholders, which has not been done over the twenty-five years of Sosthenes Behn management."[8]

As it turned out, the confrontation wasn't necessary. Behn must have counted the votes and realized that he couldn't win in a direct clash with the Ryan group. Thus, he prepared to salvage as much as he could from a situation that must have struck him as more than a trifle bizarre, and for which he was completely unprepared by temperament and experience.

Like many leaders of large corporations (especially those who were founders as well as officers), Behn wasn't as much contemptuous of stockholder rights and interests as he was unconcerned with them. Throughout his career Behn had considered his prime constituencies to be bankers and executives allied with ITT and with governments and other businessmen important to the corporation's welfare. Not since the 1920s had he interested himself directly with stockholder interests, and then only to raise capital. On seven occasions in that decade ITT issued rights to its stockholders enabling them to purchase additional shares at prices lower than those available on the New York Stock Exchange. In order to boost the price of ITT's stock so as to make the rights more valuable (and to make certain they would be exercised), Behn would issue glowing reports and often would raise dividends. The stockholders appreciated such treatment, and the exercise of rights provided ITT with badly needed capital for expansion and acquisitions.

All of this came to an end in the early 1930s, and for the next decade and a half ITT relied on its own cash flow, banks, and governments for funds, making no call upon stockholders and providing them with no payouts. The company's directors owned relatively little stock—according to one report, Behn held only 17,000 shares—and so they didn't miss the dividends. Nor were they seriously affected when ITT's stock sold at low prices. This was a period prior to the wholesale granting of executive options; ITT's management had no direct and personal interest in causing the price of the company's shares to advance.

In essence, then, there was an almost complete divorce between the concerns of management and those of ITT's stockholders. Ryan exploited this division, attacking Behn at the point of his greatest weakness. The Colonel recognized just how precarious his position had become, and the nature of his errors, and he conceded as much by agreeing to meet and deal with the dissidents.

The price for his lesson was high. In late 1947 Behn started to lose control of his corporation; never again would he enjoy that complete authority over its direction he had exercised and been accustomed to since its founding. He wouldn't give in without a fight, however. As a result, ITT would become an arena for power struggles—struggles that as much as anything else dictated its policies for the next decade.

It began on December 29, 1947, when as a result of meetings with the Ryan group Behn shook up the board. He came out of his offices to announce that six of the directors had resigned, among them Page, Deloraine, and Sunstrom. These men and another two, Kenneth Stockton and James Fullam, spent much of their time in the field and were often unable to attend meetings, giving their proxies to the Colonel instead. Ryan, McKinney, and Kirby took places on the board, and all were rightly considered anti-Behn and would remain so throughout their tenure. Three more were agreed upon by both Ryan and Behn: Boston shipbuilder Joseph Powell; W. Randolph Burgess, of National City Bank; and George Brown, a Houston-based manufacturer of oil and natural-gas equipment. Another vacancy was filled by J. Patrick Lannan, of Federal Electric, a Behn ally who had prior dealings with and knowledge of the Ryan people.

The dissidents hardly dominated the board, but they did have sufficient power to cause Behn troubles, and they also acquired a beachhead for further penetration.

Behn was able to delay payment of the dividend until he believed ITT capable of making such a payout. He retained the confidence of the old board members on this score and also won over some of the newer ones. But the Ryan group achieved one victory in 1948, and it proved far more important than that regarding the dividend.

ITT's domestic operations remained in bad shape, and it had become evident that the Colonel and his existing staff couldn't turn things around at Federal. New leadership was needed at headquarters and in the field, the Ryan faction argued, suggesting that an outsider be named as president and chief operating officer while Behn remain on as chairman and chief executive officer. The Colonel rejected the notion but had to agree that changes were called for, and he finally conceded that his administration wasn't equipped to handle the situation at Federal.

A new president would be accepted under certain conditions: First, he would have to be a man of Behn's choosing; second, he would have authority only over domestic companies and would remain completely out of the international arena; finally, the new president wouldn't be named chief operating officer, and Behn would retain that title with all that it implied.

More than three decades later J. Patrick Lannan, who was close to the Colonel in this period, spoke of how he believed the decision was made, of Behn's thinking at the time. Others within the organization agreed with Lannan.

> I think, also, the Colonel woke up one morning and said, gosh, I started this business down in the Caribbean, and I understood that. And I understand the telephone business. American Telephone and Telegraph had it tied up in the United States. I bought their old subsidiary, International Western Electric, and I understand it. But I'm never going to be able to satisfy these devils in building up the domestic business. I just don't understand that sort of thing. I understand the manufacture of telephones; I know how to sell them to the kings and queens and the post-office department. I just don't understand this fast-moving American economy.[9]

These very well might have been the Colonel's thoughts in 1947, as he took the initial steps toward an administrative transition. Some corporations are able to carry it off smoothly, with a minimum of disruption. Such wasn't to be the case at ITT, then or later.

Although dissension on the board and difficulties at Federal played their roles in exacerbating the situation, the major problem was with Behn himself and the kind of structure he had fashioned. For all his other accomplishments, the Colonel had failed to create an orderly administration at 67 Broad. He instinctively railed against the notion of establishing the type of corporation whose lines of command and responsibility might be neatly displayed on an organizational chart, preferring instead to assign tasks on an ad hoc and highly personal basis. During and immediately after the second war, for example, Frank Page performed many of the duties usually given an executive and administrative vice-president, but he lacked the titles and authority that went with the position. This wasn't because Behn thought Page shouldn't have them but rather because he was loath to relinquish symbols of that nature to anyone, even his closest associates.

Loyalties were paramount at ITT, more so even than competence. The Colonel liked to promote from within, to surround himself with familiar faces, to work with the kind of people who enjoyed his banter and appreciated invitations to luncheon. Several of his close associates thought this was a result of the Latin element in his background, that at heart Behn was more European insofar as business was concerned than he was American. At no point had he gone outside the organization for fresh, new administrative talent. He was accustomed to delegating powers broadly, with a clear understanding that in case of failure the person involved would be gently shifted to a new job, to be replaced by another Behn ally. The Colonel hated to fire anyone, preferring instead to transfer rejected executives to obscure posts in the hope they would eventually resign.[10]

Now Behn had to locate and then acquire an outsider who would come to office with his own independent power base. Such a person would have difficulties operating in the clubby atmosphere at headquarters, where he would be a stranger among executives who had worked together for many years and who were bound to consider him an interloper and a threat, forced upon them by the Ryan faction.

Had he been of a mind and disposition to do so, Behn could have mitigated this difficulty and so steered the corporation through its transitional period. His greatest contribution would have been to exercise extraordinary care in selecting the new president, and then to have used his considerable tact and charm to win him over. This might have been accomplished initially through gestures and symbols, not necessarily outright grants of power and authority. But there would have had to be the promise of the latter as well. Behn could have made the president his heir apparent, though only after making it clear that the price would be a divorce from the Ryan group.

The Colonel failed in both regards. After a surprisingly casual search he selected as president a man he didn't really know and who was, as it turned out, unable to develop a good working relationship with the old staff. Moreover, Behn made little effort to win his loyalty and trust, to integrate him into the organization. Because Behn had the responsibility and power, the fault was his. Why he acted as he did is unclear. He was weary as a result of his problems at Federal and with the Ryan group; some of his associates claim his spirit was broken. Perhaps the failures were due to age, as others believe. Yet he did recover later on, and exhibited much of his old verve and spirit. This business of selecting a president was a new experience for Behn; it might have been that he simply didn't know how to go about it, or that he had had no one to ask for guidance. Whatever the reasons, the episode was a series of blunders.

Since ITT's president would have to be knowledgeable in manufacturing, Behn might have sought his man at firms like General Electric, Westinghouse, RCA, or even one of the automobile companies. Certainly there was no shortage of executives capable of leading ITT into an era in which it would have to compete with other industrial firms and devote fewer resources to utilities management. Apparently he made no such move. Rather, in the spring of 1948, the Colonel contacted Walter Gifford, who had recently retired from AT&T to learn if he could recommend someone for the post. Behn had always admired AT&T and liked to think that his company was somehow related to it. In addition, Gifford was an old and trusted associate, and so the approach was natural.

It happened that Gifford did have a suggestion. Leroy Wilson had just defeated William Henry Harrison in a contest for the AT&T presidency. There was nothing wrong with Harrison, said Gifford. Rather, at that time AT&T needed a financial man in charge, and this was Wilson's specialty. As for Harrison, he was an engineer with a strong background in administration. This made him ideal for Federal, said Gifford, and for the management of other manufacturing facilities ITT might acquire in the future.

What of Harrison's weaknesses, both in terms of experience and

personality? AT&T was a regulated monopoly, the kind of corporation ITT had been before the war but not what it was becoming in
the late 1940s. Harrison had no experience in the consumer field,
none at all in competing with others for markets. All of his professional life had been spent either at AT&T or in the Army; nothing
in either place prepared him for the kind of situation that existed
at ITT. As for the man himself, one newspaper called him a "genial,
blue-eyed Irishman," and he certainly was a robust, outgoing individual. But Harrison also was a natural leader with a penchant for
order and a dislike for improvisation. Moreover, he was accustomed
to command, and eager to prove himself after having been passed
over. Gifford knew his man, and realized he would be discontented
and perhaps an unsettling influence at AT&T, a corporation where
order was of paramount importance. It is difficult to avoid the
conclusion that he recommended Harrison more to get him out of
AT&T than to improve the man's chances elsewhere.

At the time, however, Harrison must have appeared a fine if not
ideal selection for the tasks ahead. At fifty-two he was a strong and
vital executive, a man who clearly knew how to lead a large organization and inspire confidence. A New Yorker born to a family of
modest means, he went to New York Telephone in 1904 as an
apprentice wireman and repairman after graduating from high
school. Eager to qualify for a higher position, Harrison attended
Pratt Institute at night, where he studied engineering, and there
were courses at other schools later on. Within a few years he was
switched to the engineering department at Western Electric, where
in the company's tradition his advancement was steady, though not
spectacular.

Harrison entered the Army as a brigadier general shortly after
America's entry into World War II and was promoted to major
general in 1943. In this period he helped direct the procurement
effort and was given important assignments in the Signal Corps.
After the war Harrison returned to AT&T where he was named
chief engineer and one of the corporation's many vice-presidents.
He knew there was no clear line of succession and that being passed
over wasn't a sign of rejection, but it stung him deeply. Thus,
Harrison was prepared to consider Behn's offer seriously.

Given the situation at ITT, Harrison might have thought he
could obtain the chairmanship within a few years. He would have
preferred to be named chief operating officer as well as president,

but under the circumstances he could afford to wait it out. There was both real and symbolic compensation for this slight, in the form of salary, which at $120,000 was twice that drawn by Behn.

The Colonel thought Harrison was worth it. Not only had he acquired someone capable of running Federal and helping direct the deployment of assets in the United States, he had captured a leading executive from the much-admired and often-imitated AT&T. Some of this came out in the press release announcing the appointment:

> In securing the services of General Harrison, the directors and management of the corporation are confident that they have obtained the best possible man, particularly because of his broad experience in the domestic field, on which the corporation is laying greater emphasis than in the past.

Several years later, in an expansive mood, Behn told one of his close associates that he was most impressed by Harrison's abilities at management: "His lack of manufacturing experience was not the critical thing."[11] Perhaps not, but in this regard, at least, he wasn't the kind of man ITT needed at that juncture, something that Behn soon realized. In addition, the two had different temperaments, which made close collaboration difficult, if not impossible. Harrison was a family man, a suburbanite with a home in Garden City, New York, and active in community affairs; the Colonel remained a cosmopolitan individual who enjoyed fine food and wine and the company of stimulating businessmen and intellectuals.

Harrison was shocked at what he considered the lax financial controls at ITT and immediately set out to rectify the situation, in effect to remake the corporation in the image of AT&T. This meant sharp economies in all areas, and Harrison thought to set an example by lunching at his desk on a sandwich and coffee while the Colonel retired to his penthouse for his customary gourmet meal. Harrison wanted to reshape the corporation before embarking upon new ventures; Behn was eager to acquire additional manufacturing operations in order to augment Federal.

Already the Colonel was close to completing his initial postwar acquisition, Farnsworth Television & Radio, which he expected would become the centerpiece for ITT's consumer-products division. That company had a fine and respected name but a weak product line and poor prospects. Its founder and leader, Philo

Farnsworth, was a talented scientist who held several of the most important patents for television. He had little interest in business, however, and almost no talent in the boardroom. His operation had come close to bankruptcy in 1938; to salvage it, he offered to sell patents to RCA, and was rebuffed. Obliged either to give up or to continue on his own, he organized Farnsworth Television & Radio, scraped up enough money to purchase the manufacturing facilities of Capehart Corporation, and began turning out radio receivers. The World War II boom enabled the company to prosper, but everything fell apart when the military orders stopped arriving. During the next few years the Farnsworth company attempted unsuccessfully to establish itself in the television-receiver field and made a feeble try at becoming a force in military electronics. After these failures the company derived most of its revenues from the licensing of patents to others.

The takeover negotiations with ITT began in 1947, though why Farnsworth interested Behn remains somewhat of a mystery. Perhaps he thought to unite his research team at Federal with Farnsworth's, and he couldn't have helped being impressed by the name alone. Farnsworth Television was badly in need of capital and management. ITT soon would have sufficient funds to rehabilitate the company, but Farnsworth was woefully short on managers capable of leading the way in consumer products. Still, the acquisition was completed in early 1949, for 140,000 shares of ITT common, worth about $1.4 million.

By then Harrison had assumed command at Federal and was in the process of trying to turn that company around, justifying Behn's confidence in him. Costs had been cut, economies instituted, and duplications of effort eliminated. A quality-control program was already showing results, and morale was high. Harrison had won the respect of scientists and technicians, for he understood and appreciated the technologies with which they were working more than had Behn. He also had a clear idea of how the company's products might best be marketed to the non-Bell telephone companies. Moreover, the independents liked and trusted Harrison, who had brought the Western Electric brand of expertise to Federal. For the first time in the postwar period, the company was making good on its delivery schedules, and new orders were flowing into the marketing division.

Harrison was erecting what amounted to a duplicate of Western

A Matter of Succession: The Heir Apparent

Electric, and although the effort was successful in terms of sales, this wasn't to have been his major task. Rather, Behn had hoped he would expand Federal's consumer business, and make it competitive with General Electric and Westinghouse, not necessarily with Western Electric. Harrison virtually ignored consumer sales, and on several occasions he stated that he had little interest in this area. Now he was to be given control of Farnsworth as well as of Federal, with Behn expecting him to unite the two and transform them into a viable entity in the consumer-electrical-products field.

ITT was a strong company in 1949, even though its profit margin remained low; net income came to $4.7 million on gross revenues of $233 million. It was capable of withstanding shocks and disappointments, more so than at any time since the late 1920s. Given a realistic set of goals, the means to implement them, and the personnel to carry out the tasks, the corporation might well have fulfilled most if not all of its potential. The problem was that top management couldn't agree on direction and unite in a common strategy to achieve objectives. Such would be the case as long as Behn and Harrison remained in command.

It wasn't a recipe for disaster; ITT certainly could survive under such circumstances. But the outlook wasn't as bright as either man thought it was at the time.

8

End of an Era:
The Death of Colonel Behn

HARRISON toured International Standard Electric's European installations during the summer of 1949 while Behn remained in New York, grumbling that Harrison hadn't the right to interfere with this portion of the ITT constellation. The General consulted with Standard Telephones and Cables executives about the possibilities of obtaining a more substantial share of the British telecommunications market, and there was talk of a new submarine cable to America. He went through West Germany to inspect the reconstruction effort there and to discover the nature of research in the newly refurbished laboratories. Then on to Paris, to discussions with some of the French scientists who had returned to their homeland after the war.

Often Harrison was greeted by men he had known from his days at Western Electric, old hands who had started with their companies when they had been part of AT&T's overseas operations. Harrison made a favorable impression on them, drawing upon common memories and clearly knowledgeable regarding their current efforts. He hinted that under his leadership the Western Electric spirit would be revived, and that he would be more appreciative of their contributions than previously had been the case.

Many of the Europeans took to Harrison; not knowing much about tensions at headquarters, they naturally assumed he was Behn's heir, surveying his holdings prior to taking complete command. Although still loyal to the Colonel, the Europeans saw in Harrison a man like themselves, an engineer as well as a manager, who might rebuild ITT around its European laboratories and factories. Even Behn's old ally Maurice Deloraine, now back at his Paris laboratories, felt this way. The Colonel had allowed him a relatively free hand, but since Behn lacked a firm grasp of the technologies involved, he couldn't truly comprehend some of Deloraine's inventions and projects. Harrison was different, and in Deloraine's view in a positive fashion. He and others in Europe were satisfied that conditions would improve for them once the General assumed full leadership.[1]

Ironically, Harrison had been brought in to take charge of domestic operations, and Behn had hoped to concentrate on those in the overseas areas. By 1950 their positions were almost reversed, with Behn, the champion of an American strategy, continuing to devote time to domestic plants while Harrison favored expansion in Europe.

The two men clashed repeatedly that year, in what seemed a prelude to a general power struggle. The New York staff remained loyal to Behn, but Harrison had won over many on the board and in addition had support among the European managers and technicians.

Usually, as it turned out, Harrison had his way. And there were symbolic victories as well, which might have meant little to him but must have shattered the Colonel's confidence. Gradually Behn lost many of his perquisites, including the private limousine and, eventually, the penthouse dining room, which was converted to other uses. The Colonel took to brooding, and there were long periods of depression, each more sapping than the one before.

Both Harrison and Behn wooed the stockholders, seeking their support in the struggle. There was much talk of a dividend, this time from Behn as well as from Harrison. Taking note of the firm's improving earnings (largely as a result of foreign operations), Behn agreed that if trends continued, there might be a small payout in late 1950 or early 1951. Harrison responded that one could be made immediately. At such rumors, and at the prospect of a Harrison-Ryan victory, the price of ITT common stock more than doubled in less than half a year. It would appear that, indirectly at least, Wall Street was backing the insurgents and considered Behn a detriment to the corporation. But the Colonel remained in control; at his insistence there was no dividend in 1950.

The Korean War broke out in June, altering ITT's fortunes in several significant ways and providing Behn with his penultimate opportunity to place his stamp upon the corporation. For one thing, Harrison was recalled to active duty in Washington, initially to take the office of administrator of the National Production Authority and then to lead the Defense Production Administration. With no small satisfaction, Behn announced he would assume the duties of the presidency. War orders helped revive Federal, and the television boom led to a period of prosperity at the recently renamed Capehart-Farnsworth. There was no way of knowing just how long the war would last, whether the economic boom would continue to benefit domestic operations, or even when Harrison would return. But the Colonel probably thought he had sufficient time to strengthen his position and to set in motion programs that couldn't be reversed later on.

Harrison came back to the corporation in May 1951, after a leave of less than a year, whereupon the rivalry resumed. In addition, Behn showed that he lacked sufficient energy and imagination to embark upon any bold new ventures. Finally, his contests with Harrison and the board insurgents, combined with the early failures at Federal and elsewhere, had shattered much of the Colonel's self-assurance. The Colonel remained as buoyant as ever with close associates, but his business activities were marked by a growing conservatism, a timidity that contrasted sharply with the audacious actions of a generation earlier. On those few occasions when he showed flashes of his old form, there was a failure to carry through, and he appeared to have lost the ability to sway others to his point of view. In this period Behn seemed more concerned with retaining the symbols of power than with exercising authority to remold ITT into the kind of corporation he had hoped it would become in the immediate postwar era.

Matters drifted while Harrison was away. Uncharacteristically,

End of an Era: The Death of Colonel Behn

Behn concentrated on improving the balance sheet and cultivating stockholders rather than on deploying assets to develop new programs and strengthen old ones.

Intensifying a process begun earlier, the Colonel drained his Latin American operating companies of as much cash as he dared and had the funds remitted to New York in the form of dividends and management fees. The same was done at American Cable & Radio, which at the time was pleading for capital with which to throw another cable across the Atlantic. Even Capehart-Farnsworth, which lost money during most of 1950, was obliged to send on a small dividend the following year. Federal was operating at capacity in 1951, when it earned more than $4 million. Its managers asked headquarters for an appropriation to increase plant capacity; Behn responded by ordering it to send $3 million of its earnings to headquarters.

ITT's domestic and overseas operations prospered in this period. Consolidated earnings rose from $4.7 million in 1949 to $15.6 million in 1950, and then to more than $18 million in 1951. A farsighted policy might have dictated the plowing back of a good deal of this into expansion and research and development; Behn opted instead for repatriation of earnings. In 1949 ITT received $3.2 million in income from its subsidiaries; in 1950, $6.3 million. Remissions came to $11.1 million the following year.

All of this appeared on the balance sheets. ITT was in the unaccustomed position of being cash-rich, with a rapidly declining long-term debt and a rising book value. As though to signal this new status and win stockholder approval, Behn declared a 15-cents-per-share dividend and a 5 percent stock dividend, both payable in late January, 1951, adding that thereafter the cash payout would be made on a quarterly basis and hinting that regular increases were being contemplated.

Behn had several options in early 1951. There remained the possibility of a takeover of Raytheon, a company that was still short of capital and rich in research capabilities and whose new management might work wonders at Federal. Major investments in Capehart-Farnsworth and in Federal might have strengthened those firms to the point where in a few years they could have become important if not dominant forces in expanding industries.

Then there was Harrison's plan for a global version of Western Electric, which seemed more attractive in 1951 than when he first proposed the idea. That year ISE reported sales of more than $180 million, and by December its companies had a combined backlog of more than $215 million—both record figures. Standard Telephones and Cables was emerging as an important force in television transmission, Le Matériel Téléphonique booked large orders for telephonic gear, and in West Germany, Lorenz and Mix & Genest were in the midst of a major expansion effort. Clearly many of ITT's European companies had gathered significant momentum. Even the Latin American telephone operations were doing well, with excellent results reported from the Cuban and Chilean operations.

The corporation was faced with two sets of choices in 1951: It might expand its domestic operations or look overseas for growth. The Colonel favored the former approach; Harrison, the latter. Then there was the matter of two competing plans to strengthen the American manufacturing sector. Harrison and the dissidents wanted to infuse Federal and Capehart-Farnsworth with additional funds, but saw no need for anything more than this. On his part, Behn wanted to make new acquisitions, utilizing part of his cash hoard and expanding his equity base by swapping stock for assets. For the time being, Behn had the upper hand. Harrison and the Ryan faction waited in the wings as Behn maneuvered for position, the latter knowing that control would be lost if he faltered badly.

In early 1951 Behn met with officials from several corporations interested in being acquired. Records weren't kept of these negotiations, so there is no way of knowing just how far they went, or even the identities of the firms approached before one or the other party backed out of the discussions. Wall Streeters who followed ITT had hints of what was happening, and the stock moved upward in anticipation of an announcement of some kind. Then, in late March, the financial press carried stories of meetings between the Colonel and Edward Noble, chairman of the American Broadcasting Company. The rumors were confirmed within a week. The two firms had agreed in principle to a merger, with ITT to be the surviving company. All that remained was the matter of price and clearance by the Federal Communications Commission.

The prospect seemed exciting. The combination of ABC with Capehart-Farnsworth and Federal would transform ITT's domestic operations into an entity that in some ways resembled Radio Corporation of America. Television was a booming industry, and ABC, which at the time had sixty-three stations, five of which were owned, was well positioned to benefit from the expansion that was certain to come. It was chronically short of capital, which might be provided from ITT's overseas operations and from the further sale of Latin American telephone companies. This seemed an excellent way for Behn to implement his domestic strategy and in the process to present Harrison with a *fait accompli* on his return to headquarters.

Negotiations soon broke down, however. The problem was price and the method of payment. Noble asked for $28 million in cash. Behn offered $22 million in ITT stock, which was selling for around $16 a share. Then Behn made another offer: a share-for-share exchange for ABC common, which then was going for $13. Noble wouldn't budge, and neither would the Colonel. Discussions were terminated in late April, and not revived, though attempts to bring the parties together were made in early 1953, at a time when Noble was considering an offer from United Paramount Theatres. Once again price proved an insurmountable barrier. ABC merged with Paramount soon after, thus depriving Behn of an important opportunity to rationalize his domestic operations.

After his initial failures at ABC the Colonel turned to several smaller and less-promising companies that carried lower price tags. One of these was the Coolerator Company, then a subsidiary of Gibson Refrigerator. An old, familiar manufacturer of a wide variety of appliances such as refrigerators, freezers, and electric ranges, Coolerator hadn't shown a profit for years. In part this was due to poorly designed products that had been saddled with ill-conceived advertising campaigns. Coolerator's major plant, in Duluth, Minnesota, was an antiquated, inefficient operation in an area far from large markets, and so shipping charges were quite high. A major rehabilitation program, both of products and of plant, had begun in 1950, but Gibson's executives had little hope they would succeed. Charles Gibson, its president, was delighted when Behn showed an interest in the firm, and they quickly came to terms. The price was low, especially when contrasted with what Noble had been asking for ABC, and it hardly put a dent in the ITT treasury; Behn obtained total ownership for $2 million in cash plus 52,893 shares of ITT common, then worth about $800,000.

The Colonel had high hopes for Coolerator. Apparently he believed its products dovetailed nicely with those of Capehart-Farnsworth and that economies might be realized by combining their

distribution operations. Both companies produced consumer durables sold through retail outlets, and each had a familiar name. But
whereas Capehart-Farnsworth had at least some chance of obtaining a foothold in the new and expanding television-receiver market,
Coolerator had already fallen behind in its old product areas, bowing to such giants as General Electric, Westinghouse, and RCA-
Whirlpool.

Behn threw himself into the task of reviving Coolerator with his
usual gusto and optimism. It was his intention to revamp operations
and bring out a new line of equipment. Coolerator's 1951 models
were sold at distress prices, while designers, engineers, sales personnel, and the advertising agency planned and then produced replace-
ments that appeared on the market during the next three years.
There were novel freezer-refrigerator combinations, the industry's
first split-door models to combine the two functions, and an advanced electric range. Coolerator put out a full line of room air
conditioners, and there would even be vacuum cleaners and floor
polishers. There is no way of knowing exactly how much money
was poured into the company in 1952 and 1953, but the figure would
appear to have been in excess of $20 million.

It all came to nothing. The products weren't well received, and
in the end many lines had to be disposed of at losses. Coolerator
posted large deficits, proving to be ITT's most troubled operation
since Postal Telegraph. By late 1953 it was evident that it was incapable of being salvaged. More than any other venture, this one tarnished Behn's reputation and provided ammunition for those who
argued for his retirement.

Behn fared better with a second acquisition, the Kellogg Switch-
board and Supply Company. The price was higher than that paid
for Coolerator. Controlling interest in Kellogg was obtained in 1951
for close to $2.5 million, and the rest of the stock was gathered in
the following year for another half a million dollars plus slightly
less than $3 million in ITT common. In return Behn got one of the
nation's best-known suppliers of telephonic equipment to the non-
Bell systems, with a substantial backlog of orders, a modern plant
in Chicago, respected leadership, and a research-and-development
unit that had recently perfected a new crossbar automatic-switch-
ing device that had been well received within the industry. Kellogg
would mesh with several of Federal's subsidiaries, and product lines
of the two companies were complementary.

End of an Era: The Death of Colonel Behn

Kellogg was a solid money-maker, and in 1953 it reported earnings of $553,000, of which $335,000 was remitted to ITT in the form of a dividend. Its executives helped invigorate several of Federal's operations, providing ITT with the kind of talent it had needed and lacked since the end of the war. That July, Behn effected a merger of Federal, Capehart-Farnsworth, Coolerator, and Kellogg, with an eye toward achieving greater efficiencies and infusing ITT's domestic nonmilitary operations with some of Kellogg's leadership.

The change was to little avail. Federal's government sales continued to be strong, and together with Kellogg it was able to make further inroads into the market for telephonic equipment. But Capehart-Farnsworth was an ailing business, especially in the area of consumer electronics, and Coolerator continued to be a drain on resources. Which is to say that Behn's domestic strategy was a relative failure.

Meanwhile the European operations continued to improve, especially at the ISE companies in Britain, France, and Germany. Behn had hoped that by the mid-1950s the domestic companies would show greater profits and earnings than those overseas; this was not to be. By any criterion—especially sales, profits, and dividends—ISE was the corporation's star performer, with Standard Telephones and Cables in particular showing outstanding results. In France, ITT's reorganized Compagnie Générale de Constructions Téléphoniques developed its own version of crossbar switching equipment, which met with wide acceptance in many markets. In Germany a restructured Standard Elektrizitäts Gesellschaft was rebuilt, literally, from the ground up, and by 1955 the company was remitting dividends to the parent corporation.

Behn's attempts to deploy assets to America were based on his experiences of the 1930s and during the wartime period, when first it was difficult to repatriate earnings and then his plants were seized and in some cases bombed out. In the late 1940s there were fears that parts of Europe might turn to communism, in which case ITT would once again suffer losses, and there was constant talk of a possible new European war, one that would ravage the Continent. None of this happened, of course. Instead, the Western European economies were rebuilt at an amazing pace, and the ISE companies shared in the general prosperity. In contrast, the domestic units faltered, unable to match the stronger competition in terms of products, prices, and management. Little wonder, then, that by this time

NET INCOME OF ITT SUBSIDIARIES, CONSOLIDATED, 1950–1955

(millions of dollars)

YEAR	TOTAL	MANUFACTURING, SALES, & LABORATORY SUBSIDIARIES				TELEPHONE & OTHER RADIO SUBSIDIARIES	
		United States	British Commonwealth	Continental Europe	South America		
1950	11.4	4.0	1.3	4.7	0.6	(0.2)	1.1
1951	18.8	0.9	4.2	7.7	1.9	—	4.1
1952	23.1	4.3	4.8	7.7	1.8	—	4.5
1953	17.4	0.1	4.6	6.3	2.1	—	4.2
1954	21.3	3.7	5.2	7.3	1.0	—	4.1
1955	23.1	4.9	6.1	9.0	(0.7)	—	3.8

Source: ITT annual reports, 1950–1955

some of Behn's supporters on the board started to turn against him, seeing in this record a vindication of Harrison's vision of where the corporation should be headed.

Behn did what he could to placate critics. The dividend was raised to 80 cents in 1952 and $1 a share the following year. Upon his return, Harrison was given greater authority, and Behn no longer protested when he made forays into Europe and attempted to convince the board of the need to strengthen operations there instead of in the United States. But as Coolerator continued to drain resources and Capehart-Farnsworth failed to capture a significant share of its markets, the Colonel's credibility diminished. By 1954 his tenure in office relied more on good will, old loyalties, and memories than on performance.

ITT'S DOMESTIC AND FOREIGN REVENUES, 1951–1955

(millions of dollars)

Year	Domestic	Foreign
1951	89.4	165.8
1952	157.1	194.9
1953	158.7	203.5
1954	158.5	214.1
1955	160.6	287.7

Source: ITT annual reports, 1952–1955

Then, too, there was the matter of age. (Some said this was the crucial point.) Behn was seventy-two years old in 1954, and he had slowed down considerably. Some of his close associates hoped he would step aside gracefully; several of them pleaded with him to do so, something they hadn't dared do prior to this time. Always he rejected their advice. Behn was convinced he could hold on, and in his undiminished optimism he clung to the idea that in the end his domestic policies would be vindicated. It was clear that he would either be ejected by the insurgents, in what was bound to be a messy and unpleasant fashion, or die in office after a period of deterioration.[2]

The turning point for Behn came in late 1953 and early 1954. By then it had become evident even to him that the new Coolerator lines were dismal failures, requiring large-scale write-offs. There were slowdowns at other American operations, partly owing to the onset of an economic recession. Increasingly ITT had to rely upon its overseas subsidiaries for growth and strength. Dividends from abroad advanced, whereas those from the domestic companies all but vanished. This emboldened the board insurgents, who by early spring of 1954 were demanding a change in both direction and management.

No single event weakened Behn's grip on the board majority. Rather, earlier in the year, several of his allies started to think less about supporting him and more about ways to ease him aside with as much tact and as little pain as possible. They spoke of the sorry state of affairs at Coolerator, the continuing difficulties at other domestic installations, and of the need for a fresh approach toward the overseas operations. At a time when Wall Street was in the midst of a major bull move, ITT common had performed badly, declining from 20 to 13 in 1953 and hovering around the 15 level during the first months of 1954 while most of the rest of the list surged ahead on strong volume. Analysts blamed this on weaknesses and indecision on the part of management. There was talk of coming demands for higher dividends and a stockholder revolt, all of which strengthened the Ryan faction.

Former New Jersey governor Charles Edison, a member of the Board since 1948 and respected by both sides, was apparently a key figure in working out the means whereby the Colonel might relinquish some of his authority but retain the perquisites of office. Behn's support on the board had continued to decline. By then most of his old associates had passed from the scene. Fred Caldwell, Wolcott Pitkin, Luke McNamee, and Henry Roemer were dead, and others had retired. Ellery Stone, Mark Sunstrom, and Paul Swantee remained on the board, and apparently cooperated with Edison, telling Behn as gently as they could that the time had come for him to take less of a hand in operations. Charles Hilles, a staunch supporter, resigned as director and received a leave of absence as vice-president and general attorney to enter government service, but not before advising Behn to accept a diminished role at the corporation.[3] Realizing that he lacked the votes to win in a showdown, the Colonel agreed to a compromise drawn up and offered by Edison.

DIVIDENDS AND INTEREST PAID BY SUBSIDIARIES TO ITT, 1951–1955

(millions of dollars)

YEAR	TOTAL	MANUFACTURING, SALES, & LABORATORY SUBSIDIARIES				TELEPHONE & RADIO SUBSIDIARIES
		United States	British Commonwealth	Continental Europe	South America	
1951	8.4	1.0	1.9	2.6	0.8	2.0
1952	10.4	2.2	2.3	2.8	1.0	2.2
1953	7.5	0.1	1.7	2.9	1.0	1.9
1954	7.6	0.1	2.4	3.0	0.6	1.6
1955	11.2	0.2	2.7	4.4	0.7	3.2

Source: ITT annual reports, 1951–1955

I·T·T: The Management of Opportunity

In early June ITT announced that the recently formed executive committee would be entrusted with defining goals and making key decisions regarding policy. Behn would serve as committee chairman, but none of his old allies were members. McKinney, Kirby, Brown, and Edison were selected, along with Harrison, who now became chief operating officer as well as president. With the composition of this committee, he was also chief executive officer all but in name. ITT was now Harrison's to lead.

As for the Colonel, he was supposed to become a shadow figure, available for speeches, stockholder meetings, and public events. He would greet foreign dignitaries, take inspection trips, and continue to hold his luncheons. Thenceforth, however, he was to have symbolic rather than actual power. Thus the Behn era appeared to have drawn to a close.

As expected, Harrison moved to eliminate unsuccessful American operations, consolidate others, and in general initiate a policy of retrenchment in consumer goods. Additional funds would be earmarked for parts of Federal and Kellogg, however, as Harrison meant to expand vigorously into the domestic market for telephonic equipment. Stress would be placed on ISE operations, especially those in Britain, France, and Germany.

It wasn't difficult to see what Harrison was aiming for, and he made no secret of his intentions. Under his guidance ITT was supposed to become an updated and revamped version of what Behn had attempted to construct in the 1920s as the International System. With his background, inclinations, and the alterations in the world scene, Harrison was far less interested in telephone-operating companies and cables. Instead he would restructure ITT around its telephonic-manufacturing plants, military operations, and electronics. He had in mind a company that would produce equipment for non-Bell units in America and compete with Ericsson and Siemens in other parts of the world. ITT would have entries in television and radio transmission, air and marine navigation, and related paths to which research pointed. With ITT's assets and tradition, it seemed not only a sensible strategy but one capable of realization with a minimum of dislocation. Perhaps it was even the kind of approach the Colonel might have taken were he not so scarred by the experiences of the 1930s and '40s. In this respect it could be said that Harrison tried to carry on in Behn's tradition. But neither man saw it that way.

End of an Era: The Death of Colonel Behn

Harrison signaled his intentions three months after achieving power. Coolerator would be sold, and a special reserve would be established to take care of losses involved with the transfer. Some of the inventories were dumped on the market for whatever they would bring. Everyone in the industry knew Coolerator wasn't worth salvaging, but Stanley Luke, who was in command there, managed to get a token payment for what was left from McGraw-Edison.

Shortly thereafter, Harrison established Farnsworth Electronics and announced that Capehart was on the block. He hoped to sell the latter company's interests in radio, television, and phonographs and to use its modern Fort Wayne plant to produce gear for Farnsworth Electronics. Given Capehart's patents and its still-respectable trademarks, Harrison expected to get a decent price, so he rejected early offers as too low and prepared to await an acceptable bid.

In late 1954 Harrison traveled to Europe on an inspection tour of ISE facilities and returned to set down a five-year plan geared to doubling output there. By then it appeared evident that a European Economic Community soon would be organized, and expectations were that this would result in an even more rapid rate of growth in telecommunications. Harrison planned major construction programs in France and Germany, and operations in other countries of the forthcoming Common Market were strengthened. Greater stress would be placed on return on capital and on sales, which were lagging, but otherwise all seemed to be going well.

Harrison also rewarded ITT's stockholders, increasing the dividend to 30 cents quarterly in October 1955 and in December boosting it to 35 cents. ITT reported record earnings that year, and the stock was selling at over 30 in early January, 1956; within three months it passed the 35 level and was being singled out by financial analysts and columnists as one of the glamour issues of the bull market, while Harrison was extolled in *Forbes* as a "superlative manager."

Meanwhile the Colonel chafed in his new role, knowing that he was being bypassed and his plans for ITT were being scrapped. "They have taken away my sword!" he lamented to one old associate. There were cutbacks at Federal and Farnsworth about which he protested but could do nothing. Behn knew there was no way he could regain his old position; that much seemed clear. But he still might return ITT to his domestic strategy and, in the process, deal a blow to Harrison.

ITT'S DEPLOYMENT OF NET ASSETS, 1954–1958

(millions of dollars)

YEAR	TOTAL	MANUFACTURING, SALES, & LABORATORIES				TELE-PHONES & RADIO-TELE-PHONES	
		United States	British Commonwealth	Continental Europe	South America	Japan	Western Hemisphere
1954	273.4	64.7	37.3	58.9	32.1	—	80.4
1955	296.0	65.7	42.1	80.5	27.5	—	80.1
1956	310.7	68.7	49.1	84.8	24.2	—	83.8
1957	375.4	75.9	50.6	99.8	24.1	6.0	119.0
1958	395.7	84.3	52.6	105.6	21.3	6.0	125.7

Source: ITT annual reports, 1954–1958

End of an Era: The Death of Colonel Behn

In mid-1955 Behn opened informal negotiations with Donald Power of the General Telephone Corporation, the goal being a merger of their companies. The two men knew each other fairly well, having met shortly after World War II, when Power was General's chief counsel and as such charged with negotiating several contracts with Federal for equipment and services. General Telephone was a minor factor in the industry at this time, operating a handful of small companies unaffiliated with AT&T and with no substantial manufacturing facilities of its own. It was expanding rapidly, however, with Power handling most of the details and planning strategies. He became president and chief operating officer in 1951, at which time he was fifty-two years old, and he immediately accelerated the acquisitions program. Power purchased Automatic Electric—the important Chicago-based manufacturer of telephonic equipment Behn had sought prior to the IWEC acquisition—along with more than a dozen telephone companies. By the mid-1950s General Telephone had been transformed by him into the largest non-Bell holding company in the industry in the United States. From 1951 to 1955 revenues rose from less than $62 million to close to $210 million, and net income went from $4 million to over $30 million.

Although Power continually expanded operations at Automatic and purchased additional equipment-manufacturing firms, his companies still had to look outside the system for some of their gear, and Federal and Kellogg were major suppliers. By 1955 the General Telephone companies constituted Federal's most important non-military customers, and Automatic and Kellogg were practically next-door neighbors. Staff members and field personnel at Federal and Kellogg enjoyed comfortable relationships with their General counterparts. Walter Wright, an old ITT hand, knew Power well, and told him that General would benefit from the infusion of the superior engineering talents available not only from the domestic companies but from the European laboratories as well. Edwin Chinlund, who remained close to Behn even after leaving ITT, had a seat on the General Telephone board and may have acted as a go-between in the negotiations.[4]

The combination seemed close to ideal. ITT could provide General with manufacturing facilities and patents it badly needed, and the takeover would bring a quick end to the deficits at domestic operations. The restructured company would have a strong base in the United States, thus challenging Harrison's overseas orientation. Power was a strong, effective leader, and Behn genuinely liked the man. The thought of working with Power appealed to Behn as the best possible solution to his unhappy circumstance.

Negotiations proceeded to the point where the matter came to the ITT board. Nothing is known of what transpired at the meetings, but the merger would seem to have been too important for its opponents to reject out of hand. Harrison opposed the idea. Not only would this involve a change in the program to which he was deeply committed, but there was the matter of who would lead the merged operation. ITT was more than twice as large as General Telephone, but the latter company earned almost half again as much as ITT. It clearly was a more efficient and better-managed operation. General appeared cohesive, whereas ITT was diffuse and, until recently, in chronic difficulty. General had a better reputation on Wall Street; its stock sold for twice the price/earnings multiple of ITT's, even with the latter company's recent advance. Obviously Power would have a claim to leadership of the merged entity, no matter whether ITT or General was the surviving partner.

For a while there was talk of Behn's becoming chairman and chief executive officer while Power might be president and chief operating officer. As for Harrison, he would be vice-chairman, and in a weak position to contest Power for the chairmanship when Behn left the scene. The board would be composed of equal numbers from ITT and General, and it wasn't difficult to see that Behn's supporters might unite with the General nominees to have a majority, thus controlling the executive committee. But this was all in the realm of rumor and surmise. More to the point, Harrison and Power were strong personalities, vigorous men with records of accomplishment and plans for the future. Neither would willingly submit to a secondary role behind the other. Harrison swayed a majority of the board against further discussions, and negotiations were broken off in early 1956.

(Ironically, Power then turned to Sylvania, which was acquired two years later to form General Telephone & Electronics. Thus, two of the companies Behn had hoped would become part of ITT were united. The chemistry must have been right; the failure was in negotiations.)

End of an Era: The Death of Colonel Behn

Harrison's victory over Behn was complete. The rejection of the General Telephone merger shattered the last semblance of power the Colonel retained. Harrison set about implementing key elements of his overseas programs, while Behn retired to his office, trying to salvage what little he could from the defeat.

On Saturday, April 22, 1956, Harrison assembled some of his staff for a special meeting at the Broad Street headquarters, presumably to discuss several foreign ventures. He appeared in excellent health and fine spirits. The following morning, while asleep at his Garden City home, Harrison suffered a massive heart attack and died before help arrived. He was sixty-three years old. Harrison's death shocked all at headquarters and of course left a sudden void on the executive committee.

Shortly after the funeral, Behn called a board meeting to decide what to do next. He urged the members to exercise care in filling the post. Harrison hadn't developed a strong staff, in Behn's view, and there were no obvious candidates at headquarters. The search might take months, said Behn, and in the interim he expected to resume the duties of chief operating officer and to reclaim authority as chief executive officer. His motives were transparent to all in the room; he made no secret of them. The Colonel hoped to take control of the corporation once again.

There was no chance of this happening. No member of the board thought that this would be a proper course of action. Behn knew he lacked support, and yet he persisted, hoping to the end to regain at least a semblance of his former authority. It was a pathetic exercise, as Behn must have realized later on.

Within a short time the board announced the appointment of Gen. Edmond Leavey as president. A career officer who had been a tablemate of Dwight Eisenhower's at West Point, Leavey had a distinguished military career and in 1952 had come to ITT as a vice-president and Harrison's special assistant. By 1954 he was president of ISE and second in command in the president's office. This selection of a Harrison associate was a clear indication that the European development program was to continue and be expanded. Moreover, Leavey was to be chief executive officer, a title that was taken from the Colonel. Charles Hilles, who had advised Behn to accept a diminished role at the corporation two years earlier, now returned as Leavey's executive vice-president.

I·T·T: The Management of Opportunity

On May 23, 1956, a month and a day after Harrison's death, ITT announced that Behn would resign as chairman. He would stay on the board and receive the title of honorary chairman. It was all over, however. The announcement merely confirmed what everyone had known for months, if not years. All that remained was a farewell tour of overseas and domestic facilities. Behn was finished at ITT.

Now he deteriorated rapidly, suffering openly from gout and lumbago. Behn seldom appeared on Broad Street, and soon it was apparent he had become quite ill. But he continued to make plans. On several occasions he talked of taking a position at Berwind White Coal, still controlled by his wife's family, and transforming it into a different kind of operation. But nothing came of this.

In early 1957 Behn suffered a stroke that paralyzed his left side, and he was admitted to St. Luke's Hospital in New York. For a while he seemed to rally, but then he fell into a coma. Occasionally he would revive, to murmur, over and over again, "I have failed." No one was quite certain what this meant.[5]

Behn died on Thursday, June 6. The funeral was held the following Saturday at St. Patrick's Cathedral. Although the rest of his family—including Hernand—had been buried in Brooklyn and the Colonel had visited their graves every Sunday when he was in town, he insisted on being interred at Arlington Cemetery. This was arranged by Adm. William Halsey, an ITT director, complete with full military honors.

The entire board and most of the staff traveled to Washington for the funeral. So did General Leavey. Then, upon his return, Leavey set about obliterating as much of the Behn heritage as he could. Papers, letters, records, decorations, mementos—all were destroyed or given away, with Leavey claiming the space was needed for more important materials. Even Behn's harshest critics on the board must have been shocked by this brutal and unfeeling display of power. But more was to come. Leavey sent down a memorandum to the effect that those who put in vouchers for the Washington trip would have to pay their own way; the funeral hadn't been company business.[6]

Perhaps Leavey wanted to indicate that ITT was entering a new period in its history and that the old had to be cast aside. But at the time he had no clear idea of where he expected to lead the corporation, or indeed whether he truly wanted the post. Nor was it possible to destroy or even ignore the Behn heritage, at least not so soon

End of an Era: The Death of Colonel Behn

and under this chief executive. The Behn years were over, to be sure, but there would be no Leavey era. Instead his administration was to serve as an *entr'acte*, during which the corporation marked time, as though awaiting the arrival of ITT's second major entrepreneur.

Entr'acte

THAT Edmond Leavey found a place at ITT in 1952 had more to do with the ways Americans reward their military leaders than with any special quality he may have possessed. This isn't to argue that Leavey hadn't anything consequential to offer his new employer. On the contrary, he was intelligent, accustomed to running large operations, capable of delegating responsibility effectively, and possessed the kind of personality one often found in the executive suites of major corporations. He was there, however, because of military record and rank and a relationship with Harrison that had begun during World War II and developed during the Korean conflict.

Men with Leavey's background were being acquired by many large corporations in this period, especially by those companies hoping to receive military contracts. For ITT, however, it was as much a matter of tradition as anything else. From the first, Behn had staffed ITT with men he had met during the war. Like him, most were reservists, experienced in management or technology, on duty during emergencies. Others were regulars, lured into the corporation by Behn, who for the rest of his life considered himself something of a military expert, and who enjoyed their company. Several of these former officers went into the field, where they demonstrated abilities at management and organization, but many remained at headquarters, on call for special assignments. In effect they were the Colonel's assistants. They had titles and the salaries and expense accounts that went with them. Such people were entertaining and attractive individuals whose contacts in America and Europe might prove useful to ITT, but they hardly could be considered essential to the corporation's well-being.

Along with other chief executive officers Behn tried to obtain some of World War II's big names for the board and his staff. Among his "acquisitions" were Adm. Frederick Furth, Adm. John Gingrich, and Gen. Francis Lanihan. His most famous catch was Adm. William F. "Bull" Halsey, one of the heroes of the Pacific war, who joined the board shortly after his retirement from the Navy. Halsey opened doors for Behn in Washington and impressed visitors to the Broad Street headquarters. He also brought celebrities, such as Gen. Douglas MacArthur, to some of the Behn luncheons. Halsey went into the field to inspect ITT installations, and these visits usually resulted in favorable press coverage. He was there, in other words, for public-relations purposes, little else, a legitimate and often important function at corporations like ITT.

Behn could hardly oppose Harrison when he suggested that Leavey come to ITT as his assistant. Behn already had his military entourage; now Harrison would have the beginnings of one of his own.

Leavey and Behn had clearly and openly disliked each other from the start. It wasn't only because they were in opposite camps, though this surely was a factor. Rather the antagonisms derived from their wholly different backgrounds, beliefs, temperaments, and values. The Colonel might have looked upon this newcomer as Harrison's ally, no more than that. Leavey's reactions were more visceral. Quite provincial in his attitudes and rigid in his morality, not only did Leavey believe Behn should step down, he disapproved of him. Behn surely was an exotic, a cosmopolitan of the type Leavey couldn't fathom.

Leavey was a twice-retired general officer at the age of fifty-eight when he arrived at ITT. Born and reared in Texas, he graduated from West Point in 1917 and soon after entered the Corps of Engineers. Advancement came slowly in the peacetime Army, and so it was for Leavey, but he did achieve a reputation as a capable engineer and manager. All of his assignments but one in this period were in the continental United States, where he supervised power-development and flood-control programs, attended and taught at several schools, and for a while served in administrative capacities for the Civil Works Administration.

Leavey's only tours overseas were in Hawaii. The first of these came shortly after World War I. The young lieutenant was entranced by the place, which he soon came to consider his home. While there he met and then married Ruth Farrington, a member of one of Hawaii's most prominent families and the daughter of a future governor. He returned in 1929 for a four-year tour of duty and at that time thought about retiring from the Army to remain in the islands as an engineer. Leavey stayed in the service, however, and was a colonel attached to the Works Progress Administration project in New York at the time the United States entered World War II.

Then came a series of overseas assignments, first in the European theater of operations and afterward in the Pacific. Leavey became known as an expert in logistical planning, and by the time the war ended he was a major general. He then took command of transportation for the War Department, and in 1948 he became Army comptroller, a post involving management and fiscal duties not dissimilar to those at major industrial corporations. Leavey retired the following year to become a consulting engineer, operating out of Honolulu, but he returned to uniform less than two years later to fill a staff position at SHAPE headquarters in Europe. It was then that he renewed his acquaintance with Harrison, whom he had met during World War II. This, of course, set the stage for Leavey's arrival at ITT.

Harrison needed a deputy to help with the development of ISE's European operations, and Leavey appeared well equipped for the task by virtue of background and proclivities. On the other hand, he had no real experince in the private sector, and Leavey had always tended to be inflexible, accustomed to having his commands obeyed without question from underlings. Perhaps a desirable attribute in the wartime Army, this was out of place and bound to cause difficulties at a civilian corporation. Moreover, Leavey had a sharp temper, and showed impatience with those who held opinions other than his own. He was a stickler for order and neatness, another hallmark of the military that led to problems when he made periodic tours of plants and laboratories. He would comment on out-of-place equipment and supplies as though he were a sergeant inspecting a barracks, and this of course led to resentment.

Leavey clearly was a transplanted military officer, not a corporation executive, at heart. This simply was the way he thought. In discussing one tour with a reporter, he remarked, "It's as important for the commanding general to be seen as to see things for himself." Later on, when he assumed the presidency of ITT, Leavey tended to refer to Charles Hilles as his "chief of staff." By then he had grown irritated with the civilians who ran the corporation, and implied ITT could use a large infusion of military talent. He denied a rumor that he intended to raid the Pentagon. "However, if a company is shopping for experienced executives—especially for men who've served abroad—I would think it logical at least to consider men retiring from the armed forces."

Leavey started out as head of Federal Telecommunications Laboratories, an assignment intended to acclimate him to the situation at ITT, and he moved on to the ISE presidency in 1954. This was taken as a sign of Behn's loss of authority. Initially Leavey attempted to streamline operations at manufacturing sites and laboratories. Frequent and detailed reports were demanded and financial controls tightened, as the former general worked at imposing a new form of discipline on managing directors who in the past had been permitted a great deal of leeway.

It didn't take Leavey long to appreciate the nature and dimensions of ISE's difficulties. Although several of its component companies were growing rapidly, these companies had lost market share to European competitors such as Ericsson, Philips, and a revived Siemens. Profits weren't keeping pace with revenues; leading ISE companies had extremely low returns both on sales and investments. Leavey hoped to turn things around by putting pressures on managers. With his powers and background, this appeared the most sensible procedure. Moreover, it meshed well with Harrison's thinking on the matter, for low margins at ISE companies continued to trouble him.

It didn't work out as hoped. Some executives accepted sufficient changes so as to keep Leavey at bay, a handful went along with him, and others tried to ignore repeated requests and then demands out of New York. Several appealed to Behn for support, and this resulted in a series of confrontations at headquarters, deepening the divisions between Harrison and the Colonel.

There was more to this than a simple power struggle. European managers who respected Harrison's knowledge and found him easy to get along with bridled at Leavey's brusque manner. Those who worked at the installations during the occupation must have felt they had traded one military authority for another, and this was greatly resented. Deloraine considered Leavey a lightweight. He was, said the scientist, a "gentleman," meaning that "he was pleasant, he was intelligent, he was well educated, and he was anything you wish, but he wasn't a big manager." Thus, Leavey was ineffectual in many ways during his stay at ISE.

After a while Leavey seemed to recognize the futility of trying to impose his brand of order and efficiency upon the overseas facilities. ISE's revenues continued to climb, but at headquarters executives and board members seemed more concerned about the Behn-Harrison conflicts and domestic operations than what was happening at ISE. Leavey had a prestigious position and a good salary, and was on excellent terms with Harrison. Perhaps he thought he could coast along for a few more years and then retire to Hawaii with a generous pension. As Deloraine put it, Leavey "had the wisdom of not interfering with the machine."[1]

Whatever ambitions Leavey might have entertained for the presidency appeared to have vanished by then. A year younger than Harrison, he wouldn't have been considered for the post on the basis of age alone. Then it happened. Almost without warning, Leavey was not only president but also virtually alone at the top. Harrison had been countered by Behn, and now both men were gone. ITT was in Leavey's command.

Those who were on the board and in important managerial positions at the time differ as to Leavey's attitude. Some believe that initially at least he looked forward to the challenge and was eager to place his stamp on the corporation. Others claim that from the first Leavey considered himself a caretaker, wanting to do little more than housekeeping tasks while the board searched for a younger man to take over. What is clear, however, is that Leavey initiated no bold new program but rather continued along the lines established by Harrison.

Leavey delegated authority with a broad hand, in a fashion unknown under Behn and Harrison. Joining Charles Hilles were two additional executive vice-presidents—Fred Farwell, for domestic manufacturing, and Robert Bender, for finance. This was a familiar enough procedure to those who had come out of the military; Leavey was fashioning a staff-centered organization, with himself at its pinnacle. Most of the actual work would fall to Hilles, Farwell, and Bender; only the most important and pressing concerns would be brought to his office.

At its best this structure often proved efficient, distributing executive power to those able to exercise it in special areas and creating a keen sense of competition in the executive suites. But there were dangers, too, especially if the three men started to circle one another, planning for the succession. As it turned out, the system worked quite well, probably because of the three, only Farwell entertained serious ambitions for higher office, and also because the Leavey administration was too brief for conflicts to develop.

Leavey brought to the presidency a clear idea of ITT's failings, as well as his own thoughts regarding how they might be overcome or at least minimized. He saw the corporation as a loose confederation of operating units suffering from sloth and duplication of effort at the bottom and indifference at the top. Except for defense-related business, the domestic companies were in trouble. Capehart had been disposed of in 1956, and this helped somewhat, but the other units showed little vitality. Even Kellogg, after a promising start, had bogged down, and lost money in 1957. That firm was intended to revive Farnsworth; instead it had contracted the latter company's ailments: duplication of effort and product lines, inefficiency in operations, and sluggishness in responding to consumer requirements. Federal's research facilities were in excellent shape, engaged in pioneering work in several key areas, such as transistors. But there was insufficient contact between the laboratories and manufacturing operations, and several fine opportunities were permitted to slip by. Then there were the foreign companies, which Leavey knew best. He had failed to turn them around while at ISE; now he would try again.

Most of the Leavey reforms were organizational in nature, the intent being to create a new set of structures in the hope that out of them would emerge a revived ITT. The German subsidiaries were brought together in an umbrella operation, Standard Elektrik

Lorenz. All of the domestic research-and-development activities were united in a new division, known as ITT Laboratories. Federal Telephone and Radio was merged with Farnsworth Electronics, to create ITT Federal. These were among the most important alterations and reforms of the Leavey period, and they weren't simply cosmetic. Some of his actions suggest that Leavey wasn't a mere cipher, that he had developed a vision of what ITT might become, even though it was never clearly articulated. Leavey thought in terms of a tough, lean, highly integrated corporation, smaller perhaps than what it had been in the past but much more profitable. This was an outgrowth of his military experience and of his penchant for efficiency and cost-cutting.

This last matter affected the tone at corporation headquarters in New York. Expense accounts were kept to a minimum, salary increases were slashed, and even research-and-development operations were affected. Leavey's attitude toward paying for executive travel to Colonel Behn's funeral reflected not only this mania for economy but his intense dislike for the lavishness of the Behn period. This resulted in some small savings but left a sour taste, not only among executives involved but also among board members. Just as some of them can recall little about Behn except his panache, so they conjure up a picture of Leavey counting paper clips and furnishing executive offices by making purchases at army-surplus stores.

By 1958 it had become evident that Leavey would soon step down. He was approaching the customary retirement age of sixty-five, and he had no intention of asking for an extension. Rather he notified the board that it should look for a replacement. Clearly he wanted to retire to Hawaii, something he had dreamed about for many years.

The board was perfectly willing to let it go at that. A three-man subcommittee was named, headed by banker Hugh Knowlton of Kuhn, Loeb, and charged with finding a successor. Hilles, Farwell, and Bender were to be considered, as were others within the organization. Most assumed from the start that the post would go to an outsider, however, and the favorite was Harold Sydney Geneen.

9

The Inheritor:
Harold Sydney Geneen

IT is one of our more pervasive myths. The imperiled individual or community is rescued by the hero, whose timely arrival prevents death or failure and who then goes on to create a shining new order, superior to all that went before. The greater the dangers, the more exalted the hero's reputation. Thus his admirers are tempted to exaggerate the difficulties that existed when he appeared on the scene and the changes and accomplishments of the new era.

It is a familiar story and process. In the American Western the hero rides out of the wilderness to save the town from villains, or the police arrive "in the nick of time" to foil the criminals. There is Abraham Lincoln preserving the Union, Franklin Roosevelt assuming command in a time of grave social and economic peril. Other countries utilize the myth in recounting sagas of their heroes, from Achilles and Moses to Winston Churchill and Charles de Gaulle.

Then there is the hagiography of great businessmen, tales of

The Inheritor: Harold Sydney Geneen

unusually capable chief executives who arrive to find the corporation in ruins and proceed to revive it, to provide the firm with new and more appropriate goals and then to show the way toward their realization. Alfred Sloan performed the tasks for General Motors in the 1920s, and recently Lee Iacocca has attempted to breathe new life into Chrysler. We are intrigued by founders and entrepreneurs, but saviors and expert managers have an allure of their own. In business as much as in politics, supporters and allies tend toward exaggeration when recounting their exploits. This isn't the product of conspiracy or even of design. Rather, such a practice is an integral part of our culture, so much so that it is engaged in almost subconsciously.

Such was and is the case with ITT during the Harold Geneen era, when he was hailed as one of the truly exceptional businessmen of his time, called by Robert Kenmore, a former associate, "basically the best professional manager we've had in this generation." Both during and after his tenure at ITT Geneen was portrayed as taking over a troubled corporation, turning it around, and proceeding to create out of its turmoil one of the most powerful economic entities in the world. *Business Week* credited him with "giving the staid old empire a vigorous shaking up and tightening that's still going on," and N. R. Kleinfield, of *The New York Times,* characterized the pre-Geneen ITT as "a baroque confederation of companies" that lacked direction and drive. Toward the end of Geneen's first decade in command, *Time* called Behn "an anachronism who had outlived his times," and continued, "About the only achievement of his immediate successors [Harrison and Leavey] was to drop the ampersand—making it ITT instead of I.T.&T." "On arrival at ITT, Geneen found a mess" was the verdict of *Vision* in 1971, echoing the prevalent belief of the period.[1]

It was a picture Geneen had helped paint, and one he probably sincerely believed was accurate. The mythmaking had begun almost as soon as he arrived to take command. Less than two years after the transfer of power, he told Walter Guzzardi, Jr., of *Fortune,* "There's a question how long it would have gone on before it cracked wide open. If this had gone on for three or five more years, maybe no one could have brought it back."[2] In his own view and by his own reckoning, then, Geneen was the necessary man, proverbially in the right place at the right time, who saved ITT from an all-but-certain collapse.

I·T·T: The Management of Opportunity

This surely was an overly bleak picture of the corporation Leavey had turned over to Geneen in June of 1959. That ITT had more than its share of problems is evident. Farnsworth remained a troubled, deficit-ridden company, and most of the other domestic units were performing sluggishly, with low returns on investment and sales. Although it was true that the foreign manufacturing companies were turning in excellent sales and profits, these often paled when set beside the records of some of their competitors. Several telephone-operating companies were quite profitable, but this was more the result of momentum gathered earlier and not of superior management from New York. ITT was, then, a loose, poorly coordinated corporation in need of an overhaul. Behn, Harrison, and Leavey had all recognized this. Each man in his own way had tried to deal with the problems, with mixed results.

But if these leaders were to be criticized for their failures, they also deserve some credit for their accomplishments. When account is taken of all its problems through the 1950s, the corporation's growth appears quite acceptable and, by some standards, even impressive. Consolidated revenues for 1959 would come to $765 million, having tripled during a decade in which there was no significant acquisition. While profits failed to keep pace owing to losses posted by domestic subsidiaries and to shrinking margins, they did come close to doubling, rising from $15.5 million to $29 million. Total current assets had expanded by $270 million in this period, and liabilities rose by only $168 million. At the close of 1959 total current assets were $471 million and current liabilities $249 million, hardly a critical ratio and certainly not that of a corporation on the verge of collapse. ITT's working capital in 1959 was $222 million; in 1950 the figure had been $120 million.

Toward the end of the decade Wall Street took cognizance of ITT's prospects. The corporation's stock doubled in 1958, a year during which the Dow Jones Industrials rose by slightly more than 20 percent. That December, Leavey announced a two-for-one split, and the dividend was boosted the following March to $2 a share (or $1 on a split basis). At one point in 1950, ITT common sold for less than 10, and there was no dividend that year; the stock peaked at 65 late in 1958, this prior to the announcement that Geneen was to assume the presidency.

Time implied that Harrison and Leavey were mere ciphers, but

The Inheritor: Harold Sydney Geneen

this view wasn't shared by its writers during the 1950s. Leavey was characterized as "clever" and "sound" in 1957, and two years earlier the magazine praised Harrison as "a man of vision." *Business Week* thought ITT a "staid old empire" in 1963; five years earlier, commenting on a Leavey tour of ISE facilities, it had written that "the results of Leavey's work look impressive."

What Geneen inherited at ITT couldn't be categorized as a "mess" by any reasonable definition of the term. This wasn't the view of most informed observers, the investment community, or for that matter almost anyone who understood the corporation. The board didn't turn to him in desperation, as though seeking a savior. The foundation was in place and secure. Geneen was expected to build on it, not to raze the corporation and then start afresh.

In no way does this diminish Geneen's accomplishments or suggest he had an easy time of it during his first years at ITT. He had to embark upon a major effort at streamlining and restructuring operations so as to make them more efficient. There was a need to reconsider the objectives and strategies followed by his predecessors and then either to refine and adopt one of them or to scrap them all, substituting plans of his own. Of course, ITT was in need of a strong and consistent manager, something it had lacked at least since the outbreak of conflicts between Behn and Harrison. It was in these areas—particularly the last one—that Geneen would make his most important contributions to ITT, and the ways he did all of this are the basis for the claims that he was the premier manager and businessman of his generation.

The outlines of Geneen's early life are familiar and accessible, although, as is usual with such prominent individuals, the subject of exaggeration and rumor. He was born on January 22, 1910, in the seaside-resort town of Bournemouth, not far from London. His father, S. Alexander Geneen, had arrived in England from Russia with his brother a quarter of a century earlier, and apparently was well into his middle age at the time of his son's birth. Harold Geneen has said that his father was an impresario, a flamboyant man whose fortunes rose and fell at a dizzying pace, but there isn't a mention of him in the entertainment pages of London newspapers of the period or in any of the monographs dealing with the operatic and concert scenes during late-Victorian and Edwardian times. In any case, he couldn't have been much of an influence on Harold or his younger sister, Eva, for S. Alexander left his wife and family before the boy was five years old, and there was little or no contact between them from that time on.

More is known of the mother, Aida DeCruciani Geneen, who emigrated with her family to the United States in 1911, separated from her husband four years later, and, together with her children, became a citizen in 1918. Although of Italian descent, Aida Geneen had been born and was reared in England. She was an independent, strong-willed, and proud woman. Of all the people he was ever to know, Harold was closest to his mother, and it was from Aida that he derived much of his own personality.

Yet the two were seldom together for long, for Harold was soon sent away to boarding school. Aida Geneen might have had some money of her own and could have been of that class of English-women who believed it proper for a boy to be raised at such places. Then, too, she was an entertainer who found employment as such in America. Away from home herself for long stretches, she might have thought it best for Harold to be at school.

Whatever the reasons, in 1917, when he was seven years old, Harold was enrolled at a private academy in Suffield, Connecticut, where he would remain for the next nine years. During summers there were camps to attend and related activities, all away from home. Occasionally he would visit his mother during winter recesses, but many of these were spent at Suffield too. Harold had difficulty making friends, but for a while he was close to Meade Alcorn, who later on would become a prominent Connecticut lawyer and chairman of the Republican National Committee. Alcorn was a day student whose family lived nearby. Harold spent some vacations and weekends with the Alcorns and admired Meade's father, Hugh, who was a famous state prosecutor. This was the closest he would come in this period to having a family life.

Harold Geneen was a small, slight, unathletic boy, shy and lacking in most social graces. By his own account he was quite timid, and traces of this would remain for the rest of his life. As a man he would be something of a loner, with many acquaintances but few close friends. Some of his colleagues claim that underneath his seeming arrogance is a vein of insecurity and shyness remaining from the early years, which occasionally surfaces when Geneen encounters other important businessmen or politicians for the first time.

The Inheritor: Harold Sydney Geneen

An outsider for most of his stay at Suffield, Geneen cultivated the talents of observation rather than participation, and his sense of curiosity was sharpened, as were his analytical skills. Everything seemed to interest him, and Geneen became intrigued with problem-solving. In this, as in all things, he was testing himself against his own or exterior standards; there were few contests with the other boys. Moreover, these talents didn't emerge in the classroom, and Geneen wasn't a particularly outstanding student.

He graduated Suffield in 1926, and unlike most of those who attended private schools, didn't go on to college. This wasn't due to lack of interest or failure of intellect. Perhaps Aida Geneen suffered a financial reversal in this period, for by his own account Harold had a difficult time of it during the next few years. Geneen told a reporter of having subsisted on a diet of taffy and bread. "They had 1-cent sales on taffy, two pounds for 9 cents, and bread filled me up."

Decades later, as leader of ITT, Geneen would express a mixture of grudging admiration and contempt for those who had easier lives in the 1920s—who attended Ivy League colleges, wore the old school tie, engaged in lively social activities, and many of whom found posts at well-established, old-line corporations. He was an outsider insofar as these people were concerned, and for that matter so was his corporation. This was a source of both pride and anxiety. Geneen sought the acceptance and the applause of these individuals, but he was not certain they measured up to self-made men such as himself.

At sixteen he found a job as page at the New York Stock Exchange, and soon he started taking night courses at New York University. This was the classic path utilized by poor boys and outsiders who hoped for financial careers. The salary was around $8 a week, and the duties consisted of accepting and delivering messages. Pages walked miles a day through the Exchange, came to know how it operated, and were put into contact with brokers and office managers who later might offer them better positions. Meanwhile they would take business courses at nearby colleges to gain a background for their next step in the financial district. This appeared to have been Geneen's plan. He discovered a love and talent for accounting at NYU, just the right subject for a person headed in this direction.

Whatever ambitions Geneen might have had for a Wall Street

career would have collapsed with the crash of 1929 and the Depression. Brokers, analysts, and even pages were being fired in the early 1930s; few positions were opening for newcomers. Geneen next worked as a salesman for the New York *World Telegram* and then as a junior accountant for Mayflower Associates, and took low-paying jobs at several brokerages where he could utilize his education as a bookkeeper. He continued to attend evening classes, concentrating on accounting and related business subjects.

It was sometime in this period that Geneen was married, though when and to whom is one of those matters he hasn't talked about for years. This marriage ended in a divorce in 1946.

Geneen didn't receive his degree until 1935, at which time he was twenty-five years old. After applying for positions at several large firms, he was taken on at Lybrand, Ross Brothers & Co., one of the best known in the accounting field. Intense, rather colorless, somewhat pudgy, and in no way impressive, Geneen remained the same kind of withdrawn and uncertain individual he had been as a boy. He asked for a salary of $20 a week, but later said he would have taken less. As it happened, the minimum at Lybrand, Ross was $30, which was what he received.

Most of Geneen's work consisted of servicing client accounts, and this involved almost constant travel, and living in a series of hotels. It was a lonely existence, even though Geneen had the opportunity to expand his horizons and take the measure of some of the country's leading businessmen. In the process of going through a corporation's books, an imaginative accountant not only learns how it functions but also can isolate problems and recommend changes. Such a person can perform for businessmen services similar to those of diagnosticians in medicine. So it was with Geneen. He would spend seven years with Lybrand, Ross, during which his initial hesitancy was replaced by confidence, and in turn by cockiness. Contacts with clients led him to conclude that he was not only their equal but in some respects their superior. He saw errors in judgment and wondered how supposedly adept executives could have blundered as they did. In the process he was becoming something of an expert problem-solver, and he gained a reputation as such in the profession. This kind of person can find employment as a consultant or be taken on as controller at one of the companies whose operations he has monitored. By the time he was barely thirty, it appeared he was headed in the direction of one or another of these careers, and he had discovered within himself a driving ambition that hadn't been evident only a few years earlier.

Geneen rose steadily at Lybrand, Ross, and toward the end of the decade he was servicing some of its most important accounts. By then the American economy was shifting gears, turning to the production of military supplies, and Geneen was well positioned to observe the changes. One of his clients, American Can, had obtained a major contract to turn out naval torpedoes but apparently had no clear idea of how to structure its operations. Geneen was brought into the discussions, primarily to provide expertise in the matter of costs. He quickly spotted bottlenecks and errors in the original plans, and then went on to produce a financial and organizational blueprint of his own. Impressed by this performance, American Can offered Geneen a top accounting position, which he accepted in 1942.

Although most of his initial responsibilities were in the financial area, Geneen soon became a manager all but in title. He participated in negotiations with government and union officials, prepared bids and handled subcontracts, assisted in establishing production schedules, and learned how to jockey for position in the executive suites. American Can was evolving from a large, stodgy manufacturer functioning in a single industry into one that was involved in several. The old management team had been adept at dealing with food companies and others that utilized containers but now had to alter operations and attitudes so as to function well in different markets. Geneen was one of those who helped oversee these changes, and he found the experience stimulating. American Can's leaders felt otherwise; they clearly were uncomfortable with the new business and yearned to return to their conventional ways. That they would do so once the war ended became evident in early 1945.

By then Geneen had become wedded to the notion that growth, not stability, should be the prime goal of any vital enterprise. His early wariness and conservatism, born of personal insecurities and deepened by the depression of the 1930s, had been replaced by what to others in the firm appeared a reckless and unfounded optimism. He urged management to utilize expertise gained during the war in other, noncontainer-related businesses, and even drew up plans for rapid expansion. These were rejected out of hand. Having taken their company through the Depression intact and then through the unsettling war, American's board and management were troubled by talk of a coming economic slump and certainly not inclined to strike out along new paths. Geneen might have remained at the firm, for his talents were recognized and appreciated, but he would have found the circumstances stifling. Moreover, he was eager for rapid advancement, and this was not possible at American Can, with its entrenched leadership and bureaucratic layers. Finally, Geneen's marriage was breaking up during this period, and he might have been eager for a change for personal reasons.

Geneen left American Can in 1946 to take the post of controller at Bell & Howell, at the time a small factor in the camera business. His ambitions were both obvious and realistic: Geneen might make an impact at Bell & Howell that wasn't possible at American Can. President Joseph McNab was an elderly and ailing man. Assuming all went well, Geneen might take his place within a few years. But his hard-driving, often abrasive personality won him more enemies than allies on the board. In addition, Geneen's plans required a larger enterprise than Bell & Howell to have full play. McNab died in 1949 and was replaced by Charles Percy. Geneen prepared to move on, but not before marrying June Elizabeth Hjelm, who had been his secretary at Bell & Howell.

The following year, at the age of forty, Geneen became the comptroller at Jones & Laughlin, the nation's fourth-largest steel company and a firm badly in need of an overhaul. J&L had one of the lowest profit margins in the industry and suffered more than most during the 1949 economic downturn. Geneen was there to root out inefficiencies, tighten controls, and recommend changes in methods of financing. All of this he did, and in addition he suggested different production techniques and management organization. As had been the case at American Can and Bell & Howell, his abilities were both evident and recognized; Geneen was given a vice-presidency and greater responsibilities.

Now Geneen was involved in long-term planning, and he soon became known as a maverick. When margins declined during the 1952 recession, Geneen started to talk about moves into new product areas. Profits from the mills could be used to begin or to purchase companies in other, more rapidly growing segments of the economy. The steel business was highly cyclical and mature, hardly the kind from which major growth could be expected. In addition, Jones & Laughlin lacked the resources of such firms as United States

The Inheritor: Harold Sydney Geneen

Steel, Bethlehem, National, and several others, and had an aged plant. Clearly it couldn't hope for much more of a market share than it already had. Thus, Geneen advocated using the existing structure as a vehicle and shaping J&L into a diversified enterprise based, but not wholly dependent on, steel.

This was heresy within an industry noted for its clubbiness and devotion to what insiders liked to call the "strong metal." No group of executives fought diversification more consistently than did the steel men, most of whom had known no company or industry other than the one through which they had risen and were suspicious of outsiders. Jones & Laughlin's chairman, Ben Moreell, was a crusty retired admiral who had been wary of Geneen from the start. The firm's president, Charles Lee Austin, was a veteran J&L executive who had arrived at the company in 1942, after only a brief stint at Mellon Securities, and he shared Moreell's views regarding the controller. Geneen encountered stiffer and more emotional resistance at Jones & Laughlin than he had known at American Can. Clearly he would have to move on once again.

In 1956 Geneen was in Boston, attending a course in advanced management at Harvard. While there he learned that David Schultz, Raytheon's financial vice-president, was leaving to accept the presidency of Allan B. DuMont, and Geneen decided to apply for the vacant post. He did so, and a series of meetings followed, at which he impressed board members and president Charles Francis Adams, Jr., with his ideas and force of personality. Geneen not only appeared capable of filling Schultz's old position but might take on some of the management burdens as well. Adams offered him the job of executive vice-president, indicating it would carry heavy responsibility for operations. "I knew he would need a lot of room," said Adams later, "and I determined to give him time to run—and all the room he needed."[3] Geneen accepted, notified Jones & Laughlin of his decision, and arrived at Raytheon that spring.

As had been the case when Laurence Marshall and Sosthenes Behn discussed a possible merger several years earlier, Raytheon possessed fine technology and had an excellent reputation but remained short of capital. The situation was turning around, however. Like ITT and several others involved in World War II defense work, Raytheon was intrigued with the potential of television. In 1945 Marshall purchased Belmont Radio, which he hoped would become the centerpiece for the firm's civilian business. This venture proved as ill conceived and poorly executed as had Behn's into Capehart-Farnsworth, for Belmont drained assets from Raytheon's highly profitable defense business and related government work.

Adams disposed of Belmont by selling it for a token amount to the Admiral Corporation, completing the transaction shortly after Geneen took office. The following year he would get $5 million for Raytheon's stake in Datamatic, a small computer company that was purchased by Honeywell. In this period Raytheon was the subject of takeover bids by several large corporations, among them Lockheed and General Dynamics. These divestitures removed some of the pressures and enabled Adams to devote more attention to the firm's major business, which was the production of military hardware. An important contractor and subcontractor for missile and guidance systems, Raytheon had to compete against some of the nation's most powerful firms, and despite the perils involved, it had managed quite well. There were cutbacks in military procurement after the Korean conflict, however, and the company's sales and earnings had been on a plateau since 1952.

Adams clearly believed Raytheon's future rested in the general area of military ordnance, which in 1956 accounted for three quarters of the corporation's revenues. He hoped Geneen would eliminate waste, help restructure the corporation, and in general do all he could to boost profit margins. With expanded capital Raytheon might bid on larger contracts and expand operations outside the United States. Initially the match of these two men appeared close to ideal. They were of the same generation, each was deemed outstanding in his own field, and their talents and personalities seemed to complement one another. The descendant of two presidents, the son of the Secretary of the Navy in the Hoover Administration, and a prominent member of one of the nation's most illustrious families, Adams had excellent contacts in Washington and on Wall Street and had been in charge at Raytheon since 1959. Adams clearly expected to determine Raytheon's general direction and to serve as its "outside" man, whereas Geneen was to handle day-to-day operations, devising tactical programs that would best serve the Adams strategy.

For a while it seemed this separation of powers and functions might work. Throwing himself into his tasks, Geneen shocked many Raytheon veterans with demands on their time and talents. Soon executives accustomed to leisurely lunches and long weekends were being asked to put in twelve- to fourteen-hour days and six-day weeks, with little time for anything other than company business. Over the years Geneen had demonstrated an increasing inability to suffer fools gladly and impatience in dealing with associates who were unable to maintain what he considered a proper pace. These attributes were more in evidence now that he was in operating command. During his first year at Raytheon he shook the company to its foundations but in the process created antagonisms and made enemies. Executives and staff members respected Geneen's intellect and recognized in him an exceptional manager, but at the same time he formed no close alliances, made few friends, and was feared by most of the veterans with whom he came into contact. Adams saw what was happening, but for the moment he said and did nothing to alter matters. Geneen was bringing about needed changes, no matter how blunt his approach, and the president was willing to let it go at that for the time being. Far too self-assured to be cowed by his executive vice-president, Adams nonetheless wasn't one of his admirers.

Geneen set about to establish a new structure for Raytheon, basing it upon the one established at General Motors by Alfred Sloan, one of his few heroes. Sloan had divided GM into divisions—Chevrolet, Pontiac, Buick, and so forth—placing a manager at the head of each, giving him a measure of autonomy and holding him responsible for results. Regular reporting and tight cost control were hallmarks of Sloan's administration, the result being that GM became the leader in its field. Geneen expected as much from Raytheon. Twelve semiautonomous divisions were created, and its managers were to report directly to Geneen. After a while he scheduled formal monthly meetings, at which the managers reported, information was shared, ideas were bandied about, and all were subjected to grillings by the executive vice-president. These were often brutal affairs, for Geneen could be slashing, sarcastic, and biting when on the attack. He was capable of humiliating managers who had blundered, and on occasion he brought several to the point of tears. Some of those who survived would later claim that it could be an edifying experience, as Geneen goaded them to higher levels of excellence in performance and rewarded his stars with rapid promotions and added responsibilities. Others who couldn't take the pace and constant tension would resign, ask for reassignment to less demanding posts, or be fired.

These changes suited Geneen, who from the start wanted to create his own staff and take on managers who shared his ideas and would be loyal to him. He brought in George Ingram from Riegel Paper as his controller and L. D. Webster from Boston Woven Hose as assistant controller, thus giving him a tight grip on what he deemed the firm's financial core. David Margolis, initially hired to maintain relations with the financial community, was later named assistant treasurer and was Geneen's man in that office. A steady stream of executives arrived from the automobile industry to assume top-management jobs. E. Douglas Graham, of Ford, was to head manufacturing operations, and several years later Richard Krafve, also of Ford, was to become Raytheon's group vice-president, functioning directly under Geneen. Perhaps the most important newcomer was William Marx, who had been director of personnel at Celanese and who took a similar post at Raytheon. Marx soon became Geneen's most trusted ally, one of the few with whom he was ever close. Some called Marx Geneen's "strong right arm," whereas others said he was Raytheon's "hatchet man." Together Geneen and Marx instilled a new spirit in operations, either by motivating the veterans or by bringing in others who could function in the Geneen style. It was an impressive performance, one that brought rewards. In 1957 the corporation created an "office of the president," which consisted of three men: Adams, senior vice-president Percy Spencer, and Geneen, who in addition obtained a seat on the board.

Raytheon was about to experience a period of rapid growth, in large part owing to the awards of several major government contracts for missiles and related hardware. In the post–Korean War years sales had fluctuated between $175 million and $182 million, with a profit peak of $4.5 million coming in 1954. Now both figures rose impressively. Revenues came to a record $259 million in 1957, and earnings (in large part because of the Datamatic sale) were $4.8 million. For 1958 the figures were $375 million and $9.4 million, and the following year they would be $494 million and $10.5 million.

In large part because of David Margolis' missionary activities, more than a few Wall Street analysts were coming to view Geneen as a management genius, and he received most of the credit for this showing. That he had instituted controls where few existed before and created a smoothly running operation was evident; without

The Inheritor: Harold Sydney Geneen

Geneen a good deal of this progress wouldn't have been possible. But it wasn't all of his doing. Adams had set the stage for the advance by disposing of Belmont and Datamatic, and most of the new contracts came in through his efforts and those of the Washington staff. Moreover, Geneen had little direct control of the research-and-development programs, though of course he saw to it they were well funded. Perhaps it could be said that others created the products and obtained the orders and that Geneen made certain they could be filled on time, profitably, and up to high standards.

By then Geneen and Adams had started to clash. Perhaps this was inevitable given their differing backgrounds and personalities. More important, however, was the fact that Adams was chief executive and operating officer as well as president, and Geneen yearned for such a post, if not at Raytheon then at some other company of approximately the same size—or larger, if possible. Occasionally he spoke of his ambitions with close associates, and almost always they involved leadership of a major enterprise. There was very little of the entrepreneur about Geneen; he wasn't the kind of person likely to start anything afresh. Rather, he had become expert in revitalizing stale or inefficient operations. He had gone about as far as he could at Raytheon. Geneen understood he had virtually no chance of replacing Adams, or even of sharing power. At Raytheon only two years, already he was chafing at the job, eager for more authority.

Part of this was a symptom of sheer ambition and a drive for power, but in addition Geneen was formulating a concept of how corporations should develop that was quite different from that held by Adams. Some of his ideas derived from his experiences and others from notions then being put forth in the business schools, Harvard in particular. Geneen had concluded that Raytheon had to diversify if it was to become both secure and vigorous, and his knowledge of and work in accounting indicated that the best way this could be accomplished was through acquisitions.

Firms like Raytheon were almost completely dependent on government contracts. Sales and profits could soar in periods of rearmament or war, only to decline swiftly thereafter. The situation bore some resemblance to that at Jones & Laughlin, a company whose fortunes rose and fell with the demand for steel. Means should be found to assure orderly growth, no matter how one or another industry was doing, and this implied expansion into areas unrelated to the original business. Thus, when a decline occurred in that segment of the economy, it might be compensated for by steadiness or growth in another.

What Geneen had in mind differed from the kinds of acquisitions and expansion traditionally sought by American businessmen. At the turn of the century, managements would attempt to purchase companies in the same field or in a closely related one. A steel plant would acquire a nearby foundry or coal mine, for example. Some big businessmen would buy out their suppliers: James Buchanan Duke, of American Tobacco, took over a variety of firms that manufactured tinfoil, machinery that turned out cigarettes and cigars, and vending equipment. Usually there was a plan, a rationale that flowed out of the initial enterprise. In the case of ITT, Colonel Behn had started out in telephone-operating companies, expanded into equipment manufacturing and cables, and so fashioned the International System, in which each unit related to others to create a harmonious whole. In his eyes Capehart-Farnsworth neatly complemented Federal, and its expertise in consumer durables meshed well with that of Coolerator. Similarly, Laurence Marshall acquired Belmont as a logical extension of Raytheon's capabilities in electronics, and the move into Datamatic and computers was a reasonable complement to existing capabilities and assets.

At the time, professors in business schools and others wrote and talked knowingly of horizontal and vertical mergers and expansion, citing examples such as these to illustrate their theories. Yet there were other examples to consider. After World War II a handful of companies, most of whose business had been in military procurement, found it necessary to enter new areas in the civilian market, the alternative being rapid shrinkage and possible disappearance. Some did so to realize tax advantages or to expand without having to be concerned about antitrust prosecution. There were a few that acquired companies in unrelated areas because they appeared underpriced. Then there was one maverick, Royal Little, of Textron, whose company headquarters wasn't far from Raytheon's. Having failed to fashion a giant textile corporation, Little gathered in a group of firms in a variety of different industries. By 1958 Textron owned a newsreel and film operation, a real-estate concern, a producer of cotton pads, a manufacturer of radar equipment, a plywood business, and a pump manufacturer that itself had diversified into chain saws.

The Inheritor: Harold Sydney Geneen

Textron was considered an oddity, but Peter F. Drucker, the noted author and business analyst whom Geneen greatly admired, thought otherwise, and in fact as early as 1949 Drucker had predicted that such enterprises might become commonplace in the future. In his book *The New Society: The Anatomy of Industrial Order*, published that year, Drucker wrote, "It is management's first responsibility to decide what economic factors and trends are likely to affect the company's future welfare." This in itself wasn't startling, but he followed this up by saying:

> It is management's responsibility to decide what business the enterprise is really in. This may seem pointless. Surely it needs no rigamarole and analysis to find out what a company's business is. Is it not even, in most cases, stated in the name of the company? Actually, the decision what business an enterprise is really in—that is, the decision what its product is, what its market is, and what its outlook is—is anything but obvious. It requires careful and difficult analysis of a very high order. It also implies a very difficult decision what business the company should aim to be in. Only a few managements have so far been able to answer these questions.

Royal Little decided that Textron's business was the management of enterprises, and not only those involved in or related to textiles. This meant that skills acquired in operating, say, a machine-tool shop might be transferred to running a fast-food chain. And there was more to it than that. He demonstrated that this diversification might be accomplished through acquisitions and not through start-up ventures. Not only did Textron know exactly what it was getting, but in this way Little was able to build on an existing base, not having to nurse the firm through its infancy. Finally, Textron purchased most of its companies with its own common shares, not with cash. Thus, there were pressures upon Little to keep the price as high as possible, so that the stock would be attractive to owners and managers of firms to be acquired. This could be accomplished in several ways, but common to all was the element of rapid and steady growth, especially in earnings.

A new generation of businessmen had accepted the Drucker formulation and were intrigued with developments at Textron. They hoped to have the opportunity to transform an old-line firm into one that functioned in several industries, to be led by a new kind of manager, a polymath whose imagination dwarfed those in more conventional companies. Theoretically such people could create multibillion-dollar corporations in a short period by taking over a multitude of other firms. By 1958 several of them were beginning to do so or were considering such a move. Charles "Tex" Thornton was busily acquiring small companies at Litton Industries, which that year had sales of $83 million. In 1958 Charles Bluhdorn, who only two years earlier had joined the board at Michigan Plating and Stamping, changed its name to Gulf & Western and started to consider takeovers for a firm whose sales were less than $9 million. James Ling was attempting to expand on the base provided by what was known as Ling-Altec Electronics, which posted sales of $133 million. As yet none of these men had ventured far from their original bases: Ling and Thornton in electronics, Bluhdorn in automobile parts. Even then, however, some academic observers of the business scene had given a name to their companies. Soon to enter their free-form period, they were known as "conglomerates."

That Geneen had thought and spoken about the possibilities of leading a conglomerate is quite certain, and in this respect he was ahead of Ling, Thornton, and Bluhdorn. Clearly he had the germ of the idea while at American Can, when he encouraged management there to diversify, and he had done the same at Jones & Laughlin. In 1958 he hoped Raytheon would become a conglomerate. Geneen spoke of his ideas to several at headquarters, among them Marx, Spencer, and veteran executive Norman Krim. These men and others began by discussing such matters at lunches, but after a while these turned into informal seminars led by Geneen. Krim became so intrigued that he brought along a secretary to take notes, while assistants created charts and diagrams to illustrate Geneen's points.

One of Raytheon's greatest weaknesses, said Geneen, was its almost complete dependence on government contracts. He would alter this through a swift series of acquisitions of firms in nonrelated areas, and in a few years there would emerge a much larger, diversified corporation. It was a carefully worked out plan; Geneen even knew which companies he hoped to attract. Krim later recalled being provided with charts sketching Geneen's vision of the Raytheon of the future. He called them "road maps stuffed with the names of other companies."[4]

By 1958 Geneen had become a conglomerateur, with expectations as ambitious as any of that breed. The others had something he lacked, however: a vehicle through which to act. At the time, Adams wasn't interested in conglomeratization, and he dismissed out of hand the suggestion that Raytheon embark upon a major acquisitions program. He told an interviewer that Geneen appeared to believe that the way to win a baseball game is to "add more outs." Adams continued, "By doing that, it doesn't matter if you are tagged out at first or second; you can add four more outs and keep the inning going forever." Geneen responded that he was being blocked by "Adams' caution." At times he felt like a person "driving at high speed," and that "every so often, without warning, somebody else would try to put [his] hand on the wheel."[5] He was allowed to acquire Allied Electronics (Apelco) in 1958 and the following year Machlett Laboratories, the nation's largest manufacturer of X-ray tubes, but that was about as far as Adams was willing to go.

At the age of forty-nine Geneen was prepared to become the leader of a large corporation. He had the intellect, ambition, and experience for such a post, and he fairly ached for power. Again he would have to go elsewhere.

Meanwhile, at ITT, Hugh Knowlton had organized his subcommittee charged with searching for the corporation's next leader. He was to be its chairman, and the others were Richard Perkins of First National City, George Brown, and Robert McKinney. The latter two had been leading insurgents and supporters of Harrison, whereas Knowlton and Perkins were considered "regulars," generally associated with Colonel Behn. Although personal antipathies remained, the issues that once divided them were no more, and all hoped for a unity candidate. Under the circumstances, they decided to seek a person outside the corporation, one who had no connection with past disputes. This was the message they gave G. Lawton-Johnson, of Boyden Associates, who was charged with seeking out such people.

As one of the leading "headhunters" in the business, Lawton-Johnson knew that Geneen was looking for a top-management post, and that in fact he had already been interviewed for several. The two men came together, and Lawton-Johnson told Geneen of the situation at ITT, asking if he was interested in coming to New York for discussions. Geneen met with the Knowlton group and made a strong impression on all four men. ITT needed a person with clear plans and a record of accomplishments, and Geneen saw in ITT a near-perfect corporation that could use his knowledge of cost control and provide the base for a conglomerate. Knowlton made the offer, something Geneen had wanted for at least two decades. Yet Geneen asked time to think it over and, uncharacteristically, went to Adams for advice. "Well," said Adams. "That's certainly better than being Number Two here," and he told Geneen to make certain he obtained "a foolproof contract." Geneen nodded his agreement, returned to New York, received assurances of a free hand and sufficient power to exercise his will, and accepted the ITT presidency.[6]

10

The Pre-Takeover Years

THE FINANCIAL DISTRICT learned of Geneen's forthcoming departure from Raytheon and acceptance of the ITT presidency on the morning of May 20, 1959. This came at a time when the securities markets were in the doldrums, with most issues trading in a narrow range. There was a slight decline at the New York Stock Exchange that day, and volume was normal. Raytheon was the most active issue there, collapsing on the news and closing at 60⅛, down 6½ points from the previous session, shaving some $19 million from the total value of its shares. By June 10, when Geneen arrived at ITT to take command, Raytheon common was at 54, but the further fall-off was more the result of a lower market than of shock waves related to the resignation.

The reason for the May 20 sell-off was evident. Several brokerages, led by Merrill Lynch, had removed Raytheon from their recommended lists, apparently in the belief that the company would have a difficult time of it without Geneen. This was done almost automatically, further indication that the financial analysts credited him with primary responsibility for the firm's success. Even Adams, who generally took such matters in stride, was impressed and at a loss for words. Later he told an interviewer, "I had not realized that he had created a constituency."

Although the analysts—the constituency to which Adams referred—believed Raytheon would suffer without Geneen, they weren't as certain about his impact at ITT. That firm's stock was selling at near its postwar high at the time, the rise owing more to interest on the part of small investors than to sponsorship from the major houses. The same individuals who advised clients to sell Raytheon apparently weren't recommending switches to ITT, for on May 20 the stock closed up only half a point, at 40⅝, and on June 10 it was selling for 37⅞. If Geneen had a following in the financial district, it wasn't one whose loyalties were easily transferred.

Clearly he had had a constituency at Raytheon. Several of the executives he had brought to that company would announce their resignations soon after, indicating they would follow Geneen to ITT. One was David Margolis, who would be charged with applying Geneen's brand of tight financial controls, and his arrival in New York must have been interpreted as such by longtime comptroller Paul Swantee and treasurer Oswald Buchanan. Another was William Marx, who was to be ITT's senior vice-president. As Geneen put it, "[Marx had] the important assignment of integrating our widespread global staff activities with our area line managements, as well as [having] responsibility for our personnel, planning, and organization functions."[1] Which was another way of saying that Marx was to help weed out those executives who wouldn't or couldn't adapt to Geneen's techniques or be counted on to meet his stiff performance criteria; to discover those within the corporation who could do so and then promote them; and finally to seek new people from outside ITT for several key positions. He was to do this on a worldwide basis, and as quickly as possible, for Geneen aspired to fashion the firm in his own image while setting into motion new programs in various fields. Now that he had the power, he meant to exercise it.

Geneen and Marx did a thorough job of housecleaning in a relatively short period. Two of Leavey's three executive vice-presidents were gone in less than a year, leaving only Charles Hilles in that post. A member of the board, Hilles was kept on partially in deference to his experience and in recognition of his influence with old friends. Also, Geneen hoped that by keeping the amiable Hilles, he would demonstrate to those ITT'ers he wanted to retain that there would be no wholesale dismissals. Furthermore, Hilles and Geneen got along fairly well together, and in any case the executive vice-president was due to retire in 1961, which he did. With this, Marx moved up to the second rung of the ladder at the corporation.

As for Leavey, he was promoted to the chairmanship but would serve for only a month and a half; as planned, he retired on July 31, 1959, leaving the post vacant for the time being. Buchanan was out as treasurer and replaced by the aging and popular Swantee. James Lillis, who had long experience at Burroughs and before that at Price Waterhouse, came on in September 1959 as vice-president as well as comptroller. Two years later, as expected, Swantee retired, and Margolis took the treasurer's office. Thus, Geneen had two of his own men in the key financial posts.

There were changes up and down the line. Louis Rader, formerly of General Electric, was named group vice-president with special responsibilities for domestic commercial markets. Harry Beggs, from Cresap, McCormick & Paget, took over as vice-president and director of manufacturing and facilities. Alfred di Scipio was the new vice-president for marketing and commercial development; formerly he had been with McKinsey & Co., the management consultants. Ted Westfall arrived from Grace Lines to fill the post of vice-president and area general manager for Latin America, and Marc de Ferranti, of General Electric, became president of ITT Europe. (But not for long. In a preview of what was to come, de Ferranti was dismissed after only six months on the job, the first of a long line of firings and resignations that marked the Geneen years.)

There were several promotions from within as well. Henri Busignies, still one of ITT's most important scientists, was advanced to vice-president and general technical director, and M. Richard Mitchell, who had been with the corporation for close to a quarter of a century, was named general counsel as well as vice-president. Ellery Stone was one of that group of World War I officers Behn had brought to ITT in its early days. At the time of Geneen's arrival he was a vice-president and a member of the board; now he was given special responsibilities in the defense area. But these were exceptions. Geneen meant to have close to a clean sweep in the executive suites. Of the eleven vice-presidents who served under Leavey, only three—Stone, Henry Scudder, and Frederick Furth—remained at the end of 1961. By then there were sixteen vice-presidents at ITT, so thirteen were Geneen's appointees, with most coming from outside.

The changes weren't confined to the New York offices, for under Marx's leadership there were reassignments and dismissals in every part of the corporation, in Europe and Latin America as well as in the United States. In early 1964, after less than five years in command, Geneen said ITT had "a dynamic management team" of some 728 executives, and of this number 118 had arrived during his tenure and an additional 131 were promoted from within the system, which would indicate that approximately one out of every three top executives had replaced Behn, Harrison, or Leavey men or held newly created positions.[2]

The arrival of so many new managers could not help but affect the attitudes and performances of those who remained from earlier times. Ordinarily the transfer of corporate power at the pinnacle results in few dismissals, early retirements, or shakeups in the executive suites. In many large corporations there is a shuffling of positions and titles, with many individuals moving up a notch. (There is an old saying at AT&T that when the leader retires, the company goes out and hires a new office boy.) Such wasn't the case in Geneen's early years at ITT, which bore more resemblance to a change in presidential administrations in Washington than to the inauguration of a new regime at an American corporation. Everyone was put on notice that even the most axiomatic of policies would be scrutinized and more than likely either drastically altered or discarded, to be replaced by ones that bore the unmistakable stamp of Harold Geneen.

In this shakedown period Geneen stressed economy, efficiency, financial performance, and aggressive salesmanship. He talked of doubling ITT's revenues and profits within five years, with much of the growth coming from radical alterations in domestic operations. Geneen told a reporter that it really was quite simple, that all he was doing was "threading the pieces together" by means of techniques developed and perfected at Raytheon and elsewhere.

There was more to it than that, of course. Now in charge of domestic nonmilitary operations, Louis Rader discovered duplication of efforts and widespread inefficiencies at Kellogg and Federal. He put in a new management team at the former company, reduced inventories sharply, and eliminated several product lines that had become outmoded while developing new ones. Kellogg had lost money in 1959; it was profitable the following year, and earnings rose steadily thereafter. As for Federal, that company underwent a long and for many a painful regimen of cost-cutting and restructuring. Geneen learned that under Busignies' direction, ITT Laboratories had developed into one of the industry's most productive units. For example, the Labs had pioneered in transistors and as recently as 1955 had a long lead over most other companies in that rapidly expanding area. But there had been little coordination between the laboratory and ITT's management in the field and at headquarters, and Busignies' recommendation that the corporation make a major push in this direction was rejected. The advantage was lost, and by the end of the decade ITT had become a laggard. Busignies' promotion to a vice-presidency was Geneen's way of indicating that greater attention would be paid to such matters in the future. Within a year of taking office Geneen signed an agreement with Texas Instruments for the exchange of nonexclusive patent licenses for semiconductors, at the same time ordering a major overhaul of facilities for the production of transistors and related electronics devices.

Federal's giant New Jersey operation had defied attempts on the part of Behn, Harrison, and Leavey to rationalize operations and create a more efficient company. Largely because of military contracts, Federal showed a profit, but margins were far below those of competitors, and its rehabilitation was crucial if Geneen's domestic approach was to succeed.

Nevin Palley, newly arrived from Temco Aircraft, where he had been vice-president for engineering, was sent to Federal with a broad mandate to reduce costs and restructure procedures. Known as a hardbitten executive who kept a bull whip on his office wall, Palley cut employment from 7,300 to 6,300, eliminated wasteful projects, and increased shipments and profits. "Geneen wants one and one to make three," he told a reporter. "They don't yet—but they do make 2.6."[3]

Geneen often appeared ambivalent about the two sectors of ITT —domestic and overseas. In itself this wasn't unusual; all of his predecessors had had the same problem. In part this was due to a fascination with the globetrotting Behn (whom Geneen had never met), the solid accomplishments of the ISE companies, and the temper of the times. Against this was placed the narrow, often parochial attitudes of Geneen, the result of a childhood, youth, and middle age spent almost exclusively in the United States.

As might have been expected, Geneen and Behn were often compared. Geneen couldn't help but realize that his accomplishments would be measured against those of the Colonel, especially in the eyes of the press and of associates who knew them both. Even though he continued to believe the corporation had been mismanaged during the postwar years, Geneen had come to admire and perhaps envy Behn's flair and audacity, and he must have been impressed with the loyalty and affection he commanded. On several occasions Geneen told associates that there would have been a place for someone like the Colonel at ITT headquarters—primarily to charm clients and court leaders of corporations being considered for acquisition. Behn excelled at such duties, which resulted from a Continental outlook that Geneen probably knew he lacked at the time. He might have sensed this in the ways European managers reacted to his suggestions and his brusque approach and reflected that they, too, were drawing comparisons, perhaps not in his favor.

From his first inspection tour, Geneen came to learn that the overseas operations were in far better condition than the domestic ones, though they, too, suffered from anemic profit margins. Usually with Marx at his side, he would rush through the factories and laboratories, asking questions, making suggestions, intending to absorb as much information as he could and then take charge. His approach surprised and occasionally shocked such veteran European managers as Frank Wright, of STC; Hermann Abtmeyer, of SEL; Guy Rabuteau, of Le Matériel Téléphonique; and Manuel Márquez Mira, of Standard Eléctrica, S.A., all of whom had come into ISE during the Behn era and were accustomed to a different style of leadership. Deloraine, who had more experience with American management techniques than most of his European colleagues, was nonetheless taken off guard in his initial encounter with Geneen. He introduced himself to the new president at Orly Airport, outside Paris. Geneen looked him up and down for a few moments and then said, "Ah, so you are Deloraine, the fellow who spends all this money on research and development."[4] Like the others, Deloraine was urged to cut back on expenses, subjected to a grilling over operations, and initiated into the complexities of the new ITT approach and culture.

It truly was a culture. Some said Geneen didn't understand and certainly didn't appreciate the ways Europeans conducted business, or that if he did, he chose to ignore or brush aside old traditions as being outmoded. Whatever the reason, he attempted to preside over what might be called "the Americanization of ISE."

Some of his innovations were symbolic. For example, American businessmen often call colleagues by their first names, even when hardly knowing one another, and so did Geneen. In Europe the effect was jarring. "It is the custom at ITT," he said (meaning of course that it would be his custom, as opposed to the old ways under Behn), "and you'll have to get used to it." Somewhat formal Frenchmen, Italians, Englishmen, and Spaniards were expected to engage in banter as did their American counterparts, and it was unsettling. So was Geneen's order that English be the only language used at the European meetings, which became monthly affairs, and that during the sessions the clocks be set at New York time. On these occasions the Europeans would make reports and discuss projects and plans. One of those who attended an early session recalled the atmosphere then: "You could sense the gasp spreading around the table. The French couldn't conceive of giving the Germans information, the Germans giving the British information, etc. This was a whole new ball game."[5]

Perhaps Geneen did all this to create internal cohesion, or it might have been another of his ways of demonstrating that a new order had arrived at ITT. This theme appears and reappears in many of his public statements and in the annual reports. Geneen constantly talked of the progress made "since 1959." Apparently he believed this to have been the crucial date in ITT history, the year during which the new corporation began to emerge out of the shell of the old, and Geneen often spoke derisively of the way operations had been conducted prior to his arrival. Many of the newcomers felt the same, and even those who had worked through the Behn, Harrison, and Leavey periods came to accept at least some aspects of the change and to see their necessity. Here, too, Geneen appreciated the use of symbols. Out went the old furnishings at Broad Street headquarters and in came the decorators to provide ITT with an "up-to-date look." "I used to like the cosmopolitan, rather fading, old-world atmosphere of this place," said Richard Mitchell, an attorney who recalled the Behn era. "Life was relaxed. Now I am alert, lively, and intrigued. The place is streamlined. It's all chromium and nickel plated and Swedish modern, with colors to stimulate you."[6]

The streamlining was not quite finished, but it soon would be. Geneen was uncomfortable at Broad Street. Perhaps it was because headquarters was far from midtown, where many corporations were located, or it might have been that he felt the building was Behn's monument, hardly suited to a firm in the process of being reborn. Probably he wanted a setting of his own, one fresh and new and not redolent of the 1920s. In 1961 ITT moved to new offices at 320 Park Avenue, a building that indeed was chromium- and nickel-plated; it even had some Swedish furniture.

For all their differences in personality, style, and outlook, Geneen and Behn shared some experiences and traits. Both were foreign-born, naturalized Americans, for example, who became intensely patriotic, though not in the usual, flag-waving sense of the term. Geneen was convinced the United States was the strongest and most vigorous nation on earth and that its businessmen were ideally suited to manage all varieties of operations far better than their foreign counterparts, and Behn would have concurred with this. Moreover, the two men commanded ITT during similar periods, when the United States was dominant and self-confident and the overseas expansion of its corporations was all but taken for granted.

Behn's International System could not have been realized were it not for America's might in the post–World War I decade. As has been seen, many of ITT's acquisitions were made after competitions with weakened European concerns, with important support from powerful New York banks eager to flex their muscles overseas, and the cooperation of a government willing to support national ventures throughout the world. American businessmen were confident, aggressive, and optimistic in this period, and Behn was a near-perfect exemplar of the breed.

The United States came out of World War II the only truly great power in the world, with its economy intact, the dollar stronger than gold, and national prestige unassailable. Western Europe was in disarray, and recovery was possible only with massive American assistance. This was a time when American corporations invested billions of dollars in Europe and elsewhere, when foreigners not only respected American might, technological expertise, and management skills but were open in their admiration and eager to learn by imitation.

It appeared a realization of the prediction made by Henry Luce, of *Time*, in 1941, when he called for an "American century," and although scholars differ as to his meaning, it implied leadership if not outright domination. Luce suggested that American technicians, scientists, and businessmen spread a gospel of productivity throughout the world while the nation's army and navy guarantee peace, stability, and well-being. In addition, the United States had to take a strong stand in defense of its version of capitalism, demonstrating to others how it benefited all who lived and worked under it. "It is for America and for America alone to determine whether a system of free economic enterprise—an economic order compatible with freedom and progress—shall or shall not prevail in this century," said Luce, who had become the apostle of a muscular and missionary American capitalism.

Echoes of this could be heard during the late 1940s and through the 1950s. Toward the end of the decade Germany and Japan had recovered, with France not far behind, and their businessmen were competing against American counterparts in many markets. Even so, the example of American business prowess remained, especially for that generation of managers who helped organize the wartime production effort and who graduated to top positions afterward.

Geneen was one of these people. Early in his ITT career he often spoke of an intention to concentrate on domestic operations, in this way implying a return to the Behn approach and a turning away from plans set down by Harrison and Leavey. His domestic strategy had different roots from those of the Colonel, who after all had vast overseas experience and who opted to bring the corporation home after the scarring episodes of the 1930s and '40s. Never before had Geneen worked at a firm with extensive foreign operations. He understood American business and intended to expand in the United States, selling goods overseas but building few new plants there. He permitted work to continue on the foreign projects initiated by Harrison and Leavey, but no additional ones were planned during 1959 and most of 1960.

Then he seemed to alter his views. Just as Harrison had been delighted with what he found at ISE companies, eventually deciding to shift his attention there, so Geneen came to appreciate the growth potential of Western Europe. This, combined with his missionary attitude, resulted in a change of mind, and he drew up an ambitious development program for ISE.

In the 1962 annual report Geneen noted the completion of fifteen new facilities, all but two of which were in Europe and each of which had been initiated by his predecessors. Then he announced his own program for twenty-two additional installations, some of which had already been started. "The major portion of our initial expansion is taking place in Europe," he wrote, "to provide needed production increases in the fast-growing Common Market." There would be six projects in Germany, five in the United Kingdom, and two each in Spain and Belgium, with others in France, the Netherlands, Portugal, Austria, and Sweden. A Puerto Rican plant was to turn out telephone equipment. Finally, there would be a single new domestic installation, one intended to expand the capabilities of Jennings Radio Manufacturing, one of Geneen's initial acquisitions.

There were few takeovers of any kind during Geneen's early years at ITT, and none of them represented a significant alteration in the corporation's general strategy. Indeed, these additions supplemented existing operations and were of the kind any of his three predecessors would have considered desirable. It would appear Geneen was doing little else but filling out product lines. There wasn't a hint of conglomeratization at the time.

Ironically, the first acquisition, which came in 1959, was of the telephone-operating company in the Virgin Islands, Sosthenes Behn's birthplace. Negotiations had begun before his arrival, however; all Geneen had to do was ratify the agreement.

The following year he obtained a division of L. C. Miller, a minor factor in the electromagnetic-vibration-equipment business, which wasn't considered of sufficient importance to mention in company publications. In 1961 ITT purchased Jennings, Surprenant Manufacturing, a producer of wire and cable, and Alpina Büromaschinen, a German manufacturer of telephonic equipment. In addition, Geneen gathered in the publicly owned shares of American Cable & Radio and purchased the minority interest in one of ITT's German operations.

Far more consequential than all of these acquisitions were divestitures of several foreign holdings in this, a time when Geneen intended to stress domestic manufacturing, as these divestitures involved a partial dismantling of Behn's International System. As noted earlier, the Colonel had obtained 23 percent of Ericsson's shares in settlement of claims against Ivar Kreuger. The firm derived no benefits from this holding, and Geneen and Margolis saw no reason to keep the shares in the ITT portfolio. After much dickering they sold the Ericsson holdings for close to $22 million. They next turned to Nippon Electric, shares of which Behn had started to accumulate in the 1920s, when he considered using that firm as a manufacturing base for Far Eastern expansion, in somewhat the same way ISE had served him in Europe and Latin America. Nothing had come of this, and so the shares remained in the portfolio, contributing little to ITT. In this, his domestic period, Geneen had no intention of expanding into Japan and other parts of the Far East, so he started disposing of the stock. In addition he wrote off an unprofitable English radio-tube factory, discontinued a data-processing unit in that country, and abandoned a North Atlantic cable facility.

The corporation experienced a confiscation in Latin America, which outraged Geneen and may have paved the way for some of his later activities there. At the time, however, it merely reinforced his sentiments regarding the desirability of domestic manufacturing as opposed to foreign telephone-company ownership.

When Fidel Castro seized power in Cuba early in 1959, it appeared he would respect foreign property rights. Soon after, however, his government took over several facilities, among them Cuban Telephone, one of the two original companies involved in ITT's formation.

It wasn't much of a loss. Cuban Telephone hadn't been permitted a rate increase during the entire period it was under ITT's control. The Colonel recognized the virtual impossibility of operating the firm on a sound fiscal basis and so elected to strip it of as much of its assets as possible. Large dividends were remitted to New York while additional working capital had been obtained through the sale of Cuban Telephone bonds. By the time Castro nationalized it, Cuban Telephone was in shabby condition, offering indifferent service through inadequate and outdated equipment, and heavily burdened with debt. ITT claimed it was worth $35 million, but the figure was clearly inflated.

Castro began formal expropriation of American assets in August 1960, and Cuban Telephone was one of the first to be seized. Under the circumstances Geneen could do nothing but issue protests and await action and support from Washington. None was forthcoming.

Instead, President Eisenhower broke relations with Castro in January of the following year, all but ending any hope of compensation. It had been a scarring experience, and Geneen vowed to have less exposure in that part of the world and to do all he could to safeguard assets against similar seizures in the future. "You have to worry over any Latin American country," he told a reporter two years later. Geneen tried to offset profits from Ericsson and Nippon Electric with the losses from Cuba, realize a tax advantage, and let it go at that.

He fared better in Brazil, where in 1960 the state of Rio Grande do Sul attempted to expropriate its telephone-operating unit, Companhia Telefônica Rio Grandense, and offered ITT the token sum of $400,000 in return for complete control. Geneen dismissed this out of hand, claiming the sum was less than one sixth the replacement value alone, and this time he received strong support from the State Department. The Brazilians responded that the company was deficit-ridden and poorly managed, and tried to defend their proposal. After protracted and often frustrating negotiations, an agreement was entered into for the sale of the properties for $7.3 million, half of which was to be sent on to New York, the rest invested in the Brazilian ISE installation, Standard Eléctrica, S.A., Rio de Janeiro, which was also to receive major contracts to upgrade equipment.

In 1962 Geneen acquired six small European firms, all of which fitted in well and augmented existing operations, and one in the United States, National Computer Products. Despite its name, the latter company specialized in electronic components and had several subcontracts for work in the expanding area of satellite communications. Geneen organized ITT Intelcom around National Computer and charged the new unit with obtaining new government orders. This was his initial venture outside of ITT's traditional domestic business, but it cannot be considered a break with the past, since there was a close fit with some work already in progress at Federal.

That year ITT's revenues passed the $1-billion mark for the first time. Geneen celebrated the landmark, which was credited to the new brand of management he had brought to the corporation. Yet ITT's growth rate wasn't significantly better than it had been during the pre-Geneen period. From 1959 to 1962, for example, sales expanded by approximately 30 percent, only a small fraction higher than what the advance had been over the preceding three years, when the corporation had been directed by Harrison and Leavey. Of course, this doesn't take into account the loss of revenues from Cuban Telephone, closure of other facilities, and the additions from acquisitions.

Other statistics tell a different story. Profits advanced in pace with revenues under Geneen, whereas they had stagnated from 1956 to 1959. Part of this was the result of a national economic quickening in the early 1960s, but a good deal of the credit is due the Geneen reforms.

Most of these earnings, along with funds realized by an increase of $134 million in the long-term debt since the end of 1959, went into additions to plant and equipment, and under the circumstances the dividend couldn't be raised. ITT's total investments in facilities expanded by 38 percent during the first three Geneen years; the balance sheet was stronger and the corporation's reputation higher than at any time since the late 1920s.

Geneen had lived up to his advance billing as a master manager and financial wizard. His penchant for hard work and decisive manner captured the imagination of financial writers. "If I had more arms, legs, and time, I could run the entire corporation," he was reported to have said, and there were many tales of how he kept briefcases filled with documents, to peruse in his "spare moments," of which there were precious few. A week out of every month was spent in Europe, overseeing operations there, and he estimated that fully half his time was devoted to travel and work overseas.

Just as he had attracted some of the nation's brightest executives to ITT, now they began to depart, several to take leadership posts at other corporations. "The pressures here—the requirements for traveling, the diversity of the company—have made many say, 'the hell with it.' " This was the opinion of William Marx, who himself had started to feel burned out and was casting about for a less grueling post. "Nothing matters to him but the job—not the clock, not your personal life, nothing."[8]

Such were the components of Geneen's fame in early 1963. Newspapers and business magazines carried stories of his idiosyncracies and brilliance, and Geneen came as close to being a "business superstar" as any American corporate leader. The journalists noted that the European companies were performing well, expanding into consumer durables successfully, and if Federal remained a problem, at least conditions there were improving. Geneen continued to stress the importance of domestic business, telling several writers that by building facilities in the United States, he was making ITT a truly international concern.

The betting at the time was that Geneen would seek to expand ITT's sales in domestic telecommunications equipment, and that a major confrontation was brewing between the corporation and General Telephone's Automatic Electric Subsidiary, followed by a challenge to Western Electric itself. "I'm not at all satisfied with the share of the market we've got," he told one reporter, while another, taking note of ITT's growing backlog of defense and space-related contracts, thought the big push would come in that direction.

Rapid growth was his primary objective. Geneen continued to claim that revenues and profits would double in his first five years at the job, but this didn't seem likely given the rate of the 1959–1962 period. It might be accomplished, however, providing the pace of acquisitions quickened.

Geneen signaled a shift in this direction late in 1962. John J. Graham, who had come to ITT from RCA, established a task force charged with identifying, studying, and then recommending take-over candidates. This group was led by Robert Kenmore, who arrived at ITT from Roth, Gerard & Co., a New York Stock Exchange firm, where he had been a partner in charge of institutional research. The group sifted through lists of small companies in areas abutting those of ITT subsidiaries, spoke with professional "finders," and discussed possibilities with bankers and representatives of brokerage firms. The actual negotiations were handled by Stanley Luke, who, it will be recalled, had disposed of Coolerator and by now risen to a vice-presidency.

None of this was out of the ordinary. As far as the business press was concerned, Geneen had taken command of a complex telecommunications and related consumer-goods empire, and was in the process of slimming it down in areas where it was weak and expanding from positions of strength, mostly through development of existing operations but also by means of acquisitions.

In early 1963 Geneen was considered a manager, not an entrepreneur and certainly not a conglomerateur. Even then, however, there were hints of change. "While Geneen likes the idea of building on existing areas of capability (i.e. electronic components, aviation radio, electrical transmission gear) he will consider a sizeable company in almost any field with good management."[9] This was the view of a *Business Week* writer in May 1963. He might have added that Geneen would have found attractive those firms that clearly needed such leadership to be turned around.

At the time, Royal Little, James Ling, and Tex Thornton were considered pioneers of the conglomerate movement. Geneen wasn't one of their number yet. But he was preparing to take the plunge.

11

The Quintessential
Conglomerateur

IN November 1969 Harold Geneen traveled to Washington with several of his officers and staff members to testify before the anti-trust subcommittee of the House Committee on the Judiciary, then investigating conglomerate corporations with an eye toward framing legislation to limit their activities. Geneen was one of several conglomerateurs examined by the congressmen. Most of the leaders were there—James Ling, Tex Thornton, and Charles Bluhdorn, among others. Each explained how his corporation was structured, his takeover programs, and in his individualistic fashion each tried to defend the concept of wide-ranging diversification.

As expected, Ling dazzled the legislators with a recitation of his financial gymnastics; Thornton spoke glowingly of an ongoing program for an intricately linked chain of small to medium-size companies, all feeding off one another; and Bluhdorn seemed vague, ponderous, and occasionally even a trifle sinister, with some of his convoluted explanations and attempts to make sense of his growing family of companies at Gulf + Western.

The Quintessential Conglomerateur

As for Geneen, his was a virtuoso performance. He was quick to respond to challenges, effective in rebuttal, often witty, and clearly in command of all aspects of his corporation's activities, which befitted his reputation as one of the nation's premier managers and workaholics, and his position as chief executive officer of the biggest conglomerate of them all. Moreover, he proved the only one of the lot capable of drawing up and presenting a rationale for his actions, which was at the same time clearly stated, plausible, and original.

Geneen wasn't uncomfortable with the term "conglomerate," but he preferred to label this strategy at ITT "diversification." This was necessary, he told the congressmen, because of the accelerating pace of technological development in a swiftly changing marketplace. Obsolescence of products, services, and techniques and the introduction and acceptance of new ones occurred over months, even weeks, where once they took years or decades. Corporations had to be nimble in order to take advantage of marketing opportunities, capitalize on discoveries and inventions, and move into new areas. The older, more familiar varieties of corporations, whose leaders dealt in only a handful of closely related products or who understood a single industry (perhaps he was thinking of Jones & Laughlin at this point) weren't equipped to appreciate opportunities available elsewhere and were too conservative to shift assets into emerging growth industries with which they had little or no experience. This wasn't a problem for the conglomerateurs, who Geneen believed were opportunists in the best sense of the term, prepared to shift ground since they weren't wedded to a single approach or strategy. Such individuals could not only comprehend and then act upon novel concepts but might reinvigorate old firms mired in stagnant industries by changing their outlooks and infusing them with new managements. A year before Alvin Toffler would make the nation aware of problems posed by what he called "future shock," Geneen was claiming that conglomerateurs were best equipped, by virtue of their outlook and vitality, to deal with that very phenomenon in business. He told the congressmen, "Diversification provides a form of security and insurance and a method of adapting to the real quickening tempo of change that we are all experiencing—change in technology, change in markets and consumers, and change in foreign competition."[1]

Although at the time, conglomeratization was associated with risk-taking by daring, innovative, and change-oriented managers, in many areas these managers were more conservative than their "mainstream" counterparts. The conglomerateurs were more concerned with finance than with the development of ongoing enterprises; they were more interested in the bottom line than in supporting extensive, long-term research-and-development programs. For example, Geneen would take great pride in a string of quarterly increases in reported earnings, but ITT lagged badly in the creation of new technologies, and R&D expenses were occasionally cut severely. Critics of conglomerates often charged that they were attempting to gobble up all of American enterprise; that in the end there would be only a handful of giants, with sufficient power to challenge even the government. In fact, a number of these corporations proved to be dinosaurs, incapable of sustaining the growth formerly enjoyed by some of their acquired companies. In the end they stifled, rather than stimulated, economic development.

Many of these corporations were searching for stability, not true internal growth. Geneen observed that by spreading risks over several industries in different parts of the world, he was minimizing the dangers of a single or even of multiple failures at ITT as a whole and protecting his corporation from some of the hazards of the business cycle. A recession in one area in which the corporation had products might be balanced by expansion in another. "Diversification is, in short, an 'insurance policy' for orderly future growth and thus has important positive values as a concept in itself." Moreover, only a stable firm such as this could afford to take risks. Geneen summarized his purposes for diversification in a logical, almost geometrical, but essentially conservative fashion:

> 1. To diversify into industries and markets which have good prospects for above average long-term growth and profitability;
> 2. To achieve a sound balance between foreign earnings and domestic earnings;
> 3. To achieve a sound balance between high risk capital-intensive manufacturing operations and less risky service operations;
> 4. To achieve a sound balance between high risk engineering-labor-intensive electronics manufacturing and less risky commercial and industrial manufacturing;
> 5. To achieve a sound ratio between commercial/industrial products and services, and consumer products and services;
> 6. To achieve a sound ratio between government/defense/

space operations and commercial/industrial/consumer products and services in both foreign and domestic markets; and 7. To achieve a sound balance between cyclical products and services.[2]

This was as well thought out a strategy as Behn's International System had been more than four decades earlier. It wasn't the first time Geneen had spoken of the need for "sound balance" to obtain what he considered strength through diversification, and he would offer variations on the theme in the future.

On the surface it appeared the kind of program that might have been conceived at a leading graduate school by a detached "management philosopher," a sketch for the "corporation of the future" that occasionally appeared in professional journals. But such wasn't the case. Rather, Geneen's seven points were derived from a blend of what he inherited at ITT, ideas he had toyed with prior to arriving in New York, and his own proclivities. For example, after World War II, both Behn and Harrison had groped toward the kind of balance sketched by Geneen, though they failed to formulate a rationale for their actions. Geneen provided one, and he proved bolder, more consistent, and better organized than either of his predecessors in carrying it out. In addition, he was less bound to a single industry and tradition than were Behn and Harrison, more aggressive than either, and he had a greater capacity for the kind of effort required to manage such a diversified collection of enterprises. Finally, Geneen didn't go about creating his new ITT from a set of blueprints, such as those he placed before the congressmen in 1969. Rather, he entered the movement gradually, over a period of several years, and even now it is difficult to say exactly when—and with what acquisition—ITT joined the ranks of conglomerates.

A plausible case might be made for selecting 1963 as the turning point. Geneen took over companies at the rate of more than one per month, three times as many as in the previous three years combined, and all through the issuance of new equity. Nine of these were small European firms; as in the past, they contributed technology, plant, and work force to augment ongoing operations at ISE installations, and none in any important way represented a departure from existing product lines. ITT added five companies in the domestic sector, two of which also were conventional, at least in terms of the corporation's current business. Cannon Electric was the nation's leading producer of certain kinds of electrical connectors that were quite familiar to Federal's managers, engineers, and salesmen. The largest of Geneen's acquisitions to that time, Cannon had six plants in the United States as well as operations in Europe, Canada, and Australia. The other firm was Gilfillan, a small factor in airport surveillance and radar, whose products weren't dissimilar to those turned out by Federal.

Geneen signaled his intention to transform ITT into a conglomerate with his other three domestic acquisitions. This could be recognized only in retrospect, however, and in any case none of the three represented much more of a break with the past than had been Colonel Behn's purchases of Farnsworth and Coolerator.

As its name indicates, General Controls was a manufacturer of a wide variety of automatic control devices, some developed for the military but most utilized in appliances of various kinds. The next acquisition was Bell & Gossett, the country's largest manufacturer of industrial and commercial pumps. Finally, ITT purchased Nesbitt, which specialized in turning out heating, ventilating, and air-conditioning equipment marketed to schools.

In speaking and writing for the general public, securities analysts, and stockholders, Geneen implied that his strategy was to balance military sales with revenues and earnings from the commercial-industrial sector, and this would account for these acquisitions. In addition, although maintained for the time being as separate entities, General Controls, Bell & Gossett, and Nesbitt were all involved in the production of climatizing equipment, and so there appeared a certain logic to their acquisition; perhaps Geneen was thinking of becoming a major factor in the industry by expanding on this base. Doubtless these factors were taken into consideration, but they weren't paramount in 1963.

In late February and early March of that year Geneen drew up a memorandum on his acquisitions "goal program." He alluded to the value of diversification, but his central concern then—as before— was in balancing foreign revenues and profits with those from the United States. Geneen spoke of "certain danger signs which are beginning to accrue in respect to long relied upon foreign earnings," especially in the face of what he interpreted as a deteriorating American position in the world. He alluded to French plans to license the export of capital and the growing anti-Americanism exhibited by Charles de Gaulle. "U.S. ownership of companies in that country will be heavily scrutinized," so he thought. Germany remained friendly but was too close to the Soviet border for comfort. Italy was rent by a wave of strikes and was drifting leftward. So was Britain's Labour Party, which only recently had circulated a document that, as Geneen put it, "called for the nationalization of certain companies, *including our STC company.*" To ITT old-timers it might have evoked memories of Behn's attitude toward the close of the 1930s. But where the Colonel feared only expropriation, Geneen was also troubled by intensified competition in bidding for telephonic equipment, which accounted for almost two thirds of ITT's European revenues. At the time, each country favored domestic producers, which was to say that STC had a large part of the British market, SEL had its share in Germany, CGCT and Le Matériel Téléphonique were major factors in France, and so forth. This was about to change. Common Market ministers were "comparing notes, cost quotations, and pricing," in what appeared to be a prelude to demands for compulsory international bidding without reference to the country of manufacture. If this occurred, the entire telecommunications industry would be revolutionized, with lower margins for all and consequent disruptions within the ISE group of national companies.

Geneen feared that if this happened, not only would revenues and earnings decline but there might even be some question regarding the maintenance of the dividend. Despite higher earnings, the dividend hadn't been raised since he took office, and a cutback there surely would bring into question Geneen's leadership of the corporation.

For these reasons, Geneen indicated that within five years he wanted 55 percent of earnings to come from domestic companies. This couldn't be accomplished through internal growth alone, and so he proposed to institute a vigorous acquisitions policy to bring to ITT some $500 million in sales from this source. For the time being, the corporation would continue to pursue a program of taking over small and medium-size firms, but Geneen thought an increase in revenues of this magnitude "probably can only be carried out by the acquisition of one or two large companies when and if the opportunities in relative stock values, management situations, etc., present themselves."

Geneen was seeking takeover candidates that exhibited rapid growth rates, which would lessen ITT's relative dependence on European telephone-equipment sales and earnings. The smaller firms (by which he meant those with $100 million or less in reve-nues) were to be somewhat related to the existing businesses, and in addition Geneen would consider taking over telephone-operating companies if they could purchase equipment from the ISE factories. Most important, however, were the large acquisitions. For such Geneen would be willing to enter areas previously unexplored by ITT, among them chemicals, pharmaceuticals, insurance, food, and office equipment.[2]

None of the takeovers to that point came close to fitting this description, but ITT was on the prowl as never before. The signs could be seen and felt in the executive suites, where rumors were rife of imminent takeovers in a wide variety of industries. Some there suggested Geneen would move swiftly, if only to make good on his pledge to double revenues and earnings within his initial five years. Also, the president was known to be distressed about the prices of ITT common and convertible preferred shares. The for-mer had barely moved from the time he had taken office, and the convertibles were priced in line with the common. Geneen wanted recognition from Wall Street in addition to what he already had from the financial and business press, but there was more to this than ego. He exchanged paper for ownership of companies, and unless their quotations rose, the takeovers could involve an undesir-able and considerable dilution of equity. All of this might be changed should ITT give an unmistakable sign of moving ahead into conglomeratization, for some of the stocks of these free-form companies had become the favorites of investors.

There were no acquisitions of any consequence in the first half of 1964, but rumors of activities on this front continued. Then, in early August, ITT made its initial foray into what was truly a new area. In exchange for close to $40 million in common and preferred shares, Geneen obtained Aetna Finance, a consumer-based organi-zation with activities in half the nation's states and whose assets came to more than $90 million. Aetna's wholly owned subsidiary, American Universal Life Insurance, came along in the transaction, giving ITT a foothold in this industry as well. Two weeks later Geneen purchased a half interest in Great International Life Insur-ance, which was based in the United Kingdom. To these he added Kellogg Credit, which financed sales for that company, and ITT Credit, which provided services for other parts of the corporation. Together these four units constituted ITT Financial Services, a new subsidiary and a foundation upon which Geneen would build in the future.

This was an important development, even a turning point. ITT Financial satisfied all of Geneen's requirements regarding major acquisitions, even though it wasn't as large as these were supposed to be. It was essentially a domestic operation that over time would lessen ITT's dependence on telecommunications equipment, and financial services was a growth area. But it wasn't seen as such by most Wall Street analysts. There wasn't much glamour in finance and insurance companies in the early 1960s, and the Aetna acquisition was viewed as little more than a prudent purchase at a reasonable price of assets that might have been undervalued. Geneen's venture into conglomeratization went unnoticed, for the most part. As for the other domestic acquisitions of that year—Terryphone and Barton Instruments — these were of the kind that had been gathered in earlier, and so they caused no great excitement. ITT also acquired fourteen small foreign companies, a record number, but these, too, were minor entities in industries already quite familiar to ITT's management.

The 1963 and 1964 acquisitions enabled Geneen to claim success in meeting his objective of doubling revenues and earnings in his first five years in office. Sales and revenues for 1964 came to $1.5 billion, against $766 million in 1959. Net income was $63.1 million against $29 million. Purists noted that earnings per share had risen from $1.90 to $3.11, and so hadn't doubled. This was due to Geneen's issuance of additional shares to pay for acquisitions. The 15.5 million shares of 1959 had grown to 19.3 million five years later, and dilution of equity was of major concern to more than a few financial analysts. Others observed that Geneen was obtaining earnings at the expense of research and development, and that these outlays hadn't risen as rapidly as they might at a high technology corporation like ITT. The stockholders had little reason to be pleased with their returns. Although ITT common advanced in 1963 and 1964, it hardly was an outstanding performer in the great bull market that developed in those years. IBM, Texas Instruments, and Raytheon doubled but ITT went up by what at the time seemed a mere 50 percent. Geneen did increase the payout to $1.10 per share, as though to celebrate his success and share its benefits with the stockholders, but ITT still wasn't considered a growth issue on Wall Street. To alter this perception would become one of Geneen's major objectives for the next half decade. In addition, he pledged to double earnings, sales, and earnings per share in the same period.

While completing negotiations for the Aetna takeover, ITT became involved in discussions with several other firms more interesting to Wall Streeters, and by early 1965 another merger appeared in the works, one that would be taken as a clear, unmistakable indication that ITT indeed was becoming a conglomerate and perhaps would end up as the most far-ranging of the group. Yet it wasn't seen as such at headquarters.

In a memorandum written for the board early in 1965, a member of the corporate-development staff, possibly Robert Kenmore, observed, "Many of the fastest growing and lowest risk areas in the U.S. are in the so-called service field ranging from consumer utilities or quasi-utilities to business and financial services," and this of course was the thinking behind the Aetna takeover and subsequent creation of ITT Financial Services. "Now a similar opportunity has come up to get a well timed participation in another rapidly growing service area—that of car rental and vehicle leasing business through the acquisition of one of the most successfully merchandised names in American industry in recent years—AVIS."

The leader in the industry, Hertz, had posted revenues of $230 million in 1964, and Avis was a distant second, with a shade less than $50 million. Avis was growing twice as rapidly as Hertz, however, and its returns on revenues and equity, though far behind those of the leader, were expanding, while Hertz's had stabilized. It was, as an ITT executive put it, "a most interesting situation."

The "fit" could be close to ideal, or so it was argued in the memo. Avis' business was capital-intensive, in that funds were continually needed to finance vehicle purchases and leases, and these might be provided by ITT Financial Services. The million or so Avis credit-card holders would constitute a "very promising market for the financial services activities we are entering into." The growing cadre of ITT executives and salesmen could provide Avis with a new source of clients, and as the largest American company in Europe, ITT might facilitate expansion of rental vehicles in that part of the world.

For its part, Avis had developed strong relationships with the automobile manufacturers, which were bound to grow more important in the future, and these could open that market to other ITT companies. The memo noted that many automobile rentals took place at airports and hotels, and so the way would be open for expansion into aviation-services facilities and hotels. "But basically what Avis represents is a high quality source of U.S. earnings, non-cyclical in nature, and rapidly growing with a well accepted brand image with the American consumer for a reliable, aggressively managed company with a reputation for quality and service."[3]

In the late 1960s some analysts would charge Geneen with having swallowed companies in a random fashion—one said "indiscriminately." Although there might have been some substance to this view later on, such wasn't the case as ITT prepared to acquire Avis. Rather, it was the result of a well-calculated, rational, and financially responsible decision, based as much on ITT's current operations as on its expectations for future development.

ITT certainly wanted the management at Avis to continue, terming it "outstanding" in every respect. The three top men were all in their early forties. President Winston Morrow had been at Avis since 1957 and was generally credited with having turned around what was then a small, deficit-ridden, and unpromising operation. Donald Petrie arrived from Hertz and Robert Townsend from American Express five years later. Petrie, who became chairman of the executive committee, had responsibilities for long-range planning, and Townsend, who by 1965 had risen to the chairmanship, was an attractive and articulate manager with a reputation for eccentricity and originality. All were offered long-term employment contracts, stock options, and the usual perquisites of high position.

Although Avis was a publicly owned company, close to a third of its shares were held by the investment-banking house of Lazard Frères & Co., which meant that its representatives had to be brought into the negotiations. There followed a three-way discussion and correspondence between Townsend, the ITT people involved, and Felix Rohatyn, the Lazard partner charged with conducting the discussions. All went well, and the Avis acquisition was announced early in 1965, to be completed on July 22. In return for their shares, Avis stockholders received approximately $55.7 million in ITT common and preferred stock, making this Geneen's most expensive takeover to that time. Lazard's fee for this operation came to $135,000.

Shortly thereafter, ITT purchased several related businesses and Avis franchisees—National Auto Rental, National Truck Rental,

Airport Parking Company of America, and Narco Parking—which demonstrated that ITT was following the strategy sketched by Kenmore in early 1965. During the next four years ITT acquired other firms in auto rental, airport parking, and the like, such as National City Truck Rental, Mears Motor Livery, and Yellow Cab of Kansas City. ITT made an initial move into motels in 1967, by purchasing Cleveland Motor Inns for stock worth $37.5 million.

At the time, the Avis acquisition was proclaimed as ITT's most ambitious and definitive move toward conglomeratization, which surely was so. But it also focused interest and attention on the way executives were leaving ITT, and on the Geneen brand of management.

Townsend and Petrie found the atmosphere at ITT strikingly different from what they were accustomed to at Avis. Townsend in particular had a marked distaste for paperwork, prided himself on his informality, and was a strong manager with definite ideas as to how a modern corporation should operate. Yet, initially at least, he seemed fascinated with Geneen and appeared to have accommodated himself to the new ways. "At first I wondered how a small company could be acquired by a large one without losing some of its spark. But I'm enthusiastic," he told a reporter, and in a paraphrase of the famous Avis motto, Townsend added, "We'll try even harder."[4]

He soon changed his mind. Increasingly, Townsend chafed at having to submit frequent reports and to perform as part of a large enterprise, each segment of which seemed to be under Geneen's constant scrutiny. Since he had come out of the acquisition a wealthy man, Townsend could afford to go off on his own, and so he did. After a few months Petrie left ITT to take a position at Lazard, and Townsend to write a book. Somewhat later Townsend said, "I would like it on my tombstone that I never worked a single day for a company like ITT," which of course wasn't really the case. Still, he became quite outspoken in his dislike of the Geneen methods and philosophy.

Had Townsend let it go at that, only a relatively small number of people would have known of these feelings, but his book became a huge success. Published five years later with the title *Up the Organization: How to Stop the Corporation from Stifling People and Strangling Profits*, it was brash, iconoclastic, witty, and an almost immediate best-seller that transformed its author into a celebrity and a popular business analyst. There was no direct mention of either ITT or Geneen in the book, but most knowledgeable people who read it or who saw interviews with Townsend came to understand that this was the corporation and individual he was criticizing so sharply. "Mergers and acquisitions are a necessary evil for some companies. Avoid them like the plague if you can," was his recommendation. "Two and two may seem to make five when a conglomerate is making its pitch, but from what I've seen they are just playing a numbers game and couldn't care less if they make zombies out of your people," and in an unmistakable reference to ITT, he recommended, "If you have a good company don't sell out to a conglomerate. I was sold out once but resigned."[5]

Townsend's experience wasn't unique, and his book did serve to focus attention on Geneen and his corporation. Most of the others who left ITT did so with respectful words for Geneen, claiming to have learned a great deal from him regarding proper management techniques. That there was a figurative revolving door at headquarters and in the field was obvious, with scores of executives leaving ITT for posts elsewhere. Their departures occasionally resulted from an inability or unwillingness to maintain the pace, but more often they resulted from a desire to assume command of organizations of their own after having survived the rigors of what one business magazine called "Geneen University."[6]

Robert Alexander, who became vice-president at Zenith, was of the former group. "The reason I left was his schedule—the all-day and all-night meeting," he said. After serving as Geneen's second in command for a while, William Marx departed to take a similar though less demanding position at Great Lakes Carbon. He, too, wanted a more settled life. But David Margolis, who like Marx had come with Geneen from Raytheon, went with George Strichman to Fairbanks Whitney and transformed that moribund collection of companies into Colt Industries, a rapidly growing conglomerate on the ITT model. By 1968 former ITT'ers were presidents of such diverse firms as P. Ballantine, Turner Corporation, Whittaker Corporation, Crouse-Hinds, Kearney-National, Esterline, Keene Corporation, Crucible Steel, and McCall, and more were on the second or third rung of the ladder at other companies.

This wasn't a unique or an undesirable situation, and in fact it reflected well on Geneen. At Litton Industries, Tex Thornton permitted his executives a good deal of leeway and encouraged them to use their own initiatives in solving problems. Even someone as individualistic as Robert Townsend might have been able to continue on in such an atmosphere. Litton, too, underwent an exodus of managers, even greater than that experienced by ITT. Its so-called Lidos (Litton Industries Drop Outs) became chairmen and presidents of such firms as Hunt Foods & Industries, Western Union, Mattel, American Export, and Republic Corporation, and Henry Singleton left Litton to organize Teledyne, a conglomerate in the Thornton mold.

Conglomerateurs like Geneen and Thornton attracted many young men eager to learn from them and then to take charge on their own. As has been seen, the professional manager was perceived as some kind of wonder worker during the early and middle years of the 1960s, and a good deal of this resulted from the mystique created by men like Geneen. Many of those who served a few years as journeymen at ITT or some other conglomerate would have been disappointed if they didn't receive offers of chairmanships and presidencies from several firms.

This isn't to suggest that ITT's executive suites were stocked with middle-aged men constantly on the alert for offers elsewhere, eager for a chance to command and demonstrate what they had learned from working with Geneen. For a variety of reasons, several were quite content to remain at ITT. Some were comfortable in a secondary role, others found sufficient challenge in their posts, and a number of them lacked an overweening sense of ambition. Three of these were Francis "Tim" Dunleavy, Richard Bennett, and James Lester, who made up Geneen's office of the president created in 1967. Ted Westfall, who became one of ITT's executive vice-presidents (Dunleavy was the other) after Marx's departure, stayed on. First one and then the other was rumored to be Geneen's heir apparent, but in reality neither was seriously considered for the post of chairman or chief executive officer. Hart Perry, who was the treasurer as well as executive vice-president for finance, was a specialist satisfied to remain as such, and there were others who, like him, might be considered ITT's equivalents of barons or dukes in a medieval kingdom, dominant in their own areas: Herbert Knortz as comptroller, Edward Gerrity as a senior vice-president charged with public relations, chief counsel Howard Aibel, and Stanley Luke, who had major responsibilities in the crucial area of business development. All were well paid and had large budgets and staffs.

The Quintessential Conglomerateur

For a while in the early 1960s it appeared Robert Kenmore might become one of this group and that he might rise faster and go further than any of the others. But Kenmore, who had been a key figure in most of the pre-Avis acquisitions, hadn't brought in a major find, and it became increasingly evident that Geneen considered him a lightweight. Kenmore was named to a vice-presidency in 1966, but he performed in a secondary role thereafter. Three years later he left ITT to form his own conglomerate, Kenton Corporation.

By then Felix Rohatyn had become the major acquisitions person at ITT, and some would say the most important figure in determining the direction of the corporation after Geneen himself. A handful went so far as to claim that Rohatyn provided the imagination and audacity at headquarters while Geneen's contribution was management, power, and authority. Even now insiders differ as to which man was more creative and dominant when it came to long-term strategic planning at ITT, and whatever the answer, the very fact that such discussions take place without clear resolution indicates how important Rohatyn was during the Geneen years.

Rohatyn was thirty-seven years old when the Avis acquisition propelled him into the spotlight, but even before then he was a respected and well-known investment banker, a partner at Lazard and heir apparent for that firm's leadership.

Rohatyn was born in Vienna, Austria, in 1928. His grandfather was an investment banker who had founded the firm of Rohatyn & Co. and who had interests in other businesses as well, and his father helped manage some of the operations. The growth of Nazism in Austria caused the family to move to the south of France in the early 1930s, and shortly thereafter the parents were divorced. Felix' mother then married Henry Plesser, a partner at Lazard. In 1942 the family fled France and came to the United States after short stopovers in Spain, Morocco, and Argentina. Recalling his hasty departure from France, Rohatyn told a reporter, "I spent our last night in a hotel room stuffing gold coins into toothpaste tubes. We had been well off, but that was all we got out. Ever since, I've had the feeling that the only permanent wealth is what you carry around in your head."

Henry Plesser was given a position at Lazard's New York office, and Felix attended private schools in Manhattan and then went on to major in physics at Middlebury College, in Vermont. In 1948 he got a summer job at Lazard, and it was then he met André Meyer, the firm's senior partner, who took an interest in Felix and in time became his mentor. The following year, after graduation, he was taken on as a trainee.

Rohatyn says he found much of the work "extremely dreary" and remained at Lazard only because it afforded him an opportunity to travel and to live in exciting places. Except for 1951–1953, when he served in the U.S. Army, he spent the next six years in London, Paris, and Zurich, working in the foreign-exchange and international-barter areas for Lazard. Rohatyn had enough of this by 1955 and asked Meyer to transfer him to New York and to give him different tasks. This was done, and he came under Meyer's direct tutelage in corporate restructurings and mergers, areas in which the older man was an acknowledged master.[7]

Now Rohatyn found an aspect of the business that interested him and in which he quickly became an adept practitioner. Self-confident, personally charming and witty, with an impressive memory for details and a knack for solving complex problems, Rohatyn had all the qualifications for such tasks, and first with Meyer and then on his own he handled some of Lazard's most important assignments. He became a general partner in 1961, one of the youngest of the group, in recognition of his obvious talents not only at servicing Lazard's existing clients but in bringing new business to the firm.

Mergers and acquisitions were increasing in frequency during the early 1960s, and both established and young firms sought suitable takeover candidates. It was Lazard's and Rohaytn's good fortune that the young man was prepared by then to take a major role at the firm. Meyer, who was sixty-three years old in 1961, was a gentleman of the old school, and although he was certainly capable of arranging acquisitions for the conglomerates, he was more at home with conventional businessmen and somewhat wary of the "new breed." Rohatyn was better suited in matters of temperament and interest to work with such individuals, and so he assumed a large share of the work in this area.

Although Hugh Knowlton of Kuhn, Loeb, continued to sit on the ITT board, Geneen felt free to utilize the services of other investment bankers when seeking acquisitions. And while the two got along well and Knowlton had been instrumental in bringing Geneen to ITT, they had clearly differing personalities and outlooks. Like Meyer, Knowlton was an older man, a native aristocrat close to retirement. He didn't protest when Geneen went to Lazard in 1961 to seek Meyer's assistance in the Jennings acquisition. It was handled by Rohatyn, and although Jennings was a small takeover even by the standards of that year, the two men impressed each other.

ITT became Rohatyn's client, and its operations would take an increasing amount of his time and attention—and bring substantial fees to Lazard. But it certainly wasn't his only client, and Rohatyn could have got along very well without it. He handled deals for a large number of major corporations, including RCA, Schenley, United Aircraft, Lone Star Cement, and Transamerica, among others. Rohatyn headed the New York Stock Exchange's Crisis Committee in 1970, when it appeared some major houses would collapse, and he was one of several Wall Streeters credited with having prevented a panic. Six years later he became chairman of the city's Municipal Assistance Corporation and a member of the Emergency Financial Control Board. For a while he had more power over New York's affairs than Mayor Abraham Beame and was hailed as the city's savior from bankruptcy. By then he had become a nationally known figure, one who was generally admired. It wouldn't be going too far to say that Rohatyn was the best known and in some respects the most influential investment banker of the past half century.

Rohatyn's efforts for ITT and his position in the corporation have to be interpreted against this backdrop, which also helps explain the relationship that developed between him and Geneen.

ITT and Lazard grew closer as a direct result of the skills Rohatyn displayed in bringing off the Avis acquisition. Geneen recognized and appreciated his abilities at formulating programs, devising ingenious approaches to tax and antitrust considerations, negotiating with all sides, and concluding the deal to the satisfaction of each party. He saw in the young banker a person who might be of great value to the corporation.

But there might have been more to it than that. Geneen might have considered Rohatyn a modern version of Colonel Behn: Both appreciated the good life and possessed grace and style. As has been noted, Geneen often remarked that Behn would have had a place in the new ITT he was creating; he would be useful in wooing businessmen whose companies had been singled out for acquisition, and in addition he could be a contact with domestic and foreign political leaders. Geneen realized he himself lacked such skills, or at least didn't care to cultivate them. Many outsiders who might prove useful to ITT were put off by his manner and reputation. Rohatyn was far better equipped than he to deal with them, which was another reason Rohatyn was needed at headquarters.

After the Avis takeover, Rohatyn became one of several asked to implement the Kenmore strategy of adding airport-services firms and hotels to augment the automobile-rental operation. Lazard's major contribution in 1966 was the acquisition of Airport Parking, which cost ITT $26.5 million in stock. The following year Rohatyn was named to the board, a clear signal that he was to have enlarged responsibilities at the firm. From then on Rohatyn's hand could be seen in both the scope and nature of the acquisitions. Up to that time the acquisitions had been fairly modest and, in comparison with what was developing at Gulf & Western and Ling-Temco-Vought (LTV), even timid. Now this would change, as ITT became the boldest of the lot.

Geneen remained the undisputed leader of the corporation, and as Rohatyn's power grew, his specific position there must have appeared puzzling to those who were unfamiliar with the structure and the functioning of the modern, complex giant corporation. As a board member he was, in theory, Geneen's equal, and since Geneen was also chief executive officer, Rohatyn was in a sense his employer. But he was also a partner at Lazard, to which he owed his primary loyalty. Geneen might give orders to Westfall, Perry, Dunleavy, and others in the corporate suites, and promote or dismiss them almost at will. He had no such power over Rohatyn. If displeased by his operations, Geneen might seek out another banking house, but Rohatyn couldn't be fired from the board, though under such circumstances he probably would have left voluntarily. All of this was moot, however, since each agreed, formally and tacitly, on the terrain to be covered and the delegation of responsibilities. It would be too much to say that Rohatyn acted as Geneen's premier, for such power wasn't to be shared at ITT. Rather, he was ambassador-at-large and foreign minister, as well as the corporation's emissary to Wall Street and a major strategist.

12

Turning Point: The Merger Not Made

THE PACE OF CONGLOMERATIZATION picked up dramatically after the mid-1960s, when shares of companies engaged in this form of diversification were the darlings of Wall Street. Let it be known that a formerly stodgy, old-line industrial corporation was about to enter the ranks (and signal the transformation by hiring executives from ITT, Litton, or another leader in the movement), and its stock would rise. Now the company was able to exchange its inflated equity for ownership of firms that hadn't participated so fully in this leg of the great bull market. Earnings per share would advance as a result of pooling of interest and other techniques that the conglomerateurs mastered; investors would take note of the accelerated growth (in many cases more apparent than real) and bid prices higher, after which the process would be repeated.

Accountants, analysts, and business critics protested that conglomerates were exaggerating their financial performance. Some of them were more akin to scams than viable operating entities, they charged, adding that insufficient information about the details of mergers was made public. They implied that deception was being practiced on individuals to whom terms like "pooling of assets" and "pro forma earnings" were bereft of meaning. Look into the footnotes to financial statements, they urged, and it would become clear that jargon was being employed to mask reality. Later the federal government would probe these allegations and others, and articles regarding illusions of growth and what was behind them appeared in newspapers and magazines.

The companies responded to charges such as these by noting that their reports had been approved by independent auditors as having conformed to generally accepted accounting principles and had been approved by the Securities and Exchange Commission. Critics responded by arguing that procedures used by auditors were badly in need of revamping in light of recent developments and that the SEC was toothless when it came to dealing with this new form of enterprise.

None of the criticisms had any discernible impact on stock prices. From 1965 to 1968, when the Dow Jones Industrial Average advanced from a low of 841 to a high of 985, or approximately 17 percent, Gulf + Western rose by more than 500 percent and LTV by 600 percent. ITT was a comparative laggard in the group, its common shares moving up by a modest 160 percent.

Conglomerates were attracting attention beyond the financial district. Their operations were dissected by professors at graduate schools of business while leading practitioners were denounced as avatars of the old robber barons by critics and hailed by admirers as bold adventurers seeking to create new forms of capitalism.

In all of this there was much uncertainty as to the specific attributes of conglomerates and how to distinguish them from old-line companies. This was troublesome, especially to attorneys and others at the Federal Trade Commission and the Justice Department charged with fashioning antitrust prosecutions. It appeared simple enough at first: A conglomerate was a corporation engaged in a wide variety of nonrelated activities. This definition was inadequate, however, for if taken literally it would mean that many familiar, established firms not generally considered conglomerates were indeed of that breed.

This became apparent when antitrusters attempted to apply old standards and definitions to determine whether any of the newly refashioned corporations were in violation of the law. Long before World War II the Commerce Department had developed what were known as Standard Industrial Classifications (SICs), which encompassed the broad spectrum of American business. There were eighty-nine major classes, and supposedly each industry could be fitted into one or another of these, with some gaps and overlaps. A company might become a candidate for antitrust prosecution if it obtained too great a position in any one SIC. Such would have been the case with firms like U.S. Steel, General Motors, Standard Oil of New Jersey, and International Business Machines.

As might have been expected, those companies generally recognized as conglomerates operated in several SICs. Moreover, none was dominant in any single business, though some became giant corporations. Finally, a number of major firms not believed to be conglomerates functioned in more SICs than did exemplars of the group. For example, Textron, the classic conglomerate, had representation in thirteen of them by 1967, but that year General Electric —which most agreed wasn't a conglomerate—functioned in fourteen SICs. Charles Bluhdorn's Gulf + Western had by then emerged as a conglomerate, and its activities could be fitted into eight SICs; nonconglomerate Firestone Tire & Rubber was in ten of them, as was Rexall, best known for its drugstores.[1]

Obviously the definition was flawed and had to be either scrapped or refined.

It then was suggested that conglomerates not only operated in many SICs but had arrived there primarily through acquisitions. This presented other problems. General Motors had entered home appliances and locomotive manufacturing by taking over operating companies. RCA had become a factor in the former industry the same way, and General Electric in the latter, mainly through acquisitions. Westinghouse, Bendix, and other nonconglomerates of the period had grown in like fashion.

Was there cause for prosecution of a multibillion-dollar corporation if it hadn't a dominant position in any single SIC? Viscerally the Justice Department's antitrusters felt such firms as G + W, ITT, and LTV should be brought up on charges, or at least prevented from carrying out some of their more audacious takeovers, but they couldn't find sufficient grounds in current law and existing definitions to do so. In this regard, Justice played a role similar to that of the reformist accountants who had criticized ITT's financial reporting but conceded it had followed the generally accepted accounting procedures of the period.

These problems stimulated a good deal of thought in Washington and at corporate headquarters in the second half of the 1960s, as legislators, bureaucrats, and businessmen attempted to arrive at some kind of consensus regarding conglomerates. The need to do so became more pressing as the decade wore on. According to the Federal Trade Commission, four out of every five mergers in 1966–1968 were of the conglomerate variety, up from one out of five during most of the 1940s. In their rush to diversify, many corporations were shifting into takeovers rather than expanding existing facilities. By 1968 almost half of new investment was accounted for by mergers and acquisitions; in 1948 the figure had been a fraction above 1 percent.[2] Extrapolating the trend, students of American business forecast a time when the economy would be dominated by a handful of enormous conglomerates, none of which had the capacity or even the inclination to fund research and development, preferring instead to purchase successful small firms by means of issuing new shares to exchange for assets. Whatever problems or benefits such a scenario involved, it certainly implied that a radical alteration was in store for the American corporate economy.

Toward the end of the decade, legislators and business analysts had come to view several of the larger conglomerates as freewheeling complexes headed by imaginative and daring operators, constantly on the prowl for bigger and fatter game. No company, however established and secure, seemed safe when it came to tender offers. George Goodman, writing under the name Adam Smith, concocted a humorous scenario in which a new conglomerate planned and successfully executed a takeover of AT&T. Wall Street didn't laugh, and instead wondered which of the group Goodman had in mind.

What had begun at Textron and Litton with acquisitions of small and medium-size companies in related fields and had then gone on to explorations into new areas through takeovers of companies in nonrelated businesses had by now evolved into deals through which conglomerates engulfed firms larger even than themselves. These were moribund companies for the most part, with static or declining revenues and earnings, low returns on investment, poor prospects, and, because of all this, unhappy stockholders. The conglomerateurs would offer their high-priced paper for the discounted assets of these ailing firms, promising to invigorate them with fresh management and to reward stockholders with ownership of a growth company; that is, they portrayed themselves as modern and innovative while the managers of the acquired firms were seen as tired, aged, stuffy, and incapable of meeting the demands of a rapidly evolving economy.

It happened first in 1966, when James Ling acquired Wilson & Co., which at the time had revenues of more than a billion dollars and was twice as big as Ling-Temco-Vought. Charles Bluhdorn didn't go quite that far, but Gulf + Western already taken had over firms as diverse as Paramount Pictures, South Puerto Rico Sugar, and New Jersey Zinc. Within a period of three weeks, G + W acquired E. W. Bliss, Universal American, and Consolidated Cigar, which represented more than half a billion dollars in revenues. Then Bluhdorn took off after Armour & Co., which posted sales of more than $2.2 billion but whose net income came to less than $25 million. At the same time he pursued Brown Co., a $215-million-a-year paper- and forest-products company. (On Wall Street the story was that G + W needed paper to wrap the meat in.) Bluhdorn next made offers for the Security Insurance Company of Hartford and the Security Connecticut Life Insurance Company, and other bids followed.

Geneen's actions appeared prudent and even a trifle old-fashioned when compared to those of Bluhdorn and Ling. He operated along more conventional lines in his takeover bids, and if ITT's acquisitions seemed adventuresome, at least there was a rationale behind most of his actions. G + W and LTV were akin to pirate vessels that patrolled the Spanish Main in the sixteenth century, seeking out targets of opportunity. In contrast, ITT followed the plan Geneen had sketched earlier in the decade. Moreover, he was far more careful to preserve his corporation's financial integrity than were most other conglomerateurs, which was why ITT maintained a steady course in the 1970s when some of the others foundered. "When a Jimmy Ling is finished his balance sheet is so bad you wouldn't want to lend him a nickel," said David Margolis later on. "When a Harold Geneen is finished his balance sheet is that much more strengthened than from where he began."[3]

For the most part, ITT sought small and medium-size companies to round out existing operations and augment existing segments of the firm, or it sought much larger firms capable of becoming the core of a new division. Those in the former group tended to demonstrate better-than-average growth but were short on capital or in some other way needed to draw upon ITT's resources to realize their full potential. As has been noted, the major companies' stock prices were usually low in relation to assets and earnings, certainly below the quotation afforded ITT's paper. Which is to say that Geneen wasn't particularly interested at this stage in making offers for successful, rapidly growing firms with outstanding managements—whose stock prices reflected their situation. The corollary to this is that the mergermania couldn't have occurred without a major bull market on Wall Street, which suggested that it would draw to an end even without Justice Department intervention once the market tumbled.

Geneen wanted bargains. He expected to nourish the small companies and revive the larger ones, mostly through the introduction of better controls and leadership, just as he had at ITT, and in this way he would not only enhance the parent's total operations but turn a good profit on his investment.

While absorbing Avis, ITT was considering more than a dozen other firms, though all but two of the acquisitions during the next year and a half would be conventional. Kebby Microwave, Electro Physics Labs, Jabsco Pump, Consolidated Electric Lamp, and others were relatively small companies, barely noticed outside the division into which they fell. Hamilton Management was one of the exceptions. This company, acquired for $17.6 million in late 1965, ran several mutual funds and in addition owned Alexander Hamilton Life Insurance, a minor but growing entity that complemented ITT's other entries in the industry and rounded out operations at ITT Financial. Slightly less than a year later, ITT announced the acquisition of Howard W. Sams, at a price of $32.4 million in stock. A Midwestern publishing complex whose best-known subsidiary was Bobbs-Merrill, Sams was expanding at a rapid pace, especially in the textbook market, and was badly in need of the kinds of cash infusions Geneen was prepared to offer. Like Avis, Sams marked an entry into a new industry, and just as Geneen followed the former takeover with a search for hotels, parking lots, and automotive service companies, so there would be a rash of acquisitions of private schools, educational-equipment manufacturers, small specialty publishers, and related enterprises once Sams was in the fold.

More important than any or even all of this would have been a merger with the American Broadcasting Companies, which would have set the corporation along a quite different path from the one it was to take. This was Geneen's longest-lived and most frustrating campaign. He would fail to carry it off, and the experience left a residue of bad feeling and mistrust that affected ITT's reputation and actions for many years.

Dreams of a combined ITT-ABC went back to 1951, when Colonel Behn and Edward Noble came close to bringing their companies together. As has been seen the negotiations broke down, and two years later ABC merged with United Paramount Theaters.

Initially it appeared a viable operation. ABC was the nation's third-largest network and also operated the country's most extensive motion-picture–theater chain. The corporation's strategy seemed clear: Revenues from the theaters would be used to develop the network. In effect, ABC planned to cannibalize its movie interests to expand the television enterprise, and for a while all went according to plan. Costs in television mounted rapidly, however, and ABC wasn't able to keep pace with National Broadcasting or Columbia Broadcasting either in winning new affiliates or in adapting technologies. Its network shows ran poorly in the ratings, and ABC still hadn't converted to daytime colorcasting when discussions with ITT were reopened. It was an excellent takeover candidate: an undervalued company with high profit possibilities in a growth industry badly in need of financing and management.

Geneen wasn't unaware of television's potential. Although ITT had divested itself of Capehart-Farnsworth before he had arrived, the industry's lure remained strong. Entry would be both sensible and logical. ITT possessed the financial resources, technological expertise, and management skills to become an important factor in television. The only question remaining was how best to begin.

In 1963 Geneen charged Kenmore with making a survey of the industry. The resulting report indicated that ITT might petition the Federal Communications Commission for new channels or purchase existing individual stations or groups. There was talk of approaching Gross, Corinthian, Storer, or Travelers, all of which were regional chains, but nothing came of this. At one point Geneen considered a takeover of Columbia Broadcasting as well, but this was dropped once he learned that ABC might be had for a reasonable price.

The idea was broached by Gerald Tsai, Jr., a Shanghai-born,

I·T·T: The Management of Opportunity

American-educated mutual-fund manager for Fidelity Group. Tsai
had emerged as one of the hottest operators in the developing bull
market on Wall Street. He performed much of his own research,
usually through visits to offices of leading executives, which was
how he came to know Geneen. By 1964, Tsai's Fidelity Capital Fund
had a large block of ITT in its portfolio, along with Polaroid, Texas
Instruments, Litton, and other electronics, glamour, and conglomerate issues. In addition, Tsai held shares in firms considered possible takeover candidates, one of which was ABC.

Leonard Goldenson, ABC's president, had no desire to see his
company acquired by a conglomerate, but he knew it was vulnera-
ble to a tender offer. Management and the board owned relatively
few shares and lacked the wherewithal to accumulate more. Already
ABC was being besieged by West Coast industrialist Norton Simon,
who had developed Hunt Foods & Industries into a wide-ranging
conglomerate with interests in groceries, paint, containers, and
magazines. Goldenson had a marked dislike for Simon, who after
purchasing close to 10 percent of ABC's common shares had asked
for and was denied representation on the board. Simon was now
buying additional stock, clearly in preparation for an unfriendly
tender. If successful, he would merge ABC into Hunt and, presumably, eject the current management.

Needing a strong ally, Goldenson approached executives in other
companies with whom he thought he might get along. Probes had
already been made at Litton, General Electric, and General Telephone & Electronics, each of which had capabilities and products
that would make for a nice fit.

In December 1964 Tsai went to see Goldenson to suggest that he
consider a merger with ITT. The ABC president indeed was interested and asked Tsai to pursue the matter. Tsai now contacted
Geneen and learned that ITT was eager to discuss the possibilities.
Meetings were arranged, and after the usual preliminaries, during
which the parties circled one another, seeking strengths and weaknesses, serious discussions began. By early winter, 1965, it had become evident that each company wanted to cooperate, with price
the only important matter to be decided. Careful observers might
have noticed the stream of accountants and lawyers shuttling between the offices of the two firms in midtown Manhattan, but at the
time, Wall Street was pondering a rumor to the effect that ABC had
just about decided to become part of Eastman Kodak.

Turning Point: The Merger Not Made

The announcement of an ITT-ABC merger was made on December 7. The terms called for the transfer of fractional shares of ITT common and a new convertible preferred to ABC's stockholders. The actual dollar figure couldn't be determined, since it depended on the price action of ITT common, but it was in the neighborhood of $200 million, or close to five times the amount that had been paid for Avis.

As it would throughout the period, Wall Street thought Geneen was paying a premium price for what was admittedly a troubled company and that the merger would benefit ABC's stockholders more than it would ITT's. ABC common sold in the high 50s when rumors regarding the acquisition appeared, and the stock was at 65 just prior to the announcement. It immediately shot up to 74 when the news was released and added a dozen more points within the next three months, while ITT traded in a narrow range. In 1967, when the way seemed clear, ABC went beyond the 100 level, only to see the price cut in half once the merger was abandoned. A union with ITT would reward ABC's stockholders and free Goldenson from fears of an unfriendly takeover as well as provide the company with needed capital.

What did Geneen expect to obtain from this acquisition? He had in mind a far-ranging operation based on but not exclusively involved in television, which was more ambitious and innovative than anything then being considered at NBC or CBS. This division would have occupied ITT's attentions and interests for many years and might have become the corporation's main area of business. As such it would require a major portion of ITT's income and would strain borrowing power, perhaps to the exclusion of other significant acquisitions.

The scaffolding was already being erected. In 1965, after the boards of both companies approved the acquisition, Geneen considered support operations into which he would fit ABC. ITT committed $7 million to construct six cable-television systems, utilizing technologies that were then used primarily to bring existing programs into fringe areas where reception was poor. An additional $10 million was budgeted for this purpose in early 1966, by which time Geneen was considering the purchase of more than twenty other cable operations at a cost of more than $100 million. ITT already had approached New York City's Board of Estimate with a proposition to bring cable into Manhattan, and plans were being fashioned to enter other urban areas. ITT also explored television in theaters and pay television, as well as other promising segments of the industry.[4]

Geneen spoke with reporters about the possibility of utilizing ABC's facilities during nonbroadcasting hours to transmit business data around the world. Noting that ITT was the second-largest owner of shares in the new Communications Satellite Corporation (Comsat), he observed that an array of television signals might be bounced off orbiting stations, with ITT the leader in the next stage of television's development.

The ITT-ABC combination would have revenues of $2.2 billion, making it larger than RCA-NBC and shaking up the industry as never before. Now CBS would be the smallest entity in the field, its network destined perhaps to fall to third place. Within weeks of the ITT-ABC announcement came rumors of a merger between CBS and General Electric, and other candidates were discussed later. Industry analysts visualized a situation in which three giant networks, each backed by a wealthy and expansionist-minded parent, would take over most of the independents and smaller chains and so completely dominate the industry in all of its aspects.

Geneen and ITT became the objects of media interest in quite different ways than had previously been the case. Prior to 1965 both had been analyzed, criticized, discussed, and written about as part of the business scene, and although this was interesting and even important to many people, it hardly excited the vast majority of Americans who knew almost nothing about the way big business and its leading practitioners functioned. Now Geneen and ITT were about to become "media objects," involved in the glamorous business of entertainment, and in its most pervasive form—television. Geneen would mingle and conduct business with actors and actresses, writers, directors, producers, and other creative artists. Perhaps he would have to shuttle back and forth between New York and Hollywood, as he already was doing for Brussels. The prospect must have been exciting.

From the first, Geneen had yearned for recognition, not only from his peers but from the general public as well. Simply stated, he liked the idea of becoming a celebrity, though it hadn't been quite so obvious prior to the ABC negotiations. This wasn't unusual; Bluhdorn had felt the same way prior to G + W's acquisition of Paramount. If such sentiments seemed out of character for Geneen, perhaps this was because he had successfully masked his interests up to that time. Those in ITT's executive suites noticed his delight at the thought of becoming involved in this industry, something he hadn't demonstrated for submersible pumps or automobile rentals, and a hitherto disguised sense of humor, even playfulness, came into evidence. Where once he had granted interviews to reporters for business magazines, Geneen now offered his ideas as to proper programming and the public taste to writers of articles for media publications, and he suddenly appeared on the entertainment pages as well as those devoted to finance. A few months after the merger announcement, Geneen was expounding on the successes and failures of ABC's much-publicized "second season," noting that although many of shows hadn't done well in the ratings, one of them, *Batman*, had been a smashing success, making the effort worthwhile. "This is the way to act," said Geneen, perhaps attempting to apply his old rationale to the new business. "Move fast, infuse money, get out of it if it's not working." The interviewer opined, "He sounds like a programming man's dreams come true."[5]

Geneen also felt that the ABC acquisition would make the general public aware of ITT and help the corporation in its other activities. "You can stop fifteen people in the street and not one will know what ITT is. That bothers me," he told a writer for *Time*. "We have to get identification through products or companies." He was quite bitter about a report that although travelers recognized the name Avis, they didn't know much about its parent. Geneen hoped this would change once ABC belonged to the corporation. It might also result in higher profits for other products. On one occasion Geneen was shown a new electronic device turned out by an ISE subsidiary. He asked the price and was told it was to be offered at $30. "If the letters on it were IBM instead of ITT," he snorted, "we could have gotten $60."

Geneen might have reflected that by acquiring ABC he would have succeeded in an area where Behn had failed, for at headquarters he continued to be compared with the Colonel. More important, however, was the view that the merger would fulfill goals he had established almost from the moment of arrival at ITT. With the ABC takeover the corporation would have more than half its revenues from domestic sources and achieve the kind of balance between manufacturing and services Geneen considered desirable.

Both Geneen and Goldenson knew they would have difficulties obtaining approval from relevant federal offices and agencies. The mergermania of the mid-1960s had attracted the attention of anti-trusters at the Federal Trade Commission, where conglomerates in particular were coming under greater scrutiny. Up to then, the commissioners had been interested primarily in the question of whether or not a merger would increase or lessen competition. The conglomerates had won almost all the contests to that time, and even one of the leading critics of takeovers, commissioner Mary Gardiner Jones, had conceded, "The law respecting the anti-competitive impact of conglomerate mergers has not been established."

The ITT-ABC merger wasn't destined to be reviewed by the FTC, however. Perhaps it would have gone through if this had been the case. Rather, the takeover was to be reviewed by the Federal Communications Commission, which would consider other issues as well as that of competition. Under terms of its mandate, the FCC might reject the merger if a majority of its commissioners decided it wasn't in the public interest. Whereas a merger of industrial firms involved transfers and other dispositions of what was essentially private property, in theory, at least, the airwaves belonged to the nation at large, with broadcasters using them on sufferance and as long as they hewed to standards of conduct established and monitored by the FCC. In many of the government's complaints to the FTC, its lawyers would argue that mergers would cause a lessening of competition. This was difficult to prove, but a rational demonstration might be made, and if everyone wasn't happy with the decision, at least it could be debated on commonly accepted ground, using fairly clear-cut standards and empirical evidence. Not so the matter of public interest, which could and often did reflect little more than the suspicions and prejudices of commissioners involved and wasn't susceptible to proof or even demonstration.

The companies' leaders and their attorneys appeared before the FCC on September 19 and 20, 1966, to present their arguments, with Goldenson the key witness and the impact of a merger on ABC of paramount concern. Goldenson presented a picture of an enterprise on the edge of bankruptcy. Although ABC's theaters and other interests were profitable, they couldn't make up the losses sustained by the network and provide funds for modernization. In each of the past four years the broadcasting company had required from $4.6 million to $9 million from its parent to continue in business. Goldenson explained that additional sums were needed to convert to full-time colorcasting, erect new studios, and upgrade equipment, without which ABC couldn't keep pace with the other networks. The bill for all this, he said, would come to $140 million, and all the company had left on its line of credit from Metropolitan Life Insurance was $6 million.[6]

ITT maintained its willingness to fund all of ABC's expenditures —and more, when required to do so. Geneen talked of an expanding network capable of competing with the others because it could draw on the support of a financially secure parent. He testified that ITT intended to enter into an arm's-length relationship with the network, unaffected by "commercial, communications, or other similar interests." Thus, he would create no nexus between ABC and his other ventures in telecommunications. Although he didn't say as much, Geneen implied that his model for all of this would be the situation already in existence between RCA and NBC, which the Commission had never challenged.

This was to be the largest merger in broadcasting history, and as such it attracted a good deal of attention and comment outside as well as within the industry. The hearings were conducted at a time when the Justice Department and the Federal Trade Commission were struggling for a way to deal with conglomerate takeovers, with little success. There would be rumblings out of Capitol Hill each time a major conglomerate announced an important acquisition, and often this would be accompanied by criticism from Donald Turner, head of the Justice Department's Antitrust Division, who asked for new legislation to permit him to deal with such mergers. "In light of the bitterly disputed issues involved, I believe that the courts should demand of Congress that it translate any further directives into something more formidable than sonorous phrases in the pages of the Congressional Record," said Turner the previous year, conceding that he lacked guidelines to prosecute conglomerate mergers. In his view, then, the Justice Department could do little to block acquisitions by conglomerates. Turner ruled out harassment tactics. "It is the duty of the Department of Justice not to bring a case simply on the basis that it thinks it *can* win, but to bring only those cases that it thinks it *should* win," he said. "I think this is far too important an element in our national economic policy to be handled that way."[7]

On September 22 Sen. Gaylord Nelson, Wisconsin Democrat and Chairman of the Subcommittee on Antitrust and Monopoly, wrote a letter to the FCC strongly opposing the forthcoming merger on grounds that it would lessen competition within the industry. This matter soon became the subject for debate, with Nelson leading one faction and a promerger force forming behind Senate Majority Whip Russell Long, Democrat from Louisiana. But new legislation wasn't passed, or for that matter even introduced. Nothing was heard from Turner or from his chief, Attorney General Nicholas Katzenbach, who shared his views regarding the need to await congressional action before moving against the conglomerates.

Ramsey Clark replaced Katzenbach the following month. A judicial activist with strong ties to prominent reformist organizations, Clark insisted on immediate action in support of the Nelson proposal, a stance that brought him into conflict with Turner. The antitrust chief did write a memorandum on the subject in which he argued that the merger raised several "anticompetitive possibilities [that] warrant serious consideration by the commission," but he added that the Justice Department hadn't decided whether the ITT-ABC combination constituted a violation of existing laws. This wasn't exactly the case. Turner was speaking for himself. As for Clark, his mind was made up on the subject: ITT must be blocked. For the time being, however, he was prepared to await developments.

It was against this murky background that the commission handed down its decision on December 21, doing so in a way that all but guaranteed a prolonged public debate on the issue. The merger was to become the battleground upon which an antitrust struggle that had been years in the making would be fought, and at times the struggle overshadowed the actual issues involved in this particular case.

The FCC approved the merger by a vote of 4–3, with the majority sounding like an echo of Goldenson and Geneen: ABC needed major infusions of capital, which could be provided by ITT. Moreover, the commissioners indicated a belief the merger would in no way adversely affect the structure or content of network programming.

Commissioner Nicholas Johnson, author of *How to Talk Back to Your Television Set* and long an articulate critic of the networks and of programming in general, entered a caustic dissent for the minority. A close ally of Ralph Nader and like him an opponent of conglomerates, Johnson cast about for a rationale with which he might attack the merger. Although the FCC had been considering the request for three months, he characterized the action as "hasty" and called the ruling "a mockery of the public responsibility . . . that is perhaps unparalleled in the history of American administrative process." He continued, "Of all the large American corporations there are few whose particular business interests are so clearly of the type which should not be joined with major broadcasting facilities as are those of ITT."[8] But he could offer no justification for such a strong and serious contention other than to say that ITT's overseas operations might interfere with the dissemination of network news.

ITT could hardly defend itself against such an allegation, but neither could Johnson offer evidence that this indeed would be the case. All he could say was, "A hint of the involvement of ITT officials in foreign affairs is conveyed by the fact that three of them are members of foreign legislative bodies, two of the British House of Lords and one of the French National Assembly." To call the House of Lords a "legislative body" was certainly stretching the point, and these officials weren't in a position to influence U.S. domestic operations. This was a thin reed, as Johnson must have realized, since RCA, Westinghouse, and virtually every American firm that owned television and radio stations and also had extensive foreign operations utilized prominent nationals in visible posts, as did ITT, and for the same reason: to obtain and maintain contacts with governments and other markets for goods and services.

Significantly, Johnson didn't raise the antitrust issue, for had he done so ITT might have responded that other multi-industry firms had acquired radio and television stations without such a challenge. General Tire & Rubber, for example, had taken over RKO General without encountering problems. Johnson's protest couldn't block the merger, of course, but it did indicate that antitrusters and critics of conglomerates had singled out ITT as the exemplar for the group and the focus of their attack. This may have been more the result of happenstance than of design. Had LTV or G + W attempted to acquire CBS or ABC, it, and not ITT, would have come under this kind of criticism. Even then, Johnson's arguments had little effect outside a relatively small circle. Ramsey Clark was on his side, as was Gaylord Nelson. Donald Turner still had no clear-cut ideas regarding antitrust action, and apparently no one in the Washington press corps solicited his opinions on the matter. Instead the minority position received most of the play in the newspapers. Still, at the time, it was considered of interest only to the FCC, with no direct bearing upon antitrust proceedings. The effective date for the merger was set for January 20, 1967, with no apparent reason to believe anything would come along to alter conditions.

Now there occurred a revolution at Justice. Clark took virtual control of the case and asked the FCC for a delay, implying that unless one was granted he would institute antitrust proceedings. The Department's central argument was novel and may have indicated this was more in the nature of a probe than anything else. Clark noted that with ABC in hand, Geneen would have to abandon cable operations, so as to hew to existing FCC regulations regarding the proper spheres of interest for network owners, and that this would lessen competition in that part of the industry. Justice also questioned the majority's contention that the merger wouldn't affect the structure of network programming.

Had Clark let it go at this, sufficient grounds might have been established for a protest, even for a court battle. But he went beyond this point, impugning the integrity and intentions of the parties. He criticized the FCC for accepting at face value "assurances of good conduct." "Moreover, rather than planning to invest large amounts in the capital improvements of ABC, ITT appears to have expected ABC to produce a large cash flow which would be available to use outside of the broadcasting industry." In other words, the merger was supposed to be more in the interests of ITT than of ABC.

Wall Street disagreed. At the news of the delay of the merger, ABC common stock collapsed by more than 14 points, whereas ITT rose a point and a half. Industry experts, analysts, and investors were saying that the merger would be far more advantageous for ABC than for ITT.

The FCC refused to budge, initiating a war of nerves between the majority there and the Justice Department, neither of which intended to back down in the face of pressure from the other. The following day, however, both ITT and ABC asked for a delay, at the same time urging the FCC to reject the motion to reconsider. Turner sent out a clear signal that he would take the FCC to court if it didn't review the situation—and, presumably, reverse the decision.

This drew criticism from Senator Long, who told reporters that if the Justice Department intended "to make a big antitrust case against this proposed merger, [it] certainly should have done it a long time ago, prior to the time that the merger was announced, and

without having a $69 million unfavorable impact upon the stock of
ITT and ABC."[9] Critics responded by noting that Long might have
been influenced by the fact that ITT had just broken ground for a
new facility in his home state of Louisiana. Tempers were heating
up and the level of argument was declining that February.

Late in the month ITT announced that it would lend ABC $25
million to ease its cash shortage; several reporters implied that the
network really didn't need the money and that the loan had been
arranged so as to reinforce the companies' repeated claims that ABC
would suffer greatly unless the merger were allowed to take place.

By early March *The New York Times* and the *Wall Street Journal*
were suggesting that the FCC was about to reopen hearings in the
belief that the Justice Department would win a case brought against
ITT in the District of Columbia, because of the liberal, antibusiness
bias of the courts there. Whether or not this was so was still being
discussed when, on March 16, the FCC agreed to a new hearing. In
reporting the story, the *Wall Street Journal* observed, "The FCC's
handling of the case has been attacked by the Justice Department's
Antitrust Division, the American Civil Liberties Union, Congressmen, journalists, and even auto safety critic Ralph Nader," all of
which was true. Perhaps not since the end of the war had so many
large groups and interests arrayed themselves against a single corporation involved in a merger. Little wonder, then, that ITT's top
management, having been frustrated at the last moment in its attempts to acquire ABC, came to look upon themselves as victims of
a concerted attack, and upon such individuals as enemies.

The second round of hearings opened on April 10 and continued
until April 26. Both sides obtained expert testimony in their behalf
and introduced voluminous documents to support contentions, but
from the first it appeared that ITT and ABC would be on the
defensive throughout. For example, an official of Metropolitan Life
said that his company had recently increased ABC's loan capabilities from $42.5 million to $70 million. "We felt our $70 million loan
would be safe," said vice-president Charles Charbonnier, who went
on to imply that even more money might be available if needed. To
this Goldenson replied that ABC would need $185 million, and that
such an amount wouldn't be forthcoming from anyone except ITT.
Geneen continued to assert that ABC's relationship with ITT
would be "completely unique," and that the parent would make no
attempt to influence news coverage. Once again, ITT's critics

brought in materials relating to its activities in foreign countries, some of them military dictatorships. Might not ITT try to kill network reports criticizing such regimes? Geneen denied this would happen; his opponents indicated their disbelief.

This was followed by testimony by several reporters who told of having been approached by ITT officials who claimed their coverage was unfair and slanted. One told of being "badgered" and subjected to "nasty and accusatory language." Eileen Shanahan, of *The New York Times*, said that on February 1 ITT's vice-president for public relations, Edward Gerrity, and another official came to see her to deliver a company statement, at which time she and Gerrity talked about the fairness of her reporting. "He asked if I didn't feel I had a responsibility to shareholders who might lose money from what I wrote," said Shanahan, for both ITT and ABC common were gyrating wildly on reports written by her and others. "I told him no," she reported. Apparently this meeting wasn't too unusual or unpleasant; businessmen and others who feel they were treated badly often discuss the matter with reporters, and both sides are familiar with the give-and-take. A former newspaperman himself, Gerrity certainly appreciated this point. But other encounters ended badly. John Horner, ITT's public-relations director in Washington, called Shanahan, who testified that he said her coverage had been "unfair from the beginning." The reporter said she yelled at him that he was insulting both her and the *Times* editors and that she hung up the phone.[10] Such testimony tended to cast doubt on Geneen's claims that ITT wouldn't interfere with ABC news, and indicated the growing friction between the corporation and the media.

The second round of hearings may have influenced legislators, reporters, and the general public, but it didn't alter the situation at the FCC. On June 22 the commission once again approved the ITT-ABC merger, again by a vote of 4–3. "It's our firm judgement," said the majority, "that the merger, by providing ABC with a stronger financial base, will significantly assist ABC in making the necessary long-range plans and in taking the risks in this area [of news and cultural programming] so vitally important to the American public." As expected, the minority responded with a strongly worded attack, longer and more biting than the rejoinder that followed the initial approval, in December 1966, in which ITT was roundly castigated. It charged that many of Geneen's statements had to be taken

Turning Point: The Merger Not Made

with "a mound of salt." "[Some company testimony] has been so lacking in candor, so careless of the need to inform us in an honest and forthright way, that it is simply incredible that the majority can place such abiding faith in their every word." As for news policy, the minority contended, "There is a very significant danger that ITT's other interests will be allowed to intrude on the journalistic functioning of ABC and subvert the proper use of this electronic outlet for independent information, news, opinion, and public affairs programming." The following day some of ITT's defenders observed that if this occurred, the FCC would have the power to take away ITT's licenses, in which case the corporation would suffer a great financial loss, but such arguments had little impact within this highly emotional atmosphere.

Now it was the Justice Department's turn to act. Somewhat reluctantly, Turner recommended antitrust proceedings on July 20, and the department announced it would oppose the merger on these grounds and seek a reversal of the FCC decision. ABC common stock promptly lost 32 points on heavy trading. Spokesmen for ABC and ITT said they were "deeply disappointed" and would contest the action. Four days later, however, the companies agreed to delay their merger until the court ruled on it, and this was taken as a clear sign that Goldenson and Geneen weren't eager for a prolonged legal struggle. So was the news that ITT planned to acquire the home-building firm of Levitt & Sons and, a few months later, Rayonier, the forest-products company. Geneen was turning in another direction, bitter at having failed to obtain ABC but apparently coming to terms with the idea. The matter simply dropped from the headlines, with little more about the acquisition and the controversy surrounding it heard from either company.

On New Year's Day, 1968, ITT and ABC announced they had decided to abandon plans to merge. Goldenson said he now would seek some other large, financially secure firm that might be interested in taking over at ABC, pointedly suggesting there had been a vendetta against ITT. He added that the network was continuing to lose money and that immediate and major cash infusions would be required. As before, the corporation's critics charged that this was a scare tactic designed to promote a takeover, and that ABC not only was viable but really throwing off profits. This certainly wasn't so. Goldenson was obliged to go to the capital markets several times in the next few years, borrowing money at what were then high rates. In early 1968, ABC's funded debt came to $84.4 million; a year later it would be $143.5 million, and would peak at $177.4 million in 1970 before declining. Perhaps Goldenson had exaggerated ABC's need for additional capital, but that such was the case could hardly be doubted in the light of subsequent events.

A spokesman for Geneen offered some routine thoughts on the matter but soon turned to plans for future acquisitions. The corporation wanted to put the matter behind it as rapidly as possible. The following day the FCC asked the federal appeals court to dismiss the pending suit, and this was done. The most hotly contested merger in recent history had been thwarted by the Justice Department, the FCC minority, and their allies.

Even then this was recognized as a turning point for ITT. Had the merger gone through, Geneen would have been obliged to mount a major effort in telecommunications and entertainment. As Wall Street noted in appraising the merger, this would have resulted in lower earnings per share for ITT and a major dilution of equity, which in all probability would have been translated into declines in the prices of the corporation's common and convertible preferred stocks, making them less attractive to potential takeover candidates. Conglomeratization would have slowed down at ITT, with Geneen obliged to move ahead with what he already had—which is to say that ITT would have resembled a more coherently structured corporation than what it was to become. Finally, the domestic businesses would have been more important than ever and in time might have overshadowed the foreign sector—management's hope since the end of World War II.

The Justice Department had won an initial victory against the conglomerates, but it was incomplete, flawed, and unsatisfactory for all involved. No new legislation had been passed or guiding principle established. The case hadn't been tried, and even had Justice won its point in court, the victory would have been on the narrowest of grounds. Thus, nothing had changed insofar as the government's approach to conglomeratization was concerned. But a beginning had been made, and there was also a target: ITT. In 1968 it appeared likely there would be another round in the struggle, perhaps after the next big acquisition—or the ones that followed.

ITT had attracted other opponents in the course of its efforts to acquire ABC. Many reformers, led by the American Civil Liberties Union and Ralph Nader's public-interest organization, had come to

Turning Point: The Merger Not Made

view the corporation as the symbol of much that was unjust and perhaps even evil in American business. A number of journalists, angered by clashes with ITT's public-relations people, entertained similar sentiments, which would surface in their writings. ITT's attempt to become a media-oriented corporation ended with its having an extremely poor reputation among several of the leading practitioners in the field. This was dangerous in a period when advocacy journalism was coming into vogue.

Finally, much had been made of ITT's overseas interests, which had been painted by Johnson and others as somewhat sinister, even against the national good, though why this was so hadn't been made clear. ITT was being castigated as a conglomerate at the time of the initial announcement of merger, even while many who did so—at Justice and elsewhere—weren't certain why this form of business organization was to be feared more than any other. By 1967 interest had been focused on ITT's activities as a multinational corporation, which to some appeared vaguely undemocratic and in a way associated with repressive forces. Perhaps this had to do with growing opposition to the Vietnam conflict and the arguments put forth by some critics that the United States had entered the struggle there at the behest of businesses that profited from the war. Such allegations had been made regarding participation in World War II, and at the time, Colonel Behn was portrayed as a stateless individual with little concern for anything but his corporation, which he would defend even at the expense of the national interest. And, of course, ITT had been one of the firms charged with collaborating with and even supporting Hitler before and during World War II. Every twentieth-century war had nourished fear and hatred of American firms with overseas operations, and it was happening again in the late 1960s.

In seeking ABC, Geneen had hoped to enter a growth industry that would provide ITT with a greater stake in the domestic economy and make it less of a multinational. This was his clear intention from the time he arrived at headquarters, and Geneen's aspirations in this regard had been reinforced by the Cuban expropriation. As it happened, everything went wrong. Geneen and his staff turned once again to the tasks of conglomeratization in 1968, but the struggle wouldn't be forgotten. Not at ITT or the Justice Department, in the press or among pressure groups. Ironically, Geneen's most important acquisition turned out to be the one he didn't make.

13

Annus Mirabilis: 1968

ITT set about dismantling its cable and other television operations shortly after Geneen abandoned hope of acquiring ABC. The decision to do so appeared to have been made hastily, more in dismay and anger than a result of careful reflection as to consequences and possibilities.

Neither the Justice Department nor the FCC minority had challenged the corporation's right to own and develop cable properties; on the contrary, Turner had implied that ITT might prove a beneficial force in that part of the industry. It already had a beachhead in several segments, and the financial and management skills to become the leading force in an area that a dozen years later was to challenge the networks themselves (and may yet dominate the medium). More so even than industry veterans and prominent show-business executives, Geneen had demonstrated that he possessed a set of clear, imaginative ideas on how television's future might best be shaped and on the relationship between content, technology, and management. He obviously had the intelligence and drive to perform the necessary tasks. Yet he decided to clean house. Within less than a year, ITT had shut down or sold off all of its television and related holdings, with nothing to show for the ventures but sour memories, bruised feelings, and a tax write-off. Among these companies were several that were to become parts of large, rapidly growing systems. In addition, ITT divested itself of Cablevision, which under different ownership would become the leader in pay-television programming during the late 1970s.

In retrospect, the decision to leave the cable field appears one of Geneen's major missteps, perhaps as significant to the development of his corporation as had been the failure to acquire ABC. It may have come as a reaction to that setback, the product of sheer frustration, but there was more to it than that. This was an unusual, even bizarre period, not only for ITT and business in general but in virtually all aspects of American life. Geneen couldn't help being affected by the supercharged atmosphere of the time. A turning point in American affairs came in 1968, which was for the post–World War II generation what 1929 had been for an earlier one.

A decade later novelist and critic John Hersey would write, "There had been no other year in our history with such multiple seismic tremors as '68 was to bring." Surprises abounded. "No single one of its shocks was to turn the country around," he continued, "but the shocks were to keep coming, and coming."

The year opened with the usual spate of peace rumors out of Vietnam, which were quickly dispelled. American forces crossed over into Cambodia, and later the North Vietnamese and Viet Cong launched the Tet offensive, a daring attempt to take Saigon. Meanwhile the North Koreans seized the USS *Pueblo* and imprisoned its eighty-three–man crew. Not only was the Vietnam War expanding but there were indications the United States might become involved in a second conflict on the Asian mainland at a time when national demoralization was obvious and weariness with the struggle was on the rise.

Then came the shocks: Johnson's withdrawal from the presidential race, the assassinations of Martin Luther King and Robert Kennedy. The disastrous Democratic National Convention in Chicago was the most important but by no means the only sign that the nation was cracking apart at the seams, its political life veering out of control.

I·T·T: The Management of Opportunity

All of this diverted some attention from a badly overheating economy. Early in the year Johnson imposed mandatory curbs on investments abroad and pressed for a tax increase to stem inflation while at the same time presenting Congress with a record $186-billion budget. Without additional taxes, he said, spending would far outrun income, resulting in greater inflation, much higher interest rates, and problems with the balance of international payments. The Europeans and Japanese welcomed the President's initiatives. For years they had seen a rising tide of dollars engulf their economies. Once the world's most prized currency, it had become a glut on the market, contributing to other countries' own inflationary spirals and threatening their well-being. A flight from the dollar that had begun earlier now accelerated, with central bankers obliged to permit gold not in their vaults and utilized in international settlements to float. Some of these dollars were used to purchase the metal, a traditional storehouse of value in troubled times, but more was sent to the exchanges, to buy stocks, in what was the last and wildest stage in the great bull market. Thus it appeared that while the rest of the country was in agony, Wall Street was celebrating.

Henry Luce's "American Century" was one of the victims of the national malaise of 1968. Foreign difficulties and an endless war cast doubt on the ability of the country's leaders to steer America through in safety, while domestic problems in such matters as race and "life-styles" threatened the social fabric. Certain basic, shared truths that had gone unquestioned since the end of World War II now came under attack, and one of these was a belief that a variant of capitalism not only best served the nation but was at harmony with essential democracy. To some critics the system represented much that was wrong with the society and its people. To antiwar activists, businessmen had finagled to prod America into the Vietnam War in order to obtain profits. Ecology-minded reformers drew attention to the destruction of the landscape by commercial interests. Ralph Nader and other critics condemned capitalism for having created what they deemed to be a shabby, reprobate civilization. In the jargon of the time, many were "turned off" by the profit motive.

The ingredients for an antibusiness crusade were in place by 1968, with the multinational and conglomerate corporations the most visible and hence the most likely targets, since they had come to symbolize modern American business. But the mergermania continued, with most corporate leaders apparently unaware of ominous portents. Gulf + Western, Teledyne, Walter Kidde, and Litton announced or entered into discussions for important acquisitions. James Ling took over another conglomerate, Greatamerica, at a cost of over $500 million in new bonds. Then, without waiting to digest it, he made a tender offer for the stock of Jones & Laughlin (Geneen's onetime employer). Within a few months he had more than 60 percent of the steel company's shares at a cost of another $500 million. Yet even this paled in comparison to the explosion of activity at ITT.

In 1968 Geneen acquired twenty domestic companies with combined assets approximating a billion dollars at a cost of slightly more than that in securities and cash, and in addition he took in a handful of foreign concerns while accelerating the development of properties already under the ITT banner. In 1963 Geneen had promised to double revenues and earnings in his second five years there, and he had done far better than that. By any yardstick, this was an impressive performance, carried out at a dizzying pace. During one board meeting, that of June 12, 1968, he presented the members with proposals for the acquisitions of such diverse firms as Continental Baking, Pennsylvania Glass Sand, Speedwriting, and Tarabochia Marine Hydraulic. The board also learned of a plan to augment ITT Consumer Services by purchasing interests in Airway Lodge of Columbus, Airway Lodge of Tulsa, and Hospital Parking Company of America. Geneen discussed the creation of a new division, ITT Aerospace/Optical. He sketched a plan for the purchase of Gotham Lighting and the proposed sales of hotels in several states and one in Sweden, as well as the purchase of land in Key Biscayne, Florida.[1]

Five of the 1968 acquisitions were of considerable size and future importance to the corporation. In addition to Continental Baking and Pennsylvania Glass Sand, these were Levitt, Sheraton, and Rayonier. At the time, all appeared to fulfill several of Geneen's objectives: to stress domestic rather than overseas operations, to diversify out of telephonic and electronic products, to seek service-oriented firms, and to deemphasize reliance on military orders. Each had impressive resources and was well known in its field, and Geneen must have believed these entities capable of becoming major profit centers and meshing well with other ITT holdings to which they were related. He indicated as much in that year's annual report, confidently asserting, "We have shown the unique capability to handle new problems and new opportunities, and to continue to build constructively at a high rate of profitable growth as our diversification broadens and the company grows in each area."

By then there were five general categories in which ITT participated: Telecommunications, Consumer Products, Consumer and Business Services, Natural Resources, and Defense-Space. From Geneen's words and actions it appeared additions were being contemplated. Readers and listeners might understandably have concluded that the corporation had penetrated all corners of the globe and become omnipresent. As Geneen himself said, "ITT is constantly at work around the international clock—in 67 countries on six continents." The scope of the corporation's activities extended "from the Arctic to the Antarctic and quite literally from the bottom of the sea to the moon. . . ."

Later on this would be recognized as Geneen's high noon of self-confidence.

As it turned out, several of the acquisitions proved unwise and one a conceded mistake. Even those operations that had creditable showings in the early 1970s didn't do so because of any major alteration brought about by ITT, and in at least one case the company performed poorly as a result of the parent's programs. Of course, all of this can be appreciated only in retrospect. In addition, many of the developing problems stemmed from domestic and world conditions, as well as government actions, over which Geneen had no control. Taking all of this into account, however, one must conclude that Geneen's reputation as the most successful and innovative conglomerateur and manager of his time was tarnished by some of the moves he made in 1968.

Levitt & Sons was the initial and, by any standard, the most misbegotten of the takeovers. Negotiations were protracted, marked by delays and interruptions and the clash of two colossal egos.

They began in late January, 1966, with what was supposed to have been a social meeting between Rohatyn and an old Middlebury classmate, Joel Carr, who was a Levitt vice-president and general counsel. Talk turned to business after a while, and Carr said that William Levitt, the company's president, might be interested in a merger if the terms were right.

Annus Mirabilis: 1968

As the most famous name in home construction, Levitt & Sons could be expected to command a premium price. Sales for 1965 had come to $60 million, having doubled over the past three years. The backlog was at a record; revenues would rise to $74 million in 1966. It was a most profitable operation as well; earnings for 1965 had been $2.6 million, another record, and would go to $3.3 million the following year. Despite this, Levitt's stock had performed indifferently during the bull market, in large part because housing and related issues weren't deemed glamorous at a time when most of Wall Street's interest was concentrated on high-technology, conglomerate, and specialty issues. At $13 per share Levitt had a price-earnings ratio of 15, which was low for that period.

Levitt must have known that the value of his own holdings would increase should his firm become part of a conglomerate whose stock was a feature at the exchange, but that was not the only consideration. By nature, the housing industry required large amounts of capital, which could be tied up for years in unsold units, those under construction, and land. This was one of the major reasons that housing, one of the nation's largest businesses, hadn't spawned a single dominant firm. Given sufficient capital, Levitt might grow to major proportions, something Rohatyn was quick to appreciate. He dictated a memo on the subject to André Meyer, indicating his belief that this was an attractive acquisition candidate in almost every respect. There were some difficulties, however. "The problem will undoubtedly be Mr. Levitt's personal ambitions and requirements for continued unquestionable control over the operation once the company is owned by somebody else, and possibly an overinflated idea of value." Rohatyn mentioned several firms that might be approached, among them Gulf Oil, Holiday Inns, Georgia Pacific, and Kaiser Industries. ITT wasn't on his list, perhaps through oversight, or a belief that Geneen was too concerned with the ABC acquisition to consider Levitt at that time. Or it might have been that he believed that two strong, self-assured leaders like William Levitt and Geneen couldn't work together in harness. "Mr. Levitt is apparently a rather mercurial individual," he wrote to Meyer, "with a highly developed sense of his own importance and requiring a somewhat highly personalized approach."[2] People such as this didn't last long at ITT, and Rohatyn may have sensed the match would be wrong. Nonetheless, he prepared a memo on Levitt for Hart Perry, for transmission to Geneen. "I basically do not believe that this is a business ITT should get into," commented Perry, adding, however, "The record certainly suggests that Levitt has done a better job than most in producing a record of steady growth in recent years." Geneen agreed with the assessment, and the matter was dropped for the time being.

During the next three months Lazard continued to seek a possible partner for Levitt. One of the firm's associates, Peter Lewis, was assigned to the project, and he concluded that the most likely candidates would be found in the defense and utilities industries, the former because they could use Levitt as a means to diversify out of a business bound to suffer once the Vietnam War was ended and the latter, utilities, because with regulatory constraints it paid for them to diversify. Lewis wanted to approach such firms as Boeing, Douglas, North American, and General Telephone. Like Rohatyn, he was cognizant of William Levitt's inflated ego, and he felt, for example, that the top executives at Lockheed would be able to deal with him. "Levitt and Lockheed talk the same language," wrote Lewis, who believed a merger between the two might be worked out.

Geneen, too, was focusing on Levitt. Believing ABC was safely aboard, he was casting around restlessly for other takeover possibilities, preferably in an industry that like television would break new ground for ITT. He asked Rohatyn to prepare another memo as to projections, possibilities, and terms. This was done, preliminary negotiations were commenced, and additional reports on Levitt were delivered to both parties on May 10. In one of these, Rohatyn indicated that Levitt & Sons would benefit from having ITT's considerable financial resources at its disposal, and in addition could expect a premium price for its stock. ITT would also be well served by such a takeover. Rohatyn wrote that Geneen would be acquiring "a professionally managed company in a service business with considerable world-wide growth potential." William Levitt's reaction to this indicated that Rohatyn's assessment of his temperament was on target; he edited it to read that Levitt & Sons had "an *almost unlimited* world-wide *and domestic* growth potential."[3]

Now the companies entered into direct negotiations. By then it had become a familiar process at ITT; Stanley Luke, Robert Kenmore, Hart Perry, and others swung into action, as they had so often during the past few years. This was a new experience for Levitt & Sons, however, and apparently proved jarring for its senior executives, Richard Wasserman, Norman Young, and Norman Peterfreund, all relatively young men who were alternately impressed and disturbed by the ITT approach. William Levitt wasn't particularly pleased with the way he was treated by ITT counterparts, accustomed as he was to being the central figure at the firm that bore his name. Now he was being asked to permit it to become a relatively small segment of a huge international corporation, and at a time when Geneen seemed far more interested in television than in home-building. In many ways it was the Avis–Robert Townsend experience all over again, but Levitt proved far more determined to retain his independence and had an even greater sense of self-esteem than did Townsend. That he was having second thoughts about the takeover became evident that late summer and autumn, when he took offense at what he deemed cavalier treatment from the ITT hierarchy. Levitt wanted direct and usually immediate access to Geneen, whom he considered equal in status, and more often than not he had to deal with Perry, Luke, or others at headquarters. It was a foretaste of what might be expected once Levitt & Sons became part of ITT, and Levitt didn't like the feeling. A king in his own company, he would be a duke—perhaps less—at ITT.

Levitt met with some Lazard executives, including former Avis leader Donald Petrie, on November 1, and indicated irritation at all the time Geneen was devoting to ABC, implying he didn't value Levitt & Sons as much as he should. He told Lazard that unless ITT concluded its deal with him without awaiting the outcome of the ABC merger, he would prefer to be free of all obligations. Geneen said he was willing to proceed on that basis, and the negotiations continued.

More aware than before of Levitt's easily ruffled feelings, executives at Lazard and ITT wooed and flattered the man. Geneen expressed embarrassment at the delay, apologized for the amount of time he had to spend on the ABC matter, and assured Levitt of his dedication to home-building. Moreover, he promised to make it up to the people at Levitt in the form of a higher price for their shares. But the delays continued. Finally, in early January of 1967—after the FCC approved of the ITT-ABC merger—Geneen told Levitt that their merger could be completed in less than ninety days, to which Levitt replied, somewhat irascibly, "Harold, don't tell me any dates in the future. Call me when you are ready and we will do the deal in twenty minutes."[4]

Rumors that Levitt was about to be acquired had reached Wall

Street by then, and its common stock rose sharply, hitting an all-time high of 19 in February. Geneen had said ITT would pay a good price for Levitt, but Rohatyn didn't think Geneen would go much beyond the present quotation, inflated as it had become by merger-mania. Late that month, as William Levitt was becoming even more exasperated by delays, Rohatyn prepared for a breakdown of negotiations. By April, Lazard had decided that Levitt might use some of its stock to acquire other firms in related businesses, perhaps to salvage something from what was deemed an end to hopes of an ITT takeover. News of this reached ITT, which reacted with hurried conversations with Levitt, who was assured of Geneen's continued interest. The FCC was expected to decide on the ABC merger by June 30, said Geneen, who told Levitt that their combination would take place shortly thereafter. Levitt was willing to accept this at face value but said that he would go ahead with his own acquisitions program.

June 30 came and went with no decision, and Stanley Luke went to Levitt's Long Island headquarters to ask for yet another delay, this time until the end of July. Levitt agreed, but by his manner and his choice of words he indicated he didn't believe anything would develop and that chances for a successful merger were dim. In effect, he told Luke that Geneen would have to fish or cut bait—and that he expected he would do the latter. As though to underline his feelings, Levitt left the meeting early, implying that his other affairs were more important than yet one more fruitless negotiation with ITT.

Geneen now decided to plunge ahead and told Luke to negotiate the deal even though the ABC matter was unresolved. A merger was announced on July 22, with the actual date to be determined later. As it happened, completion was delayed until the ITT-ABC merger was abandoned. Levitt & Sons became part of ITT on February 11, 1968, at which time its stockholders received fractional shares of the new parent. As Geneen had promised, Levitt's stockholders were rewarded for their wait. The price came to more than $30 per share in ITT common, for a total of slightly less than $92 million. (This appeared a gross overpayment, but it should be considered that ITT's paper was every bit as inflated as Levitt's in early 1968.) Geneen told reporters, "[Levitt is] the ideal vehicle for ITT to participate in the United States and abroad in the revolution in housing which will take place in the next decade and of which we intend to be a part." Levitt was much more expansive. He spoke of large projects on four continents and predicted that his company—which had yet to gross $100 million a year—would have annual revenues exceeding a billion dollars by 1980. This implied that large cash infusions would be needed from ITT, perhaps as much as would have been required had Geneen succeeded in acquiring ABC. Instead of pouring funds into programming and television facilities, ITT would be asked by Levitt to purchase large tracts of land for new communities, and perhaps even to underwrite mortgages.

It is doubtful Geneen appreciated just what he was getting into when he acquired the home-building company. Nor did he fully gauge how difficult it would be to work with William Levitt, who almost immediately after the takeover provided ample evidence of his continuing independence. Although he had some kind words for his new "partner," Levitt indicated he would remain in charge at company headquarters. "We will become part of ITT, but we'll operate autonomously with the same management, same everything," he said, adding ominously, "We may or may not even use the ITT logo. It's optional."[5]

It had been a trying period for Rohatyn, Lewis, and others at Lazard involved with the merger, and the reward was commensurate with the effort. The bank's fee for its services came to more than a quarter of a million dollars.[6]

ITT's next important acquisition, Sheraton Corporation of America, met all the criteria Geneen had established for major takeovers destined to become cores of new divisions. Sheraton was the nation's largest hotel chain and in addition owned Thompson Industries, a supplier of automobile parts. It was a stagnant corporation, many of whose properties were run-down, outdated, located in declining areas, and badly in need of repairs. Returns on capital and sales were among the lowest in the industry, and prospects for a turnaround under existing management were bleak. All this was reflected in the price of its stock. Sheraton had revenues and assets each exceeding a quarter of a billion dollars, but the value of its common stock in late 1966 came to less than $60 million.

Geneen's interest in the industry probably developed during the Avis negotiations; he would have been quick to recognize the relationship between hotels and automobile-leasing. There was a similar nexus for construction and hotels, and this might have surfaced in discussions with Levitt. Whatever the origins, Kenmore was asked to investigate several hotel operations during the late spring and early summer of 1966, and by July he had settled on Sheraton as the most likely takeover candidate. The chain needed large amounts of capital for refurbishing and expansion as well as additions to management, both of which ITT could contribute. Moreover, the corporation's financial strategy was badly outdated. Sheraton was essentially a real-estate company, realizing large benefits from depreciation accounts that didn't show up as profits, and this contributed to the generally sluggish performance both within the industry and on Wall Street. Changes in this area alone could result in dramatic increases in cash flow and return on investment. The pruning of old properties might provide substantial sums and eventually lead to increased earnings. "It may now be possible for us to gain entry into this field on a broad basis at an extremely advantageous price through a vehicle which already operates in all aspects of the field simultaneously," wrote Kenmore. "Furthermore, we think significant potential exists for materially increasing the earnings of the company so that our ultimate cost of entry shouldn't prove to be very expensive indeed." The thought pleased Geneen, who marked off this segment of the report with a heavy pencil.[7]

Exploratory talks with Sheraton began soon after, and from the first it was evident that top management there was interested in a takeover. The aging president, Ernest Henderson, had recently taken a new bride and was showing more concern for his private life than for the corporation he had founded. He didn't think his son, Ernest Henderson III, capable of running the operation, and in any case the young man was more interested in starting out on his own than in managing the decrepit chain. In addition, both may have realized the ITT people hadn't a particularly clear notion of just how much capital would be needed to revive the corporation, or for that matter how to operate a hotel chain and its related enterprises. Others at Sheraton were delighted with the idea of becoming part of ITT, especially since the Hendersons were notorious for paying low salaries and Geneen was known to be quite generous when it came to remuneration.

ITT's offer was made in late October, by which time rumors regarding a takeover had reached Wall Street, causing Sheraton's stock to rise to 25, which was two and a half times what it had been a year earlier. As had become his pattern, Geneen offered fractional shares of ITT common and convertible preferred for Sheraton's common. Then followed several months during which details were settled and employment contracts entered into, and the actual acquisition was completed on February 28, 1968, slightly more than two weeks after the Levitt deal. The price in ITT paper came to $193 million, or $35 per Sheraton share, a level the stock had never been able to achieve on its own.

Geneen promptly renamed his new subsidiary ITT Sheraton, and the initials appeared prominently in all of the hotels. He had hoped to make the public aware of ITT through the acquisition of ABC. Now Sheraton was supposed to provide this visibility. The ITT letters would be affixed to other acquisitions made later on, and were even added to some earlier ones. Levitt wouldn't be one of these, on orders from William Levitt himself. This proved a forerunner of problems to come.

As expected, Geneen dispatched squads of managers and accountants to Sheraton, giving them a mandate to whip the company into shape. The newcomers elbowed aside veterans, many of whom were shocked by such a display of dynamism and force and proved incapable of adjusting to this kind of treatment. "There were constant reviews," recalled one of them in horror. "There must have been thirty-odd ITT task forces. We had reports coming out of our ears. The ITT people wanted to know too much. They were overdoing it, and our people, especially operating people such as hotel managers, rebelled. We lost a lot of them before ITT saw the light."[8]

This may have been precisely what Geneen had wanted—a general housecleaning. He either discharged redundant or unsatisfactory officers and managers or permitted them to resign, eliminated unnecessary and uneconomical divisions, and began selling off several of the run-down properties. Then he developed a five-year plan to expand into Europe and the Near East, updated facilities, and tripled the number of rooms.

Ernest Henderson died in 1967, before much of this could be seen, but even had he lived, there hardly would have been a place for him at the new ITT Sheraton. Ernest Henderson III resigned a year later to enter the nursing-home business. To take his place, Geneen selected Philip Lowe, an aggressive specialist in investments who had virtually no direct experience in the industry. Blunt and often harsh, Lowe knew how to prune a decaying operation. His heavy-handed approach antagonized those professionals remaining from the Henderson era, resulting in a steady stream of resignations.

Lowe had Geneen's support, however, as he slashed costs and instituted efficient controls, obtaining short-term results that showed up in the balance sheets. These helped mask the large infusion of funds into ITT Sheraton, which caused belt-tightening in other parts of the corporation.

In 1969 ITT announced a five-year plan to invest some $865 million in an expansion program plus an additional $81 million in new hotel properties constructed for Sheraton to manage. By then some Wall Street analysts had concluded that the hotel chain was a white elephant, and rumors abounded that Geneen would dispose of it given a chance to do so with a modicum of grace. One industry observer dubbed Sheraton "ITT's Vietnam," surely an exaggeration but one with at least a grain of truth. Solace was derived from the growth of Thompson Industries, where revenues and profits increased, but this detracted little from the embarrassment caused by Sheraton's performance in the late 1960s. In time the chain would recover and prosper, but only after alterations in plans, changes in management, and the development of new approaches. Even then, Sheraton's rebirth was due at least as much to a brightening of the industry picture as to anything instituted by ITT. Geneen might have done better by entering the field fresh, rather than trying to revive Sheraton the way he did, but of course this is a matter of hindsight.

On August 13, 1967, ITT announced that discussions were under way for the acquisition of Rayonier, a medium-size forest-products company being shepherded by Felix Rohatyn. The news caused no great stir, either on Wall Street or within the industry, since ITT was constantly on the lookout for takeovers, and Rayonier had considered several offers, the most recent from Owens-Illinois, before coming to Geneen. Negotiations proceeded smoothly, and the acquisition was completed the following April at a cost of $293 million in ITT common and preferred. This worked out to more than $47 per Rayonier common, double what it had been selling for prior to the announcement. For its assistance, Lazard received a fee of $600,000.

Rayonier possessed several attractive assets, which accounted for ITT's interest and the price paid, but the company was also troubled, and this was the reason management sought a merger partner. There were several modern, up-to-date facilities recently completed; close to a million acres of land in Georgia, Florida, and

Colonel Sosthenes Behn, who founded ITT in 1920 and led the corporation for more than a quarter of a century, at the height of his power.

Sosthenes Behn started out as a banker at the Morton Trust Company in New York, and at the time he grew a beard so as to look older and more mature. This picture was taken around 1902, when Behn was 20.

Hernand Behn, the Colonel's brother, was chief operating officer of ITT in all but title until his death in 1933.

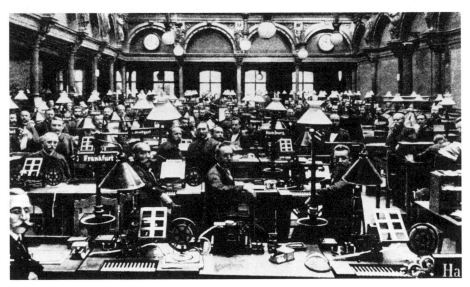

The "traffic room" of the Berlin main telephone central office, circa 1900, which used a large amount of equipment manufactured by companies later to become part of ITT.

In the early 1920s most tele-communications equipment was put together at workbenches, as at this French ITT installation of the period.

ITT's New York headquarters until 1961, the 67 Broad Street building commanded a sweeping view of New York Harbor, and to-day remains headquarters for ITT's worldwide telecommunications companies.

In 1928 ITT acquired the Mackay Companies, one of which was Commercial Cable, which owned a worldwide submarine cable service, set down by cable-laying ships such as this one.

Many of Behn's more important decisions were made in this famous oak-panelled board room at 67 Broad.

Clarence Mackay, founder and head of the Mackay Companies, joined the ITT board in 1928 and provided Behn with additional prestige in the investment community.

John Merrill, whose All America Cables became part of ITT in 1927, became the guiding force in the corporation's global telecommunications operations.

ITT's top leaders in the early 1930s. Seated from left to right are John Merrill, Sosthenes Behn, J. L. McQuarrie (an ITT vice president), and W.H. Pitkin (vice president and general counsel). At the extreme right, standing, is Frank Page.

Frank Page, a longtime ITT vice president and a key figure in the late 1930s and during World War II.

Henri Busignies, ITT's top scientist in France, escaped to America and helped develop many electronic devices used by the Navy in World War II.

E. Maurice Deloraine headed ITT's research and development efforts during World War II, and afterward took charge of European R & D operations.

Behn acquired Spain's telephone company, CTNE, in 1924. Four years later CTNE celebrated its first interconnect with North America. From left to right: the Marqués de Urquijo, CTNE's president; José Tafur, Spain's Director General of Communication; and Colonel Behn.

A view of the top of a telephone central office building in Madrid, showing the confluence of overhead lines prior to ITT's acquisition and subsequent modernization of the telephone system.

Geoff Ogilvie, who was one of Colonel Behn's closest confidants during his entire career at ITT.

Behn returned to France shortly after the Normandy landing in 1944. He is shown here with Deloraine, who accompanied him part of the way.

ITT concentrated its manufacturing in New Jersey after Hitler overran its continental facilities. Operations were expanded rapidly and the Nutley facility was continued after the war. This microwave tower was completed in 1948.

Colonel Behn looks on as President Juan Perón signs an agreement selling the United River Plate Telephone Company to Argentina in 1946.

William Henry Harrison, left, who wrested command of ITT from Behn after a bitter and divisive struggle, shown with Behn at the 1955 annual meeting. Geoff Ogilvie is at Behn's left.

After Harrison's death the presidency went to Gen. Edmond Leavey and Behn retired as chairman. The two men attended the 1956 annual meeting, which was Behn's last.

Harold Sydney Geneen arrived at ITT in 1959, inaugurating the second major era in the corporation's history.

Under Geneen corporate power came to be centralized in the Office of the President—Operations, which in the late 1960s consisted of Richard Bennett, Francis Dunleavy, Geneen, and James Lester.

Geneen moved ITT's headquarters from Broad Street to 320 Park Avenue in 1961.

One of the stormiest episodes in the Geneen era was the acquisition of Hartford Fire Insurance, completed in 1971 after months of bitter controversy. Geneen met with Hartford's chairman, Harry Williams, in an attempt to iron out differences.

Edward Gerrity, Jr., ITT's senior vice president and director of corporate relations and advertising, has been a key figure in interpreting the corporation to the public and the government from the early years of the Geneen era.

ITT acquired Sheraton Corporation of America in 1968, sold off such properties as the former Stonehaven Hotel in Springfield, Massachusetts (left), and erected new ones, such as the spectacular Doha Sheraton in Qatar (right).

The technological range of ITT companies goes from Bell & Gossett, the old line pump manufacturer (left), to Qume Corporation (right), which turns out printers for computers and related equipment.

The flamboyant Dita Beard was a central figure in controversies regarding Sheraton's role in the 1972 G.O.P. convention.

John A. McCone, who after leaving his post as head of the Central Intelligence Agency became an ITT director, advised Geneen during the Chilean crisis.

The Justice Department's antitrust chief, Richard McLaren (left) and then Deputy Attorney General Richard Kleindienst (right) were leading White House figures in the ITT antitrust cases.

ITT's System 12 digital switching equipment is the corporation's key product in the worldwide competition in the telecommunications market.

Lyman C. Hamilton succeeded Geneen as chief executive officer and helped set ITT down a new road. He stirred opposition on the board and was obliged to resign in 1979.

Rand Araskog became ITT's chairman and president in 1979, and by stressing telecommunications has opened a third era at ITT.

In 1975 present, past, and future ITT leaders posed for this unusual picture. From left to right, seated, Vice Chairman Francis Dunleavy, Chairman Geneen, President Hamilton. Standing, from left to right, executive vice presidents James Lester, Rand Araskog, and Richard Bennett. Behind them are portraits of the Behn brothers.

Washington; and a strong, aggressive management headed by Russell Erickson, who had just recently been elevated to the presidency and soon proved to be attuned to Geneen's methods of operation.

Almost all of Rayonier's problems related to its principal products. The company was one of the world's leading producers of wood cellulose, used primarily in the production of acetate and, as the company name indicates, rayon. Each was losing ground to nylon and other synthetics in its major markets, such as tire cord and textiles. Revenues and earnings moved in harmony with the general business cycle, which is to say that Rayonier was a laggard company in what generally was perceived as a growth industry. It had a weak balance sheet and, until Erickson took over, an indifferent management incapable of developing and implementing plans to alter the situation.

That Geneen had grandiose plans for the new ITT Rayonier became evident shortly after completion of the merger. First, there was the obvious "fit" with Levitt. The latter company needed land upon which to construct homes, and Rayonier had not only properties suitable for housing units but experts in the acquisition of additional tracts. More important, however, was the perceived future of rayon. The price for cotton had been rising, and there were no signs of a decline, and in the late 1960s some experts were predicting a similar increase for petroleum and natural-gas feed stocks used to create synthetic fibers. This implied that rayon might not only recapture old markets but develop new ones. Such was Erickson's perception of the situation, and one that Geneen came to share.

Old development plans formulated but never implemented owing to the lack of capital were revived, updated, and presented to ITT. The most important of these involved the construction of a new mill in Georgia, which would have a capacity of 175,000 tons annually of cellulose and would increase Rayonier's production of that material by some 30 percent. The need for such a facility had long been recognized at headquarters, but Rayonier lacked the approximately $85 million needed for its construction prior to being acquired by ITT. According to Erickson, work on it might begin in 1969 or early 1970, and the plant would be in operation just as the price for cellulose started to rise.

Not only did Geneen readily approve of the expenditure; according to those present he asked, "What else have you got?" Erickson was somewhat surprised, for he now realized Geneen hadn't a clear concept of the difficulties involved with bringing such a facility into being; nonetheless he presented Geneen with a plan for the acquisition of a huge tract in Canada—"about the shape and size of Tennessee"—upon which to construct a major processing complex. The costs involved would be enormous, even by ITT's standards, but Geneen gave his approval to the venture, which consumed almost as much capital as that employed in reviving Sheraton, though with a far less fortunate conclusion.

The hotel chain eventually turned a profit, but there would be none for the Port-Cartier operation, which suffered losses from the beginning and a decade after its first stirrings was written off at a loss of $320 million.[9] By then the increasing prices of land and of wood products cast a glow over the Rayonier acquisition, but as would be the case with Sheraton, this couldn't alter the fact that ITT had made grave errors in developing the company during the early 1970s.

Rayonier was ITT's initial commitment to natural resources, a major diversification out of the manufacturing-utilities-services nexus that had emerged during the Geneen era. The next significant takeover, Pennsylvania Glass Sand, reinforced it. The least known of that year's major acquisitions, and certainly lacking the visibility and glamour of some of the others, PGS proved the best of the 1968 crop.

The company was pretty much what its name implied, the producer of silica, the basic raw material used in the manufacture of glass, and it was the leader in its field. In addition, PGS was the nation's second-largest factor in adsorptive earths, utilized in filtering operations in the production of petroleum and natural gas and as a base for fertilizers and pesticides. For most of its history the corporation had been run by two families, named Andrews and Woods, who also owned large blocks of common stock and maintained effective control. In 1967 PGS was undergoing a generational change in management, as Hale Andrews and William Woods, Jr., succeeded their fathers as chairman and executive vice-president respectively. The Andrews family was more interested in becoming party to a takeover than was the Woods family, but both were willing to listen to offers made by Rohatyn, who once again served in his familiar role as corporate matchmaker.

The company had no important problems. Revenues, income, and dividends rose steadily in the 1960s, and returns on investment and sales were high for the industry. The business outlook was excellent, and PGS had no pressing need for financing. Hale Andrews later indicated he supported the deal more for personal reasons than for business reasons, telling a reporter, "I like to think of myself as a professional manager, not an owner."[8]

PGS differed from almost all of ITT's other acquisitions, then, in that it would require from the new parent neither capital nor operational changes.

Because of this, it commanded a premium price. Levitt and Rayonier had been sold to ITT at approximately net-asset value, whereas Sheraton's assets were almost half again what they fetched in ITT paper. In contrast, PGS required $112 million in ITT common and preferred, for assets valued at $46 million. The takeover was completed on June 27, and Lazard's fee for its services was $250,000.

Andrews braced himself for directives from headquarters and scores of experts demanding a shakeup in operations; such was the picture of Geneen's methods he had obtained from the financial press and other businessmen. None of this happened; there was little change as a result of the new ownership. "ITT did not bring an influx of its people," recalled Andrews. "The opposite is true. People wondered when ITT would show up." Apparently headquarters knew better than to interfere with an obviously successful business. PGS continued to grow, in terms of both revenues and profits, and rarely had to call on its parent for assistance or advice. It proved a worthwhile acquisition in almost every respect, but the company's successes owed more to what it had been prior to the takeover than to any changes wrought afterward.

The last of the year's major acquisitions was also the largest in terms of revenues, and in some ways the most puzzling of the group. Continental Baking was without a doubt the class in its field. A $620-million-a-year firm in 1968, the corporation operated bakeries in all parts of the nation and was a growing factor in snacks and frozen foods as well. Among its branded goods were some of the more familiar names in their categories: Wonder bread, Profile bread, Morton pot pies, Hostess cakes, and Twinkies. Its facilities were the most modern and efficient in the industry, and the marketing operations were widely imitated. Management was strong and experienced, and finances were in good shape.

In part because of all this, Continental didn't seem the kind of corporation Geneen would have wanted to acquire. As was the case with PGS, there was no need for major capital expenditures or a management change. Unlike that company, however, Continental was in an industry noted for intense competition, low profit margins, and hardly much in the way of potential growth. Although revenues had doubled during the past decade—largely because of a number of acquisitions and several successes in marketing new cakes—the basic bread operations were stagnant. Profit margins slipped below 6 percent in 1956 and declined steadily to 3.2 percent in 1965 before turning upward, but they still were below 4 percent in 1968. Unlike Sheraton, Continental had no inefficient units that might be sold so as to raise capital and increase returns on investment and sales. In fact, there was little that could have been done to improve what already was the best operation in the industry.

Continental appeared the classic case of a corporation going as far as it could in its markets. Yet such was the nature of the merger-mania of the late 1960s that it became the subject of bids from several conglomerates. In 1967 rumors abounded regarding potential candidates, and they continued into the next year, when the company's earnings advanced smartly and margins increased, stimulating interest on Wall Street. The common stock, which had traded in a narrow range for eight years, now shot up from a low of 20 to over 40, and by midyear it was at the highest price in its history.

What did Geneen find attractive in Continental? Foodstuffs might have seemed a logical extension of the hotel business, and some synergy might have developed between it and Sheraton, but this was rather farfetched. Any attempt to expand Continental out of its bakery base into other segments of the food industry would have brought ITT up against some of the world's toughest marketers, without much hope for success. The snack business was capable of better-than-average growth, but by itself this hardly would have justified the takeover. Later some observers suggested Geneen had been lured by Rohatyn's visions (Lazard received a fee of $400,000 for helping bring the parties together), and such might have been the case. More likely the acquisition resulted from a combination of factors: Continental's apparent revival in 1968; Geneen's desire to expand domestic operations; plus the heady business climate of the times, a period when it appeared conglomerateurs could work magic. By late 1968 some of them had started believing their own press notices, and Geneen might have fallen into the trap.

ITT transferred $280 million of its common and preferred for Continental—about the same as it had for Rayonier, which had $100 million more in assets and a superior potential for growth. This came to better than $68 per share, or 19 times earnings, for stock that traditionally sold for around 11 times earnings. Other conglomerates had paid similar amounts for poorer properties. It should also be noted that in late 1968 ITT common was fetching close to 30 times earnings, approximately twice the multiple it had commanded at its low point the previous year, so that in reality Geneen was only exchanging his bloated stock for similarly inflated Continental shares. This notwithstanding, one still has to wonder as to the reasons for the acquisition. Continental made no striking contribution to ITT in the years to come. As would be the case with PGS, it underwent no important changes as a result of becoming part of ITT. During the 1970s, as before, Continental was a well-managed, efficient firm in markets that at best were expanding slowly—more slowly than those of most other ITT operations.

SELECTED STATISTICS, ITT, 1962, 1967, 1968

(dollar amounts in thousands except per-share figures)

	1962	1967	1968
Sales and revenues	1,090,198	2,760,572	4,006,502
Income	40,694	119,221	180,162
Per share	1.21	2.27	2.58
Return on equity	8.6	12.2	11.7
Dividends per share	.50	.77$^1/_2$	.87$^1/_2$
Gross plant additions	114,584	238,141	362,069
Plant, property, equipment	462,323	1,305,829	1,835,793
Total assets	1,235,781	2,961,172	4,022,400
Long-term debt	266,815	744,675	931,772
Stockholders' equity	483,531	1,143,568	1,652,092
Outstanding common shares (000s)	33,258	49,940	59,059
Equity per common share	14.11	17.39	16.83

Source: ITT annual report, 1968

At the time of their acquisition, Geneen knew that Levitt, Rayonier, and Sheraton would require important capital commitments, but he was confident they soon would make significant contributions to ITT's net profits, though clearly he was mistaken as to how long it would take. Pennsylvania Glass Sand was too small a unit to make much difference initially, and what Geneen had in mind for Continental remains a mystery.

It was evident that ITT couldn't finance all of these companies' internal expansion through cash flow alone and that additional borrowing would be required, perhaps a further dilution of equity. In 1968 the corporation had taken over operations that by themselves were larger than the ITT of only six years earlier. Prudence would have dictated a period of consolidation, a moratorium, or at least a slowing of the pace of acquisitions. The economic signs weren't good in early 1969, and they worsened as the year wore on. Prices finally collapsed on Wall Street, in the most severe sell-off of the post–World War II era. It was a situation that called for caution, but it would have been out of character for Geneen to have held back.

ITT plunged ahead, planning acquisitions on a vast scale, with apparently no thought the mergermania could end. Nothing short of government action could halt the conglomeritus of the late 1960s, and this was on the way. As Geneen eyed his next acquisitions, plans were being made at the Justice Department to renew the campaign that had begun with the ABC affair, and to do so with a frontal rather than a flanking attack. The first target was to be James Ling, but all knew that ITT was the department's prime objective.

14

The Siege Year: 1969

IN the autumn of 1968 Richard Nixon and Hubert Humphrey criss-crossed a nation whose people were badly divided, demoralized, and bitter. They sought votes in the November presidential election by promising to find some honorable way to end the Vietnam War and to heal domestic wounds. The consensus seemed to be that neither man was particularly popular but that Nixon would win. A number of public-opinion polls indicated that many Democrats who had supported Robert Kennedy and Eugene McCarthy wouldn't vote that year. Liberal Republicans remained unenthusiastic about Nixon but were expected to fall into line before Election Day.

For all the confusion and the charged atmosphere of the times, these two men did symbolize differing philosophies, and it appeared basic issues were at stake. For the better part of two decades Humphrey had been one of the nation's most prominent and consistent spokesmen for liberal and progressive causes, ranging from civil rights to antipoverty programs to criticisms of big business. Nixon presented a more complex image, since he tended to shift ground as the American mood changed, but in 1968 he clearly was the candidate of his party's conservative wing and as such was counted on to be favorable to business interests.

This was Nixon's inclination. He had spent the past five years as a Wall Street lawyer specializing in corporate affairs and had become friendly with many of the nation's leading businessmen. His campaign manager and law partner, John Mitchell, was one of the financial district's most respected bond experts, and the firm, known after 1967 as Nixon, Mudge, Rose, Guthrie, Alexander & Mitchell, had a roster of corporate clients and performed financial services of various kinds for others. ITT Continental Baking fell into this second category.

In common with leaders at most major corporations, a large number of ITT's officers and directors were Republicans. Presumably most supported and voted for Nixon for a variety of reasons, one of them a belief that his election would prove beneficial for business in general. Nixon certainly sent out signals to this effect. On several occasions he chided the Johnson Administration for what he saw as an antibusiness bias, and in October, Nixon told a financial-industry group that if elected he would seek to relax regulation of the securities markets. Certainly there was no reason to believe that business would fare worse under a Nixon White House than it had when the Democrats were in control. Still smarting from the ABC loss, ITT looked forward to the time when Ramsey Clark would leave the Justice Department. Rumor had it that if he won, Nixon would name Mitchell as his attorney general. The prospect was pleasing, for such a nomination would imply an easing of antitrust pressures.

Nixon was elected in November, sparking celebrations at corporate headquarters in New York and elsewhere. As expected, Mitchell was given the post at Justice, and there were other friendly and familiar faces in the Cabinet. Liberal newspapers predicted an end to reforms started in the Kennedy and Johnson administrations, a rollback if not to the Coolidge years then at least to those of Eisenhower. Republican theoreticians described a generation of conservatism resulting from the fashioning of a new coalition headed by the first true conservative to occupy the White House since Herbert Hoover.

This wasn't to be. Not only was the Nixon presidency to end in disgrace and humiliation, it demonstrated an unusual lack of internal consistency while disappointing, alienating, and occasionally even betraying many who had been among its earliest and most enthusiastic supporters.

The conglomerates and their leaders were particularly hard hit, and none more so than ITT and Geneen. In 1968 the corporation's harshest critics had attacked the firm as a grasping acquirer out to dominate large sectors of the economy, and they hinted that ITT was a malevolent, un-American force overseas. Five years later some of these people charged Geneen and others with attempted bribery, unsavory financial manipulations, complicity in the overthrow of a foreign government, and criminal collusion. Not since the turn of the century, when a generation of publicists castigated the Standard Oil Trust and John D. Rockefeller, had any corporation and its chief been portrayed as so evil a force. The image was crystallized in a best-selling work, Anthony Sampson's *The Sovereign State of ITT*, published at a time when the company was under strong attack in the press and by government. Biased and riddled with exaggerations, it nonetheless was a vivid indictment of ITT and its leaders, and it firmly implanted the picture of a heartless, corrupt, and thoroughly amoral entity headed by a veritable automaton. This barrage of unfavorable publicity created a siege mentality at headquarters and in the field, an attitude which wouldn't be dissipated as long as Geneen remained in command and traces of which remain to this day.

In the beginning, at least—in late 1968 and early 1969—many of ITT's difficulties derived from the behavior of the stock market, the direction of the economy, and the business environment, not from any set of problems peculiar to ITT.

There was a feverish atmosphere and trading was hectic on Wall Street in the aftermath of the Nixon victory, as stocks shot to new highs. At the time, it appeared certain there would be another spectacular leg to the aged bull market, which would take the Dow Industrials beyond 1000. Not only were Americans rushing to purchase shares in established blue chips as well as in esoteric new ventures, but the Europeans were joining in, as news of financial stringencies in France sparked a rush to New York. But although most Wall Streeters were celebrating, some were troubled by talk of a Nixonian campaign against inflation, which at 4.7 percent was the worst in seventeen years. This would imply tight money and high interest rates, which together would result in a market decline and perhaps in an economic recession. Such was the situation on December 2, when the Dow reached an interday high of 995 and failed to crack the 1000 barrier.

That afternoon the Chase Manhattan Bank boosted its prime lending rate to 6½ percent, and others followed, setting the stage for a sell-off, which took the Dow to an interday low of 962 on December 17. The next day the Federal Reserve raised the discount rate to 5¹/2 percent, and the banks promptly upped the prime to 6 ³/4 percent. This was followed by another collapse, a brief rally, and further declines. The recession had begun, and the post–World War II bull market was ended. The bear phase was to last for a year and a half, the Dow striking bottom in June 1970, at 628, before turning upward again.

Virtually every stock suffered a sharp decline, but none was harder hit than the conglomerates. From its 1968 high of 86, Litton fell to 13 by summer of 1970. In the same period G + W went from 29 to 4 and LTV from 136 to 7. ITT did better than most, declining to 30 from a peak of 62, this in recognition of the firmer foundation erected by Geneen during the 1960s.

As has been seen, one of the ways conglomerates expanded was by exchanging their high-priced paper for that of companies whose assets weren't richly valued on Wall Street. Shares of some conglomerates were selling at discounts from their own assets by 1971, and by itself this might have ended the mergermania. Moreover, the performance of these companies suffered during the recession, with longtime critics observing that this was further proof that they had been little more than balloon operations, incapable of thriving unless puffed up by earnings of acquired firms. Such wasn't the case at ITT, where records continued to be set in the face of recession, a striking indication that Geneen's management methods were working and a vindication of his claim that acquired firms generally performed better after coming under the ITT umbrella than they did on their own. But this was hardly noticed or taken account of in the general bloodbath on Wall Street.

Conglomeratization had entered a new and what proved to be a final phase in late 1968, one that had been prefigured in some of Ling's actions and takeovers attempted earlier in the year. Now bold, aggressive managers sought acquisitions larger even than themselves, with some of the targets familiar, old-line companies.

The Siege Year: 1969

Gulf + Western (1968 sales: $1.3 billion) failed to complete a deal for the Great Atlantic & Pacific Tea Co. (A&P; 1968 sales: $5.4 billion) and had turned to Sinclair Oil (1968 sales: $1.5 billion). A&P soon had a new suitor in Data Processing Financial & General (1968 sales: $17.4 million), which was a small fraction of its size. At the same time General Host (1968 sales: $201 million) wooed Armour & Co. (1968 sales: $2.4 billion). And so it went. Walter Kidde made a bid for U.S. Lines, Susquehanna tried to absorb Pan American Sulphur, Continental Can acquired Miehle-Goss-Dexter, and stories regarding offers, proxy battles, and the like were features on the financial pages, and rumors as to which large enterprise would become the next object of a "raid" helped sustain interest and activity on Wall Street during the last days of the bull market.

While defenders of conglomerates were united in their belief that they represented a dynamic and invigorating element for an evolving American capitalism, critics were divided in their attacks. Liberals and radicals talked of the unwholesome influence of large aggregates of money and power, in terms similar to those heard in earlier antibusiness crusades. Within the business community, however, were conservatives and moderates who believed the conglomerates were an unsettling factor because they introduced new elements of uncertainty at a time when stability was required. Moreover, many of the conglomerateurs were "new people"—foreign-born, Catholic or Jewish, or from the South and the Far West —whose background and upbringing were different from those of the majority who had dominated most industries prior to World War II. The more "conventional" officers of large corporations, a group that tended to be self-perpetuating, often found the newcomers exotic, brash, and somewhat vulgar. This could be seen in the ways they reacted to men like Bluhdorn and Ling. It wasn't as obvious with Geneen, but he certainly wasn't out of the old mold, and this was one of the reasons he had difficulties at American Can, Jones & Laughlin, Bell & Howell, and particularly at Raytheon. The Charles Francis Adamses of this world didn't relish the idea of being displaced by such as Geneen. In their own way they were even more strongly opposed to the conglomerates than were the liberal reformers. After all, they had more to lose.

The national magazines carried stories regarding opposition to conglomerates on the part of liberal reformers, and articles about them appeared on the front pages of important newspapers. Spokesmen for this point of view were sought after as guests for television talk programs, and some became celebrities in their own right. Far less space was devoted to criticisms by conservatives, and most of these were found in specialized magazines and on business pages. Such opponents of conglomerates hardly were the type to be asked to appear on the Johnny Carson and Merv Griffin shows. Nonetheless they existed, and were quite powerful within key segments of the business community. More to the point, they held dominant positions in the Republican Party.

These men considered Nixon one of their own, a conservative who would defend them not only against liberal reformers like Ramsey Clark and Ralph Nader but also against conglomerateurs. The distinction between the old-line, traditional corporate executives and officers and the new conglomerateurs eluded most reformers, who clung to the conventional belief that big business was more or less homogeneous in its essential attitudes and values and that Nixon would do all he could to assist that community. Such individuals were caught off guard by the President's willingness to stand by while the conglomerates underwent attack by the Justice Department, in what was to be the most significant and far-reaching antitrust campaign since the end of World War II.[1]

As expected, Nixon nominated John Mitchell as his attorney general. Soon after, Mitchell told reporters, "This country is going so far right you won't recognize it." His deputy was to be Richard Kleindienst, one of Sen. Barry Goldwater's closest allies, and if anything more conservative than his chief. Together, and with the president's blessing, Mitchell and Kleindienst selected Richard McLaren to be assistant attorney general in charge of the Antitrust Division.

There was every reason to believe McLaren was as moderate and probusiness as the others. Not only did he possess impeccable Republican credentials, but for close to twenty years had defended corporate clients in antitrust actions and had often criticized the Justice Department for excessive zeal in bringing indictments. He was a partner in the Chicago law firm of Chadwell, Keck, Kayser, Ruggles, and McLaren, which occupied a position in that city roughly analogous to Nixon and Mitchell's firm in New York. Prior to joining the administration, McLaren had served as chairman of the antitrust section of the American Bar Association, a decidedly probusiness group. He was known to have ambitions for a federal judgeship, which indeed he was to receive after his service in the Justice Department. Thus, McLaren could be counted upon to hew to the Nixon-Mitchell line in most matters.

McLaren had been critical of conglomerate takeovers, perhaps because several of his clients considered themselves likely targets. He indicated as much to Mitchell and Kleindienst when they offered him leadership of the Antitrust Division. McLaren predicated acceptance on three conditions. He expected support for a "vigorous antitrust program"; he would "decide all matters on the merits"; and "there would be no political decision." He added, "We would follow my beliefs with regard to what the Supreme Court cases said on conglomerate mergers, and the restructuring of the industry that I thought was coming about in an almost idiotic way." Mitchell not only agreed to all these conditions but in public addresses would echo McLaren's attitudes toward conglomerates. In June 1969 he decried "super-concentration" in American business, and so that no one could mistake his meaning he added that it "discourages competition among large firms and establishes a tone in the marketplace for more and more mergers."[2]

All McLaren needed now were carefully selected targets and a strong rationale under which to bring his indictments. The former presented no serious difficulty. The major conglomerates were all actively seeking acquisitions in early 1969, and a number of other firms were developing their skills at the merger game. For his test McLaren could select from among more than a dozen proposed takeovers.

Developing a plausible doctrine presented a more difficult problem. Although the courts had acted against several important mergers during the past decade, no clear, unmistakable principle applicable to future actions had emerged. Nor had Congress enacted the kind of amendments to the antitrust laws Donald Turner had pleaded for, and without which he claimed no significant prosecutions might be undertaken. McLaren could draw little from two recent studies on the subject. The first of these, a product of the Ramsey Clark years at Justice, came from a commission headed by University of Chicago Law School Dean Philip Neal. Although critical of the mergermania, the study concluded there was nothing in existing law to prevent it. The Neal Commission recommended legislation to prohibit large firms (with annual revenues in excess of $500 million or assets of more than $250 million) from acquiring "leading firms" (those that had over 10 percent of their markets). In putting forth this plan, the Commission implied that without it, antitrust prosecutions of conglomerates would be difficult to bring.

The second study was far more outspoken on the subject. After Nixon's election but prior to his inauguration the Republicans asked prominent University of Chicago economist George Stigler to organize a commission to look into the matter. A noted believer in free markets and no friend of big businesses that tended to confine them, Stigler was expected to be harshly critical of the conglomerates. To the surprise of many who hadn't kept informed of his development, Stigler argued for the abandonment of attempts to limit conglomerate activity, which according to the final report posed "at most a minor threat to competition." Furthermore, the Stigler Commission urged the Justice Department "to resist the natural temptation to utilize the antitrust laws to combat social problems not related to the competitive functioning of markets."[3]

With almost no support from the political right and center and what he deemed the wrong kind from the left, McLaren had to fashion a rationale on his own, which he proceeded to do early in 1969. It was based on a well-established antitrust principle and a somewhat nebulous attitude toward economic concentration.

The antitrust principle was the old stricture against reciprocity, which meant a corporation couldn't oblige one of its divisions to sell or buy from another without offering equal access to potential competitors. This had special meaning for conglomerate managers, who were sensitive to charges that they operated a grab bag of companies and who spoke of how their corporations operated synergistically, meaning the various units meshed to create a harmonious whole. As has been seen, Geneen perceived the interrelationships between such firms at Avis and Sheraton, Levitt and Rayonier, and there were similar relationships at other conglomerates. As Columbia University law professor Harlan Blake put it, "Reciprocity is as inevitable a result of widespread conglomerate structure as price rigidity is a consequence of oligopoly structure." Did these companies indeed afford preferential treatment to one another? If so, they might be indicted under existing statutes.

McLaren had what amounted to a visceral dislike for the way conglomerates piled companies one upon the other, which he considered to be unwholesome, quite different from the internal growth exhibited by the corporations he had once defended in antitrust actions. Out of this came a claim that size alone could result in a restraint of trade under the terms of the Clayton Antitrust Act. This was a new approach insofar as conglomerates were concerned, one hardly considered during Turner's administration of the Antitrust Division. This came to be known as the theory of "aggregate concentration." Later McLaren would say, "What we were shooting for, from the beginning of 1969, was to stop this merger trend that was leading more and more toward economic concentration." He also hoped to "protect [the] political system by promoting a broad dispersion of economic power among the many, rather than concentration in the hands of a few," and he characterized conglomeratization as "a merger movement where concentration of control of manufacturing assets will be substantially increased and the trend to further concentration will be encouraged."

Critics charged there was no basis in law for this view, that since McLaren had been unable to base his opposition to large mergers on statutes and precedent, he had turned to economics and politics for justification. McLaren denied this vigorously, claiming the Antitrust Division was merely enforcing the statutes. Apparently the charges did have some effect, for little was heard of aggregate-concentration theory after it was enunciated, and McLaren dealt instead with the matter of reciprocity. Moreover, he insisted his approach was more firmly rooted in law than that of his predecessor had been. On one occasion he somewhat disingenuously remarked that whereas Turner "had analysed the thing in terms of an economist looking at markets," he looked at it "perhaps more as a lawyer interpreting the legislative history going back to 1950 and the Supreme Court decisions," and he later observed, "The law is written by Congress, and definitive interpretation comes from the Supreme Court." But no new legislation had been written and passed, and, as it turned out, the courts rejected McLaren's views of such mergers.[4]

Despite this, his anticonglomerate crusade proved most effective. The Antitrust Division was able to block several significant mergers, and conglomerateurs were obliged to make compromises in order to avoid long and frustrating legal battles. In this, as in most other contests involving the conglomerates, ITT played a central role.

Geneen accumulated companies at a near-frantic pace in early 1969, and all of them augmented existing operations. Six were added in March alone, ranging in size from the smallish Peterson School of Business, the price for which was less than three quarters of a million dollars in cash, to an important regional construction firm, United Homes of Seattle, which took $13.6 million in stock. Five more were added the following month. One of these, the Electronics Institute of Technology, was an insignificant correspondence school that cost only $50,000, indicating that ITT was either casting a very fine net or gobbling up whatever came its way in a haphazard fashion. On the other hand, Canteen Corporation, a dominant factor in vending machines and one of the largest suppliers of on-site feeding services, took close to a quarter of a billion dollars in stock, and was a major acquisition by most standards.

Canteen was a strong company whose revenues had risen steadily from $117 million to $322 million during the past decade. It was a growth company in several rapidly expanding and highly competitive industries, with sufficient capital to finance ongoing operations and borrowing power to enter new ones if it so desired. Canteen's management was somewhat aged, however, with several key executives coming up for retirement. Thus, in late 1968 they were willing to consider Rohatyn's offers, which as usual included a premium price for their stock.

As was customary, ITT filed notice with the government of its intention to acquire Canteen once it appeared negotiations would be successful. At the time there seemed little reason to expect a challenge. McLaren's views on conglomeratization still weren't well known, and no one expected an antitrust crusade from the new Nixon Administration. The only conglomerate that seemed in trouble was LTV, then in the process of attempting an unfriendly takeover of Jones & Laughlin. McLaren indeed was preparing to file against LTV, but he wanted to couple this with an action against the ITT-Canteen merger. Mitchell approved the former suit but disqualified himself from dealings with ITT, since he had acted for Continental Baking only a few months earlier. He turned the matter over to Kleindienst, and a meeting was arranged between him, McLaren, and ITT's general counsel, Howard Aibel, for the morning of April 14.

As it happened, that was the day McLaren filed a Justice Department complaint to block the LTV-J&L merger, charging it would lessen competition in the steel industry, involve reciprocity, and result in an increase in aggregate concentration. The first two allegations would be difficult to demonstrate, and the third was vague and imprecise. Nonetheless, a beginning had been made.

Aibel was willing to negotiate a compromise in the ITT-Canteen matter. Conceding nothing insofar as principle was concerned, and observing that McLaren's interpretation of the antitrust statutes was without precedent, he nonetheless suggested that if the merger were allowed to proceed, ITT would maintain Canteen as a completely separate entity, so that divestiture could take place with a minimum of problems if it were so ordered by the courts. Then followed a series of skirmishes that involved the White House, as John Ehrlichman, who was assuming an increasingly large share of authority in domestic affairs, questioned whether McLaren truly was exceeding earlier guidelines. In the end all parties agreed to accept Aibel's offer. Canteen was acquired on April 25, and three days later McLaren initiated his antitrust suit, the charges being the same as in the LTV-Jones & Laughlin action.

McLaren filed a third complaint the following month, in effect supporting B. F. Goodrich in its fight to repel an unwelcomed overture from Northwest Industries, a railroad turned conglomerate. Once again he used arguments based on reciprocity and aggregate concentration, claiming that for these reasons the merger would be against the public interest. Now he received his first setback. The Justice Department's request for a preliminary injunction was denied in July, with the court deciding McLaren hadn't sufficiently demonstrated that any reciprocity involved in the merger would be illegal, thus casting serious doubt over the use of aggregate concentration as a reason for blocking mergers. This was welcome news at ITT, where the drive for acquisitions continued, with five companies added in May and eight more in the next four months, all of which were comparatively small and none evoking a challenge from the Justice Department.

McLaren struck next in an attempt to block ITT's acquisition of Grinnell Corporation, and this time he appeared to be on firmer ground. The nation's leading manufacturer of fire-protection systems and related plumbing and foundry products, Grinnell was an old and large operation whose annual sales of $340 million would make it the largest of ITT's takeovers in this category to date. This certainly would fit McLaren's concept of aggregate concentration. Moreover, Grinnell's systems might be used in Sheraton hotels, Levitt homes, Continental bakeries, and many other ITT factories and offices, thus bringing reciprocity into question. Grinnell had just lost an antitrust case and had been obliged to divest itself of several properties and to abandon attempts to acquire additional companies in its industry, so the Justice Department was experienced in dealing with the company. Finally, McLaren expected to tie the Grinnell case to another he then was preparing, an action to block a proposed merger between ITT and Hartford Fire Insurance.

The fire-and-casualty insurance industry hardly appeared a growth field. Rates were set with reference to state authorities, competition was fierce, and returns on underwritings could be devastated in bad years. Earnings on operations were historically low, and in fact Hartford had shown deficits in this area throughout the late 1960s. This was more than compensated for, however, by returns from its capital reserves, much of which was invested in common stocks. In reality, then, these insurers were twin operations, one part insurance, the other what amounted to huge pools of investment capital; and the latter had done quite well during the bull market.

It was these capital funds that attracted the attention of several conglomerates, who sought and then merged with large casualty companies, obtaining them for prices above their market quotations but below asset values. The best known of these had been the take-over of Reliance Insurance by Leasco Data Processing the previous year. Leasco's founder and president, Saul Steinberg, had explained how he intended to utilize Reliance's reserves in "a more creative way," thus increasing earnings and making the company more profitable. But there was more to it than that; Leasco's expanding leasing operations might be financed by Reliance, which in this way would be transformed into a captive private bank. Thus, Steinberg might divorce himself from the money markets and achieve a greater degree of independence.

Just as Reliance had appealed to Steinberg, so Geneen saw great advantages in a merger with Hartford. The nation's sixth-largest property, casualty, and fire-insurance company, Hartford had assets of close to $2 billion and premium income of $969 million in 1968. A well-funded, conservative operation, it had a capital excess of some $400 million, which theoretically might be remitted in the form of dividends. For a corporation such as ITT, whose long-term debt had tripled from $310 million in 1964 to $932 million at the end of 1968, Hartford must have appeared a ripe plum.

The Siege Year: 1969

Did Geneen intend to have Hartford declare such a payout once it became part of ITT? He repeatedly declared this wasn't so, but suspicion that this would happen couldn't be easily dispelled. Still, there would be other ways for ITT to get the money. As has been seen, several of ITT's more recent acquisitions had embarked upon important long-range expansion programs, and the Hartford reserve might be used by them as a form of money pump. That this was Geneen's intention could be seen in the "Tobacco Memorandum"* of November 2, 1968, in which were sketched ITT's plans for Hartford, in terms that would later suggest reciprocity violations to Justice Department attorneys. Sheraton's expansion program, expected to add 30,000 rooms to the system during the next four to six years in addition to upgrading the franchise operations, alone might require close to a billion dollars, and some of this could come from Hartford in the form of loans. Funds were needed for Levitt's land banks and to finance construction. Avis and Airport Parking could use Hartford's resources as well, and the insurer might even help in the refinancing of a portion of the parent corporation's long-term debt.

For its part, ITT could offer Hartford an outlet for its services. In a section entitled "Marketing Opportunities Within the ITT System," the memo noted that the corporation was "a vast consumer of insurance products" and that virtually all of its employees required "various forms of casualty insurance which would readily be included in the salary savings program." The Hamilton and Hartford sales forces might distribute each other's products. All units could share customer lists:

> There are several opportunities for the marketing of insurance programs to special ITT interest groups: (a) Sheraton has 1.2 million credit card holders; (b) Avis has 1.5 million credit card holders; (c) 100 million APCOA parking transactions; and (d) ITT has over 200,000 shareholders. It is suggested that various types of insurance programs could be offered through the mail to this captive audience. There are undoubtedly other areas of specific service that could be offered that may or may not prove

*The use of a code word to signify a merger candidate at this stage in the negotiation process was somewhat theatrical but nonetheless common. When Steinberg was holding discussions regarding Reliance, he referred to it as "Raquel," borrowed from the actress Raquel Welch, to indicate a desirable property. The tobacco referred to by ITT derives from the fact that Hartford was near the Connecticut tobacco-growing area.

advantageous (Avis cars for salesmen, Sheraton hotel arrangements, etc., TDI, travel advertising locations, etc.).

Finally, "Levitt has sold homes to 80,000 homeowners and is building new homes at the rate of 6,500 per year. Within five years this figure will exceed 11,000. These purchasers require homeowners and mortgage insurance, which may be offered through special marketing programs."[5]

The possibilities for reciprocity violations were all but self-evident, and of a piece, especially when the Grinnell acquisition was taken into consideration. Later McLaren was to imagine a Sheraton hotel, financed and insured by Hartford, using Grinnell fire-protection devices, with Canteen providing food services and Avis having a preferential position in rental cars, and with a number of its rooms occupied by ITT officials traveling on business. He wouldn't even require a direct demonstration of intentions to violate reciprocity restrictions; the various companies would utilize one another's services and products as a matter of course, without direct orders from headquarters. "Where the large diversified company makes substantial purchases from many suppliers, these suppliers are going to feel a 'reciprocity effect' even without affirmative use of reciprocity by the purchaser. . . . The creation of such power, regardless of whether it is overtly exercised, may have a serious anticompetitive effect."[6]

Geneen often claimed that unlike many other conglomerates, ITT never made an unfriendly tender offer. Perhaps so, in the strictest sense of the word, but if negotiations with Hartford weren't unfriendly, they were at least cool, formal, and to a degree forced, and some of the insurance people made no secret of their dislike for the idea.

Along with many other large casualty companies, Hartford feared a takeover in the wake of the Leasco-Reliance merger. The company's chairman, Harry Williams, asked his investment banker, Roger Baldwin, of Morgan Stanley, to see if a proper partner might be located, one with whom the Hartford management might live. Rohatyn learned of this and approached Baldwin with a nibble on behalf of ITT while ordering the drawing up of the Tobacco Memorandum. He was told Hartford wasn't for sale, but Geneen's interest had been aroused, and he ordered the accumulation of the company's stock. Some 1.2 million shares were obtained from a mutual fund, to which another 500,000 were added later on, giving ITT 8 percent of the total outstanding.

On November 1 André Meyer notified a Hartford director of ITT's action and arranged a meeting for the following day between Geneen, Rohatyn, and himself and several of the directors. (The fact that Meyer had been brought into the discussions indicated the importance ITT placed on this merger.) Others followed, with Geneen outlining the many advantages that would accrue from such a combination. Using the Tobacco Memorandum as his base, he spoke of an invigorated Hartford maintaining its independence within ITT while enjoying the benefits that would come from being part of the larger organization. He seemed to be suggesting this would be more a marriage of equals than the takeover of one company by another.

The Hartford directors either weren't convinced or didn't like the arrangement. Williams approached Baldwin with a suggestion that Hartford acquire other firms in a variety of industries, preferably by issuing new stock for assets so as to dilute the ITT holdings. Rather than see Hartford become a unit under Geneen's control, he was prepared to transform it into a conglomerate. Thus, the engulfed would become the engulfer. Shortly after his initial contact with the ITT people, Williams asked the board to increase Hartford's authorized shares from 22.4 million to 40 million, "to provide greater flexibility in making acquisitions."[7]

Now Geneen realized Hartford might elude his grip. Casting aside his earlier approach, he mounted a frontal assault against Hartford. Aibel arrived there on December 23, with an offer: approximately $750 million in ITT paper, which worked out to close to $70 per share, for stock that only a few weeks earlier had been selling for half that amount and which on that date closed at 46 on takeover rumors. It was a large premium, which Geneen suspected would be too tempting for the directors to reject. Even if they put up a battle, ITT could obtain sufficient shares by means of an open tender offer to control the company, with the rest to be gathered in later on.

The stock moved to the mid-50s on the news and stayed there. This was a respectable advance, but not as much as might have been expected were it not for fear of complications, of which there were three.

The most obvious of these was opposition from the directors, a number of whom were strongly opposed to the merger. Then there was the matter of winning approval from the Connecticut Insurance Commission. As a result of the recent takeovers, the state had passed a tough law giving that body broad powers to delay or halt such acquisitions, and there were indications that commissioner William Cotter, a liberal Democrat, would so act. Finally, Wall Street seemed to think the Hartford merger could cause some problems with Washington, though in late 1968 this still wasn't considered a major concern.

The Johnson Administration was winding down by then, and at the Justice Department Ramsey Clark prepared a series of cases for filing prior to the inauguration, more to create a record and an agenda for a future Democratic government and to embarrass the Nixonians than in any expectation of their being carried through. As has been seen, Richard McLaren had already been offered leadership of the Antitrust Division and had accepted the post, but few expected the kind of activism he was to evidence.

So ITT continued to plan its approach. On January 2, 1969, senior vice president Charles Ireland sketched the strategy he thought should be adopted for the Hartford campaign. It was cast in quasimilitary terms—Ireland was a former Marine officer, and this was his style—and consisted of a four-point program, which would exert "inexorable pressure" on the Hartford board.

First, open-market purchases of shares should continue, "because it adds a real if intangible thrust to our posture of determination that will not go unnoticed in appropriate places." Next, "Ned Gerrity's troops should be exceptionally alert for any moves in the political arenas of Hartford and Washington" and refrain from "embroiling ITT in any legislative or regulatory controversy that could be used by Hartford as a rationale for finding affiliation with ITT 'not to be in the best interests of Hartford shareholders at this time.'" Ireland thought Geneen should watch for counterattacks in the form of "phony (but nonetheless troublesome) derivative suits against the Hartford or the ITT Board (or both), the creation of shareholder and/or policy-holder committees, etc. etc.—all deploring the proposed affiliation on one ground or another, and some, at least, seeking to create an atmosphere under which—again—the affiliation could be said to be 'not in the best interests of Hartford shareholders.'" Finally, "Our full panoply of contacts, connections (direct and indirect) should be delicately used to ensure an appropriate frame of mind on the Hartford Board. . . ."[8]

The Siege Year: 1969

For the most part Geneen followed Ireland's program, but with some amendments of his own. He wooed not only the company but the city of Hartford itself, with promises of construction there involving large capital infusions into the economy and the creation of thousands of new jobs. In addition, Hartford's officers would receive assurances of continued employment along with stock options and bonuses. He would do all in his power to convince them the merger was in Hartford's best interests as well as those of ITT, while at the same time applying the kinds of pressures Ireland had recommended.

Events moved along a predictable path during the next few months. The combined pressures from ITT and its own stockholders proved too much for Hartford's board to bear, and general agreement as to terms was announced in early March. Soon it became apparent that just as Ireland had suggested, this was a delaying tactic; the following month the directors asked for the first of several postponements so as to study the possibilities of an antitrust action. Thereupon a stockholders' group was organized to press for an immediate vote on the merger, while Geneen and others visited Hartford to promise additional favors for the city and bolster support on the board. On June 24 McLaren announced his intention of filing a suit within the next few weeks. Now ITT asked Donald Turner, a Harvard professor by then, for his opinion on the matter, and he obliged, holding the combination unquestionably to be within the law. McLaren obviously disagreed; on August 1 he filed separate complaints against the Grinnell and Hartford acquisitions.

ITT was now engaged in a struggle on three fronts. While pressing Hartford's board for a vote, it had to contend with both the Justice Department and the Connecticut Insurance Commission. The acquisition would fail unless there was victory in all three campaigns.

As expected, the board was the first to bow. Those opposed to the merger were able to win postponements in August and early October, but they caved in when, on October 21, a federal district court denied McLaren's motion for a preliminary injunction to block the takeover. A special meeting was held on November 10, at which time the merger was approved by a substantial majority of the stockholders.

Interest now turned to the Insurance Commission's deliberations taking place in Hartford. Cotter and his associates rejected the merger on December 14, arguing that it would benefit neither the company nor its policyholders. Moreover, they complained about the methods used by ITT during the negotiations, especially the offering of stock options to Hartford directors, presumably to influence their votes. The report left no doubt that the commission considered ITT an unwholesome influence, and by his actions and statements Cotter indicated that under no circumstances could his opinion be altered.

Nonetheless, ITT launched an offensive. First came an announcement that a revised plan would soon be presented, together with a request that the hearings be reopened for its consideration. As it turned out, the new offer wasn't materially different from the original one, but it did serve its purpose—namely, to keep the discussions alive. Then leading ITT executives descended on Hartford for meetings with Cotter and other commissioners, hoping to hammer out some kind of compromise. Geneen himself arrived in early March, 1970, just prior to the second hearings, with new offers to launch a construction program to help revive the local economy and increase employment. In some ways it was a replay of the ABC affair, with Geneen promising that Hartford Fire would have its own board and a considerable amount of autonomy. Rather than intending to strip Hartford of its capital, ITT would invest additional funds in operations and expand their scope. Cotter and the others were submitted to barrages of affidavits, testimonials, and rebuttals to their objections, as well as arguments from local politicians eager to obtain that construction program. Matters were complicated by Cotter's intention to run for Congress, which meant he needed organization support. It was against this background that the hearings took place. Still, toward their conclusion, Cotter appeared as firm as ever in his objections to the takeover.[9]

It was about this time that Cotter met Ralph Nader, perhaps the nation's most famous and articulate critic of corporate capitalism. Nader had come to view Geneen and ITT as a malevolent force, symbolic of the kind of private power he considered a national blight. Ideologically a socialist, Nader favored a wide variety of programs to restrict the activities of large corporations, from stiffer regulatory controls to passage of a national incorporation law that would give the government the means to pass on a company's right to operate in interstate and foreign commerce. By early 1970 he had come to consider prevention of the ITT-Hartford merger a priority, and one of his "raiders," Reuben Robertson III, was assigned full-time to the matter.

In a submission to the Senate Judiciary Committee two years later, Robertson sketched his version of what next transpired. According to him, Cotter spoke with Nader of the "tremendous pressures [that] were being brought to bear upon him, through both business and political channels in the community, to rule in ITT's favor." Geneen himself was coordinating the campaign, including visits to Hartford's chamber of commerce and similar organizations, which then approached Cotter on ITT's behalf. "Cotter even complained that he had been the subject of an 'investigation' by ITT." Cotter needed support and assistance, and Nader said he would supply both.

During the next month, Robertson submitted memoranda to Cotter in which it was claimed that ITT's financial strength was questionable and overstated, implying Geneen expected to use Hartford's assets in other parts of the corporation. These charges were contained in a brief and memorandum filed with the Insurance Commission on April 27, at which time Nader and Robertson believed Cotter to be as committed as ever to opposing the merger.[10]

They were mistaken. ITT intensified its pressures, and the commissioner was weakening. Through a local lawyer, Joseph Fazzano, Aibel contacted Cotter hoping to arrange some form of settlement. Geneen returned to Hartford for additional conversations, repeating his offer to construct new facilities in the city. Observing that it was an election year, local Democrats urged Cotter to change his mind. So he did. On May 24 the Insurance Commission announced its approval of the merger.

ITT now went ahead with its tender offer. The corporation was to issue 21.7 million shares of a new $2.25 cumulative convertible preferred stock for Hartford's common. These shares were worth more than a billion dollars, making this the most expensive acquisition by an American corporation to that date. This was also a premium of approximately 28 percent over the net value of Hartford's shares on the day the Insurance Commission approved the merger. Hartford's net assets came to $486 million, meaning that ITT was paying a 122 percent premium to obtain them. In this light, it becomes evident that Hartford didn't come cheaply. But with its industry position and potential, and what it might contribute to

ITT in the form of stability and services, it appeared a sensible move.

Things seemed to be looking up for ITT. Starting on June 16 and continuing through December, the corporation conducted its exchange for Hartford's shares. During the same period, Geneen picked up four small European companies and ten American ones, the largest and best known of which was Gwaltney, the producer of Smithfield hams and other pork products.

On the last day of the year the district court for Connecticut upheld the corporation in the Grinnell case, with Judge William Timbers issuing a biting rebuke to McLaren, implying the action should never have been brought and coming down in favor of the Turner interpretation of the antitrust statutes and their limitations. "The Court declines the government's invitation to indulge in an expanded reading of the statutory language and holds the statute means just what it says. It proscribes only those mergers the effect of which 'may be substantially to lessen competition.' " This clearly wasn't the situation this time, said Timbers. "The government has not sustained its burden of establishing that ITT's acquisition of Grinnell may have the effect of substantially lessening competition," and he concluded, "If that standard is to be changed, it is fundamental under our system of government that any decision to change the standard be made by the Congress, and not by the courts."[11]

This wasn't the end of the matter, however. Nor did the completion of the exchange offer mean that Hartford was safely in the ITT family. McLaren intended to press ahead with that case, and Nader would continue his pursuit. Already there were questions as to whether the former Hartford shareholders had any tax liability as a result of the transaction. In order to obtain a favorable ruling from the Internal Revenue Service, ITT had to divest itself of the 1.7 million Hartford shares it had purchased prior to the merger. This was done, in an unusually complicated set of maneuvers that involved the Italian financial institution Mediobanca di Credito Finanziario; another Italian firm known as Way Assauto, which manufactured auto parts; and Lazard, with 100,000 shares given to international businessman Charles Engelhard for his help in arranging the deal.[12] The Hartford tax problem was still to be resolved, and ITT's activities in obtaining the merger would be raised in government investigations later on. For the moment, however, the corporation's critics were on the defensive, and in early 1971 their prospects weren't particularly bright.

In the 1970 annual report Geneen celebrated the corporation's fiftieth anniversary and—by implication, at least—its twelfth year under his leadership. He observed that ITT was continuing to establish new records in most areas, the hallmark of his administration. "At the 1970 year-end we had completed a continuous record of *46 consecutive quarters* in which sales, net income, and earnings per share have increased over the corresponding period of the previous year." To underline his own contribution, Geneen added, "In the 1959 annual report we noted our commitment to build the long-term future of ITT but also our commitment to steady year-to-year growth." He saw no significant problems ahead, either with the economy or with governments. But he did note that discussions were being held with recently elected Chilean president Salvador Allende for the sale of ITT's telephone operations in that country. All was proceeding well, said Geneen. "Our discussions at this time are cordial and reflect a sincere interest on both sides in reaching equitable solutions."

Geneen had achieved all of the goals he had established for ITT upon arriving there a dozen years earlier, and at the age of sixty he was in his prime, apparently destined for additional victories before stepping down. Domestic operations were strong and developing according to plan, and there was good news from overseas as well, where the ISE companies were setting records. If Geneen was troubled by the prospects of defending ITT in the Hartford and Grinnell suits, he did not let it show. Rohatyn and others continued to feed large and small companies into the acquisitions machine, which functioned as smoothly as ever.

Never again would the situation appear so bright, the prospects so inviting. As a result of several factors—economic difficulties at home, legal complications, but most of all a corporate hubris that had developed in the late 1960s and was most evident in Geneen himself—ITT was about to enter a time of troubles more difficult and complex than anything it had known since the early 1930s.

The immediate cause was the way the corporation dealt with the Hartford and Grinnell antitrust cases, in the process of which it became deeply and inextricably involved with the Nixon Administration. Managers and executives who had proved themselves skillful in business blundered badly in political matters and demonstrated remarkable insensitivity in other areas. Geneen was able to win several major skirmishes, especially those in the courts and conference rooms, but much more was lost before congressional committees and in the arena of public opinion. Even now ITT is erroneously associated in the public mind with the shabby activities and multiple deceptions known collectively as "Watergate." That some of the criticism of the behavior of ITT's leaders during the next three years was ideologically biased, exaggerated, or simply false is demonstrable. Notwithstanding this, a number of the allegations had substance, and altered significantly the public image of the corporation.

15

Friends in High Places: White House I

AS had John Kennedy and Lyndon Johnson before him, Richard Nixon attempted to centralize power in the White House and his staff, and more than his predecessors he accumulated power at the expense of others within the executive branch. Members of the initial Cabinet weren't as much undistinguished as they were without a great deal of influence. Of this group only two—Attorney General John Mitchell and Secretary of Labor George Shultz— were able to wield considerable authority, and this was more the result of access to the Oval Office than of any powers derived from their official posts.

Counselor to the President Arthur Burns held Cabinet rank and in the view of many observers had more direct control over domestic affairs than anyone else in government except Nixon himself. Within a short period Henry Kissinger, then at the National Security Council, would overshadow Secretary of State William Rogers, and both Burns and Kissinger operated from positions close to

Nixon in the White House. Assistant to the President H. R. Haldeman and Counsel to the President John Ehrlichman controlled access to Nixon, and by mid-1969 they had effectively transferred to themselves a good deal of authority that had once been exercised by Cabinet officers. Haldeman had become White House chief of staff, and Ehrlichman would soon receive a title more descriptive of his true role: Assistant to the President for Domestic Affairs.

While Burns and others concerned themselves with wide-ranging social and economic matters, Haldeman and Ehrlichman became involved in the politics of power. Those interested in obtaining executive action on virtually any matter came to understand that little might be expected without their approval. It wasn't surprising, then, that these two—Ehrlichman in particular, because he was the more approachable—came under a great deal of attention from Washington's lobbyists. Ehrlichman would use them, and anyone else necessary, to consolidate his position and enhance his authority, elbowing aside even such prominent old associates as John Mitchell. That this wasn't perceived at the time is understandable. Later, with the release of the Presidential Transcripts, it also became obvious that Nixon himself had been manipulated, and on several occasions played Othello to Ehrlichman's Iago. But, then, there were several like Ehrlichman in the White House during this period. As for ITT, its executives and public-relations people conducted conventional lobbying campaigns, but to Ehrlichman they were pawns to be used in his play for power, or at best unwitting allies in his struggle to achieve domination over the Justice Department.

ITT maintained a large, experienced, and expensive public-relations operation in the capital. The office there was headed by William Merriam, a mild, genial, veteran lobbyist. Merriam reported directly to Ned Gerrity, of course, but he had more independent authority than any other subordinate, in recognition of which he was one of the few public-relations men to hold an ITT vice-presidency. His deputy, John Ryan, was well known for his ability to be either gregarious or tough as the situation demanded, and he positioned his people with a fine hand. A goodly number of these people were familiar figures in the capital but hardly known outside their own circles. Dita Beard was the exception.

Dita Beard arrived in Washington in the early summer of 1961 to take a job as secretary in ITT's public-relations office. The daughter of an Army officer, she had been raised in various parts of the world.

Friends in High Places: White House I

Twice divorced and the mother of five, she was unusually resilient, shrewd, and, most of all, flamboyant. Large, loud, and often vulgar in language and manner, Beard was a "character" in a city where certain kinds of eccentricities are not only tolerated but often encouraged. That she drank heavily and swore mightily soon became obvious. In some places this might have transformed her into a pariah, but not in the ones she frequented, where a straightforward approach combined with a sense of humor was looked upon as refreshing, and even attractive. "Mother Beard," as she liked to call herself, already knew some people in Washington, especially military officers, through whom she met others. "Within less than six months," she later said, "I began making contacts on Capitol Hill." Soon she was promoted to lobbyist, with a wide range of duties, "from sweeping the floor on up," but most of her work was with legislators and governors. In her words, the job involved finding out "what was going on, why, and to whom—and when it is going to happen to us."[1]

Beard was supposed to influence congressmen and others to consider legislation and regulations affecting ITT in ways that were favorable to the corporation. She did this well, and within a few years had become perhaps the best known-figure in the Washington office, on good terms with and personally loyal to Geneen, whom she regarded as a genius. In 1966 *Fortune* wrote that Beard was one of the city's most skilled lobbyists, "with a reputation for picturesque language and knowing what makes Congressmen tick."

Merriam, Ryan, Beard, and others saw the centralization of power in the Nixon White House, though at first they hardly could have known of the power struggle then developing. They took this into account when considering methods of applying pressure against McLaren and others at the Antitrust Division and elsewhere. Ordinarily they might have appealed only to Kleindienst, McLaren's superior, since Mitchell, who in the spring of 1969 was considered friendly to the corporation, had bowed out of the Continental Baking case. Thus, the initial approach followed more or less a conventional pattern. In April, Aibel went to Washington to meet with administration representatives in an attempt to dissuade the Justice Department from opposing the Canteen acquisition. Not only did nothing come of this, but two months later McLaren notified Aibel that briefs would be filed to prevent the Grinnell and Hartford takeovers as well.

I·T·T: The Management of Opportunity

With this ITT turned to the White House, utilizing two arguments against Justice in addition to the legal ones, points that would be made over and over again during the next few months. ITT was an important contributor in the area of foreign sales, earning money abroad at a time when balance-of-payments deficits were receiving a great deal of attention. The corporation would be severely damaged—so it was alleged—if these mergers were blocked, and it would be harmed overseas as well as in the United States. Then too, ITT remained a major supplier of a wide variety of military ordnance, and such operations might be affected by corporate disruptions growing out of the legal actions.

Geneen himself raised the issue of foreign dealings. Working through Secretary of Commerce Maurice Stans, he tried and failed to obtain an appointment with Nixon, nominally to talk about balance-of-payments problems. Beard had better results in her efforts. Drawing on an old friendship with Col. James Hughes, the military assistant to the President, she was able to meet with Ehrlichman, who in late April called Kleindienst to ask for a report on the ITT-Canteen suit, thus indicating he had an interest in the matter. This was provided, and now Kleindienst and McLaren knew that the White House was concerned with the litigations. Sensing she had found a way to put pressure on McLaren, Beard next contacted Secretary of Defense Melvin Laird, whom she had known when he had been a congressman, presumably to raise the issue of damage to ITT's ability to produce military supplies, and she maintained contacts with Hughes, bringing up a new issue in her own blunt way. "The IT&T position is that they have done nothing wrong and in particular have violated no policy of this administration," wrote Hughes in a memo to Ehrlichman on September 19, adding, "On the emotional side Deta [sic] cites a heavy financial support given by IT&T to the President's election."[2]

If Hughes was reporting accurately, it would appear that Beard was asking for a quid pro quo, perhaps hinting that additional donations would be forthcoming if the litigation were halted. That such offers were made in Washington was well known, but they were almost always made in a more oblique fashion. This wasn't Dita Beard's style. Defenders of the corporation would hear echoes of her words two years later, when ITT once again employed money in matters relating to presidential politics.

In early 1970, as the Canteen and Grinnell cases proceeded and the

Connecticut Insurance Commission considered the Hartford merger, Geneen traveled regularly to Washington to promote his cause with White House insiders. There were meetings with Stans, Mitchell, Treasury Secretary David Kennedy, Arthur Burns, and Chairman of the Council of Economic Advisors Paul McCracken to discuss the impact of the litigations on the balance of payments, and Ehrlichman assured Geneen the administration wasn't against bigness per se.[3] All the while, Geneen was drawing closer to Nixon himself, hoping to obtain a commitment from him on the issue.

On July 17 Geneen was one of several businessmen who dined with Nixon aboard the presidential yacht, *Sequoia*. Among the subjects discussed were ITT's antitrust problems and the balance-of-payments issue. Geneen even raised the matter of the ABC merger, perhaps thinking ahead to a time when it might be reconsidered by a friendlier FCC. Apparently the President was sympathetic, or at least Geneen could claim to have had his ear and derived some benefits from that. In any case, ITT now mounted a major effort to press for action to block McLaren.

Geneen, Gerrity, and others from headquarters arrived in Washington in early August to begin a concerted assault against McLaren. Two of Canteen's attorneys, Hammond Chaffetz and William James, attempted to dissuade McLaren from continuing his case against their merger with ITT, while Geneen and Merriam talked with Ehrlichman and Special Counsel Charles Colson and Gerrity had a luncheon meeting with Vice-President Agnew, hoping to enlist him in a campaign to persuade John Mitchell to do something about McLaren. In a memo to Agnew a few days later, Gerrity wrote, "It was plain that McLaren's views were not consistent with those of the Attorney General and the White House. We are being pursued . . . not on law but on theory bordering on the fanatic." Observing that McLaren seemed to be "running all by himself," Gerrity asked the Vice-President for advice on how best to proceed with Mitchell, in an apparent attempt to isolate the antitrust chief from others at the Justice Department.

Ehrlichman and his allies were doing the same, but for their own purposes. At the White House meeting Ehrlichman reiterated Nixon's belief that by itself bigness wasn't sufficient reason for prosecution, to which Geneen replied that McLaren seemed to think otherwise. Chaffetz and James sparred inconclusively with McLaren. In a letter to Colson shortly thereafter, Thomas Casey,

ITT's director for corporate planning, reported that in the course of their discussions McLaren had made several remarks that placed him at odds with White House thinking on the matter. For example, wrote Casey, McLaren had said something to the effect that "mere power is enough" when deciding to bring an antitrust action. Moreover, he had noted that ITT was continuing to make acquisitions, that it had to be "stopped," thus implying the corporation was being subjected to a personal vendetta.

Colson pointed out the differences between McLaren and those in the White House in a letter to Ehrlichman. "If indeed the facts here are correct then we might be riding one horse and McLaren another," he observed. "How do you think we should best proceed? My own thought would be that you might want to discuss this again with the Attorney General to be sure that he has made known to Mr. McLaren our policy toward the bigness issue." Ehrlichman agreed, and the material was forwarded to Mitchell.

The attorney general later testified that he met with Geneen shortly thereafter to thrash things out, implying he refused on that occasion to intercede for ITT. McLaren's actions had been brought on "anticompetitive grounds," said Mitchell, and not those of bigness alone. "Was Mr. Geneen persuaded at all by your arguments?" Sen. Edward Kennedy was later to ask during the Kleindienst hearings. "I would doubt it very much," replied Mitchell. Nor would the attorney general retreat as a result of pressures from Ehrlichman, who attempted to intercede for ITT. "I would appreciate your reexamining our position in the case," wrote Ehrlichman, who, referring to the *Sequoia* conversations, remarked, "[Geneen] is, of course, entitled to assume the Administration meant what it said to him."[5]

Whatever else he might have done, Mitchell didn't apply pressure on McLaren or bow to Ehrlichman. The antitrust actions continued without interruption, and McLaren later said Mitchell and Kleindienst supported his efforts in late 1970.

As has been seen, Judge Timbers ruled in favor of ITT in the Grinnell case on the last day of the year. Undaunted and without interference from Mitchell or the White House, McLaren announced that he would ask Solicitor General Erwin Griswold to approve an appeal to the Supreme Court. Given the Court's makeup at the time, and in the light of previous decisions, McLaren had reason to hope for a reversal.

Friends in High Places: White House I

In sum, the intense lobbying effort of 1969–1970 had failed in its primary objective—namely, to blunt the Justice Department's antitrust campaign—but in the process the corporation had managed to form alliances, even communities of interest, in and with the White House. True, Ehrlichman occasionally referred in his memos to "Gineen," and after a March 1971 meeting Merriam had to apologize to Ehrlichman for Geneen's having called him "Chuck" on several occasions. But there were memos and meetings; the contacts were maintained. Then, too, though Ehrlichman hadn't suffered an important defeat, the episode had demonstrated that Mitchell could reject his strong suggestions more or less with impugnity. This didn't sit well with individuals intent on concentrating power in the Oval Office. Ehrlichman needed a victory in the ITT matter, if only to signal his domination even of Mitchell. In other words, the attorney general, Kleindienst, McLaren, and others at Justice would have to be brought to heel.

McLaren held a series of meetings with Griswold in January to discuss the Grinnell appeal, knowing that without his assent there could be no further action in the case. A holdover from the Johnson Administration, Griswold was thought to agree with Turner regarding the problems of prosecuting conglomerates, and so was reluctant to join with McLaren. "We felt that it would be very difficult to win it, not only because the law with respect to conglomerate mergers is far from clear, but also because in this particular case there had been sharp conflict in the evidence before the District Judge, and the District Judge had found all the facts against us."

McLaren persisted nonetheless. Perhaps an outright reversal wasn't obtainable, he argued, but at least the Court might clarify several murky matters insofar as conglomerate takeovers were concerned, thus providing guidelines that might be useful in future prosecutions. McLaren's hand was strengthened when a district court acted to prevent the merger of White Consolidated and White Motors on reciprocity grounds, but Griswold wasn't convinced he should act until early April, when he was swayed—"reluctantly"—by McLaren's "dogged determinism to go ahead, and an engaging optimism."[6]

Meanwhile, ITT did all it could to prevent the appeal. Two of the corporation's attorneys went to see Griswold in order to argue against a continuation of the suit. Merriam contacted Assistant to the President for International Affairs Peter Peterson, claiming that antitrust actions such as this would cripple ITT in foreign markets and would thus be detrimental to the national interest. Ehrlichman told Peterson the President wanted him to meet with Geneen, the clear implication being that he was expected to endorse the ITT position. Discussions were held on April 16—four days prior to the deadline for filing the appeal—but Peterson skirted the issues; his memo on the subject was vague and imprecise, not at all what Ehrlichman had wanted.

Better results were obtained by Lawrence Walsh, perhaps the most distinguished member of ITT's longtime counsel, Davis Polk & Wardwell. A well-known antitrust attorney who had formerly served as a federal judge and an ambassador, Walsh discussed the ITT case with a number of Washington insiders in early April, and on April 16—the same day that Geneen met with Peterson—he submitted a detailed argument to Kleindienst in a "Dear Dick" letter. Elsewhere in Washington calls went out from the White House supporting ITT, both directly and indirectly putting pressure on McLaren and Griswold. Neither man gave in, but Kleindienst was showing signs of weakening, for like the others, he knew Nixon had taken a special interest in the affair, though he was not quite certain why.

For a while ITT's critics claimed that this resulted from a corrupt bargain of some kind, by which the President intended to reward ITT for favors both given and expected, and circumstantial evidence seemed to support this view. Not until the presidential-tape transcripts were released three years later was it realized that Nixon had little interest in or feeling of obligation to Geneen, that as far as he was concerned the crux of the matter was McLaren's seeming disregard of his wishes, and little else. Nixon might have reacted as strongly had some other corporation been involved. As it happened, it was ITT.

On April 19, the last day before the deadline for the filing of an appeal in the Grinnell case, Nixon discussed the situation with Ehrlichman and George Shultz.

President: I don't want to know anything about the case. Don't tell me a—

Ehrlichman: Yeah, I won't.

President: thing about it. I don't want to know about Geneen. I've met him and I don't know—I don't know whether ITT is bad, good, or indifferent. But there

	is not going to be any more antitrust actions so long as I am in this chair.
Ehrlichman:	Well, there's one—
President:	God damn it, we're going to stop it.
Ehrlichman:	All right. There's this other one that you are going to talk to John about tomorrow on the networks.
President:	Well, I don't want him to do that, for other reasons.
Ehrlichman:	Well, that's right. This, that's—
President:	This is the wrong time.
Ehrlichman:	These are all coming together.
President:	We wanted to do that at another time.
Ehrlichman:	Okay, but that's all coming together you see at this point in time, so uh, uh, it's, it's (unintelligible)—
President:	Where's Kleindienst? Isn't he in town?
Ehrlichman:	Yeah, he's in his office. I just talked to him about an hour ago. And, uh—
President:	Well, we'll take care of it.
Ehrlichman:	Okay. Beyond that, uh—
President:	(Unintelligible) cut out this damn thing, Bob—John.
Shultz:	In this, uh, talk that I am making speeches—
President:	Yeah, you talking economic.
Shultz:	Yeah—
President:	(Unintelligible) great.
Shultz:	which I quote you with, uh—I'd like to get you to riffle through it when I'm done to—
President:	Sure I will.
Shultz:	see what kind of share, but there is a section on the question of is there something new about the economy today. Has business become more monopolistic, and so on. And I go through the various studies of (telephone buzzes) concentration and the vertical integration and—
President:	(Picks up telephone) Yeah.
Secretary:	Mr. Kleindienst, Mr. President.
Kleindienst:	Hi, Mr. President.
President:	Hi Dick, how are you?
Kleindienst:	Good, how are you, sir?
President:	Fine, fine. I'm going to talk to John tomorrow about my general attitude on antitrust.
Kleindienst:	Yes, sir.
President:	And in the meantime, I know that he has left with you, uh, the IT&T thing because apparently he says he had something to do with them once.
Kleindienst:	(Laughs) Yeah. Yeah.

President: Well, I have, I have nothing to do with them, and I want something clearly understood, and, if it is not understood, McLaren's ass is to be out within one hour. The IT&T thing—stay the hell out of it. Is that clear? That's an order.

Kleindienst: Well, you mean the order is to—

President: The order is to leave the God damn thing alone. Now, I've said this, Dick, a number of times, and you fellows apparently don't get the me—, the message over there. I do not want McLaren to run around prosecuting people, raising hell about conglomerates, stirring things up at this point. Now you keep him the hell out of that. Is that clear?

Kleindienst: Well, Mr. President—

President: Or either he resigns. I'd rather have him out anyway. I don't like the son-of-a-bitch.

Kleindienst: The, the question then is—

President: The question is, I know, that the jurisdiction—I know all the legal things, Dick, you don't have to spell out the legal—

Kleindienst: (Unintelligible) the appeal filed.

President: That's right.

Kleindienst: That brief has to be filed tomorrow.

President: That's right. Don't file the brief.

Kleindienst: Your order is not to file a brief?

President: Your—my order is to drop the God damn thing. Is that clear?

Kleindienst: (Laughs) Yeah, I understand that.

President: Okay.

Kleindienst: (Unintelligible)
    (President hangs up)

Shultz: Anyway, looking—

President: I hope he resigns.

Shultz then turned to the matter of concentration and the role of conglomeratization in contemporary American business, but Nixon wasn't interested in a philosophical and economic disquisition at that time. Rather, he interrupted the secretary to turn once again to the matter of McLaren, with Ehrlichman prepared to step in and reinforce his negative attitudes toward the antitrust chief.

President: This is, this is the problem. The problem is McLaren's a nice little fellow who's a good little antitrust lawyer out in Chicago. Now he comes in and all these bright little bastards that worked for the Antitrust Department for years and years and who hate business with a passion—any business— have taken him over. They haven't taken him over. Then of course McLaren is the man. They go into —Kleindienst is busy appointing judges; Mitchell is busy doing other things, so they're afraid to overrule him. By God, they're not going to do it. I mean the point is that on this antitrust they had deliberately gone into a number of areas which have no relationship with each other, to—whether it's a question of operating more, more efficiently than the rest. There's simply a question of tactically, they've gone off on a kick, that'll make them big God damn trust busters. That was all right fifty years ago. Fifty years ago maybe it was a good thing for the country. That's my view about it, and I am not—We've been, been through this crap. They've done several of them already about—They have raised holy hell with the people that we, uh, uh—*Well, Geneen, hell, he's no contributor. He's nothing to us. I don't care about him. So you can—I've only met him once, twice—uh, we've, I'm just, uh—I can't understand what the trouble is.* [Emphasis added.]

Ehrlichman:	Well—
President:	It's McLaren, isn't it?
Ehrlichman:	McLaren has a very strong sense of mission here.
President:	Good—Jesus, he's—Get him out. In one hour.
Ehrlichman:	He's got a—
President:	One hour.
Ehrlichman:	very strong—
President:	And he's not going to be a judge either. He is out of the God damn government. You know, like that regional office man in San Francisco. I put an order into Haldeman today that he be fired today.[7]

With this, Nixon abruptly changed the topic, not to refer to the antitrust problem for the rest of the meeting. Both Ehrlichman and Kleindienst understood what was expected of them. McLaren was to be stopped. In the power contests of the Nixon Administration, ITT had become an important symbol, though this didn't appear to have been appreciated by Geneen, Gerrity, Merriam, or anyone else at the corporation—save, perhaps, Dita Beard.

Now Kleindienst either had to turn McLaren around or lose

status in Nixon's eyes. Kleindienst was in a difficult position, for he knew that McLaren might resign in a blaze of publicity were he ordered to drop the case. Fortunately for him, there was a way out. Walsh had just filed for an extension, so Kleindienst was able to ask McLaren to consider the request favorably and not arouse suspicions. And, without knowing the pressures on his chief or what had transpired between him and Nixon, McLaren agreed. Equally unaware of these developments, Griswold filed for a thirty-day extension the following day, and the request was granted automatically. Thus, Kleindienst was able to buy time.

By then Mitchell had come to appreciate the seriousness of the situation, and he knew that his status in Nixon's inner circle had been jeopardized. Essentially in the same position as Kleindienst but with more at stake, Mitchell decided he had to back McLaren, but in such a way as to retain Nixon's confidence. He would do this by stressing the political rather than the legal aspects of the matter while shifting the blame for it to those outside of the Justice Department. In addition, Mitchell would offer a strategy to deal with the situation that would defuse it in Nixon's mind.

Mitchell met with the President the following afternoon, and the two men spent close to two hours discussing a variety of subjects, most of them political. Toward the end Mitchell brought up the ITT case. "I would like to get some time to talk to you, Mr. President, about this antitrust business, because this is political dynamite." Nixon agreed, and as before indicated that McLaren was the source of most of the difficulties, giving the attorney general the opening he needed:

Mitchell: And it wasn't McLaren, you know, that started all this. It was your Council of Economic Advisors and Arthur Burns, and it was done in order to help cool this economy and the stock market and I could go on to a lot of other things. And, uh, the things that they're accusing McLaren of are just, uh, uh, made out of whole cloth. It's just not true. There are antitrust cases here, but what I want to talk about is the political aspects of it. And if, uh, if this thing should be turned off, it, I mean the general concept of it, you've got a review going now —intergovernmental—well, it's time to do it. But you just can't stop this thing up at the Supreme Court, because you will have Griswold quit, you will have a Senate investigation—Hart [Sen. Philip Hart, D-Michigan] will just love this—and we don't need it. There are other ways of working this out.

With obvious reluctance Nixon agreed to the Mitchell approach; clearly he would have preferred to fire both McLaren and Griswold. Mitchell assured him all would go well, saying, "And we can get rid of this ITT thing, I think," to which Nixon replied. "I don't care about the ITT. I don't even know what it is."[8]

So much for the effectiveness of the corporation's massive lobbying effort. The net result was that the Domestic Council Committee, which was part of the executive branch, would engage in a study of antitrust policy, to be directed by Ehrlichman, while the Grinnell case would be appealed to the Supreme Court.

That Nixon or almost any other president would devote so much attention to an antitrust matter was surprising, but even more so at this particular time. The economy was in disarray, with a combination of rising prices and high unemployment, which was coming to be known as "stagflation." The dollar was under severe and growing pressure, with foreigners turning dollars in for gold at an accelerating pace. Within a few months Nixon would institute wage and price controls and, in effect, take the country off the gold bullion standard. The administration would do all it could to safeguard the interests of those corporations that earned substantial amounts of foreign currency, for these alleviated pressures on the dollar. Or at least this was the view at ITT, whose strategists now decided to place greater emphasis on the impact of the antitrust cases on the corporation's viability overseas, especially in Europe.

Representations to this effect were made to John Connally, the new Secretary of the Treasury, for whom Nixon had great and obvious respect. Others received letters, memos, and articles pertaining to the subject, usually from Merriam. Peterson, who by now had become quite accustomed to these ITT barrages, sent one on to Ehrlichman and his assistant, Egil Krogh. "You probably have received a similar letter," he wrote, "but if you don't here it is."

Political considerations and the contest for power, and not legalities and troubles with international accounts, would determine the White House's attitude toward the matter.

Ehrlichman made his move on April 28, by which time he apparently felt the moment had arrived to come out into the open. On that day he drew up a memo to the President, in which he attempted to obtain an increased share of responsibility in this case and others. In a direct attack on the Department of Justice, he wrote, "The ITT cases have surfaced what we have known to be a problem for some time. Your strong views on how the Administration should conduct anti-trust enforcement are not being translated into action." Ehrlichman suggested the Domestic Council Committee be granted greater authority, presumably at the expense of Justice, so as better to represent Nixon's views. "You should authorize us to require all government-wide anti-trust work to be coordinated through one White House office, preferably the working group under Krogh that has been at work on this for the past 90 days."

The President agreed, providing Ehrlichman with an important personal victory and dealing Mitchell a blow. The Attorney General was duly informed of the transfer of power—but nothing was said to McLaren and Griswold. Nonetheless, one of the results of this change was that further pressures would be brought to bear to settle the ITT cases out of court.

As it happened, ITT's attorneys had already met with McLaren on several occasions to explore possibilities of a pretrial settlement, not only of the Grinnell case but also of those involving Hartford and Canteen. There wasn't anything unusual about this; in fact it was, and is, the general practice in such litigations. What the ITT contingent had in mind this time was a compromise similar to the one McLaren had agreed to in the LTV case, which had been concluded in June 1970.

Ling's attorneys had argued that LTV no longer would be a viable corporation if forced to divest itself of Jones & Laughlin. Since the company had lost more than $40 million the previous year and there was no sign of a turnround, this claim appeared justified. The Penn Central had just gone bankrupt, the largest corporate failure in American history, and Wall Street was close to panic. Believing an LTV collapse would further undermine confidence, McLaren agreed that the corporation might retain Jones & Laughlin on the condition that it divest itself of properties roughly equal to it in value. LTV agreed, and subsequently sold its majority interest in Braniff Airways and Okonite as well as several smaller entities.

In the aftermath of the LTV settlement, ITT brought in a new attorney, Ephraim Jacobs, who had previously served in the Antitrust Division and was adept at working out compromises. Jacobs met with McLaren in late November, 1970, and presented him with an offer. In return for dropping all three suits, ITT was prepared to divest itself of parts of Grinnell, Canteen, and Levitt, in addition to three of its insurance companies. Moreover, it would accept a strong stricture against reciprocity between Hartford and other ITT companies, and guarantee that the insurer's assets wouldn't be used for intercorporate loans or investments. McLaren rejected the offer, seeing in it a sign of weakness. The following month, however, Judge Timbers decided for the corporation in the Grinnell case, and Griswold's initial reluctance to press on to the Supreme Court with an appeal caused him to reconsider Jacobs' proposition.

Talk of compromise continued in early 1971 and was raised at a meeting between McLaren, Kleindienst, Rohatyn, and others on April 29. Once again the ITT people stressed the problems divestiture would create, especially to the corporation's position as an earner of foreign currencies. Rohatyn raised the issue in a letter to McLaren four days later, adding that there was no simple way of separating the two companies. "The point is that in the event a divestiture of the Hartford was carried out by ITT through some kind of spin-off, ITT would be placed in a very difficult cash position which would severely impact its ability to compete in markets abroad. There could be as much as a 45% reduction in cash available to ITT." The corporation would then have to cut back on overseas commitments, losing market shares to such firms as Hitachi, Ericsson, Siemens, and others. "It would appear contrary to the national interests of this country to take consciously actions which would have such an adverse impact on the balance of payments."[9]

McLaren's position was starting to soften. Whether because of political pressures, fear of losing the case on appeal, personal ambition, or simply a feeling that a settlement made sense at that juncture, he was coming around to that belief. He asked Richard Ramsden, a White House fellow who had previously been a securities analyst, to prepare an opinion on the subject. Ramsden had been instrumental in working out the LTV compromise, so McLaren must have had a good idea of what he would produce. The Ramsden Report, delivered on May 17, agreed almost wholly with the ITT contentions. Were the Hartford stock spun off to ITT's shareholders, the corporation would be left with a significant burden of payments on the preferred shares. "The divestiture of Hartford would have a negative impact upon the ITT parent company and consolidated balance sheets. The result would be a reduction in ITT's incremental parent company debt capacity and possible credit rating." Moreover, "there could be some indirect negative effect upon ITT's balance of payments contributions."[10]

On June 17 McLaren sent a memo to Kleindienst proposing settlement along the LTV lines. "We have had a study made by financial experts and they substantially confirm ITT's claims as to the effects of a divestiture order. Such being the case, I gather that we must also anticipate that the impact upon ITT would have a ripple effect —in the stock market and in the economy." McLaren outlined the terms to be presented, and anticipated no important difficulties in coming to an agreement. Fearing ITT would claim victory, he wrote that the Justice Department should insist on the right to approve the corporation's press releases on the matter. "We want no great protestations of innocence, government abuse, etc., etc."[11] Which is to say, McLaren recognized that the settlement would constitute a vindication of the ITT position. And though he couldn't have known it, it also meant a victory for Ehrlichman.

By the spring of 1971 everything was in place for an out-of-court agreement whereby ITT would retain Hartford. Had this been all there was to the affair, little more would have been heard of it. But there were complications. Whether related or not to the Hartford matter (ITT said it was not; others thought differently), the corporation had moved closer to the administration on yet another front. The result was that ITT was to become deeply enmeshed in presidential politics in 1972, and in a part of the Watergate syndrome that followed. What started as legitimate lobbying would end with the corporation's reputation at its nadir, the result of a series of developments that began in San Diego and ended in Santiago.

16

San Diego to Santiago:
White House II

AS had become the practice for many large American corporations, ITT held its annual meeting at different places each year, and in 1971 it was San Diego's turn. The choice was understandable. Geneen had said California had been a "good home for ITT," and the corporation had greater representation in San Diego than in any other city in the state. It owned two Sheraton hotels and was just completing construction of a major new cable plant, making it one of the more important factors in the city's economy. A third hotel, the Harbor Island, was in the process of going up, and there was talk to the effect that after its completion Geneen intended to move Sheraton's headquarters from Boston to San Diego. Moreover, one of the local congressmen, Bob Wilson, was close to Geneen, having helped arrange for the cable plant to be constructed in the city. An ambitious Republican, Wilson was considering a run against Democratic mayor Frank Curran, and getting the ITT annual meeting would help local business and, presumably, his own chances of being nominated. Geneen might have had this in mind when approving the selection of San Diego.

On the evening of May 12, after the session had ended and Geneen was relaxing and celebrating with associates and friends, Wilson approached him with a request for yet another favor. During the past few months he had been attempting to interest Curran in making a bid for the 1972 Republican Convention, with no success. This wasn't surprising, since San Diego lacked an adequate number of hotel rooms, restaurants, and other facilities needed just to enter the competition. Furthermore, local financing would be required, at least $1.2 million in cash and services, and Curran didn't believe anything near that amount could be raised.

Only days prior to the ITT meeting it appeared the Republicans had narrowed the choice to San Francisco, Houston, Chicago, and Miami, all of which had submitted bids, with Louisville, St. Louis, Detroit, and Philadelphia also in the running. But two of those involved directly with site selection—the director of administration for the Committee to Re-elect the President, Robert Odle, and William Timmons, who was coordinating White House planning for the convention—favored San Diego.

So did Nixon. He wanted to return to California in triumph, but not to San Francisco, generally considered the most liberal city in the state. San Diego was solidly conservative and close enough to his San Clemente home for him to commute to the convention. With his approval, the requirements both for facilities and for financing were lowered, the latter to $800,000, so that San Diego might qualify.

This was what Wilson and Geneen discussed on the evening of May 12, when the ITT chairman was in an expansive mood. According to Wilson, "We kicked around the idea of my going to leading businessmen and putting together a bid package. He then suggested if I would take the lead he thought Sheraton would underwrite up to $300,000 and would, of course, be willing to actually commit for their fair share of the total amount of the money needed." A few minutes later, said Wilson, Geneen indicated that he would see that Sheraton backed him personally "for half the total amount needed, which would be $400,000."[1]

ITT wanted a quid pro quo, in the form of the designation of the new Sheraton Harbor Island as headquarters for the Republican Party. Without the donation some other hotel might have had the honor; although Geneen couldn't have known it at the time, Timmons had recommended both the Town & Country and the Hilton Inn to Haldeman only one day earlier.

Later the amount to be committed was scaled down to $200,000, and the actual sum pledged was to become a matter of some contention. But a breakthrough had been made, and from that point on everything fell into place. On June 26 Timmons formally recommended San Diego as the site, and the City Council submitted its bid on the 29th. In a wire sent to the San Diego Convention and Visitors Bureau on July 21, Sheraton pledged a firm $100,000, and a like sum, if needed, contingent upon matching donations, and this was followed by an announcement of the selection of San Diego by the Republican National Committee.

Although the timing was coincidental, that was the day ITT released news of a settlement regarding the Hartford acquisition. Actually, the matter had been all but resolved more than a month earlier, but McLaren had had to go to Europe on business and the Justice Department and its attorneys had to hammer out a few compromises over specific terms. As expected, these were based on the LTV model, which meant that ITT had to divest itself of businesses with a revenue volume roughly equivalent to that of Hartford, a formula the ITT people had advocated for more than half a year. Canteen, Levitt, and Avis were to be divested, along with portions of Grinnell, and in addition ITT was to be prohibited for ten years from acquiring any domestic corporation with assets of $100 million or more without special approval from the Justice Department. In return the company would be permitted to keep Hartford, and the Canteen and Grinnell suits would be discontinued.[2]

McLaren announced that this was a major government victory, a vindication of his approach that would mean an end to the merger-mania that had afflicted American business. ITT's stock price declined sharply at the news, indicating the investment community thought likewise. Ralph Nader didn't see it that way. He castigated McLaren for what he termed a "sellout," an abandonment of a suit that might have resulted in ITT's dismemberment and possibly that of other conglomerates as well. Nader indicated he might file a complaint of his own in the matter. Such allegations were repeated six months later when McLaren was nominated and confirmed for that federal judgeship he had wanted, and of course would be raised again when news of Sheraton's contribution to the Convention and Visitors Bureau became known.

Had McLaren been party to a deal? On the surface it might appear unlikely, since at the time of the settlement ITT was in a stronger position than was Justice. On July 2 Judge Richard Austin had decided in the corporation's favor in the Canteen case, handing down a ruling almost as scathing as Timbers' had been in the Grinnell litigation. Judge Joseph Blumenfeld was to hear both the Hartford case and the Grinnell appeal and was considered favorably disposed toward the corporation's arguments. Under the circumstances, then, one might conclude McLaren acted prudently. His action seemed vindicated shortly thereafter, when Judge Blumenfeld rejected objections to the settlement, observing that the consent judgments were "carefully tailored to eliminate the aspects of the acquisitions which the original complaints alleged to be illegal." The judge continued, "Within the limits of existing statutory law and judicial power, the provisions of the proposed decrees constitute a commendable achievement toward safeguarding the public interest."[3] So reading between the lines, it would appear that had the cases gone to trial, ITT would have won both.

Four years later a special Watergate task force headed by Richard Davis reported there were "serious possibilities" that Kleindienst, Mitchell, McLaren, California lieutenant governor Edward Reinecke, and possibly Griswold had lied under oath at the hearings. The Davis report said that Griswold had provided information that the Nixon White House had made "an attempt to influence the antitrust cases" involving ITT. By then Mitchell and Kleindienst were in disgrace, and McLaren was dead.[4]

From ITT's point of view, the settlement was highly advantageous. The decree against further large acquisitions meant little in 1971. The merger movement had all but died during the stock market's collapse of 1969–1970 and the subsequent failure of the Penn Central. At the time of the announcement, ITT had no plans for additional significant acquisitions and was concentrating instead on developing those already in hand. Geneen had put his conglomerate together through financial exchanges of various kinds, and although he was proud of having improved on their performance, much of his time had been devoted to takeovers. This period was drawing to a close. Most of the corporation's future growth would come through the nurture of existing holdings.

San Diego to Santiago: White House II

Clearly Hartford was meant to be the centerpiece of the new ITT. In no year during the 1970s and early 1980s would it contribute less than 20 percent of the corporation's net earnings, far more than would have been realized by the divested properties. Of these only Avis and possibly Canteen would be regretted.

At the time, Avis was a profitable, expanding unit. This company had prospered under the ITT umbrella and doubtless would have continued to do so had it remained there. Wall Street recognized this, for Geneen was able to sell less than a quarter of its stock for a price higher than he paid for the entire company six years earlier. Avis remained independent for a few years but then joined another conglomerate, Norton Simon Inc.

Regrets over the loss of Avis were compensated for by getting rid of Levitt, which Geneen later admitted was his worst acquisition and biggest corporate mistake. This wasn't because of a decline in housing starts and management blunders, though both transpired in the late 1960s and early 1970s. Nor was it due to the departure of Bill Levitt, who soon discovered that mavericks had no place in the huge conglomerate. Rather, home-building didn't lend itself to the large-scale plans Geneen had in mind when the firm had been purchased. Even prior to the Hartford settlement he had tried to sell it back to Levitt, with no success. Now he was able to rid himself of what had proved an embarrassment, though ITT retained a large amount of Florida real estate, sold to Levitt by Rayonier and now transferred back to that company, and the real estate would increase substantially in value.

By then Geneen had realized that Canteen had limited growth potential, low profit margins that were difficult to expand, and that it was a dull performer in a highly competitive industry and likely to remain so. Still, the operations had been revamped and streamlined while part of ITT, and a turnabout was in the works. Geneen was quite content to spin it off, and Canteen functioned smoothly as part of its new corporate parent, Trans World Airlines, as one of the few consistently profitable parts of that erratically managed corporation.

Apparently the ITT personnel involved with the San Diego Convention and Visitors Bureau knew nothing of what was transpiring on the antitrust front. Later the corporation would claim that the two matters were completely unrelated, and this lack of coordination would support the assertion. But credulity was strained in the light of a memorandum allegedly sent by the outspoken Dita Beard to William Merriam on June 25, while McLaren and the ITT attorneys were discussing the final settlement and a day prior to Timmons' recommending San Diego as a convention site. In it Beard referred to a "three hundred/four hundred thousand commitment" that was to be made by ITT as part of its "participation" in the convention. Other than a handful of top people in the White House, the Republican Party, and ITT, she wrote, "*no one* has known from whom the 400 thousand commitment had come." She drew a clear connection between the money and the antitrust cases. "I am convinced . . . that our noble commitment has gone a long way toward our negotiations on the mergers coming out as Hal [Geneen] wants them. Certainly the President has told Mitchell to see that things are worked out fairly. It is still only McLaren's mickey-mouse we are suffering." Beard realized that the nexus between the payments and the cases had to be kept secret. "If it gets too much publicity, you can believe our negotiations with Justice will wind up shot down. Mitchell is definitely helping us, but cannot let it be known." As though to underline this, she ended the memo with, "Please destroy this, huh?"[5]

Later on ITT would attempt—unsuccessfully—to discredit the document. Beard would testify—unconvincingly—that she couldn't recall having written entire portions of the memo, and she further alleged that her "D," which was the way she signed such things, had been traced. The memo appeared genuine, however, and clearly implied that in the minds of all concerned a direct relationship existed between ITT's contribution and the Hartford settlement.

On August 5 the Sheraton Harbor Island Corporation sent its $100,000 check to San Diego, and arrangements proceeded for the convention. Disclosure of the pledge led to charges that it was a "payoff" for ending the suit, that McLaren had somehow been influenced by the White House in coming to terms. Kleindienst denied this vigorously, saying, "The settlement between the Department of Justice and ITT was handled and negotiated exclusively by Assistant Attorney General Richard W. McLaren." The story quickly disappeared from the newspapers and was forgotten in a period when debate was intense regarding the Vietnam War, the economy was in disarray, and attention was focusing on the coming presidential campaign.

San Diego to Santiago: White House II

Mitchell resigned as attorney general on February 15, 1972, to take charge of Nixon's reelection drive, and, as expected, Kleindienst was named to take his place. Little trouble was expected in obtaining his confirmation, which was approved by the Senate Judiciary Committee by a vote of 13–0. But Sen. Edward Kennedy expressed "some extremely serious reservations about this nomination," which he intended to pursue before the committee sent its recommendation to the full Senate.

On February 22, while the Judiciary Committee was considering the Kleindienst nomination, syndicated political columnist Jack Anderson obtained a copy of the Dita Beard memo from an unknown source at ITT. Immediately realizing the implications of its contents, he turned it over to an associate, Brit Hume, who confronted her with it the next day. Shocked and flustered—and perhaps a trifle wary since there were two other ITT people in the room—Beard claimed to have had nothing to do with the Hartford settlement, but at the same time she didn't deny having written the memo. Hume didn't pursue the matter, asking instead that she check her files and discuss the matter with those involved.

Beard contacted Hume the following morning, asking him to come to her Virginia home to discuss the memo. When he arrived Hume found her much calmer but clearly still upset after a sleepless night. According to Hume, she admitted having written it and went on to describe how she had discussed the Hartford case with Mitchell at Kentucky governor Louis Nunn's home, where they met after the running of the Derby. Beard told Hume that Mitchell subjected her to "a scathing, hour-long scolding in the bluntest language for putting pressure on the Justice Department on the mergers via Capitol Hill and other means instead of coming to see him." She was overwhelmed by Mitchell's diatribe, but recovered sufficiently to discuss a settlement. According to Hume's notes, it was arranged while moving down a buffet line.

> Finally, she said she asked him, "Well, do you want to work something out," or words to that effect. She said he replied in the affirmative. She said he said, "What do you want," meaning what companies did ITT wish to retain in the merger case settlement. She said she told him they had to have the Hartford Insurance Company "because of the economy." And she added that they also wanted "part of Grinnell." She said she couldn't

remember what else she asked for, but it was exactly what the company got in the settlement.[6]

Beard conceded she had been involved in both the Hartford talks and the donation to the San Diego Convention and Visitors Bureau. But, according to Hume, she denied the existence of a tradeoff, or that the contribution had been made to obtain the settlement.[7]

The following day Hume telephoned Mitchell's office but was unable to speak with him. Press officer Jack Hushen admitted the attorney general had met Beard at Nunn's home but said he had only spoken with her for a few moments. Hushen insisted that Mitchell could prove the memo to be false in what it said about him.

This was a serious matter, as both men realized. Mitchell had bowed out of the action because of his prior relationship with ITT Continental Baking, and he and Kleindienst had insisted repeatedly they had nothing to do with McLaren's activities in the Hartford settlement. Indeed, Kleindienst had just testified under oath to this effect. This added to the explosive nature of the documents in Hume's possession.

Hume now had sufficient material for his article. The story appeared under Anderson's name in the "Washington Merry-Go-Round" column on February 29. "We now have evidence that the settlement of the Nixon administration's biggest anti-trust case was privately arranged between Attorney General John Mitchell and the top lobbyist for the company involved," it began. The article took note of Beard's denial of any relationship between the Hartford case and the San Diego donation, but Hume was skeptical. "This clearly contradicts her memorandum, which was written about six weeks after the Kentucky Derby dinner." The Anderson-Hume position was stated flatly. "The memo, which was intended to be destroyed after it was read, not only indicated that the anti-trust case had been fixed but that the fix was a payoff for ITT's pledge of up to $400,000 for the upcoming Republican convention in San Diego."

Other articles followed, in which Anderson and Hume drew the net tighter, in the process arming Senator Kennedy and others who had doubts about the Kleindienst nomination. "We have now established that Attorney General-designate Richard Kleindienst told an outright lie about the Justice Department's sudden out-of-court settlement of the Nixon Administration's biggest antitrust case" was the lead for the March 1 column, and the lead sentence two days later was "The Justice Department and International Telephone and Telegraph are now trying to lie their way out of a scandal over the suspicious, sudden settlement of a landmark antitrust case against ITT."

All the government officials named by Anderson and Hume issued prompt and in some cases plausible denials. Immediately after the appearance of the initial article, ITT said, "There was no deal of any kind to settle our antitrust cases. It is unfair to the individuals involved to even suggest such a possibility. Agreement was reached with the Justice Department only after hard negotiations between our outside counsel and the then-Assistant Attorney General Richard McLaren and his staff." Hume had alleged that ITT had shredded pertinent documents to avoid having them subpoenaed by the committee; the corporation responded that this had been done a full week prior to the appearance of the February 29 column and in response to clear evidence that the files had been tampered with, but the image of a company engaged in a hasty cover-up was firmly implanted in the public mind.

Although he had already testified and probably would have been confirmed by a majority of the committee without further comment on his part, Kleindienst offered to return to a reopened hearing in order to respond to the allegations. So he did, and now the sessions turned to a detailed exploration of both the antitrust and San Diego situations. Through March and April of 1972 a parade of witnesses appeared, including McLaren, Rohatyn, Wilson, Merriam, Gerrity, Anderson, and Hume. Beard had vanished, but soon it was learned she was under constant medical attention at an obscure osteopathic hospital in Denver. Later it was revealed that Howard Hunt, of the White House "plumbers unit"—who was to mastermind the Watergate break-in—had flown there on March 15 to induce Beard to sign a statement disavowing the memo and suggesting that Anderson had had it forged. She refused to do so, but afterward she did issue a statement denying its authenticity. The committee tried to bring her to Washington to testify, but Beard's physicians claimed she was in no condition to travel. So on March 26 the committee members and their staff appeared at the hospital to receive her reluctant testimony, which was evasive, confused, and wholly unconvincing. The implication drawn from all this was that ITT had sequestered Beard and had put pressure on her so that she wouldn't incriminate the corporation.

ITT's position at the hearings was that it had engaged in open, legitimate lobbying efforts. "Mr. Geneen's right to place his views before any and all members of the government involved in national policy is a constitutional right of all American citizens," read a press release dated March 13. "It is the duty of any businessman or citizen to express his views when he feels he has a wrong that needed redress." According to the ITT witnesses, the corporation was primarily interested in making its position known regarding antitrust affairs, and nothing illegal had been done or suggested insofar as the Hartford litigation had been concerned. Moreover, there was no connection, direct or otherwise, between that case and the San Diego donation, which was portrayed as an advertising cost. In his testimony on March 29, Geneen said that bringing the Republicans to San Diego would place that city on the national convention circuit and thus attract other gatherings there, all to the benefit of the Sheraton hotels. He claimed that the total commitment had been $200,000—$100,000 in cash, the rest contingent on the raising of an additional $200,000 by San Diego. This wasn't a large amount to spend for publicity in introducing a new hotel. "For example, the Waikiki-Sheraton which was opened in July in Hawaii had cost about $250,000 in promotional expenses and Sheraton has in the past incurred over $200,000 on many occasions in opening expenses of new hotels. Moreover the news value of the convention with the presidential headquarters situated in the new hotel was of inestimable value to not only the San Diego hotel but other hotels in the Sheraton chain worldwide." To put the sum into perspective, Geneen added that $100,000 could purchase a little less than three minutes of prime time on a television network, and during the convention, cameras would be trained on the Sheraton name, in effect advertising it to a vast audience. "This was a solid business expense," he concluded. "It has absolutely no connection with our antitrust problems with the Department of Justice."[8]

It was a plausible argument, but under the circumstances not given much weight. Most observers considered that there were connections between the donation and the litigation. In recognition of this the Republicans decided to move the convention from San Diego to Miami, and this was taken by some as a tacit admission of wrongdoing.

It remains to be noted that Kleindienst reappeared before the committee on the last day of its hearings, April 27, once again to deny having intruded in behalf of ITT with McLaren or anyone

else. That afternoon almost all of the questions revolved around
ITT. The last exchange was pointed:

Senator Kennedy:	Just one question.
The Chairman:	We are going to quit at 5 o'clock.
Senator Kennedy:	As Attorney General, Mr. Kleindienst, given your background on the whole case, if there were a corporation that had a major fundamental problem in antitrust and they made this proposal of a contribution, either to the site committee or a national political organization, do you think under those circumstances that you would advise either the political organization to turn such a contribution down—
Mr. Kleindienst:	I do not think it would ever get that far. If Mr. Rohatyn, when he came to my office—
Senator Kennedy:	Just irrespective of the past now, just if we— I would just be interested in how you would react to a situation where a company or corporation has a major kind of legal question to be decided by any administration, Republican, and offers a contribution—
The Chairman:	Ted, I cannot go beyond 5 o'clock. (Laughter.)[9]

Kleindienst's nomination was approved by a vote of 11–4 and was
reconfirmed by the Senate as a whole. He served less than a year in
office. In May 1974 Kleindienst pleaded guilty to a misdemeanor
charge—failure to provide full information to the Judiciary Committee—and received a one-month suspended sentence and a suspended fine of $100.

Three members of the Davis task force resigned in protest over
the decision not to seek a felony indictment.

No other indictments came out of the Hartford–San Diego affair,
in part because the government was for some reason unwilling to
act. Perhaps more important, though, was that for all their pyrotechnics, Anderson and Hume could produce only circumstantial
evidence. Criminal actions might have been brought had only one
or two of the allegations they made been provable. Such wasn't the
case.

In essence, ITT's leaders had offered suspect explanations for
their actions in San Diego and Washington. Given the nature of the

times and ITT's previous problems, many didn't believe them. By 1972 Geneen was primarily known not for his management feats but for his difficulties with government, and ITT's reputation suffered as well.

This would have been bad enough, but at the same time that the corporation was explaining itself in courts and before the congressional committee, it was becoming involved in yet another sticky situation, one with more serious ramifications—namely, the internal affairs of Chile.

In this as in other episodes there would be strife, contention, and close contacts with the Nixon Administration, with which ITT was becoming identified in the public mind. There were two important differences, however. In the antitrust and San Diego episodes ITT functioned as a corporation in conflict with government agencies. The Chilean matter involved the corporation in the nation's foreign policy and covert operations, leading to charges that Geneen had arrogated to himself rights and powers usually reserved for heads of state, and that in the process he had subverted the Constitution.

In order to appreciate why ITT behaved as it did, one must first understand the situation in Chile, the temper of the times, conditions in Latin America since Fidel Castro took power in Cuba, and, finally, Geneen's perception of the meaning of the Cold War and of the proper behavior of American firms in that struggle.

It will be recalled that Sosthenes Behn obtained control of the Chilean telephone system in 1927. Three years later he organized Compañía de Teléfonos de Chile (Chiltelco), which was granted a fifty-year concession. Chiltelco was profitable and grew steadily. Telephone systems being capital-intensive, ITT had to expend large sums for additional lines and improvements. During the 1960s it provided Chiltelco with $40 million in new financing and also reinvested all of the earnings except $19 million, which was taken in dividends. As a result the value of the company's assets increased sharply. As a regulated public utility, Chiltelco submitted to annual audits. Its net worth in 1970 came to some $200 million, a figure accepted by both the government and ITT.

In 1964 Christian Democrat Eduardo Frei and Salvador Allende Gossens, candidate of the Popular Action Front, contested for the right to succeed outgoing president Jorge Alessandri. A moderate dedicated to bringing about needed social and economic changes without revolution, Frei was hailed as the democratic alternative to

San Diego to Santiago: White House II

Castro. Allende was a Marxist whose program included nationalization of the American-owned copper mines, the banks, utilities, and several industries. After a campaign during which each candidate labeled the other as the tool of outside interests, Frei won easily, receiving 56 percent of the popular vote against Allende's 39 percent. As expected, the large American firms with interests in the country—Anaconda, Kennecott, American Electric Power, and Ralston Purina, along with ITT—applauded his victory.

Shortly after taking office, Frei embarked on a program, conducted through the Corporación de Fomento de la Producción (CORFO), of compensated full and partial nationalization of several foreign-owned companies. In 1967 he signed an agreement with ITT providing for the continued expansion of Chiltelco and the gradual sale of up to 49 percent of its stock to CORFO and Chilean nationals. The money was to be reinvested in Chiltelco, which eventually was to come under full Chilean control. By 1970 ITT's interests had been reduced to 70 percent, worth approximately $153 million.

Frei's gradualism pleased the Americans, but it caused dissension within his own party and strengthened the opposition, which also won supporters because of a weakening economy. Under terms of Chile's Constitution, Frei couldn't run for a second term in 1970, by which time the moderates were divided between two candidates, former president Alessandri and Frei's rival within the Social Democrats, Radomiro Tomic. Allende planned another campaign, once again with backing from the Popular Action Front.

In the election, held on September 4, Allende received 36 percent of the popular vote, less than his share six years earlier but more than Alessandri or Tomic. According to the Constitution, the selection of the president was to be made by the legislature if no candidate obtained a majority. Such was the situation in September and October, as all three men jockeyed for position, and behind them—especially Allende and Alessandri—were foreign interests, Cuba and the Soviet Union for Allende and the United States and American businessmen for Alessandri or some other moderate alternative.

As has been noted, the Vietnam War raged in 1970, the United States was badly divided, and a president with impeccable anticommunist credentials was in office. Some considered the "domino theory" discredited by events in Southeast Asia, but others—many of whom had voted for Nixon—felt otherwise, and they yearned for vindication. Looking southward, they saw Castro's influence expanding in the Caribbean, and the Cuban had cadres of supporters in such countries as Venezuela, Bolivia, and, of course, Chile. That Castro had supported Allende in 1964 was hardly a secret, and he was in his camp six years later. His election would be seen as a major victory for Marxism, not only in the hemisphere but throughout the world. It would be the first time a communist had achieved power by election in a democratic nation. Allende's success would bolster the spirits of communists elsewhere, in Western Europe as well as within the Soviet bloc, and would provide their cause with an enhanced legitimacy. This was appreciated in Washington, and also at ITT's New York headquarters.

Geneen always considered himself a staunch patriot and anticommunist. This didn't mean ITT would refuse to do business with communist nations, or that Geneen had developed a consistent and clear rationale with an understanding of all its ramifications. His sentiments on these matters were visceral rather than intellectual, and in addition he tended to identify (and on occasion confuse) the interests of the nation with those of his corporation. Nowhere was this more evident than in Latin America.

Geneen viewed the election of Allende as a threat to both the United States and ITT, whose properties might be seized if Allende came to power. He was determined to do all he could to prevent this. It seemed the sensible thing, given the corporation's experience in the past decade.

Geneen had failed in his attempt to prod the Eisenhower White House into action when Castro expropriated Cuban Telephone. He had had a difficult time of it in Brazil, obtaining a satisfactory settlement months after that country and one of its states seized the telephone companies there. When a military junta took over in Peru, it nationalized Peruana de Teléfonos, but after protracted negotiations the generals paid ITT $17.9 million for the property, on condition that $8 million of the sum be invested in that country. This Geneen did, by erecting a Sheraton hotel there. His experiences in Latin America had obviously been troublesome.

By 1970 all that remained of Colonel Behn's telephone-operating companies were those in Puerto Rico and Chile, with Chiltelco by far the most important and largest ITT holding in Latin America. In addition, there was a small ISE factory in Santiago, which manufactured equipment for Chiltelco; there were two Sheraton hotels, worth approximately $8.4 million; there was an All America cable installation that handled international telegrams; a publishing house that put together and printed telephone directories; and a unit of ITT World Communications that operated long-distance radio telephones, 10 percent of which had already been sold to the government under an agreement similar to that at Chiltelco.

Geneen saw little future in Latin America for ITT, and had virtually no interest in expanding operations in that part of the world. But he meant to hold on to what he already had and not sell out at low prices. Wary of the Eisenhower White House after the Castro takeover of Cuban Telephone and other properties, he was cheered by John Kennedy's more vigorous foreign policy, especially the early attempts to overthrow the government in Cuba, and he felt the same about Lyndon Johnson's intervention in the Dominican Republic. In common with other heads of large American corporations doing business in Latin America, Geneen saw nothing wrong with intervening in the domestic affairs of countries there so as to further American business interests. It had been common practice, going back at least as far as United Fruit's activities in Central America at the turn of the century. Moreover, he believed Washington had an obligation to protect American investments—an echo of the "dollar diplomacy" prevalent in the pre–World War I era.

The United States government had formally renounced such practices by the 1960s, and most corporations gave lip service to the concept of national sovereignty, but interventions continued, though in a more covert fashion than previously had been the case. Funds were funneled into the pockets of friendly politicians by businessmen and White House agencies. In the Overseas Private Investment Corporation (OPIC), organized in 1969, the United States government provided insurance against expropriation under certain specified conditions for those firms operating in developing nations. In addition, even then there was strong evidence that the Central Intelligence Agency engaged in supporting friendly governments and harrassing others to the point of bringing them down. In defending both governmental and corporate intervention in Chile during a 1973 congressional investigation of the matter, former CIA director and then ITT board member John McCone said there wasn't anything unusual about it.

> This is not an unfamiliar role for the United States. If you go back to World War II, the Truman doctrine in Greece and Turkey was designed to support the political institutions that were somewhat consistent with our own as opposed to the

Communists. The Marshall Plan, indeed, had as its foundation the same idea. The Berlin airlift which James Forrestal so courageously carried out was part of it. The action of President Eisenhower in Lebanon and in Guatemala, these were all part of a situation that this country confronted where international communism had publicly, the spokesmen for international communism had publicly, time and time again, said it was their objective to destroy the free world, they were going to do it politically, economically, and, if necessary, militarily, and that was what this country and its policymakers were trying to offset.[10]

The American corporations had their holdings to protect. By 1970 these amounted to more than $1.1 billion, more than those of all other foreign companies combined. Chile's trade was financed through American banks, and on a per capita basis the country received more foreign aid than any other in Latin America. In the face of an expanding Cuban presence in that part of the world, Washington intended to make certain Chile remained both democratic and pro-American. Thus, the interests of the government and the corporations were united, in a fashion somewhat reminiscent of the way Behn had developed his nexus between the government, the banks, and ITT in the 1920s.

Starting in 1962, the CIA supported Frei's candidacy for the presidency, though without his knowledge. The exact figure expended is unknown, but $3 million was authorized in 1964, most of which went to local organizers and political journals, and probably several times that amount poured into Chile in the successful attempt to block Allende. The American corporations, ITT included, were more than willing to make contributions to the CIA effort, but the funds were rejected on the grounds that the agency couldn't accept private funding, though later it was revealed that donations had been made to friendly Chilean politicians.[11] There was ample precedent six years later, then, for government and corporate involvement in the elections.

By 1970 National Security Adviser Henry Kissinger controlled the secret Forty Committee, which in turn supervised CIA activities. In March of that year the committee authorized the expenditure of $125,000 for anti-Allende propaganda, and three months later the amount was raised to $300,000. (The CIA estimated that in this period Allende received $350,000 from Cuba and an undetermined amount from the Soviet Union.) In defending his action, Kissinger was alleged to have said, "I don't see why we need to stand by and watch a country go Communist due to the irresponsibility of its own people." Money was also sent by American banks and the copper companies, and there was an unspecified sum from ITT, all of this in the summer of 1970.[12]

As in 1964, ITT was prepared to offer the CIA a generous sum to be used in Chile. Working through McCone and CIA director Richard Helms, Geneen was able to arrange a meeting with William Broe, who was in charge of clandestine operations for the Western Hemisphere, to ask if a contribution would be accepted. During discussions on July 16, Broe told Geneen it was out of the question, citing agency policy, but the fact that at the time it appeared Alessandri would defeat Allende might also have played a part in the discussion. Broe did brief Geneen on the situation in Chile, however, and told him how funds from ITT and other corporations might be channeled to the anti-Allende forces. The two men held a short telephone conversation on July 27, and in addition McCone —still a CIA consultant, though this wasn't known at ITT headquarters—maintained his contacts with Helms, thus keeping the way open for future collaboration.[13] Such was the situation on September 4, when Allende won his victory in the first round of the presidential election.

Despite ambassador to Chile Edward Korry's warnings and indications from others that Allende had gained support, official Washington was caught off guard by his victory. Kissinger later wrote that had he known what was to happen, he would have recommended that Nixon consider "a covert program of 1964 proportions, including the backing of a single candidate." From that point on he advocated a strong line in Chile, one that involved direct and important intervention in that country's election. Kissinger indicated as much two weeks later at a background briefing for the White House press corps, which had overtones of the domino theory, with Chile functioning in Latin America the way Vietnam did in Southeast Asia. "I don't think we should delude ourselves that an Allende takeover in Chile would not present massive problems for us, and for democratic forces and for pro-U.S. forces in Latin America, and indeed the whole Western Hemisphere," he said. "So we are taking a close look at the situation."[14]

There was an interesting political dimension to all of this. At the

State Department, Secretary William Rogers was saying that little could be done or might be gained by intervening, while Ambassador Korry favored an information program and turned aside suggestions of covert action by the CIA. Thus, both men opposed Kissinger's approach. In foreign affairs, then, just as in domestic, there developed a division between a Cabinet officer and a White House insider. ITT had become an unwitting pawn in the power contest between Ehrlichman and Mitchell. Now it would play a somewhat similar role in the more open parrying for influence that had surfaced between Kissinger and Rogers, with ITT all the while attempting to preserve its ownership of Chiltelco.

Kissinger used the Chilean crisis to ingratiate himself further with Nixon, to whom the idea of a communist victory in the hemisphere during his administration was anathema. Moreover, the president blamed the State Department and Korry for letting affairs get out of hand in that country, and was inclined to favor Kissinger's approach. From that point on, the CIA, not the State Department, was in control of policy-making in that part of the world.

Under Kissinger's guidance, the Forty Committee developed a two-track program to prevent Allende's coming to power the following month. Track One was political, with the United States supporting what some called the "Alessandri formula" and others the "Frei gambit." Developed by Korry, it involved a large-scale propaganda campaign to induce sufficient Chilean legislators to vote for Alessandri, who would become president with the understanding that he immediately would resign, thus setting the stage for a new election, in which Frei might legally be a candidate. There seemed little doubt Frei could defeat Allende in another contest, and so he would retain executive power for another six years. Neither Alessandri nor Frei indicated much enthusiasm for the plan, but it was put into operation, financed by an initial $250,000 from a contingency fund, most of which was used to place advertisements in pro-Alessandri newspapers in the hope of keeping them viable.

Track Two, which was kept secret from Defense and State Department officials as well as from Korry, involved direct American support for a program of economic and political disruption in Chile, including, if necessary, a *coup d'état*.

When it appeared Track One wouldn't serve to prevent Allende's election, interest turned to the alternatives. On September 15, after consulting with Kissinger, Helms, and Mitchell, Nixon gave what came to be known as the "green light" for a massive CIA intervention in Chile.[15] Korry received only the slightest hint of what was involved. From that point on, the CIA had more knowledge, influence, and contacts with the White House in the Chilean intervention than did the State Department or the American ambassador on the scene.

To complicate matters further, there was a division between the CIA and the Defense Department, the latter allied with State in opposing covert actions. The Pentagon was refusing to encourage a strongly pro-American general, René Schneider, from engaging in a coup, this at a time when the Chilean military had all but come out against Allende. Ten days after the "green light" had been given, Korry sent a cable to Kissinger and Rogers in which he said, "I am convinced we cannot provoke a military coup and that we should not run any risks simply to have another Bay of Pigs. Hence I have instructed our military and [the CIA office in Santiago] not to engage in any encouragement of any kind."[16]

Thus, not only wasn't there a coordinated effort in Chile, but one part of the American government didn't fully understand what the other was attempting to accomplish, which resulted in bungling. The State and Defense departments were often unaware of CIA activities, and in fact these government agencies generally acted at cross purposes in Chile. Finally, there was confusion within the CIA itself as to what it intended to do.[17]

For example, in early October, Gen. Roberto Viaux, who worked with the CIA, was planning a coup, which was opposed by General Schneider, who was in close contact with the State Department. To complicate matters, Gen. Camilo Valenzuela also hoped to overthrow the government, and he received CIA encouragement as well. So it was that one American surrogate clashed with another, while a third waited on the sidelines, and none of them truly understood all of the developments, in large part because of confusion in Washington.

On October 15 the CIA decided to "defuse" the plot temporarily. Viaux was assured of continued American support but discouraged from taking action against Allende. Kissinger later testified that as far as he was concerned, this ended Track Two. The following day, however, CIA headquarters in Washington cabled its Santiago office that it was "firm and continuing policy that Allende be over-thrown by a coup," and that Viaux was to be encouraged in his efforts.

On October 17 several Chilean officers from both groups were provided arms by the American military attaché, and Valenzuela informed Viaux that everything was in readiness for the coup. Then, on October 19 and 20, there were two bungled attempts to kidnap Schneider, who continued to support the government publicly and was the nation's senior officer. On October 22—two days prior to the parliamentary vote—Schneider was killed during yet another kidnapping attempt. Riots erupted, and President Frei declared a state of national emergency, as rumors flew regarding American complicity in the assassination. Allende was now recognized as the intended victim of a plot, and his popularity soared. Alessandri asked his supporters to throw their votes to him, "in order that Salvador Allende may take office in a climate of tranquility." As a result, the October 24 vote was for Allende by a margin of 153 to 35, with seven abstentions.[18]

It is against this backdrop that ITT's role in the Chilean elections must be viewed. That Geneen, his staff, and the corporation's representatives on the scene were eager to become involved in Track One operations is demonstrable. Equally so is the fact that ITT opposed Allende's election. It was approached more than once by the CIA and asked to participate in Track Two programs, but these overtures were turned aside. That at one point in 1970 ITT contributed some $400,000 to Chilean politicians opposed to Allende is fairly certain; it was done through a dummy corporation, the Lucky Star Shipping Co., and written off as a public-relations expense.[19] Beyond that, ITT played a relatively minor role in the complicated and often confused and turbulent Chilean political maneuverings in September and October of 1970, but one couldn't have told this from a cursory scanning of correspondence that passed between Santiago and New York, which at times read like parts of a spy thriller. In fact, there was much talk, a great deal of elaborate and convoluted planning, but virtually no action. This clumsy effort at intrigue on the part of the CIA was misbegotten and misdirected, and it backfired. In these memos the ITT personnel were reporting on developments, not on the corporation's involvement in the affair, a distinction often overlooked by those who later would confuse the two. Yet this is understandable. Even if one recognizes that ITT had a legitimate concern for its investments, its interest in and tracking of what were in fact covert and illegal activities required more explanation than was offered or extracted during future investigations.

All of this provided Allende with a convenient scapegoat: the wicked capitalist trying to thwart the will of the people. ITT and Geneen would be so portrayed throughout the Allende years and blamed for that country's problems whenever they surfaced. Because of this attempted intervention, Allende's power and prestige were enhanced, while Geneen's reputation fell to its nadir.

17

Nadir: Track One in Chile

ITT held its regularly scheduled board meeting on September 9, 1970, and after the usual corporate business was transacted, there were reports on special problems. Aibel reviewed the status of the Grinnell and Canteen cases, and Geneen brought the members up to date on developments in Chile, where, "as a result of the recent election of a Presidential candidate who advocated the nationalization of basic industries," Chiltelco was in danger of expropriation.

This was a signal that ITT was about to become even further involved in Chile's internal affairs.

Geneen knew that two days earlier the Forty Committee had formulated its two-track approach, and that Track One was being set into motion. Without asking the board's approval or even discussing the matter, he indicated a willingness to commit ITT to direct financial participation. John McCone recalled the discussions two and a half years later, and although his memory wasn't com-

pletely accurate regarding details, he was correct on the central
points.

> What he told me at that time was that he was prepared to put
> as much as a million dollars in support of any plan that was
> adopted by the government for the purpose of bringing about
> a coalition of the opposition to Allende so that when confirma-
> tion was up, which was some months later, this coalition would
> be united and deprive Allende of his position.
>   Now, I would like to emphasize that this occurred after the
> election, and that it was not in support of any government
> plan. It was not a plan generated by ITT or in Mr. Geneen's
> mind. He said that this idea had been transmitted to Mr. Kis-
> singer's office, and he asked if I would support it, and I did.[1]

Two days later Jack Neal, a former State Department official and
now in charge of international relations for ITT, telephoned Viron
Peter Vaky, Kissinger's assistant for Latin American affairs, to tell
him that Geneen was willing to come to Washington "to discuss
ITT's interests" in Chile with Kissinger, and that ITT was "prepared to assist financially in sums up to seven figures." Neal also
offered to interest other companies in cooperating with the CIA,
but indicated he hadn't much success along these lines. Vaky told
Neal he would pass on the information, but in fact he didn't do
so. At the time, he considered Neal's conversation "a normal lobbying effort to establish a position, to establish a point of view of
things," and didn't think Kissinger should be bothered by such
matters.[2]
Geneen liked to attack on several fronts simultaneously, and he
so acted in the Chilean affair. To underscore the importance of the
issue, he asked McCone to go to Washington to sound out his contacts there, and the former CIA chief agreed to make the effort.

> I came to Washington a few days later and I met with Mr.
> Helms and I told him of this availability of those funds and I
> also met with Mr. Kissinger and I told him, if he had a plan
> —now Mr. Kissinger thanked me very much and said that I
> would hear from him again and, therefore, I assumed that no
> such plan was adopted as a matter of national policy and that
> was the end of it so far as I was concerned.[3]

Kissinger confirmed this in his memoirs, which contains this sole reference to ITT, in its 1,496 pages, in the form of a footnote:

> I learned later that some representatives of the CIA had informally advised some American business interests in late July and August where to channel funds during the election. This was not known at the White House or in the State Department; at any rate, it also was too late. My own attitude was that any covert action in Chile should be carried out exclusively by our government; this was not a field for private enterprise. Accordingly, I turned down ITT's offer of $1 million to help influence the election. I may have agreed with the objective, but certainly not the vehicle.[4]

Kissinger's statement was accurate, but it did not imply that ITT had no role at all in Chile or that there weren't important contacts throughout this period between the government and the corporation.

What these contacts were is still a matter of some dispute. Felix Rohatyn testified as follows: "Mr. Geneen, as far as I know, has always taken the position that the company did not participate in the plot in Chile." In a carefully prepared statement, Geneen has said under oath that "ITT did not encourage or participate in any way in any alleged plot for a military coup in Chile to block the election of Dr. Allende." Moreover, the corporation "didn't contribute money to any person or to any agency of any government to block the election of Dr. Allende." Finally, Geneen claimed, "ITT did not take any action to cause economic chaos in Chile in an attempt to block the election of Dr. Allende, nor did it advocate that any others take such steps."[5]

There is no doubt today that ITT's field representatives were in continual contact with CIA operatives and Allende's opponents, and that they often knew more of what was transpiring in Chile than did Ambassador Korry. The key figures in this were Robert Berrellez, a former newspaperman who had specialized in Latin American affairs, who was director of inter-American relations and had been on the job in Buenos Aires since January; and Harold Hendrix, a Pulitzer Prize winner for his reporting on Cuban developments, who had been director of public relations for Latin America since 1967. Both men had excellent credentials, and they went to

Nadir: Track One in Chile

Santiago that summer to report on the situation there and to represent ITT. Indirectly they were under Gerrity's control, and Gerrity became a central figure in the Chilean negotiations.

As their correspondence indicates, the two ITT representatives soon got caught up in the complex, behind-the-scenes maneuverings, and headquarters tended to see Chilean developments through their eyes. In addition, ITT's high command was in constant, almost hourly contact with the State Department and had equally intimate relations with the CIA.

What emerges from the correspondence and memos is a picture of a corporation concerned about the nationalization of its one remaining important property in that part of the world and of some individuals who, as anticommunist Americans rather than as ITT'ers, were deeply troubled by what they perceived as the growth of totalitarianism. (In an October 20 memo to Geneen, apropos of nothing and quite uncharacteristically, Gerrity wrote, "Freedom is dying in Chile and what it means to Latin America, and to us—to free men everywhere—is not pleasant to contemplate.")

Still, ITT's actions in Chile were confined to supporting opposition candidates and several anti-Allende publications and related activities. Quite simply, there is no evidence that the corporation became involved in Track Two operations.

The connection began innocuously enough, though it would appear otherwise later on. Shortly after the September 4 election Berrellez met with Arturo Matte, who was Alessandri's chief adviser as well as his brother-in-law, to learn how the corporation might best help in the election effort. Apparently without the candidate's knowledge, Matte suggested a propaganda campaign, redolent of the CIA's Track One operation, and on September 17 Gerrity proposed one to Geneen. The anti-Allende newspapers, which were failing from lack of support, would be assisted through the placement of advertisements, and there would be a radio campaign as well. Attempts would be made to convince the European press of the dangers posed by an Allende victory. Finally, some fifty families of "key personnel involved in the fight" would be relocated temporarily, presumably to avoid retribution at the hands of Allende's supporters.[6]

This was the full extent of Gerrity's recommendations at that time, though by then contributions had been made via Lucky Star

Shipping. It should be kept in mind that Geneen's offer to gather funds to block Allende's election already had been rebuffed. Hendrix and Berrellez were reporting that Allende's election was "almost certain" and would be followed by attempts at expropriation. Even so, on September 17 ITT wasn't prepared to go further than this.

What the corporation's leaders couldn't have known at the time was that two days earlier Nixon had given the "green light" for Track Two. Nothing significant changed in Santiago, but in the United States, William Broe, who, it will be recalled, headed clandestine operations for the CIA, would now assume additional powers.

Recalling his earlier conversations with Geneen and ITT's apparent willingness to assist the government, Broe contacted Geneen and asked for a meeting. At the time, Geneen was in Brussels, attending a regularly scheduled corporation conclave, and so he asked Gerrity to talk with Broe as soon as possible. So it was that the CIA operative came to New York on September 29 to present his suggestions. At the time, Broe later said, "I explored with Mr. Gerrity the feasibility of possible actions to apply some economic pressure on Chile."[7] This included a wide range of covert operations, to be funded by American corporations that would be contacted by ITT.

Broe did this with the full knowledge of his superiors, indicating either he or Kissinger was lying about whether the CIA involved the corporations in Track Two. In light of what was to transpire and the nature of the power nexus in the White House, it would appear Broe was telling the truth and that he came to New York with the specific purpose of inviting ITT to participate in a CIA plan to unsettle the Chilean situation.

Gerrity had grave doubts as to the wisdom of such participation, and would retain these throughout the next few weeks. Nonetheless, that afternoon he transmitted Broe's thoughts to Geneen in what was to become an important and well-publicized message:

> Subsequent to your call yesterday I heard from Washington and a representative called on me this morning. He was the same man you met with Merriam some weeks ago. We discussed the situation in detail and he made suggestions based on recommendations from our representative on the scene and analysis in Washington. The idea he presented, and with

which I do not necessarily agree, is to apply economic pressure. The suggestions follow:

1. Banks should not renew credits or should delay in doing so.

2. Companies should drag their feet in sending money, in making deliveries, in shipping spare parts, etc.

3. Savings and Loan companies there are in trouble. If pressures were applied they would have to shut their doors, thereby creating stronger pressure.

4. We should withdraw all technical help and should not promise any technical assistance in the future. Companies in a position to do so should close their doors.

5. A list of companies was provided and it was suggested that we approach them as indicated. I was told that of all the companies involved ours alone had been responsive and understood the problem. The visitor added that money was not a problem.

He indicated that certain steps were being taken but that he was looking for additional help aimed at inducing economic collapse. I discussed the suggestion with [Jack] Guilfoyle [an ITT vice-president, group executive for the Western Hemisphere division]. He contacted a couple of companies who said they had been given advice which is directly contrary to the suggestions I received.

Realistically I do not see how we can induce others involved to follow the plan suggested. We can contact key companies for their reactions and make suggestions in the hope that they might cooperate. Information we received today from other sources indicate that there is a growing economic crisis in any case.

I advised the visitor that we would do everything possible to help but I pointed out in detail the problems we would have with the suggestions he had made.

Finally, Bob Berrellez has just sent a report which is pessimistic as to the outcome next week. This report is being delivered to you by Mr. Barr of the technical department who is leaving for Brussels this evening.[8]

Apparently Geneen agreed with Gerrity's reservations regarding direct cooperation in such a destabilization effort. The following day, in a message to the Washington office, Gerrity said, "I will call you later to discuss HSG's reaction to my telex in some detail. He agrees with me that Broe's suggestions are not workable. However, he suggests that we be very discreet in handling Broe."

At the same time, other ITT officers were exploring the possibility of obtaining compensation from OPIC in the eventuality of Chiltelco's nationalization. This might be construed as the behavior of a corporation resigned to an Allende victory, seeking to salvage what it could from a bad situation. Merriam and others did sound out several businessmen regarding Broe's suggestion, and they reported no interest there. These firms, too, appeared to believe the prudent policy would be to watch and wait.

As the Chilean legislature prepared for the election, Broe met with ITT executives, still attempting to draw the corporation into covert operations, with no success. Korry was also involved in this, though he still didn't know the full extent of Track Two. According to Neal, "Mr. Korry said if Mr. Geneen had any ideas about U.S. policy toward Allende's government he hoped this would be relayed to the White House immediately. He said other companies with Chilean investments should do the same. He feels any complaints or ideas should be made now rather than after October 24."[9]

None was forthcoming. Instead, ITT attempted to learn what the State Department's reactions would be to a Chilean nationalization effort. Gerrity had in mind little more than the usual official protests and a cutoff of American aid programs to that country.

Allende was elected by a wide margin, and took office on November 3. That his would be a radical government was evident from the start. Most of the key economic posts—finance, public works, labor —went to Communist Party members, and the minister of economy was a communist in all but name. Castro sent his congratulations, and diplomatic relations with Cuba were restored. A few days later a statue of Che Guevara, hero of the Cuban revolution, was unveiled in Santiago. There were indications, too, that Allende would soon act to nationalize those properties belonging to American companies, and so he did. On November 20, while the Chilean legislature considered measures to broaden the scope of existing nationalization laws, the government seized subsidiaries of Ralston Purina and Indiana Brass. Six days later, before a Communist Party group, Allende spoke of his intention to nationalize American-owned copper, utility, and banking institutions. Informed he couldn't do so, even with a new law, Allende announced that he would propose a constitutional amendment establishing state control of large mines and the expropriation of the foreign firms working them.

This prompted an immediate CIA response. It began modestly

Nadir: Track One in Chile

enough on November 13, when the Forty Committee approved an initial $25,000 for support of Christian Democratic candidates in the forthcoming local elections, and on November 19 the committee authorized the expenditure of $725,000 for a new covert-operations program in Chile. In late January, 1971, it authorized the use of an additional $1,240,000 for the purchase of radio stations and newspapers to support anti-Allende candidates, and shortly thereafter the Committee started subsidizing Christian Democratic activities. None of this was done with contributions from American companies, though some of them—ITT included—were kept informed.

During these early months of the Allende presidency, ITT pursued a three-front program: one with the State Department, another with OPIC, and a third with the American corporations. Geneen and Gerrity pressed Secretary Rogers to make it clear to Allende that the United States expected "speedy compensation in U.S. dollars or convertible foreign currencies as required by law" if Allende expropriated American property, while executive vice-president Francis Dunleavy, Aibel, and others tried to pin down OPIC on the specific terms of its guarantees.

ITT helped form the Ad Hoc Committee on Chile, which brought together other large American companies with Chilean interests in a unified lobbying team, and at the same time the corporation considered approaching Allende to discuss what amounted to a "showcase deal," a proposal that would be made on several occasions.

In a memo to Geneen on February 11, Gerrity proposed, "We [might] suggest strongly to Allende that he make an agreement with us on the best possible terms we can arrange so that when he has to come to grips with the problems which will flow from his treatment of other American investments in Chile, he will be able to point to a satisfactory arrangement with us." This would imply breaking ranks with the other American companies. What Gerrity had in mind regarding Chiltelco was a variant of arrangements worked out in earlier years by Colonel Behn and more recently by Geneen when ITT was threatened with expropriations—namely, the sale of the company with an understanding that ITT would plow the money back and receive a management contract for the firm. "I believe that if we take a very pragmatic approach insofar as the telephone company is concerned, we might even be able to secure a contract to maintain and operate as well as supply the company." Both sides could claim victory, thought Gerrity. "Allende could erect a facade of 'Chileanization' in taking over Chiltelco but he would have to recognize that he does not have the know-how to run the company efficiently and that it could be in his interest to maintain a relationship with us."[10]

It seemed a reasonable formula, one that very well might appeal to the new president. ITT officials in Santiago sought a meeting with him in early March, presumably to raise the possibility of adopting some such arrangement. Berrellez noted that economy minister Pedro Vuscovic had told a group of Santiago businessmen that Allende wasn't interested in controlling private enterprise through nationalization or expropriation at that point, but rather "would prefer control over corporate decisions on new investments, expansion, and general policy."

The outlook for an accord appeared favorable on March 10, when Allende and two of his aides discussed the situation with Dunleavy and Guilfoyle, who flew down for the meeting, and Benjamin Holmes, a native Chilean and ITT's managing director at Chiltelco. Talks began amicably enough at eleven-thirty and lasted for an hour and a half. The give-and-take was occasionally pointed, but Hendrix was able to describe the atmosphere as "very cordial, relaxed, pleasant, and amiable."

From the outset Allende attempted to dispel his visitors' fears regarding expropriation, on several occasions stating he wasn't considering a Chiltelco takeover, emphasizing he would prefer a "partnership arrangement of some sort." To a degree this was due to the new government's position that nothing radical should be attempted until power was solidified and the military placated. But, in addition, Allende had little knowledge of telecommunications, and since Chile had an obvious need for foreign capital, he was in no position to alienate any outside source of funding.[11]

Dunleavy went on the offensive from the start, indicating he was not there as a supplicant but rather was prepared to discuss Chiltelco's future as an equal. He talked of "our mutually owned company," and Allende interrupted to comment, "You have the biggest part of it," to which Dunleavy shot back, "You can take it all any time, Mr. President," meaning he could exercise CORFO's right to purchase the remaining 70 percent. As it happened, Allende wasn't aware of this option, and appeared pleased when informed of it. For the moment, at least, the ITT'ers must have thought Gerrity's plan could prove a basis for negotiations.

Allende was more concerned with acquiring capital than with nationalization, and talk soon turned to the need for additional financing. Dunleavy observed that ITT was putting $6 into Chiltelco for every $1 it took out in the form of dividends, and he implied that the corporation was prepared to continue doing so, but only if ironclad guarantees were made. In his view, Allende had three options: He might purchase ITT's shares directly; he could do so through CORFO; or he could "grab the company," which is to say expropriate it illegally. Should Chiltelco be seized, Dunleavy added, "We go right to AID [Agency for International Development]" and seek compensation from OPIC. Allende assured him that the government planned to work with ITT to find a fair solution, and with this the discussion turned to other matters: the future of the Sheraton hotels in Santiago, complaints that government wires were being tapped, and even an invention developed by Allende that would indicate an incoming call while a person was speaking on his telephone.

Before leaving, Dunleavy reiterated the benefits that might be derived from an outright purchase. "If this were done, his credit rating would go up around the world." If he did it properly, Dunleavy said, "we would go to the banks and tell them how fairly we had been treated."[12]

Two weeks later Berrellez reported he had "reliable information" that Allende would accept Dunleavy's suggestion, offering between $80 million and $100 million for ITT's remaining interest in Chiltelco. According to the plan, the government would announce nationalization in harsh terms ("This would pacify the hotheads") while conducting conventional negotiations with ITT in regard to final price and conditions.[13]

Nothing of the sort happened. Apparently Allende was playing for time, consolidating his power in order to make a bold move against the American companies. That he was succeeding became evident in early April, when his Popular Front coalition won a major victory in the municipal elections, obtaining almost half the votes cast.

This signaled the beginning of the nationalization campaign, with ITT the initial target. On April 28 the government proclaimed it would take over Chiltelco the following week and pay a price of slightly more than $13 million. This clearly was unacceptable to ITT, which continued to maintain that the company was worth $153 million and whose OPIC insurance covered only $92 million of that amount. The announcement was meant as an opening move and little more, however. ITT lodged a protest with the State Department, notified OPIC, and asked for another meeting with Allende. Little was heard from Santiago for almost a month, but Chiltelco wasn't seized, an indication that the government wanted to preserve its options.

Allende met with ITT representatives on May 26 to tell them of his intention to nationalize Chiltelco as soon as possible. He named a special commission to meet with ITT experts to determine price and conditions. Nothing came of this, as the government claimed Chiltelco's net worth was $24 million while ITT held to the $153-million figure, and neither would budge.

Meanwhile the government moved leftward. Allende delivered bellicose speeches attacking "Western imperialists," Soviet experts were flown into Santiago, and from there to the copper mines and smelters, an indication these had been targeted for seizure. On July 11 the Chilean legislature approved a constitutional amendment permitting the nationalization of the copper industry. Despite all this, the Chiltelco negotiations continued, and in mid-July there was another meeting with Allende. A month later the Chileans suggested arbitration on price by members of the International Telecommunications Union coupled with an immediate takeover of the company, which ITT rejected.

The talks were broken off on August 31, and now direct action was taken. The government froze Chiltelco's bank accounts the following day and on September 16 established a three-man team to manage the company. Announcement of intervention was made a week later. Fearing a further erosion of Chilean-American relations and a bankruptcy of OPIC, Korry attempted to work out a last-minute compromise, under which Chile would pay the nationalized companies in long-term bonds guaranteed by the United States Treasury. Allende seemed interested, but in the end he rejected the plan, which in any case might not have been approved by Washington.

This was Korry's last significant act in Santiago. On September 29 he was replaced as ambassador to Chile by Nathaniel Davis, considered a hard-liner at the State Department, whose appointment was taken as a sign of worsening relations to come.

Chiltelco passed into government hands on the same day. The company's books were seized, and Benjamin Holmes and three other ITT managers who were also Chilean nationals were jailed on charges of "fraud against the government."

As anticipated, ITT filed protests both in Santiago and in Washington and set into motion its claims at OPIC. In so doing the corporation followed the route blazed by Ralston Purina and Indiana Brass and then taken by the copper companies and other members of the ad hoc committee. Together they mounted a large-scale lobbying effort in Washington, the goal being the adoption of a strong stand by the American government. In an angry memo Neal set forth a fanciful eighteen-point program designed to disrupt the Chilean economy, which was promptly discarded but would later cause the corporation embarrassment.

There were some results. The Export-Import Bank denied yet another Chilean loan request. Both Nixon and Rogers spoke out against the expropriations. The Forty Committee approved a $815,000 commitment to Chile's opposition parties. But that was all. ITT continued reviewing reports from Berrellez on developments in Chile, there were meetings with the copper-company executives to discuss lobbying and share information, and the claims were working their way through the bureaucracy at OPIC.

The Chiltelco expropriation was hardly forgotten. Geneen referred to it at the annual stockholders' meeting on May 8, 1972, noting that ITT had established a reserve to cover the uninsured portion of the investment in Chiltelco, as well as for all of the other properties in Chile. "Consequently, an extraordinary charge of $70 million, equal to 60 cents per share, has been included in our 1971 financial results as a special, *non-recurring* charge." By then, however, such matters were no longer of major concern, not at a time when ITT was under attack at the Kleindienst hearings, responding to charges that it had attempted to bribe its way out of the Hartford case and had made improper donations during the political campaign.

Then, on March 21 and 22, ITT's involvement in Chile once again became front-page news and a major topic of discussion in Washington, New York, Santiago, and elsewhere. As had been the case with the antitrust–San Diego matter, the story was broken by Jack Anderson in "Washington Merry-Go-Round." It was based on leaked documents—perhaps, but not necessarily, leaked by the same person who provided him with the San Diego material.

The revelations were, as one reporter called them, "an exposé fancier's delight," combining as they did foreign intrigue with the machinations of big business. In this period it was fashionable in some circles to look upon the United States as a malevolent force in the world (as in Vietnam), its foreign policy manipulated if not actually dictated by major corporations, especially the multinationals. Now Anderson had given critics evidence that, as he put it, "portrays ITT as a virtual corporate nation itself," free from ordinary constraints. Anderson also provided journalists with eighty pages of confidential documents drawn from the ITT files. A careful reading of these would illuminate ITT's activities in the propaganda area, its excellent intelligence operation in Santiago, and the manner in which information was utilized at corporate headquarters and in the field. In addition, there were glimpses of ITT's lobbying efforts in Washington, though there wasn't much of this in the released papers.

Other than Geneen's offer of a "seven figure amount" to prevent Allende's election, however, there was no direct evidence that ITT had actually done anything but participate in Track One efforts to support pro–Christian Democrat newspapers. But much of the press wrote it up as an "ITT-CIA plot," which was what it came to be known as in the weeks ahead. Out of the combined Chile and San Diego operations came two different pictures of the corporation, neither of which was flattering. On the one hand there was ITT the powerful manipulator, and on the other ITT the bungler, unable to use its vast powers—whether in the United States or Chile —to achieve its objectives.

The Anderson articles and release of the documents had an electric effect in Santiago. Ever since Chiltelco's nationalization there had been sporadic discussions between ITT and Allende's representatives regarding compensation. These were now terminated. The economy was in bad shape at the time, with escalating inflation, unemployment, a serious balance-of-payments problem, and declines in production. Allende now castigated ITT, blaming the corporation and other foreign interests for his country's difficulties. The Anderson documents were quickly translated into Spanish by both the government and the newspaper *El Mercurio*, and tens of thousands of copies were sold throughout Chile. Revelation of the "Frei gambit" led to attacks on the former president, who a few days later went on radio to deny there ever had been "direct or indirect contacts" between his government and ITT during the election campaigns. He said the Anderson papers merely repeated "a mass of rumors which, everyone will remember, were circulating all over Chile at that time," and he added, "It was sufficient to stand on any streetcorner in downtown Santiago to know everything that those documents contained."[14] Frei might have added that the same rumors were heard in New York and Washington, but this isn't to say Anderson's revelations had no important impact. They confirmed some of the suspicions of CIA and ITT activities in Chile during the election, and in addition spawned new rumors about the corporation that had no foundation in the evidence presented.

Most of the story came out the following year, when the Sub-Committee on Multinational Corporations of the Senate Committee on Foreign Relations investigated ITT's role in Chile in 1970 and 1971. In seven sessions held in late March and early April, the senators questioned most of the major participants from government and business, with the largest contingent from ITT—Gerrity, Merriam, McCone, Rohatyn, Berrellez, Hendrix, Neal, Ryan, Guilfoyle, and, on the final day, the last to be interrogated, Geneen.

Throughout the hearings the ITT people insisted they had done nothing wrong and hadn't participated, directly or indirectly, in Track Two operations. This was confirmed by Broe and others from the CIA and State Department. But there were two points where ITT had problems, one of which was general, the other specific, and both dealt with the offer of funds to the CIA after Allende's initial victory in the popular balloting.

Was it proper for an American corporation to seek assistance from the government if its overseas interests were threatened? The ITT'ers claimed there was nothing wrong with this, but senators Frank Church and Edmund Muskie had trouble with the idea. The issue was raised during Sen. Charles Percy's questioning of Jack Neal:

Senator Percy: As a former State Department employee, do you consider it improper for an American company to make representations to the American Government at the highest levels in order to do something about the fact that this American company is about to lose or could lose its investment if the Presidential candidate pledged to nationalize is elected; to take whatever action could be appropriately taken through Government channels to stop his election?

Do you consider that improper?

Mr. Neal: I do not consider that improper. In fact, Senator, I think we would have been remiss in this case and in all cases not to keep the Government informed. This is a company policy.

Senator Church: Mr. Neal, Senator, may I interrupt because I am not sure Mr. Neal understood the way you phrased the question. I want to be sure that you are in contact here. As I heard Senator Percy's question, he was asking you about the company's urging the Government to take any action that could appropriately be taken to stop the election. I think that was the way you phrased the question.

Will you please read the question again because I want you to be sure you understood the question before you stand on the answer.

Mr. Neal: Thank you.

Senator Percy: I will rephrase the question and save the reporter doing it if I can phrase it exactly the same way.

Did you feel that there was anything wrong in the company, an American company, going to its own Government and pointing out the danger that the company was about to lose, or the possibility existed of its losing, a very large asset owned by American stockholders, and asking that whatever action could be taken would be taken in order to prevent this loss?

Mr. Neal: Not by any means, Senator Percy. As I said a while ago, I believe we would have been remiss if we had not done this. This is a standard practice in the U.S. Government.[15]

Now Percy questioned Neal about the $1 million Geneen had offered, which, it will be recalled, McCone had said was earmarked "for the purpose of bringing about a coalition of the opposition to Allende so that when confirmation was up, which was some months later, this coalition would be united and deprive Allende of his position." McCone implied ITT was prepared to intervene in Chilean politics. Neal said otherwise:

Senator Percy: Would you wish to state categorically that the figure of up to $1 million was not intended for political activity as such?

Mr. Neal: I would be happy to, yes, I do.

Senator Percy: And it is your understanding that it was to be part of some sort of an investment or development fund?

Mr. Neal: Right, this is what I said in several cases, Senator.

Senator Percy: And you would expect it to be matched by government funds or funds of other companies that may see likewise?

Mr. Neal: Other companies which wanted to do so.[16]

McCone's stance to the contrary notwithstanding, this was to be ITT's essential position in regard to the meaning of the offer, which was the most damaging evidence of the corporation's willingness to intervene in Chile. Corporation officials testified that the money was to be used to further economic development so as to undercut the Marxist position. Gerrity claimed that what Geneen had in mind was a program to demonstrate to Allende the willingness of American corporations to assist in the development of the Chilean economy. Several subcommittee members, Frank Church in particular, found this difficult to accept. Neal was obliged to back down somewhat from this position after a barrage of questions from associate counsel Jack Blum. "It was not for a development plan?" asked Blum toward the end, to which Neal replied, "It was not for development purposes necessarily."[17] Church made his beliefs clear when examining McCone:

A million dollars is a very significant amount of money if it goes to finance covert political activity directed toward forming such [a] coalition [to oppose Allende], but it is utterly insignificant for the purpose of building houses, particularly in view of this long sustained and costly aid program that had gone on for many years by which we pumped $1.4 billion or thereabouts into Chile for that purpose and the end result was the election of Mr. Allende. This just doesn't make sense.[18]

Church returned to this theme in his examination of Gerrity, who argued, "You are saying a Government-directed program failed, maybe private enterprise should have a swing at it." Church and Muskie found this implausible:

Senator Church:	We have three volumes of documentation here that we have been questioning witnesses about for the last two days and we cannot find, in poring through these three volumes of documents that relate to intercommunications from staff person to staff person, that relate to the conversations between ITT and CIA, that relate to the recommendations which you in writing made to the government for an action program in Chile. We cannot find in these three volumes of documents a single reference to any plan that had as its purpose the building of houses or giving the technical assistance to Chile. Is that not a peculiar thing?
Mr. Gerrity:	I do not think so. I think this is a program that we talked about among ourselves. It was a sort of quick term program, a spur of the moment thing. I think it is significant, too, that despite all the discussion, Senator, nobody did anything. There was no overt action taken in any way, shape or form to subvert Mr. Allende.
Senator Church:	And the documents here are replete with the written words that describe the reason why, because in the end it was decided the plans were unworkable. But there is no reference anywhere here in any of these documents to a plan to build houses in Chile or give technical assistance or some other constructive gesture, not a single reference.
Mr. Gerrity:	There is a very simple reason for that. When we talked to the Government about this, you know, apparently they found nothing was viable so there is no sense in setting down on a piece of

	paper plans to build housing or plans for import or anything.
Senator Muskie:	No, the destructive proposals were not implemented either and they are down on paper.
Mr. Gerrity:	Well, sir, I am not aware of any destructive proposals, Senator.
Senator Muskie:	Really?[19]

That ITT would set aside so large a sum in this fashion for such innocuous purposes strained credulity. OPIC announced that the $92-million claim wouldn't be paid because the corporation hadn't disclosed material information and had "increased OPIC's risk of loss by failing to preserve administrative remedies." "It just doesn't hang together," said Percy. "It's just unbelievable," Church said, adding, "It is obvious somebody is lying; and we must take a serious view of perjury under oath."

Yet the senators didn't ask the two most important and obvious questions, the first of which was, why did ITT discuss its intervention with the CIA rather than, say, the State or Commerce Department if it didn't have covert operations in mind from the start? For that matter, because of its intimate relations with the White House, there might have been approaches to Ehrlichman, Peterson, or any of a half-dozen others who were close to Nixon. The opening to the CIA indicated Geneen had more in mind than propaganda in March and September of 1970.

The second question deals with the point made earlier: What exactly had ITT done, as opposed to having considered doing, in Chile? That Gerrity thought this crucial came out in his testimony, but the issue wasn't pursued as assiduously as it might have been. Both he and Geneen had said that ITT hadn't participated in Track Two covert operations and had rejected the opportunity to do so when approached by Broe. First Berrellez and then Gerrity denied that the corporation had made contributions to political candidates, in particular Alessandri, through Matte or anyone else.

Mr. Berrellez:	. . . I could not approach Dr. Matte bluntly, and I thought I would—
Senator Church:	You mean, you could not just go and say to him, here is some dough?
Mr. Berrellez:	I could not say, first of all, I could not say, that, sir. I am not authorized to offer money.

Senator Church: What did you mean when you said "at the end when it was mentioned we were, as always, ready to contribute"? What do those words mean?

Mr. Berrellez: The words are these, sir. I am addressing Dr. Matte. He had not mentioned money or any other needs up to this point. I am anxious to know.

Senator Church: What you can do?

Mr. Berrellez: There must be something here. But I cannot tell Dr. Matte, "Look, Buster, what is your game, how much money do you want?" I could not do this.

Senator Church: Of course not, but what you did—

Mr. Berrellez: I used, sir, classic Spanish, the conversation was all in Spanish.

Senator Church: So there is a way in Spanish to get this point across. [Laughter.]

Mr. Berrellez: No, no, sir, look, you are pretty close to it but this is not what was then.

Senator Church: All right. Tell us then.

Mr. Berrellez: You say when you leave a person and I am going to translate rather literally, you say, "Dr. Matte, or so and so, good evening, remember that if we can be of any service to you we are willing to contribute and so forth."

Now, in English it is going to sound awkward and forgive me, at least the way I see it in Spanish it is not, sir. I understood that Dr. Matte would understand, and his answer to me was you will be advised.

Mr. Levinson (committee counsel): Mr. Gerrity, on this point, if I might, we heard Mr. Berrellez' and Mr. Hendrix' testimony yesterday, that in addition to reporting they made recommendations and, indeed, Mr. Berrellez recounted how he promised support, whatever support was necessary, to Dr. Matte. You got that cable, it is addressed to you, I believe, or if it is not addressed to you, you certainly got a copy. As their immediate superior, is there any record of your having sent a message to Berrellez or Hendrix telling them,

	"For God's sake stop promising these people," or anything to the effect of, "Stop leading them to believe that we will support them or that we are increasing advertising in or contributing to or anything"? Is there anything on the record, any written communication, from yourself to them saying, "What are you guys doing?"
Mr. Gerrity:	There was no need to, Mr. Levinson. I understood what Mr. Berrellez meant. I thought he explained it very thoroughly here yesterday. Mr. Berrellez was not authorized to make any contributions. I was not authorized to make any contributions, if you are talking about financial support, and he knew that and I knew that. There is no point in sending him a message saying "Knock it off."[20]

Were these false statements, as Church had suggested? Perhaps so, but at the time there were no indictments for perjury.

As indicated, Geneen was to have the last word, appearing before the subcommittee on April 2. Like Gerrity, he asserted that ITT had done nothing to intervene in the elections, and defended the lobbying efforts. "There may have been better ways for us to have proceeded, but certainly American companies should have the right to seek and depend upon support from their own Government in protecting their interests abroad." He portrayed ITT as a concerned party willing to assist the United States government in Chile, and he reiterated that ITT did little after its offer was rejected.

> . . . we did not have a plan, that has been consistent in my testimony throughout. We hoped the Government would have a plan, and we felt that we had something that we could offer that might be helpful to such a plan. I don't know what that plan would be and would not know unless I sat down and somehow we became part of a group of people or a group of private enterprise and the Government with certain purposes ahead of us in which case we might know what we are going to do.[21]

Thus, ITT held to its original line, as set down by Jack Neal early in the hearings and elaborated on by Berrellez, Gerrity, and others.

Even then, interest remained focused on the weakest point in ITT's defense—namely, its early offer of financial assistance and whether or not direct aid had been given any candidate in the election. The former involved the matter of intent, the latter the degree of involvement, and Geneen continued to assert ITT was innocent on both counts.

Did Geneen and the rest of the corporation's officers think their testimony and related statements would be accepted at face value? This can't be known, but as far as much of the press and a large portion of the interested public were concerned, ITT was considered guilty of having intervened improperly in two presidential elections—in the United States and in Chile—and had blundered in each. What other undiscovered misdeeds had been committed were left to the imagination, which in that Watergate summer was already bound to be overstimulated.

ITT's troubles were compounded by the publication on April 23 of Anthony Sampson's article "The Geneen Machine" in *New York* magazine. Excerpted from his forthcoming *The Sovereign State of ITT*, it portrayed Geneen as a generally amoral, ruthless individual beyond the control of government. The lead in the magazine's table of contents was lurid. "The scandals that have raged around ITT in the past few years have made that huge corporation's name something to use for frightening children." The further implication was that this had its origins in activities during the Behn era. "From the beginning it was conceived as a superpower, dealing with nations as a nation itself, internally organized like some bizarre and complex monarchy."

The book was released a few months later, and quickly became a national best-seller as well as a selection of Book-of-the-Month. Not since Ida Tarbell wrote her sensational muckraking work *A History of the Standard Oil Company*, seven decades earlier in much the same form, had the appearance of an attack on a large corporation been so fortuitously timed or generated so much interest. Sampson's book was well reviewed, almost always by journalists and others who had no idea of ITT's history or what it did but had fresh ones of Geneen's relations with the failing Nixon Administration and activities in Chile. In effect, critics reviewed the corporation and its leader, not the book, and since the latter attacked the former, it was applauded. The public was prepared for a diatribe against ITT, and Sampson, a British journalist, provided one.

Nadir: Track One in Chile

That the book was often sketchy and may not have had adequate research was ignored, overlooked, or excused. Several reviewers did observe it had been hastily assembled, presumably to catch the crest of the anti-ITT fever, as it certainly did. Scholars noted its strong antibusiness bias, and some observed that the author seemed to lack a clear comprehension of how American corporations functioned.

None of the reviewers had gone through Sampson's documentation, so they couldn't have known that the relevant documents regarding ITT's role in Germany and Latin America prior to and during World War II presented an almost diametrically opposite picture of what Sampson had written. Also, few had sufficient legal background to appreciate the complexities and nuances of the antitrust litigations. Nor was there, in any critique in a major publication, a perspective of why conglomerates appeared, what Geneen had tried to accomplish, or an understanding of his very real managerial talents. What Sampson had produced was an exciting, fast-paced work of instant journalism, reflecting his honest opinions, which happened to coincide with the mind set of a large, literate public. ITT prepared a long essay pointing out errors of fact, but this was more for internal distribution than anything else and was generally ignored by the media.

Notwithstanding the appearance of *The Sovereign State of ITT*, questions of guilt or innocence might have faded in the light of the Nixon-impeachment issue, which under ordinary circumstances would have crowded from the front pages and from national consciousness mention of the corporation and its activities as well as almost everything else. Within a few months little would have remained except continued doubts and a vaguely poor public image. But there was a coup in Chile in September of 1973, during which Allende was overthrown and was either killed or committed suicide. A right-wing military junta took over in Santiago and soon after opened negotiations with ITT regarding compensation for Chiltelco. This, of course, stirred rumors that ITT had supported Allende's opponents, was responsible for his death, and now was about to receive its payoff. As a result, ITT offices in Rome, Zurich, and Madrid were bombed, and special precautions against similar violence were taken in New York and elsewhere. The corporation was truly under siege, literally and figuratively, in late 1973.

While this was happening, ITT successfully appealed OPIC's refusal to approve the insurance, and on December 22 it was announced that the new Chilean government would pay $125.2 million for ITT's equity and debt investments in Chiltelco, over a ten-year period, with much of this to be reinvested in the country. This wasn't quite the amount Geneen had hoped to receive, but under the circumstances it was a favorable development. As might have been expected, this led to new allegations regarding ITT's operations in Chile and additional threats of violence.

One question remained unanswered: What was ITT's role in the 1970 election, and was it improper? The subcommittee hearings created suspicions that lingered in mid-decade. Interestingly enough, Geneen himself provided part of the answer in what must have been an unguarded moment during an interview two years after the hearings had ended, though it went unnoticed by the press:

> We had this telephone company down in Chile worth $153 million and this guy [Allende] says he's gonna take it away from us and pay us beans. We went to everybody, including the State Department, and they didn't do anything—even though afterwards in the oil countries the Department got in the back door backing up the oil guys who were negotiating in the front room. But for us, *nothing.* So one of my thoughts was, don't you think we ought to get together and come up with a plan and we'll put money in. But we got nothing done. Nothing.
>
> Later on we learned they did have a plan for Chile, but didn't even tell us about it, *a plan not too different from what we were suggesting.* [23] [emphasis added.]

What precisely did this mean? To some it might be interpreted as a reference to Track One, but it might have been a Track Two program as well. To this day it remains unclear.

On March 20, 1978, hours before the statute of limitations ran out, the Justice Department charged Gerrity and Berrellez with having committed perjury in their testimony five years earlier. The specific reference was to statements denying having provided Matte with funds for the Alessandri campaign. Significant though this might have been, it still was a relatively minor issue compared with others raised during the hearings, leading to suspicions that the indictments had been sought primarily to keep the case alive until more damaging charges could be developed. Both men denied the allegations, and the case never went to trial.

As it turned out, the Justice Department, not ITT, came in for the larger share of criticism in the press. If Gerrity and Berrellez were thought guilty, what of Geneen, who also testified on the issue? Some reporters accused acting deputy attorney general Benjamin Civiletti, who made the announcement, with having focused on the "small fry," hinting that for some undisclosed reason he was holding back from attacking their chief. Civiletti bristled at this. "The law doesn't depend on whether someone is junior or senior," he said. "It depends on the facts." Jack Blum, who had been the associate counsel at the hearings, disagreed, and argued that Geneen should be charged with perjury along with the others. The ITT chairman, he told a reporter, "might be eligible for one of the great fiction prizes" for his testimony, adding he was "very disturbed that the department didn't probe further Mr. Geneen's statements."[24]

The corporation's humiliation and embarrassment regarding its role in Chile didn't end there. In November 1978 Stanley Sporkin, the vigorous chief of the Security and Exchange Commission's division of enforcement, charged that in the period from 1970 to 1975 ITT had expended $8.7 million on illegal activities, not only in Chile but in such places as Indonesia, Iran, the Philippines, Algeria, Nigeria, Mexico, Italy, and Turkey. This time the corporation didn't attempt to deny the allegations—in part because it had provided all of the material to Sporkin, but also because by then its credibility in such matters had been shattered. Rather, ITT noted that the payments were "consistent with the laws of their jurisdiction but may have been applied in a manner contrary to current corporate policies." In the response ITT added that the practices had been halted two years before. Although it wasn't mentioned in any of the newspapers or magazines that carried the story, the timing might have been more than coincidental. It was approximately then that Geneen stepped down from the chairmanship.

18

The Center Holds

ON September 9, 1970, at the same meeting at which Geneen informed the board of approaches to the CIA, the agenda was dominated by decisions regarding acquisitions. According to the compromise worked out with McLaren in the Hartford case little more than a month before, ITT agreed not to acquire domestic companies with assets of over $100 million until 1981, and there were other caveats Geneen would have to respect. But he was rolling along with other, small takeovers, as the actions that day would show.

Everything had been prepared in advance; all that was required was approval, which came with a minimum of discussion. This wasn't very different from what had gone before and would occur afterward. In other words, it was a fairly typical meeting for those assembled, and similar ones would follow during the next few months.

Eleven companies had already been acquired that year, ranging in size from Hartford to South Bend Window Cleaning, and dozens of others were in various stages of the by-now-familiar process. There would be twenty-two of them in 1971 (the most prominent being O. M. Scott, the nation's premier lawn-care company) and thirty-three in 1972, companies with annual revenues of some $400 million. For the most part these takeovers were engineered by the issuance of more ITT paper, at a time when the price for the company's shares still was relatively high.

The board agreed on September 9 to purchase Sonolar S.A., a French manufacturer of electronic gear, for $14.4 million in stock. Another $6.6 million in paper would go for Ulma S.p.A., an Italian producer of steel trim for automobiles, and a second Italian firm, Altissimo S.p.A., which turned out automobile lights and accessories, fetched $1.2 million. General Creosoting, a Gulf, North Carolina company with one small facility where wooden poles used by electric-utility companies were manufactured and treated, was purchased for $900,000 (7,166 shares of convertible series-K preferred stock and 13,160 of the common). Geneen notified the board that there would be a 237-room addition to the Sheraton Motor Inn on the outskirts of Portland, Oregon. He asked for and received approval to dispose of the Hayes unit of ITT Nesbitt for $580,000, the purchaser being Hyatt Restaurants.[1]

Geneen's decision to commit up to a million dollars to Track One operations—assuming the CIA would accept the money—has to be viewed against this background. ITT's board meetings were wide-ranging affairs, encompassing the globe and half a dozen industries within a few hours, during which discussions involving tens of millions of dollars were ratified. That the Chiltelco holding was important and valuable was obvious, but at the same time it should be realized that in this period it didn't dominate thinking at headquarters, not when Geneen was still concerned about possible litigations, future acquisitions, and the smooth and orderly running and development of a $6.4-billion conglomerate with some 230 profit centers and approximately 2,000 separate units.

In this perspective, Chiltelco may appear to be what it truly was in the scheme of things at ITT—a relatively small part of an enormous picture—and even Geneen, with his capacity for work, couldn't have afforded to devote a great deal of time to its problems. The reason he did so was obvious. He had been angered and challenged in Chile, and provoked into action. During the following decade the general public would learn more about ITT's activities there (and in San Diego and Hartford) than it would of its accomplishments in manufacturing and services, which is to say that most people read about ITT on the front page rather than in the business section of their newspapers. Readers learned of Geneen's views on the rights of American corporations abroad and proper relations with the federal government and not of his strategies as a manager of a highly diversified and huge corporation.

This unfortunate situation, though partly created by ITT, masked Geneen's performance and that of the corporation in the early 1970s, a period of increasing stress for American business. To the uninformed but interested observer, many of the large conglomerates appeared quite similar in structure and leadership. Litton, LTV, Gulf + Western, City Investing, Teledyne, and others had fine records and fairly well known leaders. ITT was the largest of the group and Geneen the best known of the conglomerateurs. Business journals wrote of his brilliance, but this wasn't evident to many outsiders. Such a conclusion certainly wouldn't have been arrived at by those who knew Geneen from his antitrust encounters, involvements in Chile, and acerbic encounters with the press rather than from his accomplishments at ISE, Sheraton, Hartford, and other parts of the ITT constellation.

Throughout the 1960s Geneen and other conglomerateurs had been charged with "cooking their books," showing excellent financial results through overt manipulation, accounting trickery, and timely takeovers of companies whose earnings, when added to their own, created a false picture of growth. Here, as in other areas, rumors abounded. For example, it was known that an analyst at the brokerage house of Smith, Barney & Co. had written a devastating account of ITT's manipulations, which was referred to by *The New York Times'* financial reporter Michael C. Jensen two years later, when the corporation was under attack. The report had never been published, said Jensen, who added, "Today the few copies in existence are jealously guarded and have become a sort of collector's item."[2]

That this could have been the case in the age of copying machines, especially on Wall Street, where they are kept running overtime, should have been rejected by anyone who knows how rapidly such material is disseminated. The report and its allegations were in fact quite well known, even to those who hadn't seen it. Among other matters, it noted that ITT was reporting as current income realized capital gains from Hartford's securities portfolio, gains that had actually accrued several, often many, years earlier. But this was hardly a secret; ITT took note of it in the financial statements, and to have reported otherwise would have been to break with generally accepted accounting principles.

What was lost in all of this was ITT's relationship with Hartford in this period. Ralph Nader and others had claimed ITT intended to strip the insurer of its assets, to use the money to develop such cash-hungry operations as Sheraton, Rayonier, and Grinnell. Not only hadn't this happened, but during the early 1970s the parent company actually provided Hartford with additional funds from its own treasury.

ITT attempted to respond to these and related charges, but with little impact. Comptroller Herbert Knortz observed, quite accurately, that no conglomerate and few other companies provided more financial data in its reports than did ITT. Instead of silencing or at least muffling critics, this resulted in a quite different kind of allegation: that the corporation was attempting to confuse stockholders, the financial press, and others by inundating them with a mass of irrelevant statistics and figures, to conceal what was truly happening. "We simply don't manage anything," said Knortz. "I'll put it in blood if that'll help. What can I say? We do it right, we do it right, we do it right."[3]

On several occasions Knortz would confront critics directly, usually by means of debates at brokerage houses and trust companies, and he often came out well in these encounters. Geneen encouraged such meetings, in part because he tended to measure his success by the price of ITT paper, which he always felt was undervalued at the New York Stock Exchange, and in part because of a belief that this kind of exposure would persuade brokers and bankers to recommend the issues. Moreover, the higher the price for ITT's stock, the less would have to be printed for acquisitions. Geneen would often lament that ITT had the second-most-outstanding growth record (behind IBM) of any large American corporation in the post–World War II period. Yet the stock didn't sell for the fifty to one hundred times earnings afforded many of the leading glamour issues during the 1960s and early 1970s. The reason usually given was an inability on the part of analysts and investors to understand the company. In some cases there was a conviction that the growth had come about through takeovers and would end once these slowed down, or suspicion that the figures were being manipulated; there were ITT's troubles with the Justice Department, its activities in Chile, its relations with the Nixon Administration, and a belief that the corporation would fall apart when Geneen—who hadn't designated a successor—left the scene.

SOURCES OF ITT'S PROFITS, 1961–1970

(millions of dollars)

Year	Total Profits	Profits Generated Internally	Increase in Internally Generated Profits	Profits from Acquisitions, Current Year
1961	36.1	34.4		1.7
1962	40.7	40.0	5.6	0.7
1963	52.4	46.2	6.2	6.2
1964	63.2	57.8	11.6	5.4
1965	76.1	71.7	13.9	4.4
1966	89.9	84.9	13.2	5.0
1967	119.2	98.9	14.0	20.3
1968	180.2	134.4	35.5	45.8
1969	234.0	202.2	67.8	31.8
1970	353.3	256.1	53.9	97.2
1971	406.8	391.4	135.3	15.4

Source: Derived from *Fortune*, September, 1972, p. 91.

Although there was no way of demonstrating how ITT might have fared without acquisitions, Carol J. Loomis provided some information to consider in a *Fortune* article, in September 1972, entitled "Harold Geneen's Moneymaking Machine is Still Humming." So it was, and without the giant takeovers that had marked the late 1960s. Surveying the previous decade, Loomis calculated that the earnings of the acquired companies had a weighted growth rate of 12.5 percent, virtually the same as the "base" companies with which ITT had begun the period. As was to have been expected, profits jumped each time ITT made major acquisitions, such as during the four-year period from 1967 to 1970, and the increase in internally generated profits leaped ahead the year following significant take-overs. Considering all of this, Loomis seemed to conclude that ITT probably would have grown at approximately the same pace had it not been so deeply involved with mergers.

Indirect support for this point of view came a year later in a report on the corporation by the Wall Street house of Coenan & Co., which held that much of ITT's recent success had been due to the outstanding performance of the International Standard Electric companies in Europe, which according to calculations accounted for 72 percent of the corporation's earnings advance. The implication here was that these results would have been posted even if someone else had been in command in New York, since Geneen tended to concentrate on domestic business. In other words, ITT's growth was due more to operations that had been part of the corporation and performing well prior to his arrival than to anything acquired or done afterward.

One might draw a different set of conclusions from these and other statistics, however. There is no doubt that Geneen managed to increase revenues and earnings at many of the properties he had inherited. That he had turned around Federal Electric by the early 1960s has been noted, transforming what had been a chronic invalid into a reliable source of profits after the successive failures of Behn, Harrison, and Leavey. ISE was a thriving operation when he assumed power, but it grew even more rapidly afterward. In 1973 ISE posted revenues of $5 billion, a fivefold expansion over what they had been when Geneen arrived, and this had been done without a major acquisition on the order of those taken by domestic operations in the late 1960s. Standard Telephones & Cables alone was half as large as the entire ISE had been in 1958, and much of this expansion resulted from alterations in structure, procedures, and leadership after Geneen took over.[4]

Similarly, Geneen had revived several of the moribund companies he had acquired. Perhaps the best example of this was the transformation at ITT Sheraton, which, as noted, had formulated an $865-million expansion program in 1969. At the time, the company was foundering, as Geneen and ITT Sheraton's president Philip Lowe learned the hotel business, sought a working strategy to turn the business around, and took on managers capable of heading operations. Nothing seemed to work, and in 1970 Geneen dismissed Lowe and brought in veteran hotel man Howard James, who, together with Hart Perry, developed a new approach. James sold off additional old properties, cut the work force to get rid of surplus personnel, and rationalized the system. Most important, he convinced Geneen of the wisdom of selling profitable hotels to investors and then assuming managerial contracts to run them. Increasingly ITT Sheraton became an operator and a franchiser rather than an owner of properties; in effect, it left the real-estate business to become a dispenser of services. As a result, James didn't need all of that $865 million, and turned instead to would-be franchisees for capital. He was able to scale down the ITT contribution to some $360 million, and he obtained approximately $4 billion from franchisees who constructed hotels and motor inns under Sheraton's direction, used the name, and paid the company substantial fees.

By 1973 only 28 of the chain's 271 domestic and 11 of its 42 overseas facilities were owned; the others were leased, managed, or franchised.[5] In this way the once-ailing company was turned into a profitable one, and through the disposal of these properties Sheraton developed a healthy cash flow. As a result of having the far-smaller asset base, it achieved the highest return on investment in history.

Of course, there were other operations not so successfully managed, as well as several outright failures, but these were compensated for by outstanding results elsewhere. Generally considered a somewhat stodgy operation prior to the takeover, Hartford now became a far more aggressive company, which led competitors to charge it was cutting rates so as to increase volume and improve cash flow. As mentioned earlier, the investment portfolio was turned over much more rapidly than previously had been the case. In 1967, for example, the insurer took only $198,000 in capital gains, and in the following year $8.1 million, its all-time high for the pre-Geneen period. In 1972 the capital gains from the portfolio came to $41.8 million, approximately one third of Hartford's net income for the year. ITT's critics noted this change in policy and pointed out this substantial increase in the capital-gains portion. Accountant Abraham Briloff, a scourge of conglomerateurs but one who rarely attacked ITT, thought this a demonstration of how the corporation was "weaving into its earnings whatever portion of the quarter of a billion dollars of security-value suppression it was able to achieve after it took over the Hartford Insurance Group."[6] Geneen's admirers observed that earnings from operations had never been higher, and that Hartford experienced a rebirth after only a short period of ITT's influence.

In her article Carol Loomis indicated that the most important question regarding the corporation's future was whether "the man widely regarded as the world's greatest business manager can go right on boosting I.T.T.'s earnings year after year, now that he's not so free to make acquisitions." She concluded, "Geneen might do just that." Loomis based this on the excellent prospects for the corporation's two major businesses, telecommunications and insurance. Geneen had developed the former to the point where it regularly set new records for revenues and profits, while margins were expanded over those of previous managements, and he had acquired and done as much for the latter. Moreover, Geneen had placed his stamp upon scores of other, less-well-known operations.

ITT had grown and flourished as Geneen had promised and predicted it would back in 1958, which is to say he had been successful in this sphere. This was appreciated by experts, even those who criticized his other activities. By 1973 it could be said that he had turned in one of the outstanding managerial performances of this century. That this wasn't recognized by the general public, and that he hadn't received the awards, honors, and plaudits afforded lesser businessmen in what was an antibusiness era in American history, must have been galling.

In late 1973 the economy faltered and then declined. Owing to a variety of factors—the sudden and sharp increases in petroleum prices, a cyclical downturn in the economy, President Gerald Ford's decision to combat inflation with a program of fiscal stringency that was reversed and then altered again, an erratic monetary policy, America's eroding position in world markets, and of course the national loss of confidence in the wake of Vietnam and Watergate—the country entered its sharpest recession since the 1930s. The Consumer Price Index soared and then fell sharply, as did the employment rate and other key indicators, causing uncertainties, unsettling business, and, in the end, resulting in revenue and earnings declines. All this was reflected on Wall Street, where the Dow Jones Industrials went from a peak of 1067 in early 1973 to a bottom of 570 in less than two years—the longest, steadiest, and most demoralizing bear market since that of 1929–1933.

The United States had entered what some analysts would later call the "Great Inflation," a new generation's reference to the Great Depression of the 1930s. More than any other group, businessmen had to deal with this phenomenon and a related one, "stagflation," the unlikely combination of rising prices and declining growth. Those deeply involved in international business were troubled by swift and often erratic changes in interest rates, currency prices, and the increase in economic nationalism resulting from the end of the dollar's hegemony in the early 1970s.

This was a major period of testing for ITT, during which the essential strengths Geneen had built into the corporation became evident, especially when its overall performance was set beside those of other conglomerates. In several respects Geneen's leadership during this troubled time was more impressive than it had been in the boom years of the 1960s.

But he had serious difficulties adjusting to the new business climate. Geneen's entire approach had been geared to rapid expansion in an atmosphere of growth and optimism. It showed in the acquisitions, the willingness to take on burdens of debt, his belief that the combination of hard work and brains could solve virtually any problem, and, most of all, his delight in establishing records and then breaking them. How could a person like this function well in a period when the combination of high interest rates, a low ITT stock price, and government constraints all but forbade acquisitions; when no amount of effort or intellect could alter a fundamentally ailing economy, and declines became more common than advances?

If the 1960s called for bold growth, the mid-1970s demanded efficiencies and cutbacks. Geneen understood this but couldn't accept some of the strictures suggested by the altered circumstances. Thus, he struggled for growth at a time when a certain amount of pruning might have been advisable. That he was to have failures appeared obvious in retrospect. Geneen's successes in several key areas were all the more remarkable considering the difficulties along the way.

An overview of his problems at that time might be gleaned from a careful reading of the 1974 annual report, a generally somber affair in which was contained a portrait of a struggling conglomerate beset by internal and external difficulties. Even the customary photograph of Geneen was different, the confident smile of the previous year replaced by a troubled look. Earnings had been flat in the first quarter and actually declined in the third, breaking that string of consecutive advances of which he had been so proud. Although revenues had risen to $11.2 billion (plus another $2.8 billion from insurance and finance), slightly less than $1 billion more than they had been in 1973, earnings fell by $451 million, down from 1972's $521 million.

Geneen attributed much of this to inflation. At Hartford, for example, the costs of claims rose sharply, premium income was unable to keep pace, and profits from the investment portfolio fell because of the decline at the stock markets. Underwriting losses came to $123 million (against $39 million the previous year), while realized investment gains were $21.8 million (versus $37.7 million in 1973). In all, there was a decrease of $44 million in Hartford's net income. To this was added a reduction in earnings of some $20 million from those parts of ITT involved with the housing and automobile industries, both of which suffered badly that year. There were increased earnings in other segments of the corporation, however—natural resources, telecommunications, industrial products, and ISE—which helped offset declines elsewhere. Thus, weaknesses in one or two segments of the conglomerate were compensated in part by strengths in others.

Geneen had spoken and written on this point in the early 1960s; in that period he had observed that if structured properly, conglomerates would be more resistant to swings in the business cycle than would single-industry corporations. The recession of 1973–1974 was the first important test of this belief, and ITT performed better than most other conglomerates during this difficult time. In this respect Geneen might have been considered vindicated, but problems at other conglomerates—such as LTV, Gulf + Western, Litton, and U.S. Industries—indicated that ITT's superior record might have been due more to Geneen's management and other talents than to any particular virtue of the conglomerate form itself. Moreover, ITT didn't do as well as Geneen had hoped it would, and the inability to come through the recession better than it did must have been another disappointment.

In 1974, for the first time since 1961, Geneen had little to say about acquisitions at the annual meeting, perhaps because there were only a handful of minor takeovers that year, and the same held true for 1975. The reason was not an absence of likely candidates but rather the drastic depreciation of ITT paper, the prime currency in the exchanges. In early 1973 ITT common sold at a fraction above 60.

The price was halved by year's end, and in late 1974 ITT sold for 12, thus wiping out the entire advance made since Geneen transformed the corporation into a conglomerate. Several years earlier he had complained when ITT common sold at a price-earnings ratio of 20. By early 1975, the ratio was less than 6.

Not only would ITT have to develop without acquisitions, but in this two-year span, earnings relinquished from divested companies were far more than those gained from acquired ones. Almost all of these sales and spin-offs were forced upon Geneen, who rarely let go of a property—especially one he brought into ITT—without a struggle, and then only grudgingly.

Exercising its option under the original agreement worked out by Colonel Behn, the Commonwealth of Puerto Rico purchased Puerto Rico Telephone for cash, notes, and bonds totaling $125 million. After the Chiltelco experience, Geneen was quite content to sell this property, especially since he retained an important share of the contracts for equipping the lines. Thus, ITT divested itself of what had been the cornerstone of the corporation in its early years. With the exception of one—a small unit in the Virgin Islands—all of the telephone-operating companies were now gone.

In October 1974 ITT's manufacturing facilities in Argentina were seized by the government, and although discussions about compensation had begun, there was as yet no sign of resolution. Geneen was still trying to find a proper method of disposing of his equity in Avis, Canteen, and Levitt. Finally, ITT quietly sold several minor firms that were incapable of being turned around or that no longer fitted into plans being developed at headquarters.

There was more bad news regarding Hartford, but nothing that wasn't expected. That March the Internal Revenue Service revoked retroactively the 1969 ruling whereby the exchange of Hartford's stock for ITT paper had been tax-free to the insurer's shareholders. This was due in part to technicalities in the law that appeared to have been breached. For months there had been discussions between the IRS and ITT seeking some form of accommodation, but none could be arrived at. ITT announced it would fight the decision in the courts, and negotiations between the parties went on. Meanwhile, Geneen said that any liabilities (at the time estimated to be around $100 million) would be assumed by ITT. Thus, the former Hartford shareholders were in no danger of suffering losses.

There were no important new problems in 1975, merely a continuation of the slide begun the previous year. Sales and revenues were up by $1.2 billion to $11.3 billion, while those from insurance and finance declined slightly to $2.8 billion. Net earnings came to $398 million, down $53 million from 1974, and earnings per share were $3.20, or 43 cents less than the previous year. The company attributed the decline to weaknesses in consumer-products and automotive sales, lower results at Grinnell, Rayonier, and Hartford, and a fall-off in foreign earnings due to the impact of the recession in Europe. In August, Geneen thought he saw signs the recession was ending, but as yet there was no significant upturn at ITT.

Geneen did increase the annual dividend to $1.52, continuing the string started eleven years earlier, a reassurance to stockholders that in this area at least their income would advance. But the dividend action—interpreted on Wall Street as a reflection of Geneen's perennial optimism and intention to maintain at least this record—didn't help the price of the stock, which, as indicated, declined sharply through most of the year.

In late 1975 Geneen appeared confident a corner had been turned. The consumer sector remained in a slump, but there was a pickup in ITT's two central businesses: Hartford, in the United States, and European telecommunications. For the first time since the recession had begun, the backlog was larger than it had been the same time the previous year.

The United States did come out of its recession in 1976, but the strong upward sweep some economists had been predicting after so severe a decline didn't occur. Nor did the inflation and unemployment rates come down to their 1973 levels. Instead of a recovery, the nation entered a new phase of stagflation, which of course affected ITT.

Earnings rebounded that year, rising to $489 million, or $3.95 per share, but were still below the prerecession levels. A good deal of the increase came from Hartford, where both underwriting and portfolio results were excellent. Revenues from insurance and finance came to $3.1 billion in 1976, a quarter of a billion dollars more than in 1975, sparking new talk of how ITT was masking its flaws by drawing on profits from Hartford's investments. This time there appeared some justification for the charge. Sales and revenues from other parts of ITT were $11.8 billion, up less than $400 million from the previous year and sluggish by Geneen's standards.

The less-than-satisfactory performance could also be seen in the figure for return on equity. Geneen had always prided himself on having squeezed maximum profits out of every invested dollar. When he arrived, return on equity was barely over 6 percent. Along with revenues and profits, this figure rose in every year of the 1960s and early 1970s, peaking at 13.9 percent in 1973. Then, along with almost every other statistic, it declined, coming in at 9.5 percent in 1975, and in the recovery year that followed return on investment was only 11.1 percent. This significant index of performance would never again top its 1973 high, which might be interpreted either as evidence of the continued sluggishness of the American and European economies or a slow erosion at ITT. Given the fact that such was the situation in almost all segments of the American economy, it would seem obvious that this was the result of factors beyond Geneen's control. Still, it detracted somewhat from his old reputation as a miracle worker.

In August 1974 Geneen received a two-year employment contract from the board, which meant he would continue to lead ITT at least that long beyond the normal retirement age of sixty-five. In good physical and mental condition (though soon after he would contract Bell's Palsy) and still enjoying his work, Geneen implied he had no intention of stepping down. According to one ITT'er, "If the board asks him to stay, he'll consider it his duty to."[7] It became increasingly evident, however, that no such invitation would be issued. Geneen might leave on a date of his own selection, and might even choose his successor, but the transfer of power was to be in 1977.

There were several reasons for this, the most obvious being the matter of age itself. Few large industrial corporations permitted their chief executive officers to remain after the age of sixty-five, and some even asked them to step down at sixty. Geneen was to remain two years beyond the normal span, and this might be interpreted as a sign of respect for his abilities and as a desire to keep him on as long as possible. But there were other factors. There was some doubt Geneen could adjust to the new business environment certain to exist in the late 1970s, a feeling that perhaps the job had become too complex for a single person—especially an aging one—to handle, and that only a new leader could alter the top structure in such a way as to make it more manageable and receptive to change. That Geneen had made some errors in acquisitions was obvious, as was his refusal to cut losses rapidly; his successor could more easily rid the corporation of these operations. There were rumblings out of Quebec, where Rayonier was constructing what initially was to have been a \$120-million complex but had escalated into what by 1975 was shaping up as a major embarrassment. Something would have to be done there, and Geneen seemed reluctant to act.

Finally, insofar as public relations were concerned, Geneen had become a liability, in large part because of the bad press he had received from the time of the ABC conflicts through the Chilean episode. Admittedly a brilliant manager, he had also become to some a symbol of much that was allegedly wrong with American business, to which was added his continued identification with the by-now-departed Richard Nixon. One writer in a liberal journal, not untypically, saw them as virtual twins, "each masterminding his own rise to eminence in separate but related domains."

> Each is a chief executive of multinational importance whose influence stretches across the world; each was elected by a constituency confident it was choosing a competent, qualified personage embodying its aspirations, responsive to its needs, an exquisitely representative trustee of its hopes and resources. . . . In many more ways than one, each of these world-renowned luminaries appears to be a model of the other—short of scruples, tenacious, devious, indefatigable, defensive, demanding, exacting subservience of subordinates, ruthless when necessary, intolerant of sloth, and single-mindedly dedicated to the retention of power. It was probably inevitable that their paths would cross and their interests merge.[8]

Such a picture, overdrawn and in many respects unfair, nonetheless was the one a large number of Americans seemed to have of Geneen in the mid-1970s, and it couldn't be erased. To the contrary, it was becoming even more sharply etched. At the 1976 annual meeting Geneen conceded the corporation "may have" paid \$350,000 to Allende's opponents, thus reversing his earlier flat denial that such funds had passed hands. Soon thereafter a grand jury met to consider whether charges should be brought against him, but nothing came of this. Former ambassador Edward Korry was suing ITT for \$4.6 million in damages, claiming the corporation had attempted to "cast responsibility" on him for its actions in Chile.[9] This case, too, soon died. But it was embarrassing, and Geneen's presence at corporate headquarters indicated that more of the same might be expected, and the defenses against such actions were weak and even implausible.

There was a general feeling in the upper reaches at ITT that

Geneen's time had passed and that he had to make way for a younger person. There was no suggestion that he was to leave the corporation entirely. Rather, he was to become chairman emeritus, have a position on the board, and receive all the perquisites owed a person of his accomplishments and stature. But despite all this, the decision was that Geneen had to go.

In addition to guiding existing operations, Geneen had two major concerns during this, the last phase of his stewardship at ITT. He would renew the acquisitions program in such a way as to open another avenue of interest for the corporation. Under the circumstances there could be no truly significant takeover, on the order of those of the 1960s. Still, this showed that Geneen was prepared to establish a beachhead that might be broadened by his successor. Furthermore, he had to officiate at the partial distribution of shares in two of his most important overseas operations. While doing so, Geneen paid a great deal of attention to the matter of who would follow him as chief executive officer.

By 1977 ITT had been formally segmented into five large groups, plus one more that might be called "miscellaneous." Had these been organized as separate divisions, each with its own bureaucracy—which wasn't the case—each would have qualified on its own for membership in the Fortune or the Forbes 500, and each was far larger than the entire corporation had been when Geneen arrived there. These groups were Telecommunications, Engineered Products, Consumer Products and Services, Natural Resources, and Insurance and Finance. During the late 1960s and early 1970s attention had been focused on Telecommunications and Insurance, the former because it was a rapidly expanding glamour industry, the latter owing to "hidden assets" and a high ratio of revenues and earnings to assets. Engineered Products, which was composed of some eighty companies in the automobile, electrical, and electronics fields, was more cyclical and exhibited a generally slower pace of advance. Consumer Products and Services was the weakest segment of the five. The appliance business often reported deficits, and the huge Continental Baking operation was stagnant insofar as revenues and earnings were concerned. The only important part of this area that exhibited growth was Sheraton, which continued to grow in the mid-1970s.

Natural Resources was the smallest group. Made up largely of Rayonier and Pennsylvania Glass Sand, it was a cyclical-growth segment whose promise at the time of the acquisitions had never been fully realized. Rayonier's assets were far more valuable than they had been when Geneen acquired the company back in 1968, but its performance hadn't come up to expectations, although this was expected to change for the better if everything went well at the large Quebec installation. As for Pennsylvania Glass Sand, it remained a solid performer, revenues and profits expanding as they had prior to the takeover.

Missing from the Natural Resources group were operations in the field of energy. Throughout the 1960s Geneen had failed to foresee the crisis of the 1970s, and of course he wasn't alone in this. But by the mid-1970s he was determined to rectify the situation, and an aggressive search was made for likely acquisitions. They would have to be relatively small, because of the constraints resulting from the Hartford settlement. Geneen would have to offer premium prices, since the energy stocks had risen as a result of shortages, and although ITT's common and preferred issues were up from their 1974–1975 lows, they were still selling for well under half of their all-time highs.

Such a policy ran contrary to the Geneen approach of the 1960s, which was to acquire companies that might benefit from management alterations or cash infusions, preferably both. Thus, ITT knew in advance that there would be no large-scale takeovers and that those that were purchased wouldn't experience important turnarounds in the short run or contribute significantly to overall corporate performance.

In February ITT announced the acquisition of Carbon Industries at a cost of more than $260 million in preferred stock. This was a medium-size West Virginia–based coal company, formed only two and a half years earlier from several profitable and marginal mines. Most of Carbon's customers were electric utilities, and there was a small but growing export- and metallurgical-coal business as well. The acquisition came at a time when many utilities in the area were converting from natural gas and oil to coal, and Carbon's revenues were expected to rise, along with the value of its reserves. In light of its industry position, the company appeared likely to grow substantially in the 1980s.

To some the price appeared excessive, and indeed it was by pre-energy-shortage standards. But the $260 million was only a fraction of the value of Carbon's assets, even at then-current quotations. The dividends on the ITT preferred stock issued to Carbon's shareholders came to $7.1 million per annum, whereas in the previous two years the company had earned $14.6 million and $23 million respectively. All considered, the move appeared prudent, and even though Carbon didn't prove a spectacular performer (in large part owing to the failure of coal to live up to expectations as to production, price, and demand, and a wildcat strike soon after the takeover was completed), its earnings and assets justified the acquisition.

Six months later ITT purchased Eason Oil Co., a small producer and refiner with headquarters in Oklahoma. At the time, Eason was turning out slightly more than 2,000 barrels of oil and 31 billion cubic feet of natural gas per day, and had gross revenues of $31 million, with a net income of $4.7 million. As expected, the price was high: $82 in ITT common for Eason Oil shares that a year earlier had been trading for less than half that amount. Such was the premium one had to offer for petroleum and natural-gas properties, but under the circumstances it wasn't unreasonable. Eason had more than 670,000 acres of undeveloped land, almost all of which were in North America and under the North Sea, and in several other promising locations. Given the prospects for oil and natural gas at the time, Eason appeared a worthwhile addition.

Like Carbon Industries, however, Eason didn't have a significant impact on the corporation as a whole. Each unit would receive new funding, but there were to be no further acquisitions in these areas. Whatever else it was to become, ITT didn't intend to establish itself as a major force in the energy industries. In 1977 the two companies accounted for slightly more than 1 percent of gross sales and revenues and 2 percent of operating income, and these figures are about the same today.

There were two other acquisitions, more in the old ITT mold, in this period. The first was H. J. Bottling Company of New Jersey, the producer of C&C Cola, a low-priced soft drink distributed in five Eastern states. The purchase was completed in late 1976 at a price of slightly more than $10 million of preferred stock. Already a rapidly expanding force in supermarket sales, C&C grew even faster after the takeover, adding new flavors, capturing a larger share of sales in established markets, and entering additional states.

In 1977 ITT purchased North Electric from United Telecommunications for $28 million in cash. This deficit-ridden firm was nonetheless capable of turning out the digital switching systems many telephone companies then were adopting. Geneen needed this expertise, since ITT's other companies in the equipment field were lagging behind some of their competitors. This resulted in claims that even in its basic business ITT experienced a research lag that had to be compensated for by acquisitions. The corporation responded that research-and-development expenditures in 1977 came to $608 million, an all-time high, and that the figure had almost tripled during the past decade, keeping pace with revenues and rising more rapidly than earnings. But the allegations, first expressed in the early 1960s regarding not only ITT but most of the conglomerates, continued to be heard with this, Geneen's last acquisition.

ITT divested itself of one of its oldest holdings, Le Matériel Téléphonique. Acquired by Behn even prior to the purchase of International Western Electric, for several years LMT had been one of the targets of French politicians eager to nationalize, or at least to bring under local control, several foreign-owned corporations. This was hardly the same kind of situation that had existed in Chile and other parts of Latin America. In 1962 some 38 percent of the stock had been sold in France, and the remaining 62 percent was relinquished in 1976 for $89 million. Now LMT came under the control of Thomson CSF, a French telecommunications firm.

In no way was this an indication that ITT was withdrawing from or even lessening its French commitments. The following year Geneen purchased a third interest in Société Claude, a manufacturer of light bulbs and fixtures, as well as three small firms that turned out telephonic gear, all of which became associated with Compagnie Général de Constructions Téléphoniques, the ISE operation in that country and one of its most important suppliers of a wide variety of communications and electrical equipment. That year the French companies were the third-largest ITT complex outside of the United States, behind Germany and the United Kingdom.

Standard Elektrik Lorenz accounted for over a third of ITT's European business, more than twice that of the runner-up, United Kingdom. Shares were sold to the public in 1977, lowering ITT's equity to 86 percent. As with LMT, this was more a matter of ridding the company of its foreign image than anything else, and in this case ITT retained control of activities. Clearly this sale had nothing to do with Geneen's constant attempts to make ITT more of a domestic corporation than it had been in the past. Toward the end of his tenure, close to 60 percent of earnings still came from overseas.

The most pressing political issue at headquarters, and the subject of the most speculation, remained the matter of succession. While bowing to the decision that he step down as chief executive officer, Geneen made no secret of his hope to remain as chairman of the board, a perch from which to oversee—and supervise, perhaps guide, and certainly monitor—the activities of the next CEO. That any individual who took that post would have a difficult time of it was obvious even before the selection was made. No matter what his intentions, Geneen was temperamentally incapable of refraining from playing a role at ITT, and in the nature of his record and personality, it would be a powerful one. Virtually anything he did was bound to detract from and distract ITT's next leader.

Speculation about the succession began in 1968, when, in response to urging that he share responsibilities, Geneen established the Office of the President-Operations, composed of executive vice-presidents Francis Dunleavy and Richard Bennett as well as himself. This was unique to ITT. Theoretically, the office of the president served as a corporate version of what at other firms was a single chief operating officer, who ordinarily also held the title of president. Three years later it was expanded by the addition of another person, executive vice-president James Lester, and in 1972 Dunleavy was elevated to the presidency, presumably the first among equals.

Of course, each of these men at different times was heralded as the heir apparent. Bennett, whose forte was engineering, had come to ITT after stints at Eaton, Weston Instruments, and Western Electric. Dunleavy, too, had been at Eaton, as well as at RCA and Crown Cork & Seal. He was a management specialist who prior to being elevated to the executive vice-presidency had headed ITT's European operations. Lester had had similar, major responsibilities in Europe before receiving the call to return to New York, and earlier he had worked at Rohm & Haas and at Standard Pressed Steel.

All were experienced, capable, and proven leaders, and although Bennett hadn't managed a major subsidiary, his other talents made up for that deficiency. All were younger than Geneen—Dunleavy by five years, Bennett and Lester by ten.

Appearances to the contrary, none came close to the chairmanship, not because they lacked abilities but because of Geneen's reluctance to bestow that designation any sooner than was absolutely necessary. Then, too, all had become accustomed to secondary posts in the organization, taking orders from a strong, demanding, and often harsh leader. There was much to be learned at "Geneen University," but independence of thought and action weren't high on the curriculum. As has been seen, would-be corporation managers usually left after a few years at ITT to go off on their own. Those who remained were content to accept subordinate roles. A person who while on the way to the executive suites might have become a fine chairman would soon leave, whereas those who served in top posts for more than a few years almost marked themselves as lacking requisite qualities. The board wanted a person who could manage and expand upon Geneen's legacy, but also one who could alter it where necessary. Dunleavy, Lester, and Bennett were part of the inheritance, thoroughly identified with major decisions and worn down by years of abrasion against the powerful chairman.

Finally—and perhaps decisively—all held key posts during the past few years, and the selection of any of them could have signaled a continuation of the old regime, associated in the public and private minds with Chile. The board wanted a Geneen protégé, but one not too closely identified with the chairman, and of a different generation, whose nomination would be perceived as a sign that a new era was opening. Finally, ITT needed a person adept at public relations, to regain the confidence of the media and Wall Street as well as of the general public.

This, too, all but eliminated Dunleavy, Bennett, and Lester. Instead, ITT would turn to one of the younger men on the rise, the kind who might leave the corporation unless he continued to receive additional power and status. There were several such individuals from whom to chose. As it turned out, the succession was bestowed upon Lyman C. Hamilton.

Entr'acte II

IN June 1976 ITT announced two additions to the office of the president. The first was Lyman Hamilton, then forty-nine years old, an executive vice-president who was also the corporation's treasurer, chief financial officer, and a member of the board. Rand Araskog, one of ITT's thirty-five vice-presidents, a decided step behind Hamilton in the pecking order and five years his junior, was the other. As the only member of the office of the president not on the board, Araskog was perceived as one of the company's rising stars. "Both are now the fair-haired boys," thought one ITT'er quoted in *Business Week*.

No one would have disagreed with this assessment. Hamilton and Araskog were to be the corporation's future leaders.

Immediately each became the subject of speculation at headquarters, where the betting was that within a year the two would advance as a team that in time would replace Geneen. Hamilton, most of whose work was in the financial area, was pegged as the next chairman and chief executive officer, while Araskog, who had more management experience, appeared destined to become president. Or so it seemed to outsiders.

The actual situation was more complex. In fact, Geneen would have preferred one of his older associates for the chairmanship. But Lester wasn't interested, Bennett had no support, and Dunleavy, the earlier favorite, was fading rapidly. For a while Geneen thought he might persuade the board to accept Dunleavy, who would become a front, while Geneen continued to run ITT from behind the scenes. But the board wouldn't go along with this. Both inside and outside directors understood there was a sense of malaise at the top, where things had been allowed to drift while Geneen defended himself against outside political attacks, which distracted him and sapped his energies. They continued to respect the man, and wanted him to remain at ITT in some important capacity. But most were firm in believing Geneen had to relinquish command.

Later some would claim Geneen wanted Araskog for the top post, in part because the younger man still lacked an independent power base at headquarters. According to this view, Geneen might use Araskog rather than Dunleavy as his front man, offering the appearance of transition with little of the substance. This seems not to have been the case. Araskog wasn't deemed ready for such a position, had his own ideas of where ITT should be headed, and in any case lacked a following at headquarters.

Over the past few years Hamilton had nourished a cadre of supporters at the treasurer's and comptroller's offices, and in addition he had some support on the board, especially among the inside directors. Bennett and Lester in particular were more inclined toward Hamilton than toward Araskog.

Whether this was so or not, Geneen accepted Hamilton as his successor, at a time when he didn't have to do so, and with as much grace as could be mustered given the fact that he had hoped to stay on himself.

Both men had demonstrated an unusual capacity for hard work, but where Geneen regularly devoted eighteen hours a day to the job and had few other interests, Hamilton had been more of a twelve-hour man while treasurer, and found it easier to relax. Each man traveled with an entourage carrying report-filled briefcases, but after he moved to the top Hamilton became less conspicuous in this regard.

Each was self-assured, ambitious, and aggressive, but in Geneen these qualities were painted in stark, often obvious primary colors. Not so with Hamilton, a far subtler person. More than was apparent at the time, both of these men, of different backgrounds and generations, yearned to occupy center stage, but they didn't share the same ideas about the corporation or visions of its future. Geneen and Hamilton disagreed as to strategies and tactics, though early on the younger man was sufficiently astute politically to keep some of his thoughts to himself.

While working under Geneen, Hamilton generally deferred to his chief but was less obsequious than others in this regard. He possessed a streak of stubborn though polite individualism, which was displayed while he served as treasurer but which ran far deeper than most suspected and would emerge full-blown later on. Even Geneen failed to take this measure of the man who was to replace him. In seeking a successor, he apparently looked for a younger, more polished version of himself, and perhaps did better than he realized with Hamilton. What Geneen hadn't fully taken into consideration was that this would be precisely the kind of CEO with whom he was bound to clash.

Hamilton lacked Behn's exoticism and the rough dynamism of Geneen. Of course, he was a product of a different age and had different experiences and ambitions. For one thing, Hamilton was equally comfortable in government and business, and for another, he always lacked the intense, personal identification with ITT demonstrated by Behn and Geneen. This isn't to suggest Hamilton was a mere bureaucrat with little loyalty to the firm. Rather, he had a wider range of interests than either of his two major predecessors. On several occasions Hamilton said that his career might be divided into three segments: first with government, then with a major corporation, and finally on his own, to initiate rather than manage an enterprise. That he would have left ITT were it not for the regular promotions was clear, and that he would attempt to reshape the corporation in his own image once in command should have been equally obvious.

Hamilton was born in Los Angeles in 1926, into a middle-class family that had relocated there from the Midwest. After attending local schools, he entered the Navy as a midshipman, and he remained in the service from 1944 to 1946. Much of this time was spent attending colleges—the University of Redlands and UCLA in California and Principia College in Illinois. Hamilton graduated from Principia in 1947 with a B.A., a major in political science and an interest in economics, and a desire to obtain a government position. He accepted civil-service posts with the State Department and the Bureau of the Budget with, as he later recalled, "my mind intent on being a good bureaucrat." He also applied to and was accepted into the graduate program in public administration at Harvard, from which he received an M.P.A. in 1949, with all the requirements for the Ph.D. completed except the dissertation. Shortly thereafter Hamilton married Mary Shepard, and four sons were born to them over the next ten years.

Hamilton rose rapidly in the federal bureacracy. The charming, tall, and handsome man had a keen sense of humor combined with an ability to inspire coworkers, and his talents were quickly perceived by others. Hamilton became director of finance for the Civil Administration of the Ryukyu Islands, based in Okinawa, in 1956, and rose to the post of assistant civil administrator for financial, economic, and political affairs. Hardly a prize assignment, it did enable him to advance faster than might have been possible in a more desirable location. Later Hamilton would look back on this as his most rewarding professional experience.

He returned to Washington in 1960 as financial analyst for the Bank for Reconstruction and Development, and then as senior investment officer with the International Finance Corporation. While there, he was recruited by Hart Perry—who had been his superior at the Bureau of the Budget—for ITT, and in 1962 Hamilton accepted the position of manager for financial planning in the treasurer's department. Thus he concluded the first part of his career and began the second.

Hamilton arrived at ITT at a time when Geneen was still stocking the corporation with his own men, most of whom, like Hamilton, were outsiders. The acquisitions program had begun; ITT was about to expand rapidly, affording opportunities to those who could keep up with Geneen's pace; and Hamilton was in one of the corporation's most vital offices.

Promotions came quickly, at the rate of almost one a year, and Hamilton's advancement was spectacular even by ITT's standards. In 1963 he was named director of financial programs and the following year director of foreign treasury operations, to which was added the title of associate treasurer. Hamilton became treasurer in 1967, a corporate vice-president in 1968, and senior vice-president and executive vice-president in 1973.

All this time he was involved almost exclusively with financial matters; Hamilton had no role in the antitrust prosecutions, the San Diego affair, or the Hartford acquisition. He had nothing to do with Chile. Rather, it was his task to keep ITT on an even keel at a time when the acquisitions program had slowed down and the corporation was struggling to maintain its growth image. In recognition of the importance of financial controls, both Hamilton and comptroller Herbert Knortz were named to the board in 1974.

That year Hamilton instituted a program known as "zero incremental debt," meaning ITT was to end the year with virtually the same amount of combined long- and short-term debt as it had at the beginning. He succeeded—in fact, Hamilton managed to reduce the debt by over $300 million—and so helped maintain the corporation's "A" credit rating, saving large sums in interest costs and furthering his career at ITT.

Not only had Hamilton established himself as a skillful financial manager, but he proved popular with Wall Street banks and trust companies and the district's financial reporters. These people were charmed by his easy manner, accessibility, obvious intelligence, and command of his material, but most of all by his candor. At a time when few at ITT possessed any large measure of credibility, Hamilton was open, believable, and persuasive. He had natural skills at public relations when they were needed. As much as anything else, these catapulted him ahead of Dunleavy and the others in the matter of succession. Yet he wasn't certain it would be a desirable change. For one thing, he enjoyed his work at the treasurer's office, and for another, he realized that anyone who succeeded Geneen would be in a difficult position, especially if the chairman remained at the corporation. Moreover, the two men had no particular affinity for each other, and this was bound to cause troubles. With all of this, in the end Hamilton could hardly resist the challenge and opportunity. Simply stated, he wanted the job.

The announcement came on February 9, 1977. Effective March 1, Hamilton would be president, chief operating officer, and a member of the executive committee of the board of directors. Geneen would retain the chairmanship and continue as chief executive officer but would relinquish the latter title to Hamilton at the end of the year. He would have preferred it otherwise. Still unsure as to Hamilton's capacity to perform well in the top post, Geneen suggested that no mention be made of the CEO post or the chairmanship. When and if Hamilton demonstrated abilities to fill these positions, he would be promoted, but otherwise he would remain where he was. The board overruled Geneen on this point, and he accepted the verdict.

The press and the business community hailed the move. Assessments of Geneen's accomplishments and reviews of his legacy were published, along with speculation about the direction Hamilton would take once he assumed command. From this one might have gathered that the Geneen era was about to come to a close, and the 1977 annual report referred to "a smooth transition in management" as one of the year's more important events.

But Geneen wasn't through at ITT, as could be seen in the restructuring of management that took place later in the year. Hamilton created the "office of the chief executive," composed of himself, Bennett, Lester, and Araskog, the last of whom moved up in what was seen as a prelude to selection as president under a future Hamilton chairmanship. Dunleavy was to become vice-chairman, and together with Geneen he would constitute the new "office of the chairman," whose task it would be to "provide support, assistance, and counsel to the chief executive." Geneen would stay on the board and remain chairman of the powerful executive committee, all of whose members (except Geneen, Hamilton, and Araskog) were outside directors personally loyal to him. Hamilton had the title, office, and responsibilities, but he still lacked true power, and wouldn't have it so long as Geneen remained in control of a majority on the board.

That this was so was apparent at headquarters, even though it eluded members of the press, most of whom thought Hamilton had taken over. There was even a hint of the true nature of the relationship at the top in a picture that accompanied the message to shareholders in the 1977 annual report. There were the two men, seated on a sofa. Geneen looked ahead, as though to the future—of which he meant to be an important part. Hamilton peered at the chairman, and the expression on his face was thoughtful, perhaps troubled. Several months later Geneen told a reporter, "[My new task is] to support Lyman in any way I can," and Hamilton said, "Geneen has let go." But an Ericsson executive, who was asked if ITT had become a trifle less competitive, observed, "We haven't noticed any differences—after all, isn't Geneen still around?"[1]

There were few substantive changes in day-to-day operations, but these were on the way. Hamilton established a task force charged with developing plans for structural alterations in the corporation. He sent all top executives to marketing seminars, indicating there would be added stress in this area—and indirectly implying that Geneen hadn't done as well as he might there. Hamilton evidently meant to consolidate some units, place his own men in important posts, and in general become CEO in fact as well as title.

Meetings in the United States and Europe were more subdued than they had been under Geneen. Hamilton was more inclined to listen than to lecture. The public grillings and occasional humiliations of executives who weren't prepared to answer often arcane questions came to an end; Hamilton meted out criticisms privately. Most welcomed the change, the new informality. It was still "Mr. Geneen" to virtually everyone at the top, especially in public, but even there, the style was to call the new chief executive officer "Lyman." Hamilton was respected, but he also elicited affection from associates. Comparisons with Geneen were inevitable, and Hamilton himself offered some. "Our mental capacities are different," he said. "If I don't have the same brilliance, I guess I have some of the judgment that is necessary for this job."[2]

The thin-skinned Geneen took this as a veiled criticism of many of his actions. He bristled when reading stories of how Hamilton was "cleaning up the company" after the Chilean scandals. He might have resented the irrelevant comparisons of their physical appearance—the tall, patrician-looking, usually smiling Hamilton and the short, stocky, grim bulldog of a man Geneen usually was pictured as being. Geneen couldn't have helped but notice that many of his former allies were flocking to the new CEO, and although he was still deferred to, it really wasn't the same. Whatever his intentions in 1978—and in his own mind, at least, Geneen seemed to have made an effort to accept the new dispensation—he still yearned for command and all that it implied. Like Sosthenes Behn before him, Geneen was constitutionally incapable of turning ITT over to someone else. The difference was that he could do something about it, whereas Behn could not.

There were two, interrelated programs that would provide Geneen with his battleground, and both involved corporate structure and a reassessment of the acquisitions program of the past decade. Was ITT a truly unified corporation or merely a collection of operating units held together by Geneen? On one occasion Anthony Sampson suggested the structure might fall apart once Geneen left, that the various divisions would assert their independence—in effect, rise up against headquarters—once he stepped down. Thus ITT would end up more a confederation of quasi-autonomous operations than a conglomerate.[3]

There was never any chance of this happening—not at ITT, or at any other large American corporation, for that matter. But Hamilton did permit divisional managers more leeway in making and implementing decisions. Geneen had wanted to be informed of everything that was happening at each of his units, and was free in offering advice to operators in the field. Hamilton was content to know who was responsible for activities and how they were progressing. He encouraged independence in action as well as in thought, with the understanding that success would be rewarded and failure in a good cause tolerated. In essence, Hamilton was more entrepreneurial and less managerial than Geneen had been, and he urged other executives to be so as well.

He was also the product of a different era. Geneen had been the undisputed star of the conglomerate movement and had remained devoted to its basic tenets even as it came to an end in the late 1960s and early 1970s. American capitalism had entered a new phase, but the man remained as he had been, stressing growth through acquisitions, concentrating on advances in earnings per share rather than returns on invested and total capital and profit margins.

In the late 1970s the stocks of most conglomerates were selling far below their breakup value. Under these circumstances it might have been wise to divest properties rather than buy them for depreciated equity, to become more rational through shrinkage rather than diversify further by purchasing other firms for undervalued paper. This was Hamilton's view, and it ran completely contrary to Geneen's basic instincts and beliefs.

Hamilton later reflected that through this entire period he concentrated at least as much on what he hoped and expected the corporation would evolve into by the late 1980s as he did on the problems of the present. By then ITT might be a $60-billion enterprise, with two or more divisions larger than the entire ITT had been when he assumed power. So vast an enterprise could hardly be managed by a single CEO, even one as dedicated and talented as Geneen—assuming such a person could be found—and because of this, Hamilton spoke of further decentralizing operations. Some business writers hailed this an another sign that he meant to restructure ITT, though they misjudged Hamilton's immediate plans, which were to continue as before during the next few years.

Far more startling was a persistent rumor that this was just a first step in an eventual dissolution of the corporation, that Hamilton intended to spin off each major unit until there were five "successor companies" to the old ITT. What he had in mind was to provide each of the large entities with its own CEO, not only to give them a more efficient management through greater autonomy but to head off what he feared might be a new antitrust crusade prompted by such exponential growth.

Much of this was the kind of long-range planning that corporation executives engage in but that is rarely realized, owing to economic and political developments. However, the implementation of such a program would certainly undercut if not demolish the structure Geneen had bestowed upon his successor. Although Hamilton spoke of his ideas only to trusted friends and associates, rumors regarding them were leaked, and they reached Geneen, who became furious. The problems were compounded when Hamilton made no effort to deny the talk or to placate the man he had replaced as CEO.

All of this related to policies regarding acquisitions, the chief bone of contention between the two. Stated simply, Geneen defended his record in this sphere and wanted ITT to continue taking over other companies, while Hamilton had little interest in this aspect of the business and was far more concerned with divesting the corporation of several unsuccessful operations. Geneen saw no difficulties in managing what had become 240 profit centers and wanted more, while Hamilton sought cutbacks. The very mention of a possible sale was enough to spark arguments at board meetings, with the chairman and the president always opposing each other. Hamilton's position was that once it was demonstrated that new or augmented management plus additional capital couldn't bring about substantial increases in profitability, a company should be divested, whereas Geneen continued to believe that effective management could work wonders on moribund enterprises. "I was the last guy to agree that it had to be sold," he said after grudgingly approving one such divestiture. "Geneen just became too sentimental about his subsidiaries," said Winston Morrow, of Avis, a company Geneen had been most sorry to see go.[4]

I·T·T: The Management of Opportunity

One of Geneen's favorite sayings was that it was possible to "manage a company to success." Hamilton felt otherwise. Fresh from his zero-incremental-debt campaign and eager to trim ITT of units not performing up to his standards, he had no such visceral commitments. This may have made good business sense, but to a sensitive Geneen, each divestiture would appear a slap in the face, a charge that yet another blunder had to be rectified.

Hamilton told reporters that ITT was trying "to identify activities with low return and low growth" for possible sale. What he had in mind were several poorly performing European food companies and a grab bag of minor firms in the United States. Around headquarters, however, there were recurrent rumors that once he had control of the board, Hamilton would dispose of some large operations, among them Continental Baking, Rayonier (where the Canadian mill still wasn't completed and costs were escalating), and ITT Publishing. He denied this, but several advisories out of Wall Street projected the corporation's performance without such laggards, and the picture was bright. Bankers and brokers were almost unanimous in support of this approach, which would not only increase ITT's per-share earnings but presumably result in a higher price for its stock.

A suspicion that Hamilton was catering to this kind of constituency must have crossed Geneen's mind and deepened his unhappiness with the situation. Such a divestiture program would cast a shadow on the Geneen record and enable Hamilton to pose as the corporation's savior, not only from such misadventures as those in San Diego and Chile but from unwise acquisitions. Geneen simply couldn't permit this to happen.

In 1978 ITT divested itself of six small units whose sales the previous year totaled $75 million, with losses of close to $6 million. Hamilton's pruning operation had begun. There would have been more, but Geneen was able to block them by rallying his forces at headquarters.

There were seven acquisitions in 1978 with combined revenues of approximately $200 million, most of which were accounted for by the two largest, Courier Terminal Systems, a West Coast electronics firm that cost $50 million in cash and notes, and Qume Corporation, a small but rapidly growing company in the business-machine field, which took 4.7 million shares of ITT common, worth close to $150 million. Both had promising futures, and Qume was already a leader in computer-printout systems, but their prices were high by the standards of that period. This was a time when in the wake of a stock-market collapse there developed a mania for acquisitions of capital-goods manufacturers whose stocks were selling at substantial discounts from net-asset values. In contrast, Qume diluted ITT's per-share earnings at a time when Hamilton's announced primary goal was to increase them and widen profit margins.

Everyone knew that negotiations for Courier and Qume had begun during the last months of the Geneen era, for each bore his unmistakable stamp. But the negotiations had been completed by Hamilton, and in a way quite different from that of the previous administration. Geneen had usually obtained an independent evaluation of the worth of companies he acquired, often relying on Rohatyn and the Lazard organization. Rohatyn remained on the board, along with fellow investment banker Alvin Friedman, of Lehman Brothers Kuhn Loeb. Neither was consulted regarding the final stages of the Qume acquisition, though Rohatyn later indicated he thought it a good move and the price reasonable.[5] In fact, Hamilton tended to ignore both men when it came to acquisitions and sales of units, in part to save commissions but also because he didn't intend to expand through takeover. In Geneen's last year Lazard and Lehman earned close to $2.2 million between them in fees; during 1978 this sum dropped to less than $200,000.[6] Thus, Hamilton alienated two powerful board members.

Rather than seeking growth through acquisitions, Hamilton wanted to commit a greater amount of money to research and development and further improve the balance sheet. The Qume and Courier purchases could be justified because these companies provided needed products and expertise to augment ITT's System 12, the key element of the telephonic digital-switching network of the future and the heart of Network 2000, the name given the entire system. In the next few years, however, Hamilton expected more new products to come in from existing holdings and fewer by means of takeovers. For example, there was no reason to believe ITT's own researchers couldn't develop and then produce Network 2000 without any important outside assistance.

Ever committed to rapid and dramatic growth, Geneen bridled at the idea. Hamilton's more cautious approach would require time and patience, and Geneen lacked both. In May 1978, less than half a year after stepping down as CEO and with Hamilton at his side,

Geneen asked a financial analyst, "Shouldn't we get back into the acquisitions business?"[7] It was a refrain Hamilton had heard regularly since taking office.

Two such strong-willed individuals couldn't work in tandem for long. Hamilton might have believed ultimate victory rested in mere survival, that he might accumulate power simply by holding on and avoiding a direct confrontation while performing well on the job. More of his people were taking prominent posts at headquarters and in the field, and he continued to receive good press. In retrospect, however, it is apparent Hamilton seriously misjudged his own strengths and was far too sanguine regarding the opinions held of his performance by the board. In essence, he wasn't particularly effective in the political sphere, a necessary aspect of modern management. Moreover, while considered by many a refreshing change from the uncertainties of the late Geneen era, he hadn't managed to create a new vitality within the corporation. Support for Hamilton had been broad at first, but never deep. It would remain so for a while and then would start to erode as results continued to be disappointing.

Hamilton hadn't fully realized that most of the outside directors and several of the inside ones as well had no quarrel with the way Geneen had run ITT before his last few years, that they were concerned only about his vitality and image. Hamilton had no mandate to make a clean sweep of things, and yet he gave the appearance of doing so. Some of his appointments disturbed this old guard, particularly that of Gerhard Andlinger, who became head of ITT Europe, one of the corporation's most important and sensitive positions. A former ITT executive who had left the corporation years earlier after having policy differences with Geneen and performing poorly in several posts, Andlinger had gone on to establish himself as an expert on mergers. His selection was interpreted as an indication not only that ITT would divest itself of many of the small companies Geneen had taken over in the 1960s and 1970s but that in the future Hamilton would rely even less than he already did on the New York bankers for help in acquisitions and related matters. Hamilton also tried to appoint his old mentor, Hart Perry, as head of the Washington office. Perry had been on a leave of absence for personal reasons, and several directors opposed the selection. Hamilton backed down this time, but the episode left a residue of irritation. Similarly, his attempt to close some recreational facilities utilized by the corporation for business purposes was resented, and once again the suggestion was withdrawn, all of this in such a way as to leave ruffled feelings.

Then, too, there was fallout from parts of Hamilton's reorganization efforts, especially those that involved dismissal or relocation of executives. Abandoning much of the Geneen apparatus for producing regular, detailed reports, and in other ways streamlining operations, Hamilton was able to cut approximately 120 executives from the New York office and another 140 from the Brussels center. In contrast, Geneen had rarely fired a person, preferring instead to utilize transfers. As might have been expected, this demoralized many who remained and who feared they might be next. With Hamilton gone and Geneen back in command, their worries would be over.

All of this might have been acceptable had Hamilton been able to demonstrate benefits from such changes, but these couldn't be discerned, at least at first. Moreover, there was a sense of drift in that portion of ITT that received much of Hamilton's attention— namely, telecommunications. Sensing this, Hamilton went into the field himself, attempting to win placements, something Geneen hadn't done while CEO. He had little success, losing out in several important contests with foreign firms for contracts. CIT-Alcatel outbid ITT in an initial drive to capture the Finnish market, though Hamilton was able to affect a partial recovery there later on. General Telephone & Electronics bested ITT in the first stages for contracts from Costa Rica, while Ericsson and Siemens increased their market shares in Western Europe at ITT's expense. There still wasn't a single placement of System 12, and work was lagging on Network 2000. Much of this was attributed, perhaps unfairly, to alterations in the Geneen structure.

Finally, some ITT'ers bridled at the way Hamilton was being portrayed in the press as the corporation's savior after Geneen allegedly had blackened the corporation's image and committed management errors. While he was CEO, Geneen had commanded respect, admiration, fear, and even adulation and hatred, but never sympathy. Now he received a measure of this, as old associates resented the way he was seeming to be treated. "Geneen deserves better than this," said one director on reading a newspaper report praising Hamilton and criticizing his predecessor. "He built one of the finest organizations in history; he deserved to go out in a blaze of glory—not like this."[8]

Such sentiment was growing in late 1978 and early 1979, and the wonder of it all was that Hamilton did so little to shore up his position, to placate and disarm critics. He was incorrect in believing time was on his side. Rather, it was working for Geneen, whose power was on the rise in this period. He couldn't have toppled Hamilton in early 1978—which in any case wasn't his desire then. A year later all he had to do was select the right moment.

After it was over, insiders claimed that four signals were given in 1978 and 1979 that indicated Hamilton would be challenged and deposed. The first came in March 1978, when the Justice Department dropped possible prosecution of Geneen for perjury in his testimony on Chile. Although not exactly a vindication of ITT's role in that country, this did serve at least partially to rehabilitate Geneen's reputation in the matter and give him more freedom of action, thus strengthening his hand.

That August, Hamilton scheduled a special management meeting to review major policy matters. For months he had clashed with Geneen over several key issues, and Hamilton hoped this would clear the air. Geneen agreed to listen to all that was being set forth and not to contribute to the discussions. In effect, this was to be Hamilton's opportunity to present his full case, not only to the executives present but to his predecessor.

Geneen took it in without comment. Then, toward the close of the session, Hamilton did something he was later to regret, and set into motion a confrontation he mishandled. He asked Geneen for his reactions to the discussions, and these were provided—in detail and profusion. As Hamilton recalled, Geneen took over, asking executives for reports, challenging statements, and setting down his own agenda. Demoralized and angry, Hamilton didn't attempt to discuss the matter privately with Geneen but instead took his problems to the board. His position was barely tenable, Hamilton complained, since Geneen wasn't permitting him to function with the full powers required by the CEO of such a complex organization. In an oblique way, this was a challenge, and on a ground where Geneen was supposed to have been strong. Yet the board backed Hamilton on this occasion, recognizing that he indeed was the chief executive officer and that he required such authority. The two men were headed toward a showdown, with Hamilton not understanding the meaning of his support from the board at the time. In fact, the majority was agreeing that ITT could have only one CEO at a time, and that he was it. But this episode troubled the members, and confidence in Hamilton eroded further.

A third signal came in the form of a rejoinder from Geneen. He prepared and distributed a lengthy critique of Hamilton's policies and performance, which was distributed to the board (but not to Hamilton) and the gist of which was soon learned by others. Corporately, it appeared that Hamilton had thrown down the gauntlet, and Geneen had picked it up.

Geneen attended the Brussels meetings in late June, 1979. This was a trifle surprising and unexpected, for he had missed a number of them since stepping down as CEO and until the last minute hadn't intended to go. But having been invited to a wedding nearby, he decided to make the trip.

Geneen was the center of attention, even more than usual, at the traditional postconference barbecue, in part because of another Hamilton misstep. Unable to cancel several important appointments in Asia, Hamilton elected to forego the Brussels conference, thus leaving center stage to the chairman. Toward the conclusion of the party, Geneen was asked to speak briefly to the ninety or so foreign and domestic executives present, and so he did. The speech was casual, witty, and informal, and dealt with the recent past and possible future. When it was over the executives gave him a long standing ovation.

This was more than a routine demonstration of respect for a revered figure out of the past. Most understood it to be a vote of confidence, their way of showing that they missed Geneen's strong, optimistic, expansionist outlook and leadership and that they felt uncertain about Hamilton's plans and performance. Geneen appeared genuinely surprised. His closest associates claimed none of this had been planned. But the story was leaked to the press, and though it wasn't deemed worthy of mention at the time, the Brussels party was written about later on and in most accounts was portrayed as the trigger for subsequent actions. The old ruler had raised his banner, and the nobles flocked to embrace his cause.

By now Hamilton understood that the Geneen loyalists had been aroused. They interpreted his stress on the balance sheet, talk of ridding the corporation of poorly performing units, and attempts to alter ITT's general direction as a concerted criticism of Geneen, and so it was. Hamilton would later argue that he was eager to set ITT on a new path, to meet the unique challenges of the 1980s, and not to denigrate Geneen's accomplishments during his tenure as CEO. But his actions were interpreted differently.

This was a period of fiscal stringency, not only at ITT but throughout the nation. Stagflation hadn't been checked by the end of the 1970s, and a wave of economic puritanism was sweeping over political and corporate America. Deficit spending was condemned, fiscal integrity extolled, and budget-balancing in vogue, the implication being that in the past, well-meaning but financially irresponsible individuals had burdened society with poorly considered programs, which now had to be cut or eliminated. What Jimmy Carter had pledged to accomplish for the United States—to end deficit spending and prune the political system—Hamilton was trying to do at ITT. It was only natural that those with professional and emotional stakes in the old ways would resent his attitude, assumptions, and actions.

As indicated, Hamilton lacked a majority on the board as the final confrontation approached. Bennett and Lester would be with him, as would Knortz, his old collaborator from the zero-incremental-debt period, and Raymond Brittenham, senior vice-president and counsel. The loyalties of a few others were divided, but the remainder of the board, including almost all the outside directors, would support Geneen—to a point. Hamilton hadn't spent sufficient time learning just where that point was, while Geneen was in close contact with most of the directors.

The showdown took place on July 11, 1979. It was a bitter, traumatic affair, opening wounds that will probably never heal. This is to be expected when the leader of a major enterprise, be it political or commercial, is deposed by close associates. It is an uncomfortable, messy, embarrassing, and angry business, in which individuals take harsh actions and use blunt language, leaving a trail of recriminations, painful memories, shame, and guilt.

As might be supposed, each party has his own version of the matter, though there is essential agreement on some of the facts. These are that, as was his practice, Hamilton met with Geneen the night prior to the board meeting, but that he had no inkling of what was to occur the following day. He learned that his resignation was expected during a business breakfast. The regular meeting took place that afternoon, after which a special one was convened and Hamilton's resignation accepted. But of course there was more to it than that.

As Geneen tells it, several outside directors, the most prominent of whom was Richard Perkins, had concluded that Hamilton hadn't performed well as CEO and would have to be replaced. On the evening of July 10 Perkins contacted Geneen and told him of plans to ask for Hamilton's resignation. Whether this occurred prior to or after the Geneen-Hamilton meeting is uncertain, but Geneen approved of the decision, in this way following Perkins' lead.

Hamilton believes Geneen orchestrated the final confrontation, using Perkins as his vehicle. These two men together with outside director Thomas Keesee had played golf together the previous weekend, and the final plans might have been formulated then. Thus, Perkins acted as Geneen's front man.

On the morning of July 11 Hamilton went to the Links Club for breakfast with members of the compensation committee, all of whom were outside directors and Geneen's allies: Anthony Bryan, Pomeroy Day, William Elfers, Alvin Friedman, Perkins, and Keesee. This was very much a part of the regular ritual preceding board meetings. Hamilton had no idea there would be a challenge to his position and devoted the first part of the discussions to the wording of a press release regarding ITT's second-quarter earnings. It was after this that Perkins said a number of the directors wanted him to step down, the reason being "policy differences." A shocked Hamilton listened as Perkins proposed this be cited by him in a resignation statement to be submitted to the board. Hamilton responded by asking each man present for specifics. What were the precise differences? No one had any to offer. The reason for Perkins' action was both simple and obvious: Geneen wanted him to go. Hamilton reacted more out of anger and surprise than in the hope of swaying the members. He knew it would be a futile exercise. This, then, was his version of the situation just prior to the July 11 board meeting.[10]

The board convened at 2:10 P.M., with Geneen presiding and Hamilton not attending. (He was in his office at the time, conferring with his attorney.) Ironically, this last regular meeting of the Hamilton era would be devoted, for the most part, to divestitures. Phillips Cable would acquire, for approximately $5 million, a small Canadian plant that turned out electrical wire, and ITT Nesbitt—

one of the first companies Hamilton had marked for sale—would go to Environmental Technologies Inc. for another $6.7 million. There were purchases to balance things out. The board agreed to buy land in Connecticut for a research facility, and upon Araskog's recommendation some 5,900 acres of coal land in Indiana was purchased from AMAX for $6.7 million. Then followed an economic review, reports on problems with Washington, a survey of European conditions, and the voting on dividends on cumulative convertible shares. While all of this was going on, directors shuttled in and out of the room, with at least some of them working on Hamilton's financial settlement, preparing the way for the special meeting that was to follow.

A recess was declared at 3:20, and the board reconvened little more than an hour later, with everyone knowing the sole business would be Hamilton's future. The dealings were perfunctory. At 6:32 the Compensation Committee withdrew to consider a proper settlement and reported back in eighteen minutes on the progress of negotiations with Hamilton and his attorney. At 7:05 the board learned that an agreement had been reached. A half hour later the board voted, unanimously, to accept this resolution:

> RESOLVED, that Rand V. Araskog is hereby elected President of the Corporation and appointed Chief Executive Officer to serve in such capacities until the next Annual Meeting of the Shareholders of the Corporation and until his successor shall have been elected and qualified.

The special meeting adjourned at 7:38. The Hamilton entr'acte had ended, and the Araskog era had been inaugurated.[11]

"It was a shootout," one of Hamilton's loyalists remarked, "and the good guy lost." At the time, however, it still wasn't clear just who had won—Geneen or Araskog.

Hamilton emerged from this experience scarred and bitter but hardly bereft of assets or opportunities. His reputation and popularity were intact, even enhanced, for within segments of the business community, anyone who clashed with Geneen was deemed a hero. And he was free to seek other positions. His salary and bonuses of some $480,000 a year would run until 1983.

Years earlier Hamilton had indicated a desire to divide his career into three segments: the first in government, the second at a large firm, and the third on his own. The second stage ended in 1979. Now, at the age of fifty-three, Hamilton could proceed to the third.

Shortly after leaving ITT, Hamilton was named chairman and president of Tamco Enterprises, a privately owned corporation of which he became an important shareholder. Tamco is controlled by the Gouletas family, which also owns American Invsco, the nation's largest converter of apartment houses into condominiums, with wide interests in real estate. After studying several major enterprises, Tamco announced it would make a bid for City Investing, a major conglomerate headed by George Scharffenberger, himself an ITT alumnus. Ironically, the man who had formerly eschewed acquisitions was attempting to take over a firm larger than any ITT might have considered while still under the court order.

For a while the rumors persisted that Araskog was only a front for Geneen, who was in full command. "The Boss is Back," said a *Forbes* headline, and in the story an unnamed ITT executive was quoted as saying, "Don't look for anything devious. It was all very simple. The Board retired Geneen in 1977, and he convinced them to bring him back. He never really accepted leaving, so he waited for the right moment, made his move, and now he's back." This sentiment was given credence by several changes in the executive suites, the most important being Gerhard Andlinger's departure and his replacement as head of ITT Europe by John Guilfoyle, a longtime Geneen loyalist.

It isn't known whether Geneen ever seriously considered staging a formal comeback, but with the deep divisions on the board and within the organization, such was hardly likely or even possible. Some of those who had been willing to support him on the matter of Hamilton's ouster did so with the understanding that Geneen would remain where he was, as chairman but not CEO. In any case, Geneen was sixty-nine years old, and not prepared to take on the responsibilities he once enjoyed. Finally, there was the negative reaction to all of this from the financial community, an important factor in a period of fiscal stringency. "There was no reason to fire him [Hamilton]," said a securities analyst who followed ITT. "I have not heard one person in the investment community who is happy about this." As though to signal this general feeling, ITT common declined in trading on the Pacific Stock Exchange when news of the resignation reached the floor, and lost ground in New York the next day.

Still, Geneen had the power to dictate a replacement, but there was only one obvious candidate, Araskog, who had served as president under Hamilton. Geneen clearly admired Araskog and demonstrated an affection toward him shown no other young ITT executive.

Araskog had been well prepared for leadership, and those who worked with him knew he was intelligent, capable, tough, and independent. A deficiency in any of these qualities would have eliminated him as a contender during the stormy late 1970s, and certainly would have dismayed Geneen. In mid-1979, however, Araskog was still somewhat of an unknown quantity outside the corporation's upper reaches and some of the subsidiary companies. Few talked of the new CEO's programs, ideas, or even personality. Rather, they simply assumed he would look to Geneen for guidance, at least in the beginning. "Geneen will stop the European divestiture program cold," thought one observer. "The old ways are back —earnings at any cost."[12]

At the time and under these circumstances, such a conclusion was warranted. But it demonstrated a lack of understanding of Geneen and Araskog and the context in which both men found themselves in the late 1970s. Moreover, the evaluation misread the sentiments on the board.

As it turned out, Geneen had been prepared to relinquish power but would do so in his own way, and to a person of his selection. Those who believed he intended to retain control to his last gasp and use Araskog as a front underestimated both men. As indicated, Geneen was looking for a modern, perhaps more sophisticated version of himself—a person of the first rank, not a subordinate— which implied a CEO with a strong will of his own, though one clearly in harmony with what had gone before. Hamilton possessed some of these qualities, but had never been personally close to Geneen and had blundered in their personal relations. There had been confrontations, both public and private, when conciliation might have been possible, and perhaps Hamilton hadn't demonstrated sufficient sensitivity insofar as Geneen's easily bruised ego was concerned. He had been served poorly by admiring outsiders, especially Wall Street analysts, who praised him while denigrating Geneen. Hamilton understood this, and on several occasions he tried to call them off, asking the analysts to moderate their statements regarding the "bright new era at ITT." They did so, but not before damage had been done.

The directors, both inside and outside, proved willing to go along with Hamilton's dismissal, though several did so reluctantly. All agreed, however, there could be no repeat performance. In the name of old times if little more, Geneen might call upon them to force Hamilton to step down, but there could be no encore without ITT appearing to be a blundering, out-of-control, and brutal giant. Thus, from the start Araskog was in a powerful position. He knew it. So did Geneen and others on the board.

19

The Succession:
Rand Vincent Araskog

IT didn't take long for Araskog to demonstrate that he had firmer and more complete control of the board than Hamilton had ever enjoyed. He was no mere front for Geneen but would pursue his own programs. Just what these were, and how they would be implemented, continued to be unknown, at least through his first two years in charge.

For that matter, Araskog himself was something of a mystery, though through no fault of his own. Rather, initially he seemed very much like many other CEOs of large corporations who took power in the 1970s—sharp, efficient, well trained, fact-oriented, with a command of public-relations techniques but lacking some vague, personal dimension.

ITT'ers who had worked under Geneen, and the few remaining old-timers who remembered Colonel Behn, couldn't help but notice the contrast between these colorful and highly individualistic leaders and the more conventional Araskog. Behn had created ITT,

The Succession: Rand Vincent Araskog

which for most of his reign seemed an extension of his personality. Geneen dominated all aspects of the corporation, injecting himself into its every corner. Initially, at least, Araskog gave the appearance of being an undifferentiated product of the current American business climate. Like Hamilton, he might just as well have wound up at such firms as IBM, Exxon, General Electric, or Procter & Gamble, and in time risen to the top there. And he might have done the same at the State Department, the Ford Foundation, or the Agency for International Development. In other words, he gave the impression of being another of that vast cadre stamped out with some regularity by Harvard's Graduate School of Business who had clambered up the managerial ladder and now, as a result of good fortune, adept tactics, and necrology, had taken top posts at huge enterprises, be they in government, business, or at foundations. The same hardly could be said of Geneen, and certainly not of Behn.

Those who perceived Araskog as being one of this mass of managerial experts were later proved wrong, but the assumptions were understandable. In 1979 the arrival of Araskog and his consolidation of power were interpreted as representing a kind of maturity at ITT. This isn't to suggest the corporation had consciously decided to work with what it already had, that he was expected to do little other than compose variations on themes created during the Behn and Geneen periods, or that earlier accomplishments somehow couldn't be surpassed or even matched. Rather, the problems and opportunities of the late 1970s were strikingly different from those of two decades before, when Geneen had assumed leadership, just as those of 1959 couldn't be compared to the prospects of 1919, when Behn planned to create ITT. Geneen appreciated this. After a few months in office he had been asked to compare himself to Behn, and replied that the Colonel had been a man for his times, and so he would prove to be a person suited to the demands of the 1950s.

Araskog might have said as much in 1979; certainly his actions during the next three years indicated this was how he felt. At a similar stage in his ITT career, Geneen had concentrated on reshaping and developing the Behn legacy. Araskog's major tasks in his early period had been to rationalize his vast and convoluted inheritance. In the process he managed to convince doubters he had the ability to direct ITT, and he demonstrated an independence and toughness some outsiders had doubted was there.

Stockholders and the press might have caught a glimpse of this at the first annual meeting Araskog presided over, which was in Chicago in early April, 1980. He was somewhat nervous at this, his initial exposure to the general public as chairman, but he fielded a series of questions with ease and humor and even managed to turn one regarding Hamilton's sacking to his advantage (in part by reading a telegram of congratulations from his predecessor). Then, when a stockholder directed a query to a senior vice-president, Araskog interrupted and politely but firmly said, "Ask me the question, and I'll decide who should answer it."

Geneen was seated with the other directors at the back of the stage. He smiled. This was how he would have reacted.

As the name implies, Araskog is of Scandinavian descent. His paternal grandfather, Nels Ohlsson, migrated to Norcross, Minnesota, from Sweden in 1886, and later moved to Fergus Falls, where he opened a dairy and ran a farm. The reasons for the Atlantic crossing were familiar. There was an economic slump in the old country, and the Ohlssons went to Minnesota seeking farmland in an area already settled by many of their countrymen. There were several hundred Swedish families there, and dozens of Ohlssons and Olsons. In order to differentiate themselves from the others, this particular family changed its name to Araskog—the name of the area in Sweden from which they came. (*Araskoga* means "great woods" in Swedish.)

Randolph Vincent Araskog, a son of the original immigrants, married Wilfred Mathilda Swanson, whose parents were also farmers. Early in life Randolph wanted to become a dentist, but his father insisted he remain on the farm. Swedish-American boys of that generation followed their fathers' wishes, and so did Randolph. He ran a small farm and dairy on the outskirts of Fergus Falls and later obtained a post as tax collector in the town itself. On October 31, 1931, one of the bleakest periods in the history of that part of the state, Wilfred gave birth to Rand Vincent Araskog.

The family survived the bad years with few difficulties. Later Araskog recalled growing up on the farm during the New Deal era. "Our neighbors, farmers and businessmen, were going bust all around us. We didn't, but the whole family had to pitch in." Seeing no future on the land and not wanting to subject his own children to the kind of discipline imposed upon him by his father, Randolph urged them to seek opportunities elsewhere. "My father didn't encourage me to be a farmer," said Araskog, "and I didn't want to be one."[1]

The Succession: Rand Vincent Araskog

Araskog attended the local schools, where he did well, becoming the class valedictorian. Uncertain as to what he wanted to do and lacking funds—as well as scope—to aim elsewhere, Araskog leaped at the chance to attend West Point when a local congressman offered to nominate him for a place there. He really wasn't interested in a military career, however, and concentrated instead on Soviet studies, becoming fluent in Russian. After graduating in 1953, he attended Harvard for a year of graduate work in this area, after which he was assigned to the Pentagon, reporting indirectly to Secretary of Defense Charles Wilson.

A year in Europe in field operations followed, after which Araskog returned to Washington with special responsibilities for Hungarian affairs. In 1956 he married Jessie Maria Gustafson, also a Minnesotan, and he remained with the government, settling in Arlington, Virginia. When the USSR launched its Sputnik satellite in 1957 Araskog was assigned to the Advanced Research Project Agency, charged with developing an American counterpart. Now Araskog became a speechwriter and one of the agency's spokesmen before congressional committees, a position long on responsibilities but short on remuneration.

Eager to return home and seeking a higher salary than possible in government service, Araskog cast about for a position in the private sector. His work had brought him into contact with representatives of defense-oriented corporations, and he considered offers from several of them. Araskog was most interested in placement at Minneapolis Honeywell, some of whose business was in areas touching upon his expertise and whose headquarters was less than three hours by automobile from Fergus Falls. He went there in 1960 as marketing director for advanced research programs, and within six years, by the age of thirty-five, he had risen to become director of marketing and planning for the aeronautical division.

Araskog was fairly content at Honeywell, sufficiently so as to turn down bids from other companies that occasionally came his way. By then, too, he was quite self-confident, having had intimate contacts with high government officials and having served in positions where he had to negotiate with some of the nation's premier businessmen. As might be expected, he wanted more rapid advancement than was possible at Honeywell, and in 1966 he agreed to go to ITT's Park Avenue headquarters for an interview. Araskog impressed the management with his credentials, accomplishments, and bearing and was asked to consider a high executive post at

Gilfillan in California. Together with his wife he visited the installations. They decided against relocation, rejected the ITT proposal, and returned to Minnesota. But not for long. Two months later ITT offered him a job as president of the defense communications division (soon to be renamed the aerospace, electronic, components, and energy group), with the understanding he would serve as director of marketing at headquarters until the presidency became vacant three months later. The work there would provide Araskog with line as well as staff experience and would make good use of his knowledge of that segment of the industry. He accepted, and started moving rapidly up the corporate ladder.

As indicated, Araskog and Hamilton were considered two of the brightest young men in the ITT stable and by mid-decade were viewed as the corporation's management team of the future, to take power when Geneen stepped down. Even then, Araskog was one of the chairman's favorites.

What there was about him that so impressed Geneen is difficult to say. That both men genuinely respected each other was and is obvious, but there is more to it than that. Certainly Geneen served as mentor for the younger man, and if Araskog lacked the chairman's almost obsessive involvement with corporate affairs, he compensated for this with efficiency and clarity of thought. Moreover, Araskog could be as tough and stubborn as Geneen, which rather than angering the older man actually pleased him. Both prized cold efficiency, and neither was a sentimentalist when it came to business affairs. In the end, however, there was a chemistry between these two that really is indefinable but familiar enough to anyone who has worked in the upper levels of any organization. It wasn't shared by Hamilton, who was more easygoing and freewheeling in his approach. All three men recognized this during the last years of the Geneen era and through the Hamilton chairmanship.

One might catch a clue as to just what this was by observing Araskog at a meeting, by holding conversations with him, or simply by noting his actions at business and social occasions. To begin with, he is a tall, somewhat slender, well-built man who looks a trifle younger than his age, carefully groomed and barbered, with strong, regular features. Even so, little of the military remains in his bearing. Araskog moves easily, with a slight stoop he seems aware of and occasionally seems to try to correct. He has a sharp, quick sense of humor, tells a story well, and is a patient listener. Still, he rarely

The Succession: Rand Vincent Araskog

gives the appearance of being completely relaxed and off guard in public. Araskog has an attractive, even boyish smile, and knows how to put people at ease. But his eyes are always alert, and his glance intense, and this is so even when he is discussing the most innocuous subject. Geneen has the same kind of look. Hamilton does not.

The business press corps knew little of Araskog when he assumed leadership, but most reporters who regularly covered ITT and who admired Hamilton were prepared to withhold judgment on his replacement. Thomas Hayes, of *The New York Times*, was typical of the breed in writing of perceived differences of opinion at corporate headquarters regarding the capabilities of the new CEO. "Araskog is an extremely bright man and a natural leader," one executive told him. "He is decisive, plays the game hard, but is not at all pompous or militaristic. He'll be good for morale." Another, identified as a Hamilton ally, disagreed. "He likes to get into the trenches, but is not a commanding personality. He works very hard, but is a lightweight who probably won't last. The perfect assistant."

The last sentence probably summed up the general feeling of reporters at the time. Although conceding that Hamilton's leadership had been deficient in some areas (many singled out telecommunications placements as the most glaring problem) and that morale was low at several subsidiaries, a number of observers concluded that the dismissal was a case of overkill, that Geneen had sought revenge for real and imagined slights, and that Araskog was and would remain little more than his tool. According to Hayes, Araskog told the board that he rejected Hamilton's program of concentrating on return on assets in favor of Geneen's of stressing earnings per share.[3] The implication was that short-term planning would take precedence over that for the longer term, there would be a slowdown if not reversal of the divestiture program, and ITT soon would revert to an acquisitions stance.

These assumptions were reasonable given Geneen's reputation, the current interpretation of the Hamilton dismissal, rumors regarding the mood of the board, and, most of all, Araskog's abilities and status, neither of which was deemed particularly promising for ITT.

Such analysis didn't take several important considerations into account. In the first place, though Araskog might not have been well known outside ITT, he had an impressive record as a group executive and had performed well, in difficult circumstances, while chief operating officer under Hamilton. He had the respect and support of the board, with the Hamilton loyalists conceding that Araskog hadn't participated in the overthrow and that he had behaved correctly through the entire episode. Then, too, he was far more secure in power than Hamilton ever could have been. From the first, many suspected that Geneen had accepted Hamilton reluctantly and was apt to help organize an opposition to the new president. Geneen had too much of an emotional and professional investment in Araskog to try to repeat the operation. Even in the unlikely circumstance that he did, support would have been lacking. Virtually everyone involved understood that after so unsettling a coup there must be stability at the top. Hamilton might have been expendable. In 1979 Araskog was not, and he knew it.

Finally, a few commentators remarked negatively on Araskog's relative youth and inexperience for so complex and demanding a post. In fact, he was precisely the same age in 1979 that Geneen had been two decades earlier when he became CEO, and of course Geneen had arrived from Raytheon a stranger and had had to undergo a period of orientation and familiarization before acting with any degree of confidence. ITT had grown more than twentyfold in revenues since then, but in this respect at least Araskog would have no problem, having spent the past thirteen years at the corporation, most of the time close to its heart and mind. Moreover, he would be ITT's first chief executive who had demonstrated both line and staff management talents. Of the corporation's other CEOs, only Harrison came close to Araskog in this respect, and even he lacked breadth of experience in the field.

Whatever suspicions existed that Araskog would prove a weak and indecisive leader, dependent on Geneen's patronage for survival, were stilled by two developments during the next half year, each of which had more symbolic than practical importance. The first offered a clue as to the course Araskog intended ITT to take, while the other was a rite of passage, a gesture that removed some of the uncertainties at headquarters and in the field.

Rayonier's Port-Cartier project had been in trouble from the first. Shortly after ground was broken in 1971, there developed technological snags, production difficulties, and labor problems. Costs escalated, and toward the end of the decade it became evident the huge installation could never be profitable. By then it had incurred pre-

The Succession: Rand Vincent Araskog

tax losses of more than $200 million, and even Geneen, ever the optimist regarding programs he had set into motion, was prepared to reconsider its viability.

Clearly something had to be done, and in early 1979 Hamilton called in an outside consultant, Sandwell & Co., for advice on how best to proceed. There were two alternatives: a continuation of the project or a writeoff. At the time, the latter seemed more practical and had growing support from the board. With Port-Cartier behind it, Rayonier's return on capital would rise, and there would be important tax credits to apply against future earnings. And, of course, the large losses finally would be staunched.

Sandwell's report suggested it might be best to complete the construction, which would require an additional $125 million or so spread over five years. Given no major production hitches and a reasonably good market for chemical cellulose, the plant might show a small profit by the mid-1980s, and more thereafter.

The Sandwell report was on Hamilton's desk when he left ITT, and Rayonier's troubles were one of the first important matters requiring Araskog's attention. That September, with the full support of the board—Geneen included—he decided to close down construction at Port-Cartier. The writeoff came to $320 million (which subsequently was reduced somewhat when the installation was sold).[4]

Hamilton probably would have acted in much the same way, but by this action Araskog sent out a signal to the business community. He was as willing as his predecessor had been to cut back in order to improve operating results, even if this required the divestiture or abandonment of projects of the Geneen era. But soon after, Araskog indicated that a deficit-ridden European television and audio project, which Hamilton had wanted to sell and which was close to Geneen's heart, would be retained.

On November 14 Geneen told the board of his intention to resign as chairman on January 1, 1980. "I have tremendous confidence in the way Rand Araskog is running the company and in its future under his direction," he said. "I think it is time for him to assume the added responsibilities of the chairmanship." In addition, Araskog was to be chairman of the executive and policy committees, providing him with all of the leading executive and operating titles at ITT. Whatever doubt there was that this was now his corporation was thus dispelled.

I·T·T: The Management of Opportunity

On the same day, ITT released its third-quarter earnings report. As a result of the Port-Cartier writeoff and currency translation, ITT suffered a $137-million loss. Net income for the year as a whole would come to $380.7 million, against $661.8 million in 1978, this on total sales and revenues of a shade less than $22 billion. Return on equity was a low 6.8 percent (or half of what it had been in the early 1970s) and far below the old standards. This is not to suggest ITT was in any trouble. In fact, telecommunications, insurance, the hotels, and several other segments of the business reported record incomes, and as a further sign of confidence the dividend was increased from $2.20 per share to $2.40, the sixteenth consecutive annual advance. Rather, Araskog and Geneen in effect had "cleaned house" to prepare for the new era.

As expected, Araskog continued to defer to Geneen, especially in public. Insofar as policies were concerned, however, his approach and strategy were closer to those Hamilton had initiated. After watching Araskog in action for a year, several important ITT'ers concluded that he somehow managed to combine Geneen's forcefulness and decisiveness with Hamilton's program, and that this was to the good, for in so doing he was drawing upon the best each man had to offer for the early 1980s.

Like Hamilton, Araskog permitted line managers more leeway than they had during the Geneen chairmanship, perceiving that they were spending too much time attempting to impress corporate managers and drawing up more complex and detailed memos than were necessary. "I think in most cases now the companies that we have are strong enough and mature enough so that the managers we have in them are looking at their competition, not at headquarters," Araskog told an interviewer in the spring of 1980. Some fifty regular reports were eliminated, and executives were given the option of reporting weekly or monthly, with most choosing the latter. "Now, watchdogs might be helpful, but I think if the line managers do it themselves, they do it with more intensity."[5] As part of this program Araskog cut back on executive overhead, eliminating many positions, especially those concerned primarily with reporting. Travel budgets were slashed, and there were fewer of the general conclaves so famous during the Geneen era.

Araskog not only continued but actually accelerated the divestiture program instituted by Hamilton, on occasion ridding ITT of companies his predecessor had scheduled for divestment, and he did so with no observable opposition from Geneen. In 1980, his first full

The Succession: Rand Vincent Araskog

year as chairman, Araskog sold sixteen companies with sales of over $460 million, in addition to Rayonier's British Columbia operations, a $215-million-a-year operation. The proceeds from these came to $564 million. (By way of contrast, in 1979 ITT disposed of seventeen companies with annual sales of $221 million for $74 million.) Araskog saw this as only the beginning; late in 1980 he told a reporter of plans to divest companies providing as much as a billion dollars in sales within the next two years.[7]

Most of the units sold in this period were foreign—Oceanique, Claude, Allied Technologies, Canadian Lighting Fixtures, and Canadian Wire & Cable—in one way or another ailing, or else they no longer fit into Araskog's rapidly developing plans. As part of a continuing program of selling nationals shares of units based in their countries, ITT offered 50 percent of SESA Rio to Brazilians, and 25 percent of CSEA was sold in Argentina, which brought in $35 million. A 15 percent divestiture of STC returned $50 million from the United Kingdom but left ITT in control of that key company.

These sales sparked rumors regarding just where Araskog intended to lead the corporation. Some old-timers might have seen in these sales and related actions a resemblance to events of the mid-1950s, when another new leader took command and the old chairman faded into the background. It will be recalled that in the earlier period Harrison sold off several units and signaled his clear intention to transform ITT into a major supplier of telecommunications and electronics equipment and, in so doing, to alter the direction Behn had established. By late 1981 some outsiders—and a number of executives as well—had concluded that Araskog intended to transform ITT from a loosely shaped conglomerate into a rational, broadly based, international electronics corporation with major stress on telecommunications.

Several signs pointed in this direction. For one thing, early in his chairmanship Araskog indicated a desire and his intention to concentrate on high technology, and of course his initial ITT experiences and much of his prior career had been in this field. He told one audience, "Probably the fastest growing business area of the next 50 years other than energy, and this may be even faster, is telecommunications and electronics."[8] He went on to paint a bright picture of the prospects for other ITT operations, but there was no doubt where Araskog's true interests lay.

There was a nice symmetry here. Behn and Geneen had been

financially oriented businessmen, each of whom fashioned ITT into a huge enterprise, one that was badly in need of pruning and by the time of their departure lacked a sense of purpose and direction. By inclination and experience, Harrison and Araskog were both geared toward production and management, electronics and telecommunications in particular.

The importance of telecommunications in ITT's future was underscored when, in early 1980, the corporation agreed to an out-of-court settlement of an antitrust action against AT&T's Western Electric subsidiary. Under the terms of the agreement, AT&T was to purchase $2 billion of ITT equipment over the next ten years and in addition provide ITT with a $200-million interest-free loan for this period. In effect, AT&T was enabling one of its chief rivals to enter the domestic arena in a major fashion while at the same time providing it with more capital to help finance the venture.

The fascinating relationship between AT&T and ITT was advanced another sizable step in early January, 1982, when the Justice Department agreed to settle its antitrust action against AT&T in return for that company's divesting itself of its domestic operating units. When this nationwide divestiture is completed, AT&T will be left with its profitable long-distance operation and Western Electric and Bell Laboratories. In effect, it will have been transformed into a manufacturing-research corporation, the largest in world telecommunications.

At the time of the settlement, most commentators predicted the coming of a colossal showdown between the new AT&T and IBM. More likely, however, is the development of a major move by AT&T into the overseas telecommunication markets, where it will have to face a newly invigorated ITT. And thus, interestingly, do two titans come full circle. In 1920 Sosthenes Behn envisaged ITT as an overseas image of AT&T, and in time both firms had operating units, factories, and research arms. Now, within a year or two, AT&T will relinquish its telephone companies, as had ITT long ago. Rather than ITT's becoming an overseas version of AT&T, the latter company will be transformed into a huge American counterpart of ISE.

Moreover, an objective that had eluded Behn, Harrison, and Geneen might now be realized by Araskog. He will have the opportunity to transform ITT into a significant factor in the domestic electronics and telecommunications businesses, not only via the

The Succession: Rand Vincent Araskog

AT&T contract but by way of the introduction of European-manufactured consumer electronics into the American market. In 1982 ITT planned to sell television sets and related products to Americans, thus countering the Japanese "invasion" with a European one from ITT's factories in Germany.

Further, all this happened at a time when there were signs of important breakthroughs insofar as System 12 was concerned. In early 1981 ITT had been awarded a major contract from Mexico, and other orders followed from Europe, Asia, and other parts of Latin America. This key project, which had taken upward of half a billion dollars in research-and-development costs alone, now seemed ready to pay off handsomely and to become the central focus for Araskog's ITT.

Understandably, there was much talk of sales to come in order to pay for the growth of telecommunications—that within a few years Rayonier, Continental Baking, Grinnell, and other companies with growing capital needs of their own might be sold, along with the entire package of publishing, educational, and related concerns. Only Sheraton, by now a true money-maker in the midst of rapid expansion financed in large part by franchisers, was spared these rumors. There was even talk of a spectacular arrangement for divesting Hartford, especially after ITT came to terms with the Internal Revenue Service over the tax liability in the takeover. (In early May, 1981, the corporation agreed to pay $18.5 million as a final settlement, which some observers took as a signal that Araskog soon would initiate the sale of the giant company.) Funds realized from such a sale might be used to reduce ITT's debt and capitalization, increase earnings per share dramatically, and permit the corporation to concentrate on telecommunications. Moreover, "deconglomeratization" was becoming the vogue on Wall Street, where analysts noted that the breakup value of a number of important firms in this category was far higher than their current prices would indicate. Among these were Teledyne, Litton, Kidde, Reynolds Industries—and ITT. The talk was that if Tamco managed to acquire City Investing, Lyman Hamilton would do just that—break it down into components and, by selling off several, recover the purchase price and still have a valuable property. In the early 1960s the financial community had watched with admiration as a generation of financially oriented managers, led by Geneen, acquired large and small properties and fashioned huge enterprises. Two decades later there was talk of another generation of businessmen who might dismantle some of these creations.

This was noted at headquarters. The brighter balance sheet and profit picture made possible by at least a partial deconglomeratization, combined with the enhanced desirability of a firm with a major focus on telecommunications, would boost ITT's stock, which had been in the doldrums since the early 1970s. In addition, some of the funds obtained from such sales might be used to purchase an important electronics corporation, further enhancing ITT's image and providing yet another signal that the Araskog era had truly begun. The stricture against large acquisitions entered into as part of the Hartford settlement ran out in September 1981, and although a spokesman called the lifting of the consent decree a "nonevent," it wasn't seen as such by financial analysts who followed the corporation.

Araskog knew of such talk, and in 1980 he went to great lengths to assure executives at several of the operating companies that he had no intention of divesting their units. Most of the rumors centered on Rayonier, since headquarters was still smarting from the Port-Cartier fiasco. President Ronald Gross told employees the company wasn't for sale, but the talk persisted.

By early summer, 1981, it appeared that Rayonier indeed might be divested, along with part or all of Continental Baking. Once again there were denials, but this time they were more perfunctory than before. Few doubted the dismantling process was about to begin.

That August three Canadian companies purchased Rayonier Canada for $355 million, and the same month some of Continental Baking's subsidiaries were sold, the most important being Gwaltney, which fetched $35 million. The following month ITT confirmed rumors that the rest of Rayonier would be divested and that "preliminary discussions" had begun with several interested parties. Others followed in 1982, including the profitable C&C Beverages.

Geneen had nothing to say regarding these dispositions, and if any reporters thought to contact him for comments, none appeared in the newspapers or business magazines. By then he was involved in several new ventures that had nothing to do with ITT. He remained on the board, but in other ways he had passed from the scene.

No one could doubt Araskog was in full command, with as much authority as Behn and Geneen had exercised at the height of their power. Like them, he will shape ITT in his own image, but this will be done upon a foundation provided by Geneen. Araskog can no more ignore this than Geneen could the Behn legacy.

It could not be otherwise. More than six decades of development and experience have resulted in an encrustation of tradition and custom that cannot be shuttled aside with impugnity. Araskog clearly appreciates this.

To paraphrase William Faulkner: The past isn't behind us; it isn't even the past.

Chapter Notes

Chapter 1. The Brothers Behn

1. A. N. Holcombe, *Public Ownership of Telephones on the Continent of Europe* (Cambridge: Harvard University Press, 1911), p. 26ff.
2. E. M. Deloraine, "An ITT Memoir: A 'Telecom' Pioneer Tells It Like It Was," *Sigma,* second quarter, 1970, p. 58.
3. *The Nation,* April 18, 1928, p. 546.
4. *Fortune,* December 1930, p. 36.
5. Geoffrey Ogilvie correspondence, September 4, 1978.
6. Charles Edward Taylor, *Leaflets from the Danish West Indies: Description of the Social, Political, and Commercial Condition of these Islands* (London: William Dawson & Sons, 1888), p. 54.
7. *Ibid.,* p. 55.
8. Ena Scott interview, June 3, 1980; Clyde Dickey interview, November 11, 1978; New York *Herald Tribune,* April 19, 1931.
9. New York *Herald Tribune,* April 19, 1931.
10. *Poor's Public Utility Manual,* 1921 edition, p. 2247.
11. *Ibid., loc. cit.*

12. *Ibid.*, p. 2245.
13. Edwin Roome interview, December 27, 1978.

Chapter 2. The Colonel

1. Louis Chereau, "New Initiatives in Industrial Technologies, extracts, Part III, Colonel Behn," manuscript on deposit in the ITT archives.
2. *Poor's Public Utility Manual*, 1921 edition, p. 2244.
3. Telephone conversation between the author and Geoffrey Ogilvie, September 22, 1980.
4. ITT annual report, 1923, p. 5.
5. Douglas J. Little, "Twenty Years of Turmoil: ITT, The State Department, and Spain, 1924–1944," *Business History Review*, Winter, 1979, pp. 450–52; ITT annual report, 1924; Ignacio Satrustegui, "Colonel Behn and the Birth of CTNE and SESA," manuscript on deposit in ITT archives.
6. Material relating to the CTNE and ISE acquisitions can be found in the Geoffrey Ogilvie mss. See also ITT annual reports, 1924–1926.
7. Joseph E. Sterrett and Joseph S. Davis, *The Fiscal and Economic Condition of Mexico*, 1928, pp. 185–88.

Chapter 3. The International System

1. Maurice Deloraine, *When Telecom and ITT Were Young* (New York: Lehigh Books, 1976), pp. 76–78.
2. Herbert Feis, *Europe, the World's Banker, 1870–1914* (New Haven: Yale University Press, 1930), p. 23 ff.
3. *Time*, December 24, 1928, p. 26.
4. *The New York Times*, May 20, 1928; *Time*, April 2, 1929, pp. 35–36.
5. Discussions of the British challenge in telecommunications were covered by the financial press and other newspapers during this period. See *The New York Times*, March 14, 1928, and subsequent issues. Also, Ogilvie conversation, September 22, 1980.
6. *The New York Times*, March 29, 1929; December 10, 1929.

Chapter 4. Fighting for Time

1. ITT annual reports, 1929–1931.
2. Activities of American businessmen and bankers in Germany during the interwar period is a dark and bloody historiographic battleground. This is particularly so for those corporations functioning there in the Hitler period. The key source is the International Military Tribunal, *Trial of the Major War Criminals*

before the International Military Tribunal, Nuremberg, 14 November 1945–1 October 1946 (Nuremberg: Secretariat of the Tribunal, 1947–1949). References to and discussion of American corporations may be found in several of the forty-two volumes. Among works most important for an appreciation of ITT's role and those of other companies are Edward W. Bennett, *German Rearmament and the West, 1932–1933* (Princeton: Princeton University Press, 1979); James Stewart Martin, *All Honorable Men* (Boston: Little, Brown, 1950); Joseph Borkin, *The Crime and Punishment of I. G. Farben* (New York: The Free Press, 1978); C. W. Guillebaud, *The Economic Recovery of Germany from 1933 to the Incorporation of Austria in March 1938* (London: Macmillan, 1939); and Robert Brady, *The Rationalization Movement in German Industry* (Berkeley: University of California Press, 1933). For a sensational but nonetheless stimulating work, see Antony Sutton, *Wall Street and the Rise of Hitler* (Seal Beach, California: '76 Press, 1976). A believer in conspiracy theories, Sutton presents a one-sided indictment of ITT, General Electric, and other American companies that, along with their banks, he claims conspired to bring Hitler to power and then helped him to rearm Germany.

3. Robert Shaplen, *Kreuger: Genius and Swindler* (New York: Knopf, 1960), p. 126.

4. Roome interview, December 27, 1978; Ogilvie conversation, September 22, 1980; Ena Scott conversation, October 22, 1980; "I.T.&T.'s Nine Lives," *Fortune,* September, 1945, p. 192.

Chapter 5. A Matter of Survival

1. Douglas Little, "Twenty Years of Turmoil" pp. 449–472 is the basic source for an appreciation of ITT's Spanish policies in this period. See also Gabriel Jackson, *The Spanish Republic and the Civil War, 1931–1939* (Princeton: Princeton University Press, 1965). Dickey interview, November 11, 1978.

2. Little, "Twenty Years of Turmoil," p. 471; Jackson, *The Spanish Republic and the Civil War,* p. 248 ff.

3. Little, "Twenty Years of Turmoil," pp. 470–71.

4. *Ibid., loc. cit.*

5. Otto Nathan, *The Nazi Economic System: Germany's Mobilization for War* (Durham, N.C.: Duke University Press, 1944), p. 161.

6. F. A. O. Schwarz speech at Lawyers' Conference, Boston, Mass., on November 3, 1972, text in ITT archives.

7. "I.T.&T.'s Nine Lives," pp. 192, 201.

8. Borkin, *The Crime and Punishment of I. G. Farben,* pp. 195–96; Martin, *All Honorable Men,* pp. 209–10; National Archives, Record Group 259 (Records of the Board of War Communications, 1940–1947), Feis to Dunn, June 19, 1941, 862.75/20.

9. Deloraine, *When Telecom and ITT Were Young,* p. 104.

10. *Ibid.*, pp. 105–106.
11. Sutton, *Wall Street and the Rise of Hitler*, pp. 83–84.
12. ITT annual report, 1937, p. 29.
13. Dickey interview, November 11, 1978.
14. Scott interview, June 3, 1980.

Chapter 6. Repatriation and Rebirth

1. "I.T.&T.'s Nine Lives," p. 192 ff.
2. Anthony Sampson, *The Sovereign State of ITT* (New York: Stein & Day, 1973), p. 31.
3. Record Group 259, 852.75 National Telephone Co/39.
4. Deloraine, *When Telecom and ITT Were Young*, p. 115; Henri Busignies interview, January 10, 1981.
5. Some of ITT's critics have alleged that Behn provided his German subsidiaries with expertise and patents, which later were used by the Nazis against American troops. Sampson writes, "In 1935 Hitler forbade the export of patents and technical information from Germany, except under special license, but ITT continued to supply its German subsidiaries with patents, and to build up the exports from Germany." At the time ITT had no domestic research facilities, so presumably Sampson was referring here to ISE patents. Yet none of them were provided to Lorenz and other German companies. Nor was Behn able to repatriate earnings or assets, which was one reason that the German companies had the capital with which to purchase the interest in Focke-Wulf and other concerns. Busignies had no contact with the Germans at any time in the decade, but did work closely with ISE counterparts in the United Kingdom. The reason was Hitler's refusal to permit German scientists to cooperate with the French arm of ITT. Had he done so, it would have been to his advantage, since Busignies was far ahead of Lorenz's scientists in direction-finder technology. Germany's inability to develop a version of Huff-Duff is proof that such technology transfers hadn't taken place. Here and elsewhere, Sampson is vague when it comes to providing evidence to substantiate his claims. Busignies interview, December 18, 1980; Deloraine interview, January 14, 1981.
6. G. Edouard Hofer interview, September 28, 1980.
7. Alexander Sanders interview, January 16, 1981.
8. Record Group, 259, 862.6463/55, August 15, 1942.
9. Record Group 259, 852.75, June 14, 1940; 852.24/1030-1/2, June 16, 1942.
10. Sanders interview, January 16, 1981.
11. Sampson, *The Sovereign State of ITT*, pp. 33–47.
12. Busignies interview, January 10, 1980.

13. Record Group 259, 821.73 AL 5/13, June 18, 1940; 835.75/52, May 31, 1942. In addition there are bundles of newspaper and magazine clippings in the Record Group 259 file.
14. Deloraine, *When Telecom and ITT Were Young*, pp. 133–41 ff.
15. Mark A. Sunstrom, "Memorandum Summarizing Incorrect and Improper Statements Made in Newspapers or by Radio Commentators with Respect to I.T.&T. and Some of Its Directors and Officers," no date, in ITT archives.
16. Record Group 259, 862.75/7-2145 CS/LE, July 21, 1945.

Chapter 7. A Matter of Succession

1. Record Group 259, 835.00/11-2745.
2. Arthur Schmitt interview, June 10, 1980.
3. Busignies interview, January 10, 1980.
4. Chereau, *New Initiatives in Industrial Technologies*, p. 37.
5. James Fox interview, December 8, 1978.
6. Busignies interview, December 17, 1980.
7. Otto J. Scott, *The Creative Ordeal: The Story of Raytheon* (New York: Atheneum, 1974), p. 202.
8. *Time*, December 22, 1947, pp. 87–88; *Business Week*, November 22, 1947, pp. 94–95.
9. J. Patrick Lannan interview, March 15–16, 1980.
10. Ogilvie among others remarked upon this aspect of Behn's personality. "Like most Latins, he wanted men around him who, number one, were loyal. If they weren't loyal, he didn't want them. Brains came second with his staff. When the time came for change, he really hadn't built up any number-two men who could take over for him. I think this is well known and understood." Ogilvie interview, September 18, 1978.
11. Schmitt interview, June 10, 1980.

Chapter 8. End of an Era

1. Deloraine interview, January 14, 1981.
2. Bertram Tower interview, September 17, 1980.
3. *Ibid.;* Roome interview, September 22, 1980; Schmidt interview, June 10, 1980.
4. Walter Wright interview, October 4, 1978.
5. William Behn interview, May 27, 1981.
6. Roome interview, September 22, 1980.

Entr'acte

1. Deloraine interview, January 14, 1981.

Chapter 9. The Inheritor

1. *Business Week*, May 4, 1963, p. 81; April 22, 1972, p. 74; *The New York Times*, December 23, 1977; *Time*, September 8, 1967, p. 87; *Vision*, September 1971, p. 56.
2. *Fortune*, February 1961, p. 112.
3. Scott, *The Creative Ordeal*, p. 266.
4. *Ibid.*, p. 286.
5. *Ibid.*, p. 292.
6. *Ibid.*, pp. 295–96; David Margolis interview, August 7, 1980.

Chapter 10. The Pre-Takeover Years

1. ITT annual report, 1959, p. 7.
2. ITT annual report, 1963, p. 5.
3. Walter Guzzardi, Jr., "I.T.T. Gets the Message," *Fortune*, February 1961, p. 115. \
4. Deloraine interview, January 14, 1981.
5. Richard Howe, "Harold Geneen: The Man at the Top of the ITT Pole," *Vision*, September 1971, p. 54.
6. "I.T.T. Gets the Message," p. 118.
7. John J. Jessup, ed. *The Ideas of Henry Luce* (New York: Atheneum, 1969), p. 118.
8. "One Man's $1-Billion Company," *Business Week*, May 4, 1963, p. 82.
9. *Ibid.*, p. 88.

Chapter 11. The Quintessential Conglomerateur

1. United States, 91st Congress, House of Representatives, Committee on the Judiciary, hearings before the antitrust subcommittee, *Investigation of Conglomerate Corporations*, Part 3 (Washington: U.S. Government Printing Office [GPO], 1970), p. 247.
2. *Ibid.*, p. 249.
3. ITT, "Acquisitions Policy, March 11, 1963," in *Ibid.*, pp. 258–63.
4. Al Kroeger, "Merger Machine in High Gear," *Television* magazine, July 1966, p. 7.
5. Robert Townsend, *Up the Organization: How to Stop a Corporation from Stifling People and Strangling Profits* (New York: Knopf, 1970), pp. 94–95.
6. "They Call it 'Geneen U.,'" *Forbes*, May 1, 1968, pp. 27–35.
7. "The Remarkable Felix G. Rohatyn," *Business Week*, March 10, 1973, pp. 133–37; *Fortune*, November 1977, pp. 117–19.

Chapter 12. Turning Point

1. Robert Sobel, *Money Manias* (New York: Weybright & Talley, 1973), pp. 319–22 ff.
2. United States, Federal Trade Commission, Bureau of Economics, *Current Trends in Merger Activities, 1968* (Washington: GPO, 1968), p. 17; United States, Senate, 91st Congress, 1st Session, Sub-Committee on Antitrust and Monopoly, *Economic Report on Corporate Mergers* (Washington: GPO, 1969), p. 63.
3. Margolis interview, August 7, 1980.
4. Harvey Levin, "Broadcasting Structure, Technology, and the ABC-ITT Merger Decision," *Law and Contemporary Problems,* Summer 1969, pp. 452–84.
5. Kroeger, "Merger Machine in High Gear," *Television* magazine, July 1966, p. 6.
6. It should be noted, however, that from 1962 to 1965 the American Broadcasting Companies on the whole earned more than $39 million, and that 1966's earnings would come to a record $17.8 million. Goldenson intended to say that the network's expenses consumed all of this and more. The figures appear to bear this out. In 1966 ABC reported cash items of less than $20 million, the lowest since the early 1950s, and down from $47.3 million the previous year. American Broadcasting Companies annual reports, 1961–66.
7. Robert Goolrick, *Public Policy Toward Corporate Growth: The ITT Merger Cases* (Port Washington, N.Y.: Kennikat Press, 1978), p. 42; Sobel, *Money Manias,* p. 349.
8. *Wall Street Journal,* December 22, 1966; Sampson, *The Sovereign State of ITT,* p. 90.
9. *Wall Street Journal,* February 6, 1967; *The New York Times,* February 6, 1967.
10. *Wall Street Journal,* April 20, 1967.

Chapter 13. *Annus Mirabilis*

1. ITT Board of Directors, minutes for regular meeting, June 12, 1968.
2. United States, 91st Congress, House of Representatives, Committee on the Judiciary, hearings before the antitrust subcommittee, *Investigation of Conglomerate Corporations* (Washington: GPO, 1970), pp. 774–75.
3. *Ibid.,* p. 814.
4. "Levitt's Secret in Change," *Business Week,* July 29, 1967, pp. 47–55.
5. *Ibid., loc. cit.*

6. *Ibid., loc. cit.*
7. *Investigations of Conglomerate Corporations,* p. 353.
8. "ITT: The View from the Inside," *Business Week,* November 3, 1973, p. 53.
9. Carol J. Loomis, "How I.T.T. Got Lost in a Big Bad Forest," *Fortune,* December 17, 1979, pp. 42–45.
10. "ITT: The View from the Inside," p. 56.

Chapter 14. The Siege Year

1. Robert Goolrick, author of a study of ITT's antitrust difficulties, takes a somewhat different point of view, holding that Richard McLaren underwent a change of heart shortly after taking office as head of the Justice Department's antitrust division in 1969. "The more he read in the voluminous literature of conglomerate mergers," says Goolrick, "the more McLaren began to be swayed by the reasoning of their critics." Given McLaren's broad experience in antitrust matters prior to taking office, such a radical alteration of opinion in so short a time on so basic an issue appears unlikely. See Goolrick, *The ITT Merger Cases,* especially pp. 51–66.
2. United States, 92nd Congress, 2nd Session, Senate, Committee on the Judiciary, *Hearings on the Nomination of Richard G. Kleindienst of Arizona to be Attorney General* (Washington: GPO, 1972), pp. 116–18; Sampson, *The Sovereign State of ITT,* p. 168.
3. Goolrick, *The ITT Merger Cases,* pp. 50–51.
4. *Ibid.,* pp. 60, 63, 81.
5. Kleindienst hearings, Part 2, p. 1651.
6. Goolrick, *The ITT Merger Cases,* p. 70.
7. *Wall Street Journal,* December 16, 1968.
8. Kleindienst hearings, Part 2, pp. 1217–18.
9. *Hartford Courant,* November 8, 1970; March 13, 1972; *Wall Street Journal,* November 19, 1970; December 3, 1970.
10. Kleindienst hearings, Part 2, pp. 1281–86.
11. Goolrick, *The ITT Merger Cases,* pp. 98–100.
12. Abraham Briloff, *The Truth About Corporate Accounting* (New York: Harper & Row, 1981), pp. 25–28.

Chapter 15. Friends in High Places

1. Kleindienst hearings, Part 2, pp. 744–47.
2. United States, 93rd Congress, 2nd Session, House of Representatives, Committee on the Judiciary, *Hearings Before the Committee on the Judiciary, pursuant to H. Res. 803, A Resolution Authorizing and Directing the Committee on the Judiciary to Investigate*

Chapter Notes

Whether Sufficient Grounds Exist for the House of Representatives to Exercise Its Constitutional Power to Impeach Richard M. Nixon, President of the United States (Washington: GPO, 1974), Book V, Part 1, pp. 137, 142.
3. Kleindienst hearings, Part 2, p. 631.
4. Impeachment hearings, Book V, Part 1, pp. 163–65.
5. *Ibid.*, pp. 153–71, 177–78; Kleindienst hearings, Part 2, pp. 183–84.
6. Goolrick, *The ITT Merger Cases*, p. 108.
7. Impeachment hearings, Book V, Part 1, pp. 312–19, 346–48.
8. Impeachment hearings, Book V, Part 1, pp. 372–76.
9. *Ibid.*, Book V, Part 1, pp. 419–22.
10. Kleindienst hearings, Part 2, pp. 103–110.
11. *Ibid.*, pp. 110–11.

Chapter 16. San Diego to Santiago

1. Kleindienst hearings, Part 3, pp. 866–67.
2. *Ibid.*, Part 2, p. 1582.
3. Goolrick, *The ITT Merger Cases*, p. 145.
4. *The New York Times*, January 22, 1978.
5. Kleindienst hearings, Part 2, pp. 447–48.
6. *Ibid.*, pp. 491–92.
7. *Ibid.*, p. 409.
8. *Ibid.*, pp. 648–49 ff.
9. *Ibid.*, pp. 1750–51.
10. United States, 93rd Congress, 1st Session, Senate, Committee on Foreign Relations, Sub-Committee on Multinational Corporations, *Hearings Before the Sub-Committee on Multinational Corporations, Multinational Corporations and United States Foreign Policy, On the International Telephone and Telegraph Company and Chile, 1970–1971* (Washington: GPO, 1973), Part 1, p. 104.
11. United States, 94th Congress, 1st Session, Senate, Select Committee on Intelligence Activities, *Covert Action in Chile, 1963–1973: Staff Report* (Washington: GPO, 1975), pp. 9–15; Laurence Stern, "U.S. Helped Beat Allende in 1964," *Washington Post*, April 6, 1973.
12. Seymour Hirsh, "Censored Matter in Book About CIA Said to Have Related Chile Activities," *The New York Times*, September 11, 1974; *Covert Action in Chile*, pp. 20–21.
13. Multinational hearings, Part 1, pp. 244–47; *Covert Action in Chile*, pp. 12–13; Paul Sigmund, *The Overthrow of Allende and the Politics of Chile, 1964–1976* (Pittsburgh: University of Pittsburgh Press, 1977), pp. 112–13.
14. Henry Kissinger, *White House Years* (Boston: Little, Brown, 1979), p. 669; Multinational hearings, Part 2, pp. 541–43.

15. *Covert Action in Chile*, p. 25.
16. United States, 94th Congress, 1st Session, Senate, Select Committee on Intelligence Activities, *Hearings, December 4–5, 1975* (Washington: GPO, 1975), p. 32.
17. Kissinger denies this. "Whatever the State Department's procrastination before the Chilean election, it strongly supported and actively implemented each subsequent 40 Committee decision." He offers no evidence to support this claim, however, and subsequent events indicate otherwise. *White House Years*, p. 672.
18. United States, 94th Congress, 1st Session, Senate, Committee on Intelligence Activities, *Alleged Assassination Plots Involving Foreign Leaders: Interim Report* (Washington: GPO, 1975), pp. 229–32, 242–45.
19. *The New York Times*, November 2, 1978.

Chapter 17. Nadir

1. Multinational hearings, Part 1, p. 102.
2. *Ibid.*, pp. 196–97, 433–36.
3. *Ibid.*, p. 102.
4. Kissinger, *White House Years*, p. 667.
5. Multinational hearings, Part 1, pp. 440, 457–58.
6. *Ibid.*, Part 2, pp. 614–15.
7. *Ibid.*, pp. 626–26. The belief that ITT instigated the plot persisted in antibusiness publications and articles, even to the present. For example, in James Petras and Morris Morley, *The United States and Chile* (New York and London: Monthly Review Press, 1975), p. 34, is found: "Realizing that the presidency in Chile would pass to a socialist in November, ITT officials began to elaborate a strategy of external economic coercion designed to lead to international economic chaos and the ultimate demise of the new government. ITT Chairman Geneen now emphasized that company officials in contact with U.S. government representatives 'should demand that U.S. representatives of international banks take a strong stand against any loan to countries expropriating American companies or discriminating against foreign private capital.'" The reference is of a memo *to* and not *from* Geneen, and dated October 20, almost a month after ITT received the CIA recommendations and rejected them.
8. *Ibid.*, *loc. cit.*
9. *Ibid.*, pp. 662–75.
10. *Ibid.*, p. 799.
11. Norman Gall, "The Chileans Have Elected a Revolution," *The New York Times Magazine*, November 1, 1970, p. 106.
12. Multinational hearings, Part 2, pp. 824–29.
13. *Ibid.*, pp. 836–37.

14. Sigmund, *The Overthrow of Allende*, p. 169.
15. Multinational hearings, Part 1, p. 73.
16. *Ibid.*, p. 75.
17. *Ibid.*, p. 77.
18. *Ibid.*, p. 116.
19. *Ibid.*, p. 186.
20. *Ibid.*, pp. 162, 177.
21. *Ibid.*, p. 475.
22. *Forbes*, May 15, 1975, p. 102.
23. *Ibid., loc. cit.*
24. *The New York Times*, March 21, 1978.

Chapter 18. The Center Holds

1. ITT, Board of Directors, minutes for regular meeting, September 9, 1970.
2. *The New York Times*, August 6, 1973.
3. Carol Loomis, "Harold Geneen's Moneymaking Machine is Still Humming," *Fortune*, September 1972, p. 212.
4. *Moody's Industrial Manual*, 1958, 1973.
5. *Ibid.*, 1973, *loc. cit.*; "ITT: The View from the Inside," p. 33.
6. Abraham Briloff, *Unaccountable Accounting* (New York: Harper & Row, 1972), pp. 104–105.
7. *Wall Street Journal*, March 28, 1976.
8. William Rodgers, "Mirror Images of Power," *The Nation*, October 1, 1973, p. 302.
9. *Wall Street Journal*, May 20, 1977.

Entr'acte II

1. *Business Week*, May 15, 1978, p. 63.
2. *Wall Street Journal*, October 11, 1978.
3. *Financial Times* (London), December 30, 1977.
4. *Business Week*, May 15, 1978, p. 62.
5. Robert Smith interview, June 26, 1980.
6. *Wall Street Journal*, July 18, 1979.
7. *Newsweek*, July 23, 1979, p. 56.
8. *Financial Times* (London), July 13, 1979; *The New York Times*, July 12, 1979; *Wall Street Journal*, July 18, 1979. Discussions with several key ITT personnel indicate that the newspaper reports of this period were accurate, and apparently based on calculated leaks.
9. Lyman Hamilton interview, September 10, 1981.
10. *Ibid.*
11. ITT, Board of Directors, minutes for the meeting of July 11, 1978.
12. *Fortune*, August 13, 1979, pp. 31–32.

Chapter 19. The Succession

1. "Rand V. Araskog: Past, Present, and Future Challenges," *Profile*, Winter, 1980, pp. 2–3.
2. *Ibid.*, loc. cit.
3. *The New York Times*, July 15, 1979.
4. Carol Loomis, "How I.T.T. Got Lost in a Big, Bad Forest," *Fortune*, December 17, 1979, pp. 44, 50, 55.
5. Willard C. Rappleye, Jr., "An Interview with Rand V. Araskog; Management Themes and Variations," *Financier*, June 1980, pp. 1–6.
6. ITT annual report, 1980, p. 2.
7. "ITT's Groping for a New Strategy," *Business Week*, December 15, 1980, p. 65.
8. Rand Araskog, "The Challenge of the 80s." Speech delivered at the opening session of the worldwide public relations/advertising conference, Key Biscayne, Florida, January 10, 1980.

A Note on Bibliography

THE most important single source for this book has been the memories of ITT personnel and others involved with the corporation. More than two dozen of them have submitted to major interviews, the transcripts of which are in the ITT archives and may be consulted with permission. Another fifty or so past and current ITT'ers have spoken with me regarding special aspects of the company's history. In addition, there have been conversations and discussions with individuals in related companies, the government, and the media who in one way or another became involved with ITT. Finally, I have been able to draw upon the experiences of a number of attorneys and reporters who have followed ITT through the years and who were particularly interested in the career of Harold Geneen.

As indicated in the Preface, this book wasn't sponsored by ITT, which did not enter into any financial arrangement with either the publisher or me in regard to the project. To the best of my knowledge, this is the first time a history of a major American corporation has been undertaken "from the inside" without such support. ITT had no control over the manuscript but did arrange for interviews and prepared transcripts of them for my use. A list of the most important interviewees is included in the Bibliography.

Not all of those who were approached agreed to be interviewed, including a former CEO and one of the book's two most important figures, Harold Geneen. At the outset I was warned he probably wouldn't see me but was also assured on several occasions this wouldn't be an insurmountable problem. "Don't worry," said one senior official. "Everything Hal knows, we know. There won't be a single question you might have asked him we can't answer." Indeed, most matters of fact regarding the Geneen era could be obtained from and verified by others, but the lack of direct contact with the central figure has been one of my greatest disappointments insofar as research is concerned.

ITT was investigated by government agencies and congressional committees throughout the late 1960s and early 1970s, and the more important hearings have been listed in the Bibliography. In addition, the corporation and its leader were reported on by the press in great detail during the past two decades. Hardly a month went by without an illuminating article appearing on the business pages of major newspapers or in such publications as *Business Week, Fortune, Forbes, Dun's Review, Newsweek,* and *Time.* All of these have been gone through carefully, and although each hasn't been noted in the Bibliography, the list may be obtained in the *Reader's Guide to Periodical Literature,* which was where I located most of them.

Of invaluable help in understanding ITT's activities during World War II are the documents on deposit in the National Archives filed under Record Group 259 (Records of the Board of War Communications, 1940–1947).

Not much has been written in book form about ITT, other conglomerates, or for that matter the businessmen who lead them. Of all the books mentioned in the Bibliography, only three are of major importance, and these are the works by Robert Goolrick, Anthony Sampson, and Paul Sigmund.

Selected Bibliography

Books

All America Cables, Inc. *A Half Century of Cable Service to the Three Americas*. New York: All America Cables, 1928.

Behn, Paul. *Genealogie der Familie Behn*. Görlitz: Druck und Berlag von G. A. Starke, 1912.

Bennett, Edward. *German Rearmament and the West, 1932–1933*. Princeton, N.J.: Princeton University Press, 1979.

Borkin, Joseph. *The Crime and Punishment of I. G. Farben*. New York: The Free Press, 1978.

———and Charles Welsh. *Germany's Master Plan*. New York: Duell, Sloan and Pearce, 1943.

Briloff, Abraham. *The Truth About Corporate Accounting*. New York: Harper & Row, 1981.

Burns, Thomas. *Tales of ITT*. Boston: Houghton Mifflin, 1974.

Churchill, Allen. *The Incredible Ivar Kreuger*. New York: Rinehart, 1957.

Selected Bibliography

Deloraine, Maurice. *When Telecom and ITT were Young.* New York: Lehigh Books, 1974.

Feis, Herbert. *The Diplomacy of the Dollar: First Era, 1919–1932.* Baltimore: Johns Hopkins Press, 1964.

———. *Europe: The World's Banker, 1870–1914.* New Haven: Yale University Press, 1930.

Ferns, H. S. *Britain and Argentina in the Nineteenth Century.* Oxford, England: Clarendon Press, 1960.

Galdames, Luis. *A History of Chile.* New York: Russell & Russell, 1964.

Goolrick, Robert. *Public Policy Toward Corporate Growth: The ITT Merger Cases.* Port Washington, N.Y.: Kennikat Press, 1978.

Guillebaud, C. W. *The Economic Recovery of Germany.* London: Macmillan, 1939.

Henderson, Ernest. *The World of "Mr. Sheraton."* New York: David McKay, 1960.

Hills, George. *Franco: The Man and His Nation.* New York: Macmillan, 1967.

Holcombe, A. N. *Public Ownership of Telephones on the Continent of Europe.* Cambridge, Mass.: Harvard University Press, 1911.

Jessup, John. *The Ideas of Henry Luce.* New York: Atheneum, 1969.

Kehrl, Hans. *Krisen Manager im Dritten Reich.* Düsseldorf: Droste Verlag, 1973.

Kissinger, Henry. *White House Years.* Boston: Little, Brown, 1979.

Levene, Ricardo. *A History of Argentina.* New York: Russell & Russell, 1937.

Lewis, Gordon. *The Virgin Islands.* Evanston, Ill.: Northwestern University Press, 1972.

Lindahl, Goran. *Uruguay's New Path.* Stockholm: Broderna Lagerstrom, 1962.

MacEoin, Gary. *No Peaceful Way: Chile's Struggle for Dignity.* New York: Sheed & Ward, 1974.

Martin, James Stewart. *All Honorable Men.* Boston: Little, Brown, 1950.

Nathan, Otto. *The Nazi Economic System.* Durham, N.C.: Duke University Press, 1944.

Petras, James, and Michael Morley. *The United States and Chile.* New York and London: Monthly Review Press, 1975.

Philips, Frederick. *45 Years with Philips.* Poole, England: Blandford Press, 1978.

Reynolds, Clark. *The Mexican Economy.* New Haven: Yale University Press, 1970.

Sampson, Anthony. *The Sovereign State of ITT.* New York: Stein & Day, 1973.

Sandford, Robinson. *The Murder of Allende and the End of the Chilean Way to Socialism.* New York: Harper & Row, 1975.

Sasuly, Richard. *I. G. Farben.* New York: Boni and Gaer, 1947.

Selected Bibliography

Scott, Otto. *The Creative Ordeal: The Story of Raytheon.* New York: Atheneum, 1974.

Shaplen, Robert. *Kreuger: Genius and Swindler.* New York: Knopf, 1960.

Siemens, Georg. *History of the House of Siemens.* 2 vols. Freiburg-Munich: Karl Alber, 1957.

Sigmund, Paul. *The Overthrow of Allende and the Politics of Chile, 1964–1976.* Pittsburgh: University of Pittsburgh Press, 1977.

Sparling, Earl. *Kreuger's Billion Dollar Bubble.* New York: Greenburg, 1932.

Sterrett, Joseph E., and Joseph S. Davis. *The Fiscal and Economic Condition of Mexico.* New York: International Committee of Bankers on Mexico, 1928.

Stevenson, William. *A Man Called Intrepid: The Secret War.* New York: Harcourt Brace Jovanovich, 1976.

Swanberg, W. A. *Luce and His Empire.* New York: Scribners, 1972.

Taylor, Charles Edwin. *Leaflets from the Danish West Indies: Description of the Social, Political, and Commercial Condition of these Islands.* London: William Dawson & Sons, 1888.

Thompson, Stewart. *The Age of the Manager Is Over.* Homewood, Ill.: Dow Jones Irwin, 1975.

Thyssen, Fritz. *I Paid Hitler.* Port Washington, N.Y.: Kennikat Press, 1972.

Townsend, Robert. *Up the Organization.* New York: Knopf, 1970.

Weil, Felix. *Argentine Riddle.* Washington: John Day, 1944.

Whitaker, Arthur. *Argentina.* New York: Prentice-Hall, 1964.

Wilgus, A. Curtis, ed. *Argentina, Brazil, and Chile Since Independence.* New York: Russell & Russell, 1963 ed.

Winslow, John. *Conglomerates Unlimited.* Bloomington, Ind.: University of Indiana Press, 1973.

Wooston, Maxine. *The Structure of the Nazi Economy.* Cambridge: Harvard University Press, 1941.

Zanartu, Mario, and John Kennedy. *The Overall Development of Chile.* Notre Dame, Ind.: University of Notre Dame Press, 1969.

Government Documents

United States. 91st Congress. 1st Session. House of Representatives. Committee on the Judiciary. Antitrust Subcommittee. *Hearings on International Telephone & Telegraph Corporation, November 20, 21, 26, December 3, 1969.* Washington. GPO, 1970.

United States. 92nd Congress. 2nd Session. Senate. Committee on the Judiciary. *Hearings on the Nomination of Richard G. Kleindienst of Arizona, to be Attorney General.* 4 parts. Washington. GPO, 1972.

United States. 93rd Congress. 1st Session. Senate. Committee on Foreign Relations. Subcommittee on Multinational Corporations. *Hearings before the Subcommittee on Multinational Corporations, Multinational Corporations and United States Foreign Policy, on the International Telephone and Telegraph Company and Chile, 1970–1971.* Washington. GPO, 1973.

United States. 93rd Congress. 2nd Session. House of Representatives. Committee on the Judiciary. *Hearings pursuant to H. Res. 803: A Resolution Authorizing and Directing the Committee on the Judiciary to Investigate Whether Sufficient Grounds Exist for the House of Representatives to Exercise its Constitutional Power to Impeach Richard M. Nixon, President of the United States of America.* Book V, Parts 1 and 2: "*Department of Justice/ITT Litigation—Richard Kleindienst Hearings.*" Washington. GPO, 1974.

United States. 94th Congress. 1st Session. Senate. Select Committee on Intelligence Activities. *Covert Action in Chile, 1963–1973: Staff Report.* Washington. GPO, 1975.

United States. 94th Congress. 1st Session. Senate. Select Committee on Intelligence Activities. *Hearings, December 4–5, 1975.* Washington. GPO, 1975.

United States. 94th Congress. 1st Session. Senate. Committee on Intelligence Activities. *Alleged Assassination Plots Involving Foreign Leaders: Interim Report.* Washington. GPO, 1975.

Interviews

Howard Aibel
Rand Araskog
Sosthenes Behn II
William Behn
Henri Busignies
Hans Carl
A. Goodwin Cooke
Clyde Dickey
Maurice Deloraine
James Fox
Michael Ganz
H. A. Hahlbeck
Lyman Hamilton
Hans Kehrl
J. Patrick Lannan

Eric McWhirter
Ray Manning
David Margolis
William Marx
Geoffrey Ogilvie
O. J. Olgiati
Edwin Roome
Alexander Sanders
Arthur Schmitt
Ena Scott
Ellery Stone
Edmund Stoner
Bertram Tower
Walter Wright

Index

Index

Index

Index

Index

Index

Index

Index